Sequel to

to

NORTH STAR GOLD

By Ella Lung Martinsen

It's a true Alaska-Klondike, gold-rush story in which the author recounts the exciting adventures of her parents, Edward B. Lung and Velma D. Lung and their rugged quest for gold while living in a primitive little log cabin on Dominion Creek, near Dawson, with their three children. Dozens of famous and colorful characters come to life, including Soapy Smith, Alexander McDonald the Klondike King, Pat Galvin, Klondike Kate, Diamond Tooth Gertie, Swiftwater Bill, George Carmack, William Ogilvie, Joaquin Miller, Robert Service, and many others. Never before, in book form, have some of these dramatic, eye-witness stories been told.

Besides being an unusual saga of family adventure, *Trail to North Star Gold* is also a valuable historical document of those momentous years when thousands of stampeders rushed north as the first earth-shaking news of "Gold in the Klondike" echoed around the globe.

When Ed Lung went north in the 1897 Stampedes, he kept diaries, and later Velma D. Lung wrote memoirs. These form the basis of *Trail to North Star Gold*. The gold fields of Alaska and the Klondike are described here in detail, including where the greatest quantities of the yellow metal were found, and the largest nuggets.

In *Trail to North Star Gold* those who like true adventure will live over again the intriguing gold rush with all its excitement and rugged pathos—and in so doing will also gain a great deal of knowledge of the country and history of Alaska, "The Great Land," the land of the mighty Yukon!

It is certain that a great gold-rush epic, like the one which began in 1897 after George Carmack discovered gold on the Bonanza, will never be repeated in all its wild, uninhibited action and color.

Velma D. Clement Lung as she looked before the Alaska-Klondike gold rush.

Trail to North Star Gold

a sequel to "Black Sand and Gold"

True Story of the
Alaska-Klondike Gold Rush

By
Ella Lung Martinsen
As told to her by her mother,
Velma D. Lung

Binford & Mort Publishing
Portland, Oregon

Trail to North Star Gold

COPYRIGHT UNDER INTERNATIONAL
PAN-AMERICAN COPYRIGHT CONVENTIONS
© 1969 BY ELLA LUNG MARTINSEN
ALL RIGHTS RESERVED INCLUDING THE RIGHT
TO REPRODUCE THIS BOOK, OR ANY PORTIONS
THEREOF, IN ANY FORM EXCEPT FOR THE IN-
CLUSION OF BRIEF QUOTATIONS IN A REVIEW.

ISBN 0-8323-0242-2 (paperbound)

Library of Congress Catalog Card Number 70-98194

Printed in the United States of America

First Edition 1969
Second Edition 1974
Second Printing 1984
Third Printing 1991

Dedication and in Memoriam

To
My beloved parents,
Edward Burchal Lung and Velma D. Lung,
and to friends, Joaquin Miller, poet-gold-rush reporter,
and to the poet-laureate of the Yukon, Robert W. Service.
Also, to all true Sourdoughs, I dedicate my writing of
"Trail to North Star Gold."

STAR-TRAIL

By Ella Lung Martinsen

Some night I'll fling myself across the skies,
And feel, and see a thousand eyes,
I'll travel, travel, swift in flight . . .
Until I reach a trail of golden, haloed light.

I'll hang my hat upon a star—the North Star!
My overcoat, a million miles afar,
The Milky Way will be my stepping stones,
I'll have a hundred million different homes!

I'll find, and wear a bright, celestial crown.
Upon the earth I'll twinkle down
And sing on moon and solar-wave,
And pray the Lord the world to save.

In flashing light I'll dance, and race
Through great galaxies of nebula, outer space,
And come to rest before His throne . . .
With loved ones, lost, in worlds unknown.

PREFACE

It is my hope that all who read "Trail to North-Star-Gold" will appreciate the tremendous effort that has gone into making this book. I hope, also, that the story will be a lasting, historical record of those hectic days when thousands of people from our country, and others, too, rushed North to seek fortune and security.

Preceding the Alaska-Klondike Gold-Rush, the Great Depression and Panic of the Nineties had swept across America, leaving great numbers of people destitute.

Lumber mills, shipyards, smelters, stores and factories were closed while men frantically walked the streets hunting jobs. Many people didn't even have five-cent carfare!

My father, Edward Burchell Lung, son of a Baptist minister, at the age of twenty-one had come West from Rochester, New York, to seek fortune in Tacoma, Washington. The year was 1890. In Tacoma he found a job as expert accountant at the Reese, Redman and Crandle Wholesale Grocery Company. A year later he met and soon afterwards married a beautiful young lady, who was destined to become my mother, Velma D. Clement, the eldest daughter of a successful hotel-owner and real estate man. But about two years later Horatio C. Clement (my grandfather), died suddenly, leaving his family almost penniless. The crash of the stock market and "Great Panic" had practically wiped him out, but the family was not aware of this until after his death.

During this chaotic time, to Edward B. Lung and Velma D. Lung a son was born whom they called Clement ("Clemy").

Clemy was only a little boy when the first cry of "Gold, Gold in the Klondike—tons of it!" was screamed by the newsboys on the streets of Tacoma, early in the spring of 1897. My father, Edward B. Lung, had just lost his position with the wholesale grocery company. It, and many others had gone bankrupt and were permanently boarded up.

And so it was only natural, that my father would be caught up in the tremendous gold-rush excitement that followed the glittering accounts of gold-discoveries in the North. On May 24, 1897, he left Tacoma with that first wave of men to form a stampede from the Puget Sound area. The S.S. Mexico was packed to the gunwales with hopeful men—all expected to become Klondike Kings within the year.

If those who read this book, "Trail to North-Star Gold," would also read "Black Sand and Gold," my first book, they would get a true picture of the drama of those hectic times, for I wrote the story from my father's diaries and the stories he told me. I also used a number of historical documents to round out the story.

I wrote "Trail to North-Star Gold" from my mother's wonderful memoirs of her days in the Klondike. Also, I used a number of my father's unpublished gold-rush diaries of 1898. Chapter XI, "Pink Flannel Heaven," tells how my father built a little log cabin in the Klondike, lining it with pink outing flannel. Naturally, this story is very dear to my heart, for I was born in that little log cabin about forty-five miles from Dawson, on Dominion Creek.

In 1951, when I was beginning to write "Black Sand and Gold" for the Alaska Sportsman Magazine (in serial), my husband and I went to Dawson and the Klondike to interview old Sourdough friends. I also wanted to locate our little log cabin where my family had lived those many long years ago and where I was born.

We found that the cabin was gone, but we had a chance to browse around. While we were there we met a Mr. A. M. Olsen, an old-time Sourdough, who had lived in the area since 1898. He remembered my family very well, as did Alec Adams, a well-known Sourdough actor of Dawson, and as did Tom Hebert, a former mine-owner, roadhouse owner and Mounted Policeman.

My husband and I spent the most interesting ten days of our lives visiting the gold fields where Dominion, Bonanza, Eldorado and Hunker Creeks are located.

While Perry and I were in Dawson we visited the office of Mr. John Dines, the Mining Recorder. (He is no longer there, but is now in Ottawa. He is the son of a well-known 1898 Dawson Sourdough.) When I told Mr. Dines who I was he was immediately interested and helpful. He pulled down an old ledger from the archives. Carefully wiping off the dust, he opened a page where my father's name appeared (in large, beautiful, Spencerian handwriting), entered by the old time Gold Commissioner, Thomas Fawcette. The record said: "Lung, Edward B.–Sept. 3, 1897, No. 7-82 Bench 2, Tier 8–Below Bonanza."

Then, Johnny Dines almost reverently turned more fragile, yellowed pages and there we found the name, O. Martinsen, Jan 24, '99, No. 19831 Hill, W. ½ Limit No. 92, Below Discovery on Bonanza Creek – Lovett Gulch, Jan. 24, 1899. (Ole Martinsen was my husband's father.)

My husband and I looked at the old ledger with a great deal of sentiment, for Perry's father, also, had gone to Dawson during the big stampedes. In fact there is mention in my father's Gold Rush diary of having met a Mr. Martinsen from California on the steamer going North–"a fine fellow!" Think of it! My father and future father-in-law met for the first time on a gold-rush steamer before I was born.

Now, as I finish this second book, I believe I have not wasted my time. I believe these stories will grow more valuable with the passing of years. At this date, most of the gold-rush generation has passed on over the Great Divide, as *have* my *beloved* parents.

Again, I say, as I did in the preface of "Black Sand and Gold" that every stampeder who headed North, into that rugged, frozen land of Gold, was making history ... leaving his imprint with the others on the sands of time. And so, to all of those intrepid Sourdoughs, I wish to dedicate this book. It is through their rugged strivings and trail-breaking that the Great Northwest was opened up at least a hundred years earlier than it would have been, had they not braved the unchartered wilderness.

Yes, I am very proud that my parents were among those who went to Alaska and the Klondike during those very exciting, thrilling epoch-gold-rush years, and that they kept records of their lives while in the North.

And now, a word about modern-day Alaska and the Klondike: While I was still working on this story, my husband and I went North to attend the Alaska and Canadian 1967-Centennials. From Fairbanks we flew by Wien and Canadian Air Lines to Dawson City, via Whitehorse. We were nicely settled in the Flora Dora Hotel when eager tourists began arriving for the Gold-Discovery-Day Celebration, August 17th! It was fascinating watching the crowds come in by car, camper, trailer, bus, plane and in the boat-flotilla. Some of them had started at Lake Bennett, over 500 miles up the Yukon; others had joined the Flotilla at Whitehorse, capital of Yukon Territory, and other points north. Those in the flotilla had the rare opportunity of living over the exciting "Trail of '98" with some of its hazards, too! The flotilla was made up of small launches, rowboats, Indian canoes, and even several amphicars—all were gaily decked with banners, flags, evergreens and bright wildflowers. They swung around a wide bend of the Yukon and headed for Dawson, coming in, in serpentine formation. (Amphicar is a car that can go on either dry land, or water.)

Bud Fisher, Alaska's well-known, colorful Sourdough was Boat-Master, leading the flotilla-procession. His bright red shirt, long, grey whiskers and Buffalo Bill haircut were conspicuous as he drew closer to the waiting throngs along the Dawson riverfront. When the modern Argonauts got close to shore they gave loud cheers to those waiting to welcome them. They had come a long way and were bronzed and tired from their strenuous boat trip lasting nearly two weeks. Many of them had come from distant parts of Canada, Alaska, and the States ... some were from as far away as New York City, even Europe.

Many of these people had already read "Black Sand and Gold," others wished to purchase copies at the Dawson Artscraft Store almost immediately upon landing. It was a pleasure to autograph books for these modern Argonauts. Every year the flotilla is part of the gold rush celebration. The large river steamers are no longer running. It's a pity, too! But the Argonauts do have a wonderful time in their individual boats and are entertained at spots along the Yukon.

As a highlight to my pleasure of being in Dawson for the celebration, I presented an autographed Centennial edition of "Black Sand and Gold" to James Smith, Commissioner of the Yukon (really Governor) on the stage of the Palace Grand Theater before a large, responsive audience. The presentation had been arranged by Garfield White, a well-known Canadian actor from Vancouver, B.C., who is a star in Fran Dowie's "Gaslight Follies," an exciting gold-rush production put on every summer in Dawson for the tourists. When the Governor and I met on the stage, there was much applause and numerous flash light pictures taken.

Another pleasant occasion was the Centennial Kiwanis dinner at which I was guest speaker (Fred Cook President). The men were already planning activities for the following year and wondering how many moose burgers they should plan on, and who would go hunting for the moose. It was a delightful pioneer group, in a unique frontier setting.

As a parting goodbye to the Yukon, Jack and Marlene Olson drove Perry and me to the gold-fields. Once more we visited Gold Bottom Creek at the Discovery Claim where the Canadian, Robert Henderson, had first found gold. Bert and Thora Bratsberg own the claim now. Next, we visited the Bremners in their hill-top house on Last Chance Creek. They were making beautiful jewelry from old mastodon tusks found in the gravels of their rich claim.

As a last goodbye we went to claim 2-B Below Discovery on Dominion Creek where I was born. The Harold Schmidt family now own the claim. Mrs. Schmidt was just taking blueberry muffins from the oven and graciously invited us to tea.

After tea, Barbara, the pretty eleven-year old daughter, took me on tour, and I poked around among the old gravels and sands. I even noted the diminutive brook which flowed down the hillside near the cabin. No doubt it was the same little stream in which I had dabbled my toes as a small child—Oh, so many years ago!

I said when I left my dear friends on Dominion Creek and in Dawson that I probably would never come back to the Klondike; and yet I know that if the call of the North becomes too overpoweringly strong, I shall return once more to Dawson and to that very beautiful Dominion Creek Valley where the lovely rainbows span the hills and where there is great tranquillity, contentment and many cherished gold-rush memories. Truly, I am glad that I was born in a little log cabin in the Klondike!

SPECIAL ACKNOWLEDGMENTS

First of all, I wish to mention my lovable friend, Robert W. Service, famed poet of the Yukon. From time to time he sent encouraging letters to me urging me to complete my two books. Just a few weeks before his death I received a fine letter giving me permission to use his poem. "Good-bye Little Cabin," which he wrote shortly before he left Dawson. When I visited his little log cabin in Dawson in 1951 (and again in 1967), I saw the handwritten, birch-bark-framed poem, tacked up close to the door. The ladies of Dawson are keeping the cabin in good repair. It is now a shrine to the Yukon poet and all tourists visit this famous spot. Usually there is someone at the cabin (at designated hours) to recite Service's poetry. In 1967, it was Wally McSween, famous Canadian actor and performer at the Palace Grand Theater in the summer season.

Next, a big thank-you goes to ex-Commissioner Col. Stewart T. Wood, former head of the Royal Canadian Mounted Police (headquarters, Ottawa, Canada). He is the well-known son of Zachary Taylor Wood, Commissioner of the Northwest Mounted Police in 1899, mentioned in Chapter XV, "Three Men In A Casket Of Ice." It was Zachary T. Wood who helped solve the celebrated mystery of the baffling disappearance of Fred Clayson and his other companions in late winter of 1899.

In another big acknowledgment, I wish to thank Emery F. Tobin, former Editor-owner of The Alaska Sportsman Magazine. It was Mr. Tobin who published my first book, "Black Sand and Gold," serially in his magazine and urged me to write the sequel.

Next, I wish to thank Mary Pullen Kopanski of Skagway, Alaska, for her letters of encouragement and data received. She is the granddaughter of Harriet Pullen, the hardy pioneer who established and ran the famous Pullen House during the epoch years of the Alaska Klondike gold-rush.

Also, to Captain C. F. Stabbert of the Marine Medical Missionaries, winter headquarters located on Thetis Island, B.C., I give a very grateful thanks for data concerning the S.S. Islander's last, fateful voyage.

There are others, too, who helped with the historical data: Archie McLean Hawks, famous Chilkoot Tramway engineer and builder. Both he and his wife were in their 90's when they passed away in Santa Barbara, California.

Then, there is my very good friend, Miss Lulu Fairbanks, of Seattle, Washington, former Editor of The Alaska Weekly. Lulu has always been keenly interested in all Alaska-Yukon history, as her uncle founded and named the City of Fairbanks, Alaska. She has been the guiding light as secretary of The International Sourdough Club and has kept it active for many years. (Lulu Fairbanks, deceased in 1968)

I must also mention (Mrs.) Margaret McRae, now of Ruskin, B.C., who went to Dawson as a schoolteacher in 1910 and married Dan McRae, an 1898 Klondike Sourdough. For twenty years Mrs. McRae taught school at the Grand Forks of the Bonanza and Eldorado Rivers and knows that country like a book. She served us (wild) strawberry shortcake in her cozy little Dawson cabin while we talked of the old days. Two old-timers—Malcolm Ross and Captain Tommy Byers—were there. Captain Byers was decorated by King George V for unusual bravery in the first World War, receiving the military Cross. He was Dawson's Postmaster in 1951.

Also, I wish to gratefully acknowledge the help of the late Mary Vogel (Nelly Daly) of Tacoma, Washington. She supplied me with some of the personal details of the Fred Clayson story. She went to Dawson in '99 with my mother and brother, "Clemy."

Again, and publicly, I wish to thank my faithful husband, Perry Martinsen, for his long suffering in eating late meals and overlooking a dusty household during the years I've been writing these stories! He is a hero, too, in his own special way!

Also, again, as in the preface of my other book, I wish to thank Juanita Miller for her enthusiastic interest. Her father, Joaquin Miller, the nationally known poet and eminent gold-rush reporter, and my father, Edward B. Lung, were frozen in together at Circle City during the famine-winter of 1897 and became good friends. Joaquin Miller figures prominently in "Black Sand And Gold," my first book, and is also in this story.

And then a big acknowledgment goes to the late Allen Rogers of Santa Barbara, who was generous with old documents which his father, Eugene Rogers, left as records of his trips into Yukon Territory.

Here, I wish to thank Mr. Thomas Binford for giving me a book called "Cheechako Into Sourdough," by Thomas Wiedemann, which Mr. Binford published in the 1940's. I was delighted with the book and later found that my father had known Wiedemann in the Klondike and had recorded that fact in his diary. Of course I have mentioned Wiedemann in this story. Another book that was helpful in telling the special marine, gold-rush-facet of the story was "Sentinels of the North Pacific," by James A. Gibbs. It's another Binford & Mort publication and very authentic.

In this spot I give grateful acknowledgments to the wonderful people of the International Alaska-Yukon Sourdough Club. Fred Hand of Santa Barbara is its present president (1969), and to the late Dick

Racine, 1959 president, well-known, famous lecturer, who kept prodding me to finish this story.

I give special acknowledgments to Otto Nordling, of Vancouver B.C., well-known Canadian public figure, who grew up in the Klondike at Gold Run Creek; was on The Bank of Montreal staff in Dawson; and later served as a member of the Canadian World War II prisoners in Japanese prison camps. He has always been very interested in my Klondike stories and has sent many messages of encouragement. It was Mr. Nordling who designed the colorful Yukon-Coat-of-Arms representing Canada's twelve provinces.

Here, I give acknowledgments to our dear old friend, Arthur (Art) Buel, famed early-day Dawson artist and newspaper cartoonist. His name gives lustre to old gold-rush days and has to be mentioned. (Now deceased)

Big acknowledgments are due The National League of American Pen-Women; the Strollers' Club of Santa Barbara; and The Santa Barbara Womens' Club. I'm indebted to all these fine fellow-club-members for their unusual interest in these stories. Also, I must acknowledge Dave Griffiths of Seattle—well-known lawyer and International Sourdough Historian—for his helpful interest and comments while he was alive. And, too, I must mention my very good friend and fellow Stroller member, Mrs. Roy W. Cheeseman, for her faithful efforts in getting the manuscript ready in typewritten form for publication. And last, but not least, I give grateful thanks to Brad Hope, Recorder of Mines in present-day Dawson, for his interest and helpfulness.

Ella Lung Martinsen

Mendenhall Glacier, near Juneau, Alaska.

Chilkoot Pass, Alaska, 1898.

CONTENTS

1. An Exciting Letter 1
2. The Rosalie 7
3. Wild Skagway and Soapy Smith 18
4. The Little Iron Horse 32
5. Perilous Journey and the Nora 39
6. The Mighty Yukon 50
7. Glittering Dawson 63
8. The Famous Bonanza and Eldorado 81
9. Deep Valley and Little Log Cabin 104
10. Alive, Warm and Bubblin' 119
11. Pink Flannel Heaven 124
12. The Two Champs 131
13. The Little Preacher 135
14. Talking Dog 146
15. Three Men in a Casket of Ice 151
16. Rainbow-Gold, Frenchie and Nelly 165
17. Great Nome Stampede 169
18. Fire in the Cabin 181
19. Goddess of the Gold-Rush 183
20. The Alaska Stork 191
21. Aunty Fanny and a Galaxy of Stars 202
22. Patsy and Pedro and Another Summer 209
23. Sourdough Tales and Yukon Romances 217
24. The North Star 228
25. Call of the Tanana and Forest Fire 238
26. The Banshee in the Haunted Mine 249
27. Rugged Ways to Riches and Romeo 261
28. A Sleigh Ride to Dawson and Blizzard 276
29. A Thousand Miles over the Ice, and Trail of '98 280
30. Thieves in the Cache 302
31. Mysterious Ten Above Lower Discovery 306
32. Riffles of Riches and Klondike Kings 320
33. Farewell to the North 329
34. Bricks of Gold and Alaska Forget-Me-Nots 336
    Index 347

Juneau, Alaska, at an early date. (Winter)

Skagway, 1898. White Pass is to right (out of picture). Chilkoot Pass is to left, in high mountains.

THE NORTH WIND

By Ella L. Martinsen

Oh, chilling, screeching, North-Wind, blow!
Play me a tune on your violin-bow,
While writhing brooks freeze and flow,
And leaden-skies drop buckets of icicled-snow.

Oh, it's good to be in a cabin, low . . .
Warmed by a fire where the embers glow,
Away from the roar of avalanche-floe,
Away from the claws of Kodiak-foe . . .

Here, in the land of the Eskimo,
Here, in the land of the Sourdough.
Oh, chilling, screeching North-Wind, blow!
Tell me your Gold-Rush tales of long ago.

Off for the Alaska-Klondike gold rush. Relatives and friends bid farewell.

Scene along the Inside Passage, Alaska.

Chapter 1

AN EXCITING LETTER

It was a sunny morning, early in August, of 1899 when the mailman brought a faded, weather-beaten letter. Immediately, I recognized the bold, unusual handwriting—it was my husband's! My heart leaped and skipped some beats as it had been many months since I had last heard from him. Hurriedly, I tore open the envelope and read the message written at Dawson, Yukon Territory, May 25, 1899.

Dear Velma:
    I'm not planning to come back to Tacoma this fall. As you know, I've trekked a thousand miles over the ice in my quest for gold. God knows how hard I've struggled! So far, I haven't been lucky, although my search has lasted for nearly two years. Yes, I could give up and come home, defeated, but I won't. Everything close to Dawson is staked solid, the Bonanza, Eldorado, Hunker, Gold Bottom, Dominion Creek, and all of the others. However, I believe that if I remain here another year or two, I may yet find fortune. Up here, in the Klondike, I've seen great riches come to fellows over night with the lucky turn of a shovel.
    I have been fortunate within the past few weeks to get a good prospect out on Claim -B Below Discovery on Dominion Creek. It's about forty-five miles northeast of Dawson, over towards the Canadian Rockies.
    I'm building a little log cabin, hoping you'll come North and join me. Dearest Vel, you can't know how much I've missed you and our little son, Clemy. If you will only come, I'll try my best to make you both happy.
    The Indians are predicting an early winter. They say ice will be running in the Yukon around the first of September, so if you're coming, you must not leave Tacoma any later than the 24th of August. I'm enclosing a list of things that you will need, also, a

list of canned goods and other things. Everything is very expensive up here. Crowd into the trunk anything extra that seems important.

Velma, my darling, please come. Answer immediately. Love to dear Clemy—and your sister and Mother Clement.

As ever, your devoted husband,

Edward

I put down Edward's entreating letter with mingled emotions. Edward building a little log cabin for us in the North? Oh, what should I do? I had never pictured myself living in the Klondike! But oh, it was so good to know that he was still alive!

My mind rushed back over the fateful events before the gold-rush—the Great Panic and Stock Market Crash of the Nineties—the heartbreaking depression. Thousands of men out of work! Edward out of a job, too! Then, the exciting news of tremendous gold discoveries in the Klondike! Like a flash of hope the word had come, in early spring of '97. It was like news from Heaven! Banks had failed. Businesses had gone broke. Factories and stores were boarded up. Hungry people stood in long lines in front of public soup kitchens, many who once had been well-to-do. Some didn't have five cent carfare! I thought of how eagerly Ed had joined the stampedes expecting to find riches quickly, and how optimistically he had promised to return home within a year.

While Edward was away, in order to make ends meet, Clemy and I had lived with my widowed mother, Mrs. Horatio Clement, and my sister, Rowena. But during all of that time, how I had wished for a home of my own! I had longed for a cozy, little cottage with a white picket fence, and bright flowers around the door—and Edward with us!

I read, and re-read his urgent letter and was just folding it up, when little Clemy (age four), came bounding into the house, his light blond, wavy hair, rumpled and damp, his freckled face smeared and streaked with dirt-smudges.

"Clemy," I said, "how would you like to see your father in a few weeks?"

Clemy jumped up and down, clapping his hands, his large grey eyes wide with excitement.

AN EXCITING LETTER

"Oh, Bamba, do you really mean we can see daddy?" (He called his Grandmother, 'mother'—and me, 'Bamba'.)

"Yes, we shall see him very soon. But we must begin getting ready this very day!"

Clemy ran from the room to tell his little playmates all over the neighborhood that he was going North where there was snow, and where he could see his daddy at least a dozen times a day!

"Velma," said my mother, as I hurriedly began assembling things and checking steamer schedules, "I know you want to see Edward, but do you fully realize the hazards of a trip like this! And, if you reach Dominion Creek safely, it will be a lonely life. Remember, you're a girl of culture; you've had every luxury—that is, until your father died."

"Oh, I know all this," I told her. "Why remind me, now?"

"But I must," exclaimed mother seriously, as she followed me about the house, literally wringing her hands over my decision to go to the Klondike.

"Velma," she said, "can you really picture yourself in a crude little cabin with probably not even a rug on the floor!" "Then too," she rushed on, with just a tinge of reproach in her voice, "you've never learned to cook, or do heavy housework! Why, you'll be washing, scrubbing, sewing and helping Edward in ways that I can't even imagine! I honestly don't think you can do it," she exclaimed, showing earnest apprehension in her expressive brown eyes. (Mother was an attractive woman in her late forties.)

"I don't care! I love him, and I'm going to him," I told her firmly. "Out of the six years of our marriage, Edward and I have been separated almost half the time. And poor little Clemy—he's hardly seen his father!"

"Oh Velma, how I envy you!" exclaimed Ena, my beautiful, blue-eyed, seventeen-year-old sister, bursting into the room. "I think it's just wonderful! Sounds so romantic! Think of the fun of living in a little log cabin, beautiful Malemutes, sleigh ridges by moonlight and starlight, fur parkas, and trips to Dawson! Think of seeing real Klondike Kings, handsome Mounties, and sacks and sacks of nuggets, and barrels of yellow gold-dust! Dawson dance-hall girls, gamblers, and Klondike Queens! And, ah yes, the great Northern Lights! They tell me it's all like living in another world. Vel, Vel, it's the chance of a lifetime! May I please come visit you?"

"Of course," I laughed, "but I can't imagine our Mother ever approving of it."

During the following hectic days, mother's home was in great disorder—people coming and going—the place littered with all kinds of boxes and crates of canned goods, and various other miscellaneous items! Needless to say, my dear mother had worked herself into a nervous stew! But finally, she gave me a helping hand when she saw I was determined to head North.

Of course Clemy's joy was boundless! I made numerous lists, and systematically checked them off. Then, over to Seattle I went to buy a fur jacket. Edward had listed a fur coat as not a luxury, but a real necessity. I decided it should be of sea otter. (Otter at that time was plentiful and inexpensive as the Russians had been slaughtering the poor animals in Arctic waters for years!)

The jacket that took my eye was a lovely, golden brown color, like gorgeous thick velvet. It had a deep, wide collar which stood high at the back of the neck and it could be rolled close to the throat for protection in cold weather. The mutton-leg sleeves were puffed at the shoulder and close-fitting at the wrist. There was a close-fitting bodice, ending in a short peplum, which rippled slightly at the hips.

"Madame, it's extremely becoming." encouraged the clerk. "The brownish-amber color of the fur is just a wee bit lighter than your eyes, and the golden sheen of the fur compliments your dark, curly hair and rosy cheeks. You say you're going to the Klondike?" asked the clerk incredulously. "Oh! how very exciting! Truly, I envy you!"

It was now August 22nd. At last Clemy and I were ready for the journey. We had been fortunate, through a friend, Dr. William Misner,* to obtain passage on a small freighter, called "The Rosalie." And so, about noon, I had our luggage moved to the dock. The trunk and satchels were to be placed in our stateroom, the boxes of canned goods stored in the hold of the ship.

The dock was heavily crowded. Soon it was time to tell neighbors and friends, (Dr. Misner,* the G. G. Chandlers, the Toziers and the Robert Walkers) and relatives, Mother and Ena, and an uncle, Foster Clement, "goodbye." Words always seem inadequate when one is under

---

*Dr. William W. Misner, well-known Tacoma, Washington physician, went North in 1897 and again in '98. He was also well-known in Dawson and points along the Yukon.

AN EXCITING LETTER

great stress. How I dreaded this parting with Mother, for I knew it was going to be a painful, emotional scene! I had never really broken away from her parental-tie although I was now twenty-four. Yes, it certainly was time! But suddenly, and unexpectedly, it was hard for me, too. Mother's fears and apprehensions rose up like challenging demons to devour me in these last few moments. All of the things she had said were true. I wasn't suited to wilderness living! I might prove a dismal failure!

For just a little bit I felt fright, and wished I had decided to stay in Tacoma. Then, too, I might never see my dear sister and beloved mother again. The Klondike was far——oh, so far away! That thought brought tears which I couldn't conceal.

"Little Clem," mother was saying, dabbing her eyes, "when I see you again, you'll probably be a big man—a real miner! Never, never forget your dear grandmother while you're away in the Klondike, and please use the box of artist paints I gave you, and send me some bright pictures."

"Vel! Vel! goodbye, and send me a nugget, will you?" asked Ena, brushing back a tear, as the shrill whistle blew its warning blast of departure. Ena and mother gave us hurried, parting kisses, and mother pressed a small Bible into my hands and told me it must be my guide, and that she would pray for a safe journey and protection for us while in the North. She sent her best love to Edward, "who is like a son to me," she said.

As the boat picked up speed, and we were several miles from Tacoma, I looked off to the Northwest.

Somewhere, in that general direction, our little freighter would be nosing her way for perhaps seven days along the Inside Passage. It would mean a thousand miles of steady salt-water travel to Skagway. Then, at last, we would be about half way to the Klondike. I had been warned when I bought my ticket, that it might prove to be a rugged trip, even hazardous. I had assured the ticket agent that I was in good health and could take the hardships should any arise. He had looked at me with a dubious expression in his eyes. Of course, I knew his thoughts—I was not the hardy pioneer type. Somehow—ticket agents had an uncanny way of sizing people up!

In Annie Wright's Seminary, in Tacoma (an exclusive school for girls), I had specialized in the Fine Arts. I had seriously studied piano, painting and drawing. Then, too, I had shown promise as a singer. But, as I began evaluating all of my background I gained courage. Why couldn't I, too, be strong and efficient like my great-grandmother Pollard and my great grandmother Davis in Oregon? I knew that when they were very young they had lived in luxury on southern plantations; one in Kentucky, the other in Virginia. In 1844, long before the Civil War, the two families had freed their slaves and moved to Missouri where they had waited to cross the plains in covered wagons with a wagontrain. While waiting, their faithful slaves had found them and begged to remain with them.

In Oregon, the Pollards and Davises had helped build a new territory, homesteading in the Willamette Valley.

As a small child, I had often visited the farms, and had eagerly listened to Grandma Davis tell pioneer tales. Her people had suffered great hardships while crossing the plains in covered wagons drawn by oxen, and had had many close calls from the Indians. A chief, when he had seen Grandmother Davis combing her golden-blonde hair, had wanted to buy her. That tale had always made my spine tingle! The whole wagon train had been in grave danger, but somehow they had come through safely.

"Well," I told myself, "if my grandmothers could meet danger and endure untold hardships, so could I!"

That night, after I had tucked little Clemy into bed, I slipped out on deck for some cool salt air. Nearly everyone had retired except the crew and a few others. It was a calm, quiet night, save for occasional, distant laughter from the other side of the boat, and the faraway sound of a violin.

Puget Sound was in one of her soft, poetic moods. The water was placid, smooth, and dark with hardly a ripple showing. Phosphorus sparkled and gleamed like jewels when a frightened fish darted away, or a stray bird disturbed the water.

Our steamer was making good headway. By morning we would be well into the famous, picturesque Inside Passage, and much farther along on our journey into the mysterious North.

Standing alone on deck, again I suffered the exquisite pain—of leaving home—while watching the dark outline of the Olympic Mountains and the ever-changing, shadowy shore-line.

Instinctively, I searched the velvety heavens for the Dipper and the

North Star, and found them, far to the North.

Polaris! The North Star! It was Edward's and my star—the star we had both watched during all of those long, heartbreaking months of separation. Yes, it was our own special link. Now it seemed to glow more brightly, beckoning me with reassurance.

"Oh Edward," I whispered. "I'm coming to you, and to our little log cabin on Dominion Creek, far, far away in the Klondike!"

Chapter 2

THE ROSALIE AND THIRTEEN RINGS

Suddenly, I awakened to hear one of my satchels sliding back and forth across the stateroom floor, making weird, scratching noises, like a cat at the door. The elements were certainly kicking up a terrible fuss!

I switched on the lamp and looked at my watch. Three-thirty in the morning! Goodness, what a change in the weather! I felt a peculiar sea sickness in the pit of my stomach, but my first thought was of little Clemy.

He was sleeping soundly in the upper bunk, his sweet face, pink, like a cherub's. It was evident he would sleep 'til morning, if I didn't disturb him, so I turned off the lamp and crawled to the porthole. There wasn't much to see through that small, oval framework (facing port side) except a wildly tossing sea.

Anxiously, I strained my eyes for a glimpse of land. Dimly, I could see a distant shore; then, at close range, colossal rocks and jagged reefs. And, as I watched, there were complete blank spaces of no shoreline at all.

Ah yes, I knew! This was the beginning of huge Queen Charlotte Sound. I had heard of its many treacherous reefs and hidden shoals, and that it could be extremely dangerous in stormy weather. There were more of those nerve-racking, scratching sounds of slipping baggage, and the rasping sounds of straining timbers.

Our little freighter began twisting and turning like a tortured thing.

Certainly a tremendous storm was raging out at sea! Waves rolled higher and higher, heavily pounding the boat. The wind had risen to a wild screech! Slowly, we were being driven alarmingly close to some of those jagged rocks while, underfoot, I could feel the freighter shudder, and hear a threatening, thunder-like roar, deep down, in the throat of the ocean. Then in almost frantic, higher pitch, the warning-clang, clang, of a lighthouse bell! Again, I felt that odd feeling in the pit of my stomach, and added to that, very real fright!

I could hear the deck hands run through the ship, checking on freight. Obviously, some of it had already broken loose and was slipping about. Fearfully, I thought of other steamers that had capsized in this graveyard stretch when heavy cargo had shifted, in stormy weather. Then, my mind flashed back to tales of wrecked gold-rush steamers. Some had even been driven against these very same rocks!

For instance, there was the S.S. Mexico which had struck West Devil's Rock, August 5, 1897 on a return trip from Sitka. The vessel had hit a reef at 4 a.m., going full speed. Sleeping passengers were thrown from their bunks; some suffered broken bones and internal injuries. Fortunately, everybody reached lifeboats, but in a dense fog many of the lifeboats became separated from the Captain, and were swept out to sea! It was only a miracle, they said, that all passengers were finally rescued. (The Mexico sank in eighty fathoms of water, 500 feet.)

Then there had been another steamer tragedy, the awful wreck of the Clara Nevada! In early spring of 1898, the Clara Nevada failed to reach Skagway. Search parties were sent out, but at first with no success. Finally, quite by chance, the body of the ship's purser, young George H. Beck was found by a passing fisherman. Beck's body had washed up against Chilkat Island and caught in the seaweed. He was fully dressed, even to a heavy overcoat, but there were strange powder-burns on the upper part of his coat. The corpse and scorched overcoat presented a baffling mystery. Where was the ship, and where were the crew and passengers? The authorities finally gave up hope of ever finding any of the sixty-five passengers or crew alive.

Then, nine miles away from Chilkat Island searchers located parts of a sunken hull which was the Clara Nevada's. It was determined that the ship had exploded and blown sky high. The tragedy had occurred because of an illegal shipment of dynamite which had been crated care-

THE ROSALIE AND THIRTEEN RINGS 9

lessly. Carrying dynamite on passenger ships was strictly forbidden by all maritime law.

And then everyone knew of another ship disaster—the needless wreck of the steamer Corona. It left Seattle January 3, 1898, loaded to capacity. Three days later the Corona struck a reef and went down minutes afterwards. Fortunately, everyone reached uninhabited Lewis Island, but they waited for five long days to be rescued in snow and freezing weather. When the victims were finally found, all were suffering from extreme exposure and starvation. Oddly, no one could give a logical reason why the Corona had struck a reef.

As a small leap ahead in the Alaska story, the horrifying wreck of the S.S. Islander was a dreadful tragedy which shocked the country. In the summer of 1901 (August 14, the S. S. Islander left Skagway bound for the States. She was carrying her largest passenger list since at the peak of the gold-rush (in '98). It was said the ship had three million dollars in gold stored in the purser's safe. Captain H. R. Foote, on that fateful night, stood two watches in the early evening, then turned the bridge over to the pilot, so that he, the captain, could get a bite to eat in the galley. While he was having a last cup of coffee, suddenly, the steamer was enveloped in a thick mantle of glacial fog.

From the galley the captain heard the pilot frantically blast the whistle in order to get his bearings through echo-soundings. To the captain's horror, the echoes bounced back with sudden promptness! There was absolutely no time for the pilot to swerve the ship. The Islander was upon one of the newest and mightiest icebergs that had ever stalked the Inside Passage. It had broken loose on this particular night from the mammoth Taku Glacier and was prowling! The steamer struck the mountain of partly submerged ice with such terrific force that her hull cracked and buckled, jamming stateroom doors and windows tight-shut. Volumes of water poured into the stricken vessel. The pumps were immediately switched on, but it was a futile effort.

Quickly, the Islander filled with water while the captain desperately tried last minute measures, and also while a few loyal crewmen ran along deck, with axes, trying to batter down doors to free screaming passengers. In the dense fog and wild confusion, lifeboats were cut loose, holding only a small fraction of capacity.

Now, as a great big leap ahead in the Alaska story: the wreck of the British steamer, The Princess Sophia, came as a dreadful shock to the entire world. At 10 p.m. on October 23, 1918, the Sophia left Skagway loaded to capacity with passengers from all parts of Alaska and Yukon Territory. The ship was also loaded with a real treasure of gold, as most of the sourdough-passengers never expected to return North.

Early in the morning, October 4, about five hours after the Sophia left Skagway, she ran into a blinding snowstorm and soon afterwards struck Vanderbilt reef, in Lynn Canal. Helpless, she remained caught on the rocks with a hole in her hull. (She was only one-half mile from shore.) Several vessels rushed to her aid from Juneau, including the Cedar. but because the sea was fairly calm, Captain Locke decided his ship, the Sophia, was in no immediate danger. Foolishly, he refused help from the Cedar and other rescue ships, saying that he would wait for a ship of his own Canadian Line*, from Vancouver, to come and take his passengers off the steamer.* But on Friday, the next day, October 25, near evening, a fierce gale forced the attendant rescue ships from Juneau to hurriedly seek shelter. At 5 p.m., Captain Locke saw his fatal mistake!

A frantic, last minute message came from the Sophia, sent by the terrified wireless operator, "For God's sake, save us! We are foundering!"

Heavy waves suddenly lifted the Sophia off the reef. Quickly, she sank in very deep water taking everyone aboard—343 souls, including whole families. Only a half-frozen, pitiful little dog reached shore!

Knowing some of the these alarming accounts already, I looked at the angry waters of Queen Charlotte Sound, with extreme fear and anxiety. We might never ride this storm out on the Rosalie. Oh, why had I risked it—Clemy's life and mine!

There were muffled cries, ship's bells clanging and the captain's crisp orders.

There was a quick knock at my stateroom. I struggled against the wind, to open the door. It was the Purser:

"Lady, don't be afraid," he said hurriedly. "But we're telling all passengers to get dressed and put on life preservers. They're in your cabin. Keep all portholes locked. Don't venture out unless we give the

---

*Vanderbilt Reef is located near Juneau, at end tip of Douglas Isle.

*The Princess Victoria answered the SOS at Vancouver, B.C., and she was speeding to the rescue when the Sophia went down. The Captain of the Sophia, as a last minute measure had emptied the ship's oil upon the waves in an effort to becalm the water around the steamer.

alarm. You could be swept overboard!"

Before I could ask a single question he was gone! I heard him hurriedly deliver the same terse message to the passenger in the next cabin, a young woman traveling alone.

I remembered seeing her for the first time at dinner the night before, sitting alone several tables away, aloof and silent; only talking to the waiter a few times. She was a fascinating person to watch, (I thought), a young woman of unusual beauty, with the bearing of a queen—tall and stately, beautifully gowned, fair skinned, velvety eyes, and a complexion like the inside petal of a lovely white lily.

After dinner I had noticed that she'd kept absolutely to herself and had spoken to no one. I had wondered, "Who is she and where is she going? Could she be the wife of a wealthy mine owner? An adventuress? An actress maybe, or was she a ——?" My mind refused to shape the last words. I had heard tales of hundreds of that kind of woman in the North. Not knowing her real name, in my own mind I dubbed her "Lady Lily."

In the lounge, for a short time that night, Clemy and I had sat near her while looking at magazines, but actually it was difficult to look at anything except Lady Lily. Clemy, frankly, stared at her! She was reading a book and never looked up. Suddenly, I was shocked to see her fingers when she turned a page.

There was a ring of all shapes and sizes on every finger, and on both hands, including her thumbs! Then, I was shocked again. I could see that she was reading one of the cheapest Dime Novels of the day, completely taboo in refined society. The main characters were depicted in suggestive poses on the garish cover!

In a few minutes, Clemy and I hurriedly left the lounge.

When we reached our cabin, Clemy remarked, "Mother, that lady was awfully pretty, but she wouldn't answer—no, not even when I asked her why she wore thirteen rings! Sure! I counted them, and I told her I thought she could move her fingers much easier if she only wore two, like my mother."

"Oh Clemy," I chided, "you shouldn't have said that! But say, young man," I asked suspiciously, "when did you speak to her, anyway?"

"Oh, when you went to get your scarf," Clemy replied guiltily. "Yes, Mother, at first I thought she was very sad and lonely and would like to talk to me, but I guess she just doesn't like little boys."

"Clemy," I said carefully, "don't you think she's the prettiest lady you've ever seen?"

"No Bamba, you're the prettiest," he had said loyally.

Well now, I could hear the beautiful "Lady Lily" stirring about, as the stateroom walls were paper-thin. She seemed to be greatly agitated—walking the floor and sobbing! She sounded terribly frightened. But who wouldn't be thoroughly frightened? I certainly was!

Quickly, I got the two life preservers down from the shelf and fastened one around my trembling body. The straps were salty, rusty and hard to adjust. Then, I gently awakened Clemy, trying very hard to appear calm, but I knew my voice shook and that I was as white as a sheet!

Clemy opened his eyes very wide and said quite unexpectedly:

"Oh Bamba, don't be afraid! Jesus will take care of us, just like he did when Peter, James and John were so afraid of the waves that time they were out fishin' on the Sea of Galilee. Remember, you told me that story once, yourself."

"Yes, Clemy," I said faintly, as I helped him into his clothes, "you're such a brave little boy to remember it right now."

While I fastened the big straps of the life preserver around his warm, moist little body, I breathed a fervent prayer for our safety.

We were both very wide awake now, and so we sat on the edge of the lower bunk and visited, desperately trying to forget the raging storm. We talked of Edward in the Klondike; of loved ones and friends in Tacoma, and then about drawing. Clemy liked to draw and paint pictures and seemed to have a natural talent for art.

"In the morning," Clemy informed me, "I'm going to draw the Rosalie, and I'm going to show the big rocks. And I'm going to draw that pretty lady in the next cabin, with all them thirteen rings."

"Those rings," I laughed softly, half amused, forgetting for the moment to be afraid of the storm.

The boat continued to roll, jerk and dive—the frightening suspense was still with us—but finally, the two of us crawled into the lower bunk, still, of course, keeping the life preservers on. (A more uncomfortable position, one could scarcely imagine!) Clemy's trusting little hand held mine. Soon he was fast asleep. I listened to the raging storm then gradually my apprehensions subsided. I was sure, I didn't imagine it—the ship was riding on an evener keel. Then, I too, dropped off into an almost peaceful slumber.

* * *

The rest of the trip was through fairly calm seas. However, we passed the rusting hulls of shipwrecked steamers. The sight of these was certainly not reassuring! No one could tell how many lives had been lost thus far in the gold-rush but they were estimated into the hundreds! Too many old derelicts had been pressed into service, and too many captains and crews had been too unfamiliar with the route.

We passed chunks of floating glacier-ice, some (with imagination) resembled castles, cathedrals, prehistoric animals, white polar bears, swans, and even log cabins.

We skimmed past green, wooded islands; high, snow-capped mountains, tumbling waterfalls, glistening glaciers, beckoning coves; tiny fisherman's settlements, and a few colorful Indian villages which had grotesque totem poles placed near the beaches.

At intervals we passed picturesque hamlets and cities, like Prince Rupert, Ketchikan, Wrangell, and Petersburg.

In no time, Clemy had made friends with the crew and passengers; that is, all except "Lady Lily." Also, he spent quite a lot of his "spare time" painting Alaska scenes which he had promised to send to his grandmother. In his childish collection were paintings of lighthouses, totem poles, spouting whales, fishing boats, Indian canoes, gold-rush steamers, sturdy tug boats, freight barges, the Rosalie in a dreadful storm, and there were several almost ridiculous views of "Lady Lily," who, he said, "still didn't like little boys, but who, he thought, might like his daddy!" As he had promised, he sketched the "Lily" with prominent fingers, in almost cartoon-like style, showing thirteen conspicuous rings sparkling on her ten long fingers. These he pinned up in our stateroom and asked me to choose the best ones to be mailed to his grandmother when we would reach Juneau.

"They will show her Alaska," Clemy said proudly. "And look at this new one. I copied it in the ship's lounge. See the head of the old

---

*Ketchikan was a thriving fishing and milling town. In '98 a rich gold-quartz outcropping had been discovered on Thorn Arm at tidewater. Six hundred men had rushed to the area. Mr. B. Cromer of Portsmouth, Oregon, made the original discovery.

Sourdough? He has a big nose and long chin whiskers and see—he's looking right out across the ocean. He laughs and almost jumps out of the picture?"

"Of course, Clemy," I said, "the old Sourdough does appear to be awfully pleased about something. Perhaps it's because you've discovered him in the map of Alaska. Or, maybe it's because you're coming North."

In just a short time we reached Juneau. The captain let us go ashore while he discharged cargo. This gave us a fine opportunity to inspect the city which, a few years later, was to become the official capital of Alaska Territory. At this early date the capital was still at Sitka even though a big part of the Territory's official business was being legally transacted at Juneau, and had been for several years.

First, Clemy and I hurried to mail letters and his bundle of pictures. Then, with several other passengers (Nelly Daly of Tacoma was in our party, also Fred and Anne Clayson of Skagway), we quickly went through the most colorful trading posts. We found a few last minute items to take into the Klondike, like thread, pins and needles. Of course we were fascinated with Juneau's quaint atmosphere, and it was good to be ashore for awhile.

Directly across from Juneau was large, green verdured Douglas Island. The distance to the island from Juneau appeared to be less than one quarter of a mile (three city blocks).

A Sourdough pointed out the famous Treadwell Mine, on Douglas Isle, to a group of us. Among the things he told us was the Treadwell was being worked continuously, day and night, with no stopping. Also, there were a number of barges waiting near the island to take the gold ore to the States, some probably to the huge smelter in Tacoma on Puget Sound.

The great Treadwell seemed to monopolize most of the beachland although two other good-sized mines stood nearby. They were "The Ready Bullion" and "The Mexican." While we were in Juneau we learned that it had had its beginning way back in 1880 when two miners from Sitka, called Joe Juneau and Richard Harris, were exploring the vicinity in canoes, accompanied by their Indian wives. They were looking for gold, expecting to find it, because in an old report to

---

*Sept. 8, 1906, Juneau finally became the official capital of Alaska. The largest peak back of Juneau was called Mt. Juneau.

Sitka, by John Muir (who had also explored the vicinity in an Indian canoe) there was mention that, according to the geology of the area, gold should be found somewhere in the surrounding region of Gastineau Channel.

The Juneau party landed and explored back in among the mountains. They soon found gold in a little stream, just behind what is now Juneau. They named the area "The Silver Bow Basin," and called the stream, "Gold Creek." When the news reached Sitka a wild stampede followed. Soon, there was a thriving little settlement at the waterfront.

At first, the community was called "Harrisburg" in honor of Richard Harris. Then, as the village grew, its name was changed to "Rockwell" in honor of a prominent naval officer. But in 1882, at a special miners' meeting, the name was changed to "Juneau" honoring Joe Juneau, who was not only one of the original discoverers, but who was also a nephew of Solomon Juneau, the pioneer who had founded the city of Milwaukee, Wisconsin. The miners were determined that at least one good American city would bear the name, "Juneau."

After finding gold in the Silver Bow Basin and other places among the cliffs, Joe Juneau speculated that there must be a rich Mother Lode somewhere in the vicinity. But where? He never once guessed that huge deposits of gold lay right under the water-channel at the city's front doorstep, across on Douglas Isle. No, nor did anyone else!

Quite by chance gold was found on the island at the beach-line. But it was in such minute quantities that the discoverers—Bean and Matthews—decided the claim had very little value. Gladly, they signed it over to John Treadwell for the consideration of $500—$5 for re-recording the claim, and $495 for a debt owed Treadwell on a freight bill. (Treadwell was a builder from San Francisco.)

Treadwell and four other partners* developed the mine, and by carefully boring under the salt water, they struck a rich vein. "The Treadwell" was world famous by 1899, and was yielding large quantities of yellow gold. Already, the miners had tunneled under the salt water to a depth of 500 feet. At this date, 1899, they expected to continue to at least 1,000 feet in one particular location. "The Great Treadwell" was making more than a half-million dollars in annual pro-

*One of John Treadwell's well-known partners was Senator P. Jones of Nevada. Treadwell Associates had to fight squatters on their claim. Joe Juneau, himself, never reaped any gold to speak of. 1898 found him in Dawson, destitute, and for a living he was washing dishes in a restaurant.

fits and was providing men with hundreds of jobs.

A deep cave had been discovered which led down under the beach and bay. A rich ledge extended 400 feet from wall to wall. Originally, they thought the hole had led to an underground chamber, and that it must have been the beginning of an ancient river bed. This cavern was known as the famous Glory Hole.

We also learned that the "Treadwell" had the biggest quartz stamp-mill in the world, and several hundred stamps had recently been added.

Another intriguing thing about Juneau was that it was almost entirely lighted by that brand new invention—electric lights, and had been since 1897.*

* * *

When the Rosalie pulled away that day there were about forty-five of us still aboard. Among them were several Skagway merchants who seemed not the least bit interested in the hard work of gold-mining. No! Nor was our beautiful, but mysterious "Lady Lily" interested, for she was still avidly reading her dime-novels and keeping very much to herself, and of course, looking more gorgeous than ever! No one had as yet found out who she was, or where she was going, and apparently that was exactly the way she wished it!

(As a leap ahead in the story) I was shocked to hear at a later date that my intriguing "Lady Lily" was none other than the notorious "Diamond Lil," (Lillian Davenport). She kept a "Luxury House" in Skagway and grew wealthy by entertaining returning "Klondike Kings," who, laden with gold, visited her after coming over Chilkoot or White Pass from Alaska-Yukon Territory! Originally, she was from the underworld of Chicago and had developed a great passion for diamonds! Certainly, nature had fashioned her into a perfect beauty and at first glance she did appear to be a person of real refinement. But "Diamond Lil" was a Courtesan in the fullest sense of the word, only entertaining the obviously rich clients who could pay handsomely for what she had to offer. Nevertheless, she was firmly entrenched in the "world's oldest profession." (Many years later, when she had wantonly spent her youth

---

*In 1917, the world's most unique and famous mine, "The Treadwell," met with disaster. The engineers tragically misjudged the slant of the deepest shaft and salt water from Gastineau Channel rushed in and flooded the mine and utterly destroyed it. This was a terrific loss to the entire city of Juneau.

THE ROSALIE AND THIRTEEN RINGS

and fortune, she died in Seattle a penniless, forgotten old scrub woman.)

Hourly, passenger vessels caught up, and passed us, also many tugboats, barges and freighters hove into sight. Two mammoth twin barges, the Ajax and Bjax from Seattle, traveled near us for a time. It was said there were over a hundred passenger vessels making regular runs to Alaska.

Newspapers had well advertised the fact that all Eastern special gold-rush trains made good connections with the largest steamers. Among the steamers we saw was the large luxury liner, The Roanoke. Others were: The City of Seattle, The Alki, The George W. Elder, The Cottage City, The Portland, The Excelsior, The Humbolt, The Topeka, The Willamette, and The Islander (that doomed ship which was to sink August 14, 1901). One could almost feel the vibrant electric waves of enthusiasm from boatloads of eager hopefuls coming across the waters. Steamers literally bulged with lively people, singing, drinking, and even dancing—crammed between all kinds of freight and equipment. Some of the smaller vessels carried unhappy sheep, cows and oxen, all cruelly herded together with barking dogs, neighing horses, braying mules and many bales of hay and crates of machinery. What a motley mess were some of those steamers and freighters—packed full of a chaotic conglomeration of everything! At least the Rosalie was a clean, neat little vessel even though a bit crowded!

"Say," said an old-timer, as we passengers stood watching Lynn Canal grow narrower, and the mountains more giantlike. "In just about a half-hour we'll be at Skagway. The buildings ain't very pretty, mostly covered with that black, ugly, tar-paper stuff. Everyone uses it—keeps that beastly north wind out. It comes a-howling down from the peaks like screaming Banshees. It's often cold in summer, but it's cold as Hades in winter! Skagway's a lot like an icebox—with a steady wind blowing through. In fact, Skagway in Indian lingo means, "North Wind." But there's something else far worse in Skagway than wind and weather. 'Tis the bad reputation of the place.

"A year ago it was considered the roughest, toughest spot on the face of the earth. But now that that scoundrel, Soapy Smith, is gone the town has improved somewhat. Yet, I'm telling ya' girl, if ya' were my daughter, I would be mighty uneasy about you going into Skagway. Be mighty careful and be sure to keep an eye on little Clem, too!"

Chapter 3

WILD SKAGWAY AND SOAPY SMITH

I quickly discovered that a boarding house was a good place to learn community news. The mere mention of Soapy Smith in Skagway had started conversation buzzing, even though he had now been dead and buried a little over a year.

Clemy and I had found lodging for the night at a small boarding house near the waterfront, owned and operated by Mrs. Harriet Pullen, an attractive widow who had several small boys and a daughter to support. She was a friendly, energetic person, and had been in Skagway since early fall of 1897, so she had seen the town sprout and grow from only a few log cabins to a lively boom town, and of course, she had known the notorious Soapy Smith, too.

"Yes, friends," Mrs. Pullen said, as she passed the sandwiches and hot coffee to a group of us soon after our arrival in town, "Soapy Smith was certainly a Wizard of Deceit! In fact, he inspired confidence that was most unusual. With his strong underworld tendencies, it's no wonder he became a successful gambler, notorious crook and sinister politician.

"How did he look, you ask."

"Well, he was not very tall—about five feet ten inches—rather on the slight side. He had almost delicate features—tried very hard to hide them behind a huge, black beard."

"And his eyes?

"Well, they were rather soft and dreamy. And, yes, he certainly had a refined nice way, too—like a real gentleman! Somehow he always gave the impression of being a sympathetic, kind, honest person—seemed even religious at times. But folks, he was really a twisted soul, an expert in the art of fraud and villainy. Yes, I should say even a genius at it!

"Well, here is his story prior to his coming North, as I've heard it, and then afterwards in Skagway, as I knew it.

"At the very beginning of the Klondike gold-rush, Soapy Smith, who was then in Denver, Colorado, cocked his ear and listened with greedy attention to the fabulous newspaper accounts of rivers of gold discovered on the Bonanza and Eldorado. First, he listened to those wildly

Lawless Skagway, ruled by Soapy Smith. (Courtesy of Dedman Photos)

Harriet Pullen and her famous Skagway gold rush boarding house.
(She bought the three-story mansion from Billy Moore
about 1900, expanding her accommodations.)

Soapy Smith, riding his horse through Skagway's streets a few days before his violent death.

Clancy's saloon (part ownership with Soapy Smith's gang in Skagway).

exciting newspaper reports telling of the arrival of the S. S. Humbolt in San Diego, in June, 1897; saying the steamer was loaded with gold from the North. Next, came the thrilling reports of the arrival of another steamer, The Excelsior, in San Francisco, a few days later. It too, was loaded with gold! And then came the astonishing account of the famous treasure ship, the steamer Portland*. It arrived in Seattle that same month, laden with a ton of glittering gold and it was all owned by just a few dozen Klondike Kings!

"Of course this momentous news rocked the world and it certainly rocked Soapy Smith to the very bottom of his toes as he wrapped pieces of soap in front of curious street-corner audiences, using clever sleight-of-hand performance, nonchalantly flourishing five and ten-dollar bills, which he pretended to include in many of the packages of his miracle soap. Gullible people who bought the soap and found that they had not been lucky, could not guess what was at the bottom of the master showman's dishonest mind. Smith had suddenly grown mighty impatient with all this 'small-fry way of acquiring riches.' He could no longer resist the tempting lure of gold 'way up North, somewhere near the Arctic Circle.

"Would he mine for the rich, yellow stuff?

" 'Certainly not,' he told his henchmen indignantly. 'We'll dig it from the pokes of successful sourdoughs. All it will take is intelligence and a little finesse.'

"And so with a selected band of hard-boiled con men, pickpockets, gamblers and swindlers, Soapy went to Seattle and boarded the S. S. City of Seattle late in the fall of '97. After docking at Skagway and looking over the place with an appraising eye, he decided they would go no further. This was it! Here was a lively, dramatic spot to fleece the 'innocents.' Sure, it was a perfect setting! Money and equipment were pouring in from the States, and bags and bags of yellow nuggets and gold-dust were coming from the North—coming over the old Indian Chilkoot Pass Trail and also over the newly opened White Pass, sometimes called the Skagway Trail."

Mrs. Pullen went on to say she had been among the first to see Soapy Smith standing on one of Skagway's main street corners loudly

---

*The Portus B. Wear and the "Alice" reached St. Michaels in late spring of 1897 laden with tons of gold from Dawson. The gold was then transferred to the steamers Humboldt, Excelsior, and Portland and rushed to the States.

proclaiming his wares and even singing ballads to attract the crowds! Of course he was surrounded by newly arrived, gawking, orey-eyed, homesick stampeders, and they, in turn, were surrounded by Soapy's men.

"Soap, soap—the miracle cleanser—soap, the heaven-sent purifier!" Smith called in a ringing voice, as he held up a bar of soap. "Men, next to Godliness is cleanliness, and I give you this nugget-like, sweet-smelling soap, for just a dollar a bar!"

"Of course," said Mrs. Pullen*, "there were always eager greenhorns who would plank down their dollars and receive five-cent packages of soap. Afterwards, and always, there would be excited commotion, accompanied by slap-happy exclamations. Sometimes as high as a $50 bill would show up! But," said Mrs. Pullen, "these lucky people were Soapy's men. Only occasionally were strangers ever allowed to win.

"When interest would sometimes lag in the soap game, our future uncrowned king of Skagway would then cleverly switch to the old-time shell game—that is—guessing under which of the three real walnut shells the hard, little green pea had finally become lodged, after it, of course, had been skillfully maneuvered around and 'round on a table-top, or on some other equally level spot in plain sight of everyone.

"And so," said Mrs. Pullen, "Soapy Smith's games flourished. People were tolerant. What harm was there in simple raffle games? The new magician soap salesman was certainly a good looking fellow, and after all, he was furnishing cheap entertainment for hundreds of homeless people who passed through Skagway's portals.

"Later on, when Soapy had become sufficiently well-known, he gradually tapered off his raffle games. Rapidly, he was becoming a prominent citizen, a man of real importance!

"But soon it was noticed that gangs of hoodlums and hardened criminals were flocking to Skagway. They were underworld characters—many from San Francisco's tough Barbary Coast.

"Now it was becoming apparent, too, that our soft-spoken soap salesman, who always dressed so fastidiously, was on easy speaking terms with these human vultures, men like Joe Palmer, Chinaman Yee, Turner Jackson, Frisco Red, Tom Candy, George Wilder, Doc Baggs, Slim Jim Foster, Charles Bowers, Old Man Tripp and many others. Then, it was whispered that Soapy Smith was actually at the head of

---

*Mrs. Harriet Pullen died in 1948 at the age of 86.

these terrible and vicious gangs."

"But no," said some of the shocked citizens, aghast, "no, this couldn't be possible! Why, how could a man who loves children and dogs and who sends donations to the poor widows and who is so conspicuous in church fund-raising be a crook? Why, the very idea! He's a kind, generous fellow!

"And didn't he (Jefferson Randolph Smith) now hobnob with Skagway's most influential citizens? And didn't he receive letters from well-known people from all over the country, complimenting him on his fine civic work in Skagway? Yes, and hadn't the Daily Alaskan praised him in editorials?

"And how about that visiting New York World newspaper reporter? Hadn't he written back to his paper that Jefferson Randolph Smith (Soapy Smith) was an unusually fine fellow, the nicest and pleasantest he had ever met! And what if Soapy Smith had become sort of a self-appointed dictator, 'The Shah of Skagway'? Wild, woolly Skagway needed someone who understood how to manage unruly crowds, flocking through to the Yukon Country.

"Soon it was noted, however, that the 'Chief' owned a saloon on Holly Street. He liked to call it 'Jeff's Oyster Bar, No. 317.' Occasionally he did serve oyster soup, but liquor flowed in the 'Oyster Bar' like water.

"Soapy's place was very small and modest. It was only about twenty feet wide by fifty feet long and was constructed of rough pine boards. It was kept spotlessly clean. Yes, Soapy believed soap would do wonders for man—would make him sleep better, would give him glowing youth—and even cleanse his ills and sins. Those who knew Soapy Smith best knew that he had really enjoyed his work of soap salesman. But when his saloon became popular he no longer bothered selling soap, even though he kept quantities of it around his quarters.

"Inside his saloon, to the left of the door, was the bar, and back towards the rear of the saloon were the gambling tables. Right behind the bar a door opened into a storeroom, and from it, another door opened out into a small back yard enclosed with a high fence. In the storeroom and back yard many evil deeds were planned and speedily carried out.

"A live eagle was kept in the yard, in a cage, as a special drawing card to many unsuspecting patriotic greenhorns who were hit over the head and robbed after having been lured to the spot to view the eagle.

"Of course, Soapy Smith claimed no knowledge of these vile deeds. He was the affable back-slapping host who greeted customers out front. But he had a private office where his lieutenants regularly met. Here, gold-dust and valuables were speedily divided up.

"Now by early spring of '98 the 'Chief' was reaching the height of his evil Skagway career. Secretly, he controlled Sheriff Taylor, also the Skagway newspaper and the Militia which he himself had organized. The Spanish American War had given him an excuse to organize this group. It was later proven that the 'Militia' were all Soapy's men. He called them his 'Tigers,' ready to do his bidding whenever he decided to declare martial law and take over the town, lock, stock and barrel.

"His men met all steamers that landed at Skagway's four elongated piers. Even before prospective victims could reach land they had been spotted, for a number of Soapy's men traveled the steamers regularly. One, Frankie Dwyer, was the most colorful crook on the steamship lines. Another was bright quick-witted Wilson Mizner*, a young Soapy Smith protege from San Francisco. This one went on to Dawson to increase his fortunes there, after only a few months in Skagway.

"Of course, it was almost impossible for newcomers to tell the difference between Soapy's 'Tigers' and legitimate Skagway business men. They posed as travel agents, telegraph operators (there was no telegraph in Skagway in '97 and '98), traders, miners, packers and even bankers, and they were very adept in the art of disguise. Most of them were nimble-fingered, quick-witted, convincing talkers. Also, there were a number of notorious pickpockets who wasted no time in lifting valuables from gaping cheechakos. Perhaps the most sinister of all the group was Rev. Charles Bowers, for he posed as an extremely religious, gentle soul!

"Not only did the crooks swarm into Skagway, they stationed themselves out on the lonely mountain trails. Some carried heavy-looking packs, but the packs were actually filled with chicken feathers! Many was the poor fellow who came stumbling into town minus his poke of gold, and many was the stampeder, or sourdough, who just disappeared, or whose body was found, dumped on the streets of town, or even

---

*Wilson Mizner became known in Dawson as "The Yellow Kid." He hobnobbed with the sporting class, became an entertainer, a gold-weigher, a boxer, a colorful rascal about town. He believed it a sin to work if one had brains. He came from the famous Mizner family of Benicia, California.

found floating in the Skagway Harbor!

"But as usual, when these crimes occurred, Soapy indignantly declared he knew absolutely nothing about them, and after some particularly revolting crime he would loudly raise his voice for tighter law enforcement; he even organized a special group, 317 to be exact, for the said purpose of enforcing law and order and cleaning up the town. These men actually posted signs on public streets threatening extreme punishment to all law breakers!

"But in late spring of '98, so much evidence had piled up against Soapy that all citizens were forced, at last, to admit that he was the real criminal-leader. Even so, there were still some who charitably excused him!

"Then, on July 8, 1898, like a thunderbolt, Skagway was suddenly swept clean of Soapy Smith. It all happened in an unforseeable, dramatic way. But, folks," Mrs. Pullen reminded us, "if you're going sightseeing, I'll continue this story and show photographs later. I have pictures of Soapy Smith taken shortly before his death and a few, right afterwards. Some are pretty gory! One thing I will add, tho'. Since Soapy Smith is gone a very peculiar thing has happened around here. Somehow, through death, our 'Alaska Jesse James' has caught the popular fancy of strangers. Now, if I don't miss my guess, someday, he'll become an Alaskan legend. A lot of children in Skagway are already playing 'Soapy Smith,' even my own boys, much to my distress!"

"Be sure you're back before dark," our hostess advised, as a group of us prepared to inspect Skagway. "Soapy's gone, but remember, there's still a lot of his breed left."

After leaving Mrs. Pullen's peaceful boarding house, we found ourselves in a giddy whirl of humanity. The town fairly bulged and groaned in the chaos of gold-fevered people and bewildered animals!

Howling dogs, braying mules and neighing horses cleft passageways through busy, bustling crowds, setting up a noisy uproar of commotion, and raising great clouds of choking dust, accompanied by nervewracking squeaks of wagon* wheels badly in need of axle grease.

Pack-train drivers yelled abusively at their helpless animals, as they cracked long bull-whips across bare flanks. Oh, it was a sickening sight!

All business places wore false fronts. Colored posters, carnival-like,

*George Brackett was the owner of the wagonroad that led to White Pass. At first he charged toll.

seemed everywhere, proclaiming steamboats, outfitters, merchandise, and even Dr. Pierce advertised himself in large print along with a number of patent medicines. Also, lawyers' names boldly fluttered on the breeze.

We were jostled past gambling houses, hotels, dark, smelly saloons (At least fifty of them were in Skagway), and a number of unappetizing looking restaurants. Numerous liquor-smelling dance halls vibrated to the throb of loud, hysterical music, where would-be "Klondike Kings" pranced and kicked up their booted heels with painted, befeathered, gold-hungry girls of the bright lights. Yes, Skagway was in a slap-happy mood, alright, like a real wild west frontier town!

Clemy and I witnessed the departure of at least a dozen heavily packed mule-trains, also saw scores of cheechakos with ungainly burdens, struggling towards White Pass. And, as if to taunt the hikers, the little "Iron Horse," with the orange-red trim, at the new Broadway Station (near salt water), whistled and snorted and clanged, calling almost impatiently to the lucky devils who had tickets, to come running and jump aboard. Clemy and I hurried to the station too, for the following day we would be among the "lucky ones" to ride the train. Thousands would still have to pack into Dawson!

After watching a heavily-loaded train pull out, Clemy and I worked our way up the main streets, passing the Golden North Hotel, the Nugget Shop (there were all kinds of beautiful gold jewelry), the Post Office, the St. Nicholas Hotel, John Clancey's Saloon, and then we were at that notorious spot called Jeff's Place, on Holly Street.

"Come in, folks, join the fun," invited a man with an easy voice, leaning in the doorway, grinning at us.

Clemy tugged at my sleeve, but I hurried him away! Plenty of carousing was going on in the Soapy Smith Oyster Bar!

Shortly afterwards we reached the Yukon Outfitting Company, and there I was glad to pause, for a small brown monkey with an organ grinder was putting on a Soapy Smith street show. The monkey was jigging up and down, doing a queer dance. He was dressed in a tiny man's suit, a red striped vest, a derby hat and high-topped boots. Across his chest dangled an imitation nugget watch chain, and in his belt was stuck a toy pistol. His little green eyes roamed furtively over the crowd, as he kept up his odd little jig.

The gypsy organ grinder energetically pumped out lively, bouncy tunes, but "A Hot Time in the Old Town Tonight" seemed to be a favorite with the crowd. It greatly pleased the monkey too, who almost went berserk when the tempo was increased to a fever pitch. Jumping up and down, flapping his arms, he grabbed up tiny pieces of soap from a container and flung them in wild frenzy at the audience, just like a jungle beast throwing coconuts!

Of course his antics highly pleased the crowd. They dodged and grabbed and got souvenir soap, and Clemy retrieved several pieces too. At quick intervals, the little fellow hopped down from his box and passed his hat among the crowd for donations. When the hat was full of nickles and dimes, the monkey would rush back to his master. Greedily, he would sweep the contents into a small tin box, then he would pat the little fellow and give him peanuts.

"Ha!" laughed an old timer at my elbow, "That monkey sure is smart, and well trained. Soapy Smith lives again in this new kind of 'Skagway Monkey Business'."

"But say now," said the sourdough, addressing himself to a nearby group, including Clemy and me, "if you-all want to see some real local color, go to the Juneau wharf. There on the very first boards of the ramp are bright red blood stains. They mark the exact spot where Soapy Smith fell during a terrible fun-fight! Yes, that episode our town will long remember!

"It all happened just four days after our extra fancy Fourth of July parade in which Soapy Smith had made himself a prominent figure. He led the big parade, riding a beautiful pale grey stallion, and at the head of his own militia! Yes, he was the grand marshal!

"Whether young J. D. Stewart of Dawson was in town for that parade, no one is absolutely sure, but he was definitely in Skagway on July 7th, for it was then that Soapy's men spotted him and planned to steal all of his gold—$17,000 worth, in dust. First, they got a lot of it at the gambling tables, then they robbed him of the rest of it, while he was seeing the patriotic eagle in the back of the saloon. The eagle had, by the way, been displayed in a cage in that Fourth of July parade.

"Perhaps Stewart should have been grateful to've escaped with his life, but he was a stubborn cuss! He complained bitterly to Sheriff Taylor. Then, when no arrests were made, Stewart rushed over to Dyea, nine miles away, and angrily laid his case before law-enforcing Marshal Sehlbrede, saying that he thought Sheriff Taylor was one of Soapy's men.

"Well, Sehlbrede couldn't deny it, but Skagway was out of his jurisdiction. It had been rumored for many weeks that Sheriff Taylor was a tool of the Soapy gang. Then, too, it was common knowledge that right after the terrible avalanche on Chilkoot Pass, on April 3rd (1898), Soapy's men had rushed over and had robbed the dead while posing as rescue workers.

"And a little while before the avalanche episode, in March, Constable Rowan in Skagway and poor Andy McGrath had been slain in cold blood! Rowan was hurrying to get Doc Whiting, as his wife was about to give birth. He had almost reached the Doc's office, when he and another fellow named McGrath were called into Rice's Variety Theater, a saloon, to settle a dispute. Unfortunately, the bartender, Fay, was waiting behind the door with a gun. Without giving any warning he pumped Rowan and McGrath full of lead. They died instantly, right there on the floor, before a horrified crowd.

"Right away Soapy claimed absolutely no responsibility for these killings, but when his henchmen rescued Fay at the very last moment from the hanging party there was no doubt whose man Fay really was! Even so, Soapy Smith did a very crafty thing. Quickly, he raised several thousand dollars as a special purse for Rowan's widow and child. This, for a time, made Soapy their temporary benefactor. But something was brewing, like the fateful 'handwriting on the wall.' Soapy Smith should have heeded that warning!

"Thousands of stampeders in early summer of '98 were bypassing Skagway in favor of the town of Dyea in order to use the new Chilkoot Pass Aerial Tramway and to avoid Skagway because of Soapy Smith's gang. The flow of traffic to Dyea and Chilkoot had to be stopped as the new White Pass Railroad had already been started. Skagway was to be the new railroad's terminus and crime couldn't be allowed to take over the city.

"The $17,000 Stewart gold dust episode acted like a spark in an open keg of dynamite—Skagway was now ready to clean house! And so, on June 8, at 9 p.m., the most important meeting in the city's history was hurriedly called to Sylvester's Warehouse at the end of Juneau

---

*The worst avalanche in Alaska history occurred on Chilkoot Pass April 3, 1898. Seventy people were buried alive under ten acres of snow. Only five lived to tell about it.

dock. The Vigilante Committee (the 101) had called together its members, and all loyal Skagway citizens. The object was to decide just how to rid Skagway of the Soapy gang. A rope was hastily stretched across the ramp-end of the dock and three men were posted there with guns to keep the crooks from passing the barricade, should they try to come to the meeting. Much to everyone'e surprise, none of the gang appeared, but who should show up but Soapy Smith himself! He came down the road toting a Winchester 45. Obviously, he had been drinking heavily, which was quite unusual for him. For, strange to say, he was a teetotaler.

"Well, immediately, I could tell there was going to be a nasty scene! Soapy's face was full of terrible rage, like an approaching thundercloud. I watched in fascinated dread as Soapy neared the barricade.

"All at once, Frank Reid, our city engineer, one of the deputized men at the rope, commanded Soapy to halt. But Soapy kept right on coming, like a mad bull. As he advanced closer, he called loudly to Brownell and another fellow on the dock, to get the H– out of his way, that he was sure coming in! Promptly, both of these fellows went over the rail and landed on the sandy beach, six feet below. From there they ran to safety.

"Soapy Smith then headed for Frank Reid, wildly brandishing his gun, waving it like a club.

"Suddenly, he lunged at Reid, striking him a wicked blow, full in the face, with the butt-end of his Winchester. At the same time he screamed nasty insults at Reid, for he had always violently hated him.

"To defend himself against a second vicious attack, Reid grabbed Soapy's gun, shoving it to one side, and with his free hand he grasped for his own revolver. Tearing it loose from its holster he took quick aim at Soapy and fired, but, unfortunately, the hammer clicked on a blank cartridge. This certainly was too bad for Reid! It gave Soapy Smith just time enough to turn his weapon and level it straight at Reid, who, by now, was taking another quick aim.

"For a brief few seconds both fellows glared fiercely, holding the bead on each other. Then, all at once, simultaneously, their guns spurted fire! To us, who were standing near, it seemed there was only one extra-loud blast. When the smoke cleared, there they lay, the two of them. Soapy Smith sprawled in a pool of his own blood—stone dead—shot through the heart! A few feet away, face down, gushing blood all over the place, lay Frank Reid. Quickly, we turned him over and saw a horrible wound in his groin.

"He was still conscious when we carried him to Doc Whiting's. He was calm—told us not to worry—said he'd soon recover. But twelve days later he died in awful agony. It was a terrible shock, for he was very popular in these parts. We lost a real hero that day. Then, we learned Reid had been a hero long before coming to Skagway, as he had been in those fierce Oregon-Bannock-Piut Indian Wars, back in 1878. Before that, he had been a school teacher and a fine surveyor. When first he came North, he helped with the survey for the famous Chilkoot Pass Aerial Tramway, working with Chief Engineer Archie McLean Hawks. Reid also helped survey the Skagway townsite.

"Yes," sighed the Sourdough, "Soapy Smith's bullet took one of our most useful citizens."

After seeing the Soapy Smith Monkey Show and hearing the story, Clemy and I, with the crowd of sight-seers, hurried to the Juneau wharf, as tho' drawn by a magnet!

"Ha, ha," laughed a stranger leaning at the rail, smoking his pipe and eyeing us with a quizzical smile. "Sorry to disappoint all ya' fine people, but the feller who keeps the bloodstains bright with red paint ain't here no longer. Yep," concluded the obliging old-timer, squinting his eyes at us, "suppose you've heard about our notorious villain. He sure was a scoundrel! But, do ya' know, some folks stuck up for the villain; called him 'Robin Hood of Alaska.' 'Twas because he fed a few down-and-outers. Never fool yourselves, many of them down-and-outers ended up becoming part of the gang, 'Soapy's Lambs,' he liked to call 'em!"

Naturally, we visitors were disappointed because we could not see the red historical marks, the beginning of 'Skagway's liberation.' But there were hobnails driven into the planks forming "Hobnail" crosses. These, the old-timer hastened to explain, marked the exact spot where Soapy and Frank Reid had fallen in battle.

Next thing I knew Clemy and I were jostled along a dusty road in the midst of a chattering, curious crowd, headed for the little cemetery. Somehow, that seemed the next logical place to go after visiting Juneau wharf!

The cemetery was just a short way back of town, on sloping ground. The place was lightly wooded, and appeared almost park-like. A frothy,

Stampeders on scow getting ready to land at Dyea, Alaska.

Dyea, Alaska, where the stampeders landed to go over Chilkoot Pass.
(Courtesy Dedman photos)

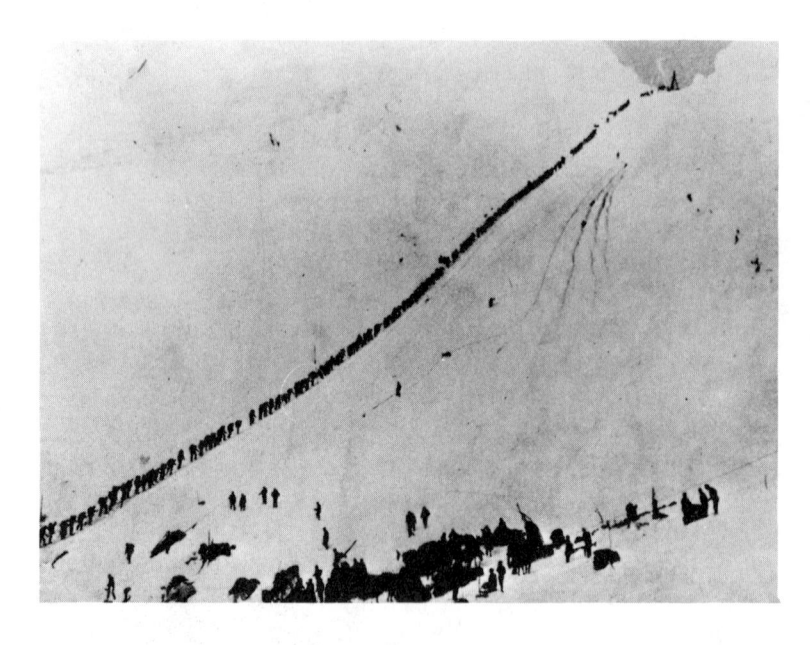

Trail of '98. Chilkoot Pass, from the "Scales" up!
(Courtesy Paul T. Mizony)

White Pass Yukon Railroad, Alaska, called the "most spectacular little railroad in the world," 1899.

lacy waterfall cascaded down from a high rocky cliff, dropping into a lovely, cool brook. Crystal-water flowed away through a deep bower of delicate maiden-hair ferns and wild mint. Somehow, the place seemed more for the living than for the dead.

Soapy's weed-choked grave sprawled in the southwest corner of the cemetery, in a lonely, melancholy spot. Only a rough wooden board identified the corpse that lay somewhere beneath.

"Why—he was only thirty-eight!" exclaimed a woman in the crowd.

"The words of his mouth were as smooth as butter, but war was in his heart; his words were softer than oil, yet they were like drawn swords," solemnly chanted a tall, thin sanctimonious-looking man in the crowd, whom someone had fittingly nicknamed "The Poet-Minister."

In a small sun-bathed clearing we found the peaceful resting place of Frank Reid, near the tumbling waterfall. A soft, almost shapeless rainbow moved gently across the clearing, like a filmy phantom, lightly treading on the weathered tombstones.

"Oh, that I had wings like a dove, for then I would fly away and be at rest," softly quoted our poet friend.

"Oh, poor Reid," sighed a woman in the crowd. "His headstone says he died July 20, 1898, and it says he gave his life for the honor of Skagway. What a pity he had to die so young! He was a handsome man—about forty-eight. His picture is in the Golden North Hotel.

"As the flower of the field, so he flourisheth—man's days are of grass . . . the wind passeth over it and the place shall know it no more," solemnly chanted the poet, in almost bitter tones.

"But there is someone in California who still remembers Soapy Smith, and cares," insisted a timid voice in the crowd. "That 'someone' has sent enough money to replace that rough wooden headboard for a marble slab. It could be Soapy's real wife, not the redheaded woman! No one really knows—exactly, tho'."

"Humph! He doesn't deserve that much consideration," snapped a lady, beligerently.

It was evident, as I listened to their remarks, that each visitor was reviewing the bandit-leader's crimes and was acting as judge and jury. They were carefully reading other headstones, too. Putting all these

*Soapy Smith's descendants live in Southern California.

together—the stones were eloquently speaking out against Soapy, these victims who lay beneath, who would never reach the Land of Gold!

After many indignant remarks, the crowd moved on down the trail, but I remained seated on a fallen log, letting Clemy dabble in the murmuring brook. He was only a small child and needed relief from the thought of death.

Soon, however, I became aware that we were all alone in the cemetery. "Clemy," I said, "I heard them say they were going to Dyea. We should try to see it, too. It was there your father landed in 1897, on his way to the Klondike."

Hurriedly, Clemy and I crossed the narrow bridge spanning the big Skagway River. We followed the trail that crossed the peninsula, through a thick forest and soon came to salt water on Lynn Canal. But it was apparent that we had permanently lost our crowd. How could they get ahead of us so fast? And now, we were in a lonely stretch!

"Oh, Clemy," I said, "we should turn back!" But Clemy jubilantly pointed to an old sourdough with his mule approaching us from Dyea.

"Say now, why that lost-nugget expression?" he asked. "No, don't tell me; you two are kinda lost now, ain't ya? Two cheechakos!! Gol darn! You kin bet your boots I wouldn't let my daughter and grandson come out on this lonely trail. Lady, this is Smuggler's Cove! Plenty of them smugglers slip in here, too.

"Nope, ya' can't make it over to Dyea and git back before dark altho' I passed a crowd two miles up that sure was a-tryin'! Why, it's sixteen miles round-trip."

"Oh mister, have you ever seen the big Chilkoot tramway?" asked Clemy eagerly.

"Oh sure, little man, lots of times. It's in them big mountains yonder, beyond Dyea. The aerial tramway runs from Canyon City up to Sheep Camp, and then to the top of Chilkoot Peak. It sure is a back-saver, a lifesaver to many a stampeder. Every day it hauls thousands of tons of supplies over to the lakes so stampeders kin git on down the Yukon to Dawson more quickly. Back in early 1897 the big tram was only an engineer's dream. By golly, I wish ya' could see it!"

"What does it look like?"

"Well, my boy, it has dozens of big iron buckets fastened onto a thick, moving copper-steel cable. The cable travels along, high in the air, above the mountainside, and it's held up, or supported by, high tripod towers, spaced at certain distances. The longest distance is twenty-two hundred feet, the longest span in the world! Yes, it's a wonderful sight, a great job of engineering.

"In places them buckets travel two and three hundred feet above the ground. Maybe higher. Each bucket carries 300 pounds. Many a feller's tried to hook rides, but I only know of one who did. Rides are forbidden mostly because of great danger. But at the very beginning of the tramway, a stampeder from Tacoma did get permission to ride in one of those buckets. Well, he had a mighty close call! When he was almost at the end of his ride, up near the top of Chilkoot, suddenly, right ahead of him, a bucket tore loose from the copper cable. It crashed to the earth with a terrible thud, just barely missing a dozen stampeders on the trail below. Man! Oh man! It was lucky for that fellow ridin' the good bucket that he hadn't chosen the ill-fated one, for if he had it sure would have been the last of him! Yep, I saw it all happen with my own eyes! Canned goods, machinery and a tangled mass of camp equipment spilled out all over the mountainside!"

"Oh, Mister, that was my dad a-riding the good bucket," cried Clemy excitedly. "He sent a letter tellin' all about it—even drew a picture."

"Well, well, bless my soul!" exclaimed the old Sourdough. "And to think I'd meet Ed Lung's little son and wife way up here in Smuggler's Cove. Yes, my boy, your dad did have a mighty close call. He musta' had a guardian angel watchin' over his shoulder that day, and no foolin'!

"Nope, lady, to see the tram, you'd have to first get to Dyea and then climb a rough mountain trail. Ya' ain't missin' much tho', not seein' Dyea. Looks like Skagway; it's about the same size, too. The Dyea Indian Village ain't much neither—just same old Indian style.

"Well now, the most important difference between the two towns is the way they're run. Dyea is very law-abiding, no rough stuff! U. S. Marshal Sehlbrede* sees ta' that. When he speaks, folks take heed! His

---

*The Hon. C. A. Sehlbrede became a U. S. Commissioner in Alaska. He was from Roseburg, Oregon, and was successor of John U. Smith in Dyea. Sehlbrede was a puritanical, shrewd lawyer dedicated to Federal statutes and for lack of disciplined Alaska law he transplanted the Oregon Code to the Territory. He was greatly feared by criminals and the sporting class. He and Frank Reid had long been friends, and in the Skagway episode it was hard for him to be impartial. Governor Brady of Alaska sent a government cruiser from Sitka to help re-establish law and order after the Soapy Smith shootings in Skagway.

guide ta' law and order is the Ten Commandments. Ain't none better. Thou shalt not do this—Thou shalt not do that—and all the rest of it.

"And, if them Bible rules don't work—well then—Sehlbrede has a mighty strong garrison of U. S. soldiers there at Dyea. It was a mighty good thing for Skagway 'cause right after the Soapy Smith shootin' fracas, Sehlbrede rushed troops over. He got there just in time to halt the lynchings. By golly, things was sure a runnin' wild; jus' like they was in them real old WILD WEST DAYS!

"But say now, Lady, I'm 'Skagway Charlie'. When you git up to Dawson be sure to tell Ed Lung 'Hello' for me. Say that I was mighty glad to meet his wife and son and escort 'em safely back to Mrs. Pullen's boardin' house.

"Here, Clem, climb aboard my good old burro, Dolly Dimples. We must be gittin' back to Skagway afore that honory ole sun drops down into Lynn Canal.

"Come on, Lady," urged the old Sourdough, "you follow Clemy, and I'll bring up the rear with my rifle. Smuggler's Cove ain't no place ta' be caught after dark."

Chapter 4

LITTLE IRON HORSE

It was now September 1, 1899.

Bright and early, muffled to our ears against the cold blasts sweeping down from snow-clad peaks back of Skagway, Clemy and I eagerly climbed aboard the little White Pass-Yukon train and scrambled for

---

*The famous "Pullen House" of Skagway was not in existence until 1900. The first three years of the gold rush (1897, '98, and '99) Mrs. Pullen ran a small boarding house down near the waterfront.

Billy Moore, an old sea captain, built the first cabin in Skagway in 1887, homesteading the area. When the stampeders came in 1897, many of them stayed and squatted on the land. Billy Moore tried to make his large homestead stick, but was unsuccessful. After a long legal battle he won twenty-five percent of the townsite value. His large three-story home was purchased in 1900 by Mrs. Pullen and became the famous "Pullen Boarding House."

seats in the center of one of the three rapidly filling coaches.

What an exciting adventure it was going to be, riding on this new, almost toy-like train! Already, they were beginning to call it the most spectacular railroad in the world!

The small, sturdy Duchess Engine, with steam puffing and bells clanging, was making ready to pull the heavily loaded narrow-gauge passenger cars, with freight, up over the steep White Pass grade to Lake Bennett where she would leave us to continue on our way to Dawson by boat.

Just six weeks earlier, in Alaska, all who traveled over White Pass had either hiked the 40-mile trail, or ridden horseback. Clemy and I were truly fortunate to be going North at this particular time, and we owed Dr. Misner in Tacoma gratitude for obtaining our railroad tickets.

Now, as we sat looking out of the window, watching Skagway disappear behind a deep bend of the mountain, I thought of our interesting twenty-four hour stopover. Certainly it had been an exciting pause, and I was quite sure that I would never think of Skagway without vivid, mental pictures of Soapy Smith which the stories that different ones had helped create.

"But why was it?" I asked myself musingly, as I watched the foothills slide into cliffs and cliffs into high craggy battlements, "that this lawless fellow should capture the imagination of so many people since his sudden death?

"Was it because Soapy Smith had used the unrestrained, wild spirit of the frontier so effectively, riding the crest of its uninhibited greeds and passions? There was no use denying it, the evil aura of Soapy Smith still lingered over Skagway. But now my thoughts were focused on the gold-seekers, moving in an irregular column, slowly picking their tedious way over the bumpy, uneven trail which in places ran almost parallel with the railroad tracks.

Slung across sagging shoulders hung bulging gunny sacks, oversized boxes, sleds, mining supplies and many other kinds of miscellaneous things. Some of the men even toted precious Klondike stoves! Yes, they were a motley crowd all right. Most of them looked more like emaciated, worn out bums than gold-seekers!

"Certainly," I thought, "not many of them are really the frontier-type!" Why, I knew that staggering along like pack-horses, were doctors, lawyers, teachers, politicians, merchants, artists and even preachers! (My husband had been an expert accountant right out of an office.)

I recalled, while at Mrs. Pullen's boarding house, I had heard that even a Rajah had come to Skagway in his regal yacht, intending to join the gold-rush. But when he climbed the White Pass trail and saw the stampeders loaded down like beasts and saw how the animals were mistreated too, he decided the lure of gold was not strong enough to draw him, a Rajah, into such a dubious adventure. So he quickly gave up the idea and returned to India.

The Rajah had come upon men frozen to death in the snow, sitting up like stones. And he had seen wild-eyed, demented stampeders who had suddenly gone mad, beating their animals, cursing and pushing and screaming at everyone in their path—even shaking their fists at God!

Now our little train slowly picked up speed. For about six miles we followed along the picturesque East Fork of the Skagway River which gushed through a deep, grey-shadowed canyon. Then, we crossed over to the right-hand side and slowly began ascending the massive Sawtooth Mountains. Gradually, we were coming into a primeval world of towering Alaska peaks, glistening snowfields, crystal waterfalls and eternal, blue-faced glaciers.

It seemed our plucky little Duchess Engine couldn't possible pull us up, and around some of the steepest curves, and clung with clutching, nervous fingers to the small iron rails. At last we reached spectacular Rocky Point, or 7 Mile Post, and caught a splendid, unobstructed glimpse of sparkling Lynn Canal, far below.

Beyond Rocky Point, we crossed and recrossed small stretches of the torturous stampede trail; caught up with, and passed, hard-pressed bands of sweating fellows, laboriously picking their way up the rough, icy grade. Wet snow had fallen during the previous night, in these upper regions, making the going difficult for hikers. We came alongside of a lone man (of all things!) pulling a canoe, sled-fashion. Of course the canoe was loaded to overflowing! No doubt if the owner could reach the lake in time to beat the ice he would transport himself and his goods to Dawson by canoe. In any case it would be a hard, precarious trip, especially in a trail-worn canoe!

"Lady, look down there, where the river flows," said a miner at my elbow as the train crawled along the perpendicular rim of a canyon. "See those objects there, at the bottom of the ravine, which appear to be large, irregular boulders? Well, they ain't rocks. Nope, they're dead, snow-covered pack-horses. Poor things! There are at least three thousand of 'em all together, and they're strewn along the White Pass trail in this ravine and another one up near the summit. It's pitiful, I tell you! Some of these pack-animals dropped from sheer overwork, or hunger, and stumbled and fell off the grade and lay in ravines for hours, maybe days, with packs still strapped to their backs before they mercifully gave up the ghost.

"But no, Lady, don't look. You must watch the marvels of this fine little railroad. There were those who said it was impossible to put one through up here and the idea became a huge trail-joke. But expert railroad construction engineer, E. C. Hawkins, and a young engineer named Michael Heney, sometimes called the 'Irish Prince' conquered these mountains. In places the workmen had to be let down with long ropes over these crags, a thousand feet, to set dynamite to blast out the railroad bed.

"Many times Mike Heney, himself, went over the brink. It was a colossal job with very few casualties. One day, tho', a terrible accident did occur. It happened right after some extensive blasting, and when it seemed that all rubble had settled. Suddenly, a huge rock loosened from the mountain-top. It came thundering down over the place where a group of men had just started working.

"When that horrible stone bounced to the second ledge below, and stopped, two workmen were missing! It was obvious they were caught somewhere beneath that giant granite boulder on the second ledge.

"Now look closely, Lady, and you'll see that ugly 100-ton rock. It stands there about two hundred feet below the railroad bed. Heney was so grief-stricken that he climbed down and painted a large, black cross on the rock. He felt doubly responsible because one of the fellows hadn't wanted to work that day, but Heney talked him into it"

Previously I had grown ill at the sickening thought of 3,000 dead horses on The White Pass. But now, at 11 Mile Post, I shivered when I saw the hideous boulder. What a frightful price the two workmen had paid to successfully put through this railroad!

Clemy sat spellbound at the window listening and watching.

Suddenly, we were plunged into darkness. Clemy drew close, and said reassuringly, "Oh Bamba, don't be afraid. I saw it coming. It's only a tunnel!"

Yes, it was a tunnel all right—black as ink!

"This is another great engineering marvel," volunteered the friendly miner in the darkness. We're going smack through the middle of a solid granite mountain. Think of it! This little train is the first in Alaska and Yukon Territory!"

While we were still in the tunnel I could hear two women behind us plotting a joke on the Canadian* Custom Officers who would board the train at the summit, where we had been told a checking station was located. Naturally, I strained my ears to catch what the women were saying. One told her companion that she was wearing a sealskin coat which had already passed the Canadian Customs in Victoria, B. C. and that she had a receipt to prove it.

Her friend replied that she was wearing a grey fur coat on which there was no duty—she said she was absolutely sure of it! The "grey coat lady" then suggested that "just for the fun of it" they ought to exchange wraps as a good joke on "those stuffy" custom officers. Her friend agreed to exchange coats after the train passed Dead Horse Gulch*, not far from the summit. They planned it all amid suppressed, tittering laughter.

Now, we were nearing the summit. Soon the train stopped, and a severe looking Canadian customs officer stepped aboard and called briskly, "Have all hand-baggage open for inspection and valuables ready to declare." Expertly inspecting all luggage, the officer quickly worked his way down the aisle O.K.'ing everyone's things, including ours.

When he reached the two women, he paid no attention to the "sealskin coat." Promptly, he demanded duty on the grey fur one. The lady wearing it at first argued mildly, then violently. She said the coat was old and recently relined and that she understood, anyway, there was no duty on this type of fur. But the officer was determined to collect duty on the grey fur coat, no matter what her arguments!

Now the real owner wasn't saying a word, just sitting back, listening. Finally, when her friend realized she was losing the battle, she exclaimed sourly, "Well, this grey coat isn't mine anyway, so there, I'm

---

*The Canadian-American boundary line is at the summit of White Pass. Yukon Territory is beyond, to the North.

*About a year later, a high cantilever bridge was substituted for a switchback used to get the train around, through, and up the yawning chasm called "Dead Horse Gulch."

Stampeders in the mountains above Skagway, Alaska, 1898.
White Pass.

First passenger train at Lake Bennett, July 6, 1899.

Stampeders at Lake Bennett (middle of picture). Lake Linderman is out of picture, to the right. Connecting river joins the two lakes.

Steamers tied up to shore to let passengers walk around dangerous Miles Canyon and Whitehorse Rapids. The Hepburn Tramway, horse-drawn, freighted baggage.

not paying duty on it!'

By this time the determined officer was very much out of patience! Reaching over the seat, he pulled the grey coat off her back, turned it inside out, threw it across his arm, and was about to start up the aisle (which meant confiscation), when the real owner snapped, "Well, you Shyster, how much do you want for it, anyway?"

The officer looked at her sternly, then named the custom price; the woman grudgingly dug down into her purse and the fur coat was returned, but when the officer went up the aisle, ugly words of abuse followed after him. The customs officer discreetly ignored her remarks. However, all of us sitting nearby got the full blast of her venomous wrath.

"Well, that joke sure fell flat," winked the sourdough across the aisle. "The old gal did have to pay duty after all!"

None of us could learn the true facts, but evidently the Canadian authorities (who are very discerning), had been watching for these women.

After passing the Customs we began the long, gradual descent towards Lake Bennett. Now, we were chugging North over a high, rather broad plateau, surrounded by picturesque, snow-capped ranges which stood off at some distance—perhaps eight or ten miles.

Often, we passed straggling, weather-beaten groups of stampeders who gallantly waved and looked longingly at us as we whizzed by. How we wished they could ride, too!

We rumbled onward, passing many little lakes and whistle-stops. First, there was a place called "Meadows." A short distance beyond, we came to Fraser, and then we reached Log Cabin* which was a very well-known stampeder's junction. From this spot the famous Fan-Tail Trail, to Lake Atlin, branched off. Here, there was a large encampment of weary-eyed people, who resembled refugees more than gold-seekers.

Not stopping at any of these spots, we continued on until we reached 37 Mile Post. Here, the train pulled to a halt, enabling us to catch a brief view of old Chilkoot Pass. The famous mountain stood off in the distance to the northwest, perhaps a dozen miles away.

---

*Between Log Cabin and Lake Bennett there were many bogs which the Stampede-trail passed through. Sticking out of the bottomless mud were often seen forelegs, hindlegs, or parts of dead horses. These pitiful animals had become stuck in the mud and left to die by their heartless masters.

"Gosh, if we just had 'telescope eyes,' we could see them poor devils toiling up beastly Chilkoot!" exclaimed a Sourdough sympathetically. With mixed emotions I stared at Chilkoot, that jagged peak rising high above the surrounding snow fields—like a colossal, white monster, viciously guarding the treasures of the Yukon. Then I shivered, for I could picture my husband lying desperately ill up there on that cold, windy peak, a night in 1897, deathly ill from ptomain poisoning! What a terrifying experiecne it must have been before he was finally rescued by a kind hearted Indian-packer and good old Stacey, Ed's Tacoma partner. Briefly, I told Clemy a little about his father's adventure on Chilkoot, but the Sourdough at our elbow began telling of his adventures, too.

"Yep, I'm telling ya, folks," said the Sourdough, "that big heap of devilish mountain sure has taken its toll. 'Taint only white men who fear it, the Indians do, too. Oh yes, I have good reason to know:

"Back in February of '98 my party of men and I tackled old Chilkoot, going up from the Dyea side. We had climbed about half-way up, when we met a band of Tagish Indians coming down the trail. We stopped to talk and it was then that a warrior noticed that his young squaw and papoose were missing. He and the Indians became quite alarmed as they had been caught for a time in a blizzard at the summit.

"Well, they hurriedly retraced their steps to the summit, and found the little squaw with her babe. Luckily, the papoose still lived, but the mother was dead. She had carefully bundled the child in its own warm blanket. Then, she'd taken hers off and had wrapped it around the child, too. Also, the mother had cradled the babe in such a way that her own body sheltered it from the storm. Oh! it was all so very pathetic—yes, and wonderful, too! The poor little mother's body was a protection to her papoose even in death."

Now the five-minute pause was over! No one spoke as the train moved quietly forward. All eyes were focused on treacherous Chilkoot.

A few miles more, and we caught a fleeting glimpse of Lake Linderman. The train crept on, and in a few minutes our conductor called, "Lake Bennett is next and it's at the end of the line."

*The last railroad spike was driven July 7, 1899, at Lake Bennett by the wife of chief-engineer-superintendent E. C. Hawkins. Michael J. Heney, and Capt. Jarvis, a Northwest Mounted Policeman, each hit a lick for luck. About 200 people were at the celebration. A banquet followed in Heney's mess house. The first trip was made on open flat-cars from Skagway and back.

As the train swung slowly downgrade, Lake Bennett hove into sight. All eyes watched expectantly at the windows as the upper end of "Bennett City" came into view: Hundreds of men were milling about among tents, shacks and warehouses, as busy as bees—hauling supplies, cutting wood, hauling water and building boats.

"Clemy," I said (with a lump in my throat), "take a good look at this beautiful lake. It's an historic spot. See what the men are doing here? Your father and his party of men made the same hectic preparations to go to the Klondike back at Lake Linderman in 1897. After we've found a place to spend the night we'll hike back to Lake Linderman, which is about a mile. There, we'll see where your father and Stacey camped with hundreds of others, while waiting for the ice to break-up and where your father and Stacey built their twenty-foot, flat-bottom boat. Your father had never done carpentry work before and I'm sure Stacey hadn't either, for he was a Tacoma policeman. It must have been a nerve-wracking job, building that boat. They knew the safety of their lives depended on the sturdiness of their craft in the dangerous waters ahead."

Chapter 5

PERILOUS JOURNEY

and

THE NORA

While Clemy and I waited for other passengers to come aboard the Nora, I was beginning to get that queer, seasick sensation from the uneasy motion of the boat. How I wished I hadn't had those heavy pancakes swimming in grease! Also, I wished that I could have slept, if

---

*A swift river, flowing through a low canyon, connects Lake Linderman with Lake Bennett. It was here that a number of stampeders lost their lives as the current was very swift, especially in the spring. Those whose bodies were recovered were buried near the canyon trail.

for just a few hours, the night before! All night long, I had turned and twisted on my narrow cot, listening to the cold wind whistle through the knotholes and cracks of the shack-hotel. It was obvious that a bad storm was brewing out over the lake and probably on down the Yukon.

"Actually," I had told myself, consolingly, during those wretched night-hours, "how very fortunate we really are to have passage on the Nora. She's very 'tiny and primitive' but a hundred times better than riding in an open boat, or scow to get to Dawson!"

When Clemy and I were at breakfast we had listened to several stampeders talk:

"Well, at last we're ready to head North," had said a hollow-eyed, skinny fellow, hurriedly swallowing his coffee and gobbling up a forkfull of pancakes. "Wish I knew just where that Johnson crowd is, now. They sailed yesterday in that lopsided tub!"

"Yea," said his companion, "last night it was the coldest yet, colder than hell! Must of snowed all over the mountains. Some of the gang crowded into that little log-church. There were fifty of us sleeping all over the floor!"

After breakfast, as Clemy and I were walking back to the shack-hotel, we heard excited cries from scattered groups echoing along the lake:

"Ready, boys. Hurry! Hoist the sail! Shove off!"

"Goodbye, gang. Will be seein' ya' in Dawson! You bet! We'll all be Klondike Kings and wearin' coon-skin coats!"

"Hey, there, save us a barrel of yellow nuggets, you lucky dogs!"

"Bonanza! Eldorado! Here we come! Just watch our dust. Brother, it will be plenty of Gold-Dust!"

All at once there was a great commotion aboard the Nora. The ship was crowded to overflowing with excited travelers, and enormous amounts of baggage. The captain loudly gave orders to deck hands, who hurriedly did last minute jobs which included lashing a large, ungainly scow, loaded with bales and bales of hay to the front of our steamer.

When all was in readiness, about 9 A.M., our captain yelled, "Shove off!" Immediately, we headed out towards the middle of the lake, pushing the scow ahead of us through very choppy water which quickly developed into the roughest lake-storm that I have ever seen!

By the time we reached the middle of the lake, and turned northward, the wind had grown into a tempestuous gale, beating at us like a thousand demons, and shaking us as if we were rags in the wind! The overloaded scow began to jerk and bounce and dance like a crazy man hanging at the end of a rope! Now it became almost impossible to keep our seats. Often, we were hurled to the floor!

"Oh," laughed Clemy, "it's fun—just like Teddy Roosevelt's Rough Riders. Gidday-ap, Nora!"

"Have a Bully good time, little boy," said one of the passengers. "Maybe soon we'll be out of this rough water." (Bully time was a slang expression of Teddy Roosevelt's.)

But my terrified thoughts were far from Colonel Theodore Roosevelt and his famous Texas Cowboy Roughriders, and the important part they had played in the winning of the recent Spanish-American War; my frantic thoughts had flashed back to my husband and his party who had been caught in a similar storm, probably out here on this very same stretch, back in June of 1897. They had almost gone down when the seams of their homemade, twenty-foot boat had suddenly sprung open, and they had only escaped drowning by frantically bailing and making for a narrow cove where they managed to land safely. There, they had repaired their boat while waiting for the storm to pass.

Well, at least, the little Nora* looked sturdy enough, but like most gold-rush crafts, she was riding too low in the water. Most of the passengers had grown soberly quiet.

With grave apprehensions, all of us watched the lashing waters around us, and the leaden skies above us. Low, ominous clouds hung heavily over the steep cliffs as if waiting, like hungry, black vultures. Everyone knew there had been many lives lost in this body of water. (I'm sure most of us said our prayers during those agonizing hours.)

Finally, after an eternity of lurching and bouncing, we reached the north end of the 26-mile-long lake. At this point all of us breathed easier, for here, at least, we were sheltered from the high winds and fierce waves.

As we approached Caribou Crossing, (a small connecting river between Lake Bennett and Lake Tagish,) we spotted the famous Tagish

---

*In 1897 Otto Partridge brought $20,000 over White Pass. The money was hidden in a bale of oakum to fool Soapy Smith's men. At Lake Bennett Partridge used the money to form a navigation company. They owned the Nora, Flora, and Ora, first steamers on the upper Yukon and lakes. It is said that these little steamers were built in the States and knocked down and freighted across White Pass and reassembled at Lake Bennett.

Indian Village, built on both sides of Caribou Crossing. Here, there were hundreds of natives living in small log cabins, and of course there were scores of little Indian children running about.

"It was at this village that Kate Carmack was born," said Jack Diehl, a courteous miner at my elbow. "I mean, of course, the beautiful Indian Princess who married George Carmack. Yes, Carmack and Kate, together with her three relatives, Tagish Charlie, Skookum Jim and Kulsin were in that historic scouting party when Carmack made the Bonanza Discovery—Aug. 17, 1896.*"

That bright seventeen year old Indian boy, Kulsin, (named "Patsy Henderson" by George Carmack) was too young to legally stake a claim, so he remained at the mouth of the Klondike River, in camp, to guard the dogs and fresh catch of salmon, while his relatives attended to the legal matter of getting enough gold to prove to the recorder at Fortymile that they had really made a significant gold discovery on the Bonanza.

"No, Patsy Henderson didn't get any gold. He has remained an unspoiled Indian, but perhaps that was his salvation, for great wealth has been the ruination of his two uncles. Much of the time they loaf around Dawson in saloons and other places, and squander their gold. Skookum Jim spends half of his time in jail and Dawsonites have nick-named the place, "Skookum House."

"George Carmack has tried to get Skookum Jim and Tagish Charlie to return to this village and settle down, but with little success. It's strange! Few white men have really influenced these Indians thus far. Yet one who did, was Jack London, that young writer-fellow from California. He stopped here for a spell, on his way to Dawson in '98, and named the place 'Carcross.'* Since then, the name has stuck.

"But perhaps the most influential white man ever to be in this village is Bishop Bompas. Often, when the mercury hits maybe fifty below zero, this tall, pioneer minister, can be seen mushing his dog-team to

---

*Kate Carmack was the daughter of the Tagish Indian chief.

*Bishop W. C. Bompas is buried in the cemetery at Carcross. He came into the country in 1867. Soon after the railroad reached Carcross, in early 1900, Tagish Charlie fell off the railroad bridge at Carcross and was drowned.
 The first passenger train to reach Lake Bennett by rail was on July 6, 1899. The train only ran to the upper end of the lake. Many important officials and financiers were aboard. The cars were flat-top freight-sections with benches placed crosswise. In 1900 the White Pass Railroad reached White Horse.

visit some sick, or dying Indian. These Indians are his flock; he is Bishop* of the whole Yukon region. Recently, I heard him say:

"'I have devoted all of my days to digging the mines of God's Holy Word and have found, in my own estimation, far richer prizes than all of the nuggets in the Klondike!'

"Yes," concluded the miner, "the good old Bishop is a real saint with a heart of gold, and I'm afraid the greatness of his work will never be fully appreciated. Surely, he's laid up his treasures in Heaven!"

The phrase caught my ear—"Treasures in heaven." Now, I reflected on my own life thus far: I had always taken religion for granted, had always attended church and had prayed when I was afraid and desperately needed Divine help. Religion had been an important part of my up-bringing. It had fitted into my girlhood surroundings, which I had so dearly loved—a mansion, servants, horses, cultural things—beautiful clothes, gay parties, formal balls, and the theatre. Oh, how I loved the theatre: I knew that I would have none of these things out on Dominion Creek. How much would I miss them?

I tried very hard to look into the future. I knew that I would be the happiest woman in the Klondike to be with my husband, but could I unselfishly leave a warm cabin, like Bishop Bompas, and trek through the snow to aid some sick Indian, or miner? Well, I couldn't honestly answer that question as yet.

As our steamer entered Lake Tagish, once more we were in danger. Again, the Nora was getting the full blast of the wind, and when we came to the much-dreaded stretch, called, "Windy Arm," the little steamer began to ship water: It was plain that the scow was a deadly menace as it jerked and wrenched the Nora, this way, and that, and with such terrific force that she literally stood up on end. Terrified, all of us clung to our seats!

"Deck hands, quick!" shouted the captain, "cut that scow loose, or we sink!"

When the scow bounced free, all of us gave grateful sighs of relief. Getting rid of that scow was the only way we could hope to remain afloat. Nevertheless, the owners, a man and his wife, wrung their hands and wept bitter tears. They had been promised over $400 for each bale of hay in Dawson. Now, their investment was a total loss.

As we watched the barge rapidly reach the cliffs and break up, it surely seemed that the angry lake had been lying in wait for that hay, and that we, too, would be its next victims.

"Yea," sighed a miner, as we glided free—into more peaceful water, "we're the lucky ones to survive. Guess there's no accurate count of just how many boats and barges have gone down in Windy Arm*. The Tagish Indians always try to cross early in the morning before wild winds blow."

Late that afternoon found us gliding into the third lake by way of a natural, short, connecting river. We were now in Lake Marsh, often called, "Mud Lake" by the early stampeders. It was quite shallow and almost swamp-like, and was more sheltered from high winds.

At Lake Marsh we spotted a few Klondike-bound Argonauts, both on the water and in camps along the shore. We hailed them enthusiastically, and they, in turn, joyously called back greetings. The captain answered with lusty toots from the ship's whistles. How very good it was to see other human beings in the deepening wilderness!

Our first night out, since leaving Lake Bennett, we dropped anchor and for my part, I slept soundly, scarcely feeling the hard, straw mattress or the narrowness of the bunk. Clemy, of course, slept the carefree sleep of early childhood.

Next morning, our steamer again churned northward. At breakfast, our self-appointed narrator, the Sourdough traveler, Jack Diehl, who said he knew the country "like a book," began describing what lay ahead.

"Well folks, after we navigate twenty miles of Lake Marsh we hit the Lewes River. Then, we have about twenty-six miles yet to go to reach Miles Canyon, a hell's caldron! Two miles below the Canyon are the mighty Whitehorse Rapids, another terror! We should reach Miles Canyon about ten a.m. Then, we'll be pullin' ashore and walkin' around that devilish, five-mile stretch.

"Now, the Mounties are trying to persuade everyone to pull ashore just above the Canyon and portage outfits on one of the horsedrawn tramways which will also haul our stuff. Both companies charge 5 cents a pound. They can even carry a pretty good-sized canoe, or boat. But the pity of it is, many poor fellers don't have the money to use the tram, and so they brave the Canyon, the Whitehorse and sometimes end

---

*In 1899, in Windy Arm cliffs, John Pooley and Josephus Stewart found a rich mineral belt of ruby silver, of stephanite, galena, and pyrite. The mines were named, Venus, Uranus, Montana, and Mountain Hero. Later, "The Big Thing Mine" was developed, and a camp sprang up called, Conrad.

up dead!

"Back in '97 there were a few men stationed above the Canyon who would pilot boats through for $100 apiece. It was then, in the same year, that two enterprising fellers saw the urgent need of getting stampeders and their stuff around this dangerous water. So they cut down hundreds of small trees, trimmed them smooth, and laid them end to end, making double-wooden-rails. These, they extended for five long miles, or until they reached a spot just below the Whitehorse Rapids. At that point, a tiny settlemen sprang up, called, "Closeleigh." It had two very good reasons for being there. It was at the end of the tramway. Also, there was a small, but important Mounted Police barracks there, with a telegraph office. The men called their crude little tramway-enterprise, 'The Macaulay.' It was placed on the east side of the river. Naturally, it has saved many lives, as has the second, or newer one which is on the west side of Miles Canyon. It's called 'The Hepburn.'

"Well, the Hepburn will be hauling our freight to the 'spanking-new,' settlement of 'Whitehorse.' It would be fine if you and Clemy could ride, and the other ladies too, but it's an unbreakable rule that the tram is for freight only."

"Oh," I said, "it will be very nice to go ashore and walk."

"It will be a long, strenuous hike, I'm afraid," cautioned the miner, shaking his head dubiously. "Be sure tho', to wear your most comfortable shoes."

After listening to the miner I settled down to enjoy the wonderful scenery. I felt a little uneasy about "wearing my most comfortable shoes" as they were packed away in my big truck, under a ton of baggage! No chance of getting them out! The river wound leisurely through a wide, tranquil valley flanked on either side by beautiful snow-clad mountains which stood off at some little distance. For the time being, at least, the ordeal of Miles Canyon and the Whitehorse Rapids seemed a long way off!

It was a clear, bright morning, and I, for the first time since leaving Lake-Bennett-Tent-City, was really enjoying the ride. But gradually the swiftness of the water became quite noticeable! There was a wild, ferocious tug, and lion-like force to the river.

Suddenly, our ears caught a low, muffled, ominous roar! Everyone was at the rail, nervously watching.

"Yep, we're coming to Miles Canyon, all right," said the miner.

"We've just about covered the twenty-six miles. Just around that bend is the Canyon and, look! There's the red-flannel flag tied to a tree. It's there as a warning. Talk about danger! Brother! It means plenty of danger!"

Without any of us hardly being aware of it, our captain had been gradually nosing the boat towards the left bank. Breathlessly, we watched, as quickly and expertly he brought the steamer in for a safe landing at just the crucial moment! Another few seconds and we would have swept hurtling through the canyon!

Men on shore at Canyon City, who had heard our ship's whistle, grabbed sturdy lines thrown to shore by our crewmen, and in a jiffy had secured the steamer to strong moorings, both front and back. Then, a gangplank was hastily pushed ashore.

"Goodbye and good luck, my passengers," called the captain in farewell. "Now I must hurry back to Bennett. You'd better start right out on your hard hike around Miles Canyon and Whitehorse Rapids. If you stop to look down, be extremely careful, for if you should ever slip in, it would be the last of you! The sister ship, 'Flora,' will be waiting to pick you up at the little village of Whitehorse. Your new captain will be anxious to get down the Yukon as far as possible tonight. Every hour counts in the mad race with the ice, so keep moving!" he advised.

Gratefully, we bade our faithful captain goodbye, then the crowd started up the trail, but Clemy and I tarried just long enough to see that our precious trunk and other luggage were placed aboard the tramway. (A team of scrawny, patient looking horses stood waiting to pull the heavily loaded carts, which were hooked one onto the other, train-fashion.)

Canyon City was just a small place, a few cabins and several warehouses, but it was an important depot. Obviously, "the Hepburn" was doing a rushing business.

Into a small wooden mailbox, Clemy quickly dropped a large envelope addressed to his grandmother, containing a letter and several of his brightest paintings. Surely his grandmother would get a rugged impression of the country. One picture depicted a gory gun-fight between Soapy Smith and Frank Reid. Another, was of the Nora in bouncing waves. After we had posted the letter we hurried to catch up with the other passengers.

The dusty trail ascended a steep slope which rapidly grew to canyon proportions. Soon we overtook the others, who had left the trail, to get a better view of the river at one of the Canyon's most spectacular spots. As Clemy and I peered over the brink, a terrifying spectacle greeted us. From where we stood it seemed incredible that anyone in a boat could ever survive the terrors of the water, rushing so wildly far below.

"Oh Clemy," I shivered, "your father passed through here in a leaky boat. It makes me shudder, and ill to think of it!"

"Mother, please come away!" cried Clemy, pulling me back to a safer distance. But, I was utterly fascinated, almost hypnotized by that raging, sucking torrent of danger, a hundred feet below!

"Yep, it was in this stretch, often called, 'Dead Man's Canyon' that a lot of 'em met their fate!" exclaimed the miner, shaking his head sadly. "I ought ta' know. I lost three of my best friends down there!"

"By George, you couldn't get me to go through that canyon for all the gold in the Klondike!" exclaimed one of the passengers.

"No, nor me either," chorused several others in the party.

"Great guns! See that hideous whirlpool! Watch its ugly, green lips swirl 'round and 'round."

"See it pull that writhing tree to its center! There it goes, down, into the river's gullet! Yes, and so it was with those poor, hapless stampeders who got caught in there."

Again, we started up the dusty trail. This time my knees were quaking! I kept thinking of Edward with his party, Stacey, Jourgensen and Crawford. They had certainly been courageous, or, was it just pure foolhardiness, mixed with a terrible urge to get to the Klondike that had made them dare these boiling waters?

It was about two and a half miles, of strenuous walking around the canyon—through a scant forest—up hill and down, but finally, we reached the stretch called Squaw Rapids. Here, the water rushed wildly over large, black rocks which had obviously taken their toll too, for wedged in between huge boulders were many pieces of splintered, broken boats and miscellaneous parts of miners' equipment.

Soon the trail led closer to the river's edge, on low, sloping banks. We were now approaching the mighty Whitehorse Rapids, which greeted us with a terrible roar, and a cold, misty spray.

"This stretch is greatly feared, too," said the miner. "It's been a graveyard for many a poor stampeder. Some, who passed through the canyon and Squaw Rapids successfully, panicked and tipped over here."

"Man, oh man, who wouldn't lose his wits here!" exclaimed someone in our party. "See how the river leaps, fights, twists and spurts in all directions! Just hear it rage! I tell you, it's the worst torrent in all the world! They say it's got the power of millions and millions of wild horses! Hundreds were wrecked here, and plunged to watery graves."

Again, I shuddered! "Clemy," I said, "never forget that your father braved the Whitehorse. He must have had a guardian angel!"

In early afternoon we lunched on sandwiches given us by the cook, of the steamer. After that, it was up and plod, on that hot, dusty trail! I was beginning to wonder if we would ever reach that waiting steamer below the Whitehorse Rapids!

Poor little Clemy was awfully tired but it was hard for us women, too. Our long, full skirts were unwieldy; our feet, thrust into narrow shoes, were in dreadful torture. None of us had comforable shoes. Mine were packed away. Yes, this was the longest and most painful hike of my life, and the other women agreed that is was for them, too.

In the distance on a low flat, by the river, a few shacks and tents finally came into view. They looked like a haven of rest! We stopped on the outskirts of Whitehorse just long enough to bathe our aching feet in cool river-water. Soon we found the steamer Flora tied to the river-bank, loaded and waiting. Painfully, we scrambled aboard and temporarily collapsed. All of us had agreed, as we trudged the river-bank, that we would like to have tarried in this new spot of Canadian civilization if we had had more time; however, we could see that the place was destined to become an important center. A few log houses were already being moved from across-river on barges, from Closeleigh (the old tramway location), to the new Whitehorse Cityside. It was quite apparent that Closeleigh was just about finished, as a settlement. Many people were camping in tents, at Whitehorse, and it was evident that many shacks and log cabins were about to be erected; a hotel, too. Also, there was much freight stored along the west river bank brought by the Hepburn Tramway.

Of course the building activity was in grand anticipation of the momentous coming of the narrow gauge White Pass Railroad. We especially noticed that the place was swarming with handsome

---

*A hotel was being erected in early fall of 1899. It was called, "The Windsor" and was owned by Dick Racine.

Stampeders going through Miles Canyon, also called, "Dead Man's Canyon."

Stampeders portaging a sleigh and freight, 1899.

A stampeder's boat headed for the rocks in Whitehorse Rapids, 1898.
(Courtesy of Eva L. Roane)

City of Whitehorse at its earliest date, late 1899. Steamer waits
to take freight and travelers down the Yukon to Dawson, Y.T.

Mounties. It was said there were at least a hundred of them stationed in the vicinity, and from there they would patrol the entire upper Yukon-region.

What picturesque, splendid looking young men they truly were with their bright red flannel jackets, trimmed with gold-braid, their long, dark trousers, with gold-braid running down the sides to hightopped boots, and their jaunty little caps perched on intelligent brows. (A few wore broad-brimmed hats to shade their eyes.) All of these men seemed to be of a very high calibre. Their presence meant law and order. All criminals had reason to fear the famous North West Mounted Police!

As our steamer pulled away from Whitehorse a miscellaneous group, including several handsome Mounties, were there to wave goodbye, and wish us "bon-voyage."

Now, as we watched the shoreline of Whitehorse recede, the grizzled old Sourdough-traveler began talking to a group of us:

"Well, folks, we have about fifteen miles of river ahead, before we enter the fourth, and last, lake in this remarkable chain of northern lakes. The captain says we'll probably make it to the far-end of Lake LeBarge, where we'll tie up for the night. There's a wicked stretch just beyond that point, known as the 'Thirty Mile River.' Yep, it's sure a holy terror! We'll go through it sometime tomorrow and, take it from me, we'll all need steady nerves! But folks, be sure to be on deck when we first reach Lake LeBarge. If there's a sunset, the scene will be fabulous, something to remember always!"

*The steamer, A.J. Goddard is reported to be the first little steamboat to go through Miles Canyon successfully; also, there was the tiny steamer, Witch Hazel, built at Bridal Veil, Oregon, which made it safely. About the same time, the steamer Bellingham also made a run through the canyon. Perhaps the biggest audience to witness a historic dash through Miles Canyon was when in early summer of 1898 Captain Barrington took his stern-wheeler steamboat through the canyon while hundreds of stampeders stood along the cliffs and cheered. Captain Barrington stood on the pilot-house of the Willie Irwin directing the use of the sweeps, two at the front and two at the stern. There were twelve men aboard. The canyon echoed to the encouraging cries of the men and the sound of the Willie Irwin's whistles. Soon afterwards the Mounties forbade steamers to go through the canyon.

*Captain Barrington died in Dawson on August 30, 1898, from typhoid-malaria. His steamer, Willie Irwin, was made of California redwood. All of the parts were freighted across Chilkoot and White Pass and then assembled at Lake Bennett.

*Lake LeBarge was named in honor of Michael LeBarge of Montreal. He was in a survey party of 1866 and '67 exploring for the proposed Western Union Tele-graph Line.

We glided into the huge, ocean-like Lake LeBarge, just as the sun was dropping to the horizon. The water was as calm as a millpond. There wasn't even a ripple! The old-timer was right—the scene was beautiful and thrilling—awe-inspiring. Glorious colors from the sinking sun shot deep down into the lake, and the water's surface mirrored back the surrounding snowcapped mountains with amazing accuracy. It was like a great mural-canvas spread out at our feet.

Truly, it seemed that the ancient Sun God, Apollo, had raced across the heavens to put on a special display.

"Oh," cried Clemy, "I'll have to paint this bright sunset for my grandmother. She'll love this picture!"

"Yep little Clemy, this sure is an artist's paradise and I hope you can make a good picture of it," drawled the miner, as he drew long puffs on his pipe and dreamily watched the lake. "Not only did the good Lord put plenty of gold up here, he spread a lot of real beauty around for us to admire."

"We'll be tying up at the north end of Lake LeBarge, announced the captain. In the morning we'll have an ordeal—the famous Thirty-Mile River—but we'll make it. But folks, you'd better get out your warmest clothing. The wireless at Whitehorse says, ice is beginning to form and run in the Yukon!"

Chapter 6

THE MIGHTY YUKON

"It was right here so many stampede-boats overturned and fellows drowned," said Jack Diehl, leaning anxiously at the steamer's rail. "Many early stampeders considered the Thirty-Mile River as dangerous as Miles Canyon, or the White Horse Rapids. Lucky for us the Canadian Government blasted out some of the deadliest rocks last spring of '99, when the river was still frozen over. Even so, it's plenty dangerous when ice is running in the river!"

The Thirty Mile River was a narrow, zig-zag, rocky outlet, from Lake

LeBarge which was part of the Lewes River proper. It had certainly earned for itself an ominous reputation from the early stampeders! When I saw it from the decks of the Flora, I recalled what my husband had written home concerning it:

It seems that he and his companions had camped at the entrance of the Thirty Mile in order to scout the river area. Then, when he and his party were about ready to shove off, fifty stampeders crowded near, wistfully watching. One of them stepped forward and exclaimed,

"Man alive, you fellows aren't really going into that devilish water in your little boat! We came through the Canyon and White Horse, but can't see ourselves risking our necks in a place like this!"

"Don't be afraid," my husband told them. "Come on boys, you'll never get to Dawson by just standing around wishing. Follow me, let's go!"

When the men saw that my husband really meant what he said, they scrambled into their boats and one by one shoved off. Ed led the way, standing in the prow of his boat, spotting the dangers and holding a long oar to guide the boat through. "Sticking out of the swift rapids and whirlpools," Ed wrote, "were huge boulders and partly submerged logs. In some places there was just barely enough room, or water for us to pass over safely without tipping over, and we knew we weren't safe until we had passed Casey's Rock."

Of course the male passengers, including little Clemy, were getting a tremendous thrill from the Thirty-Mile stretch. I was too—in my own particular way. However, I admitted to the women on the steamer, and to Nelly Daly, who had the stateroom next to mine, that I was really petrified with fright and she confided back, that she was too.

There was a visible downward slant to the Thirty Mile Valley. It seemed that all forty-four miles of Lake LeBarge were pouring into this narrow gap, and that we were riding its precarious crest to destruction. But, after thirty miles of very tense travel, the river widened and calmed.

Next place of real importance was the Cassiar Bar.

"Yep, there's gold on that bar, all right," said Jack Diehl, "but it's

---

*Some authorities claim that gold was first in chemical solution and that a huge lake, or inland sea covered the interior of Yukon Territory. As the water vanished the liquid gold became attached to iron pyrites, making fine gold, coarse gold, and nuggets. The chain of lakes like Bennett, Tagish, Le Barge and Atlin and also the Yukon River are off-springs of the land-covered water-era.

nearly always that darned, fine, 'yeller stuff.' We call it flour gold! It actually floats!

"During the heavy spring floods, it travels for miles and miles. So, a good percentage of the stuff gets caught on sandbars like this one, but the rest is lost in the main river. Someday they'll find a way to reclaim it."

Always, when we would see miners panning for the "yeller stuff," we'd rush to the side-rail and lean way over, to observe them. The Lewes River in many places was so narrow that we could call across stream and carry on "shouting conversations." (From two to three hundred feet.)

Several times, now, since leaving Lake Bennett, we had pulled ashore to refuel. Invariably, there would be numerous little Indian children shyly watching from behind cords of logs. And then, too, there were numerous dogs who always set up wild, wolf-like howls when they would hear our ship's whistle. Usually, they were famished, emaciated malemutes or huskies. Some would break loose from their chains and come running along the river banks pathetically begging morsels of food. The cook always saved scraps which he threw to them from the steamer.

"Oh, it's a crime to let poor dogs get so hungry!" I exclaimed, as I watched the animals swallow the food whole and beg for more.

"Well, if the Indians go hungry, so must their dogs!" said the purser. "You see, the natives have to hunt and fish for almost every morsel."

When we would land, in no time flat, the deck hands would roll out the large wheelbarrows and then would hurriedly begin taking aboard many cords of logs, that is, as many as the prow of our little steamer could hold. It usually took about three quarters of an hour to load up.

All thirty of us would walk briskly up and down while Clemy never wasted a moment getting acquainted with the Indian children. They would go running and jumping through the trees, whooping and yelling, playing Buffalo Bill, cowboys and Roughriders, "like Teddy Roosevelt," Clemy would tell them. Of course the Indians had no idea who these two American heroes were, but they quickly caught on to the general idea of galloping and shooting at an imaginary enemy. When we would pull away from the villages, Clemy would always leave the Indian children with sad regrets, and his pockets would bulge with a strange assortment of souvenirs—stones, sticks, bear teeth and even animal claws.

The "Flora," was really quite small, so we were cramped into very close quarters. Naturally the staterooms were very, very tiny. The bunks were just barely wide enough for a person to stretch out and lie flat.

Our dining room was quite austere—just the bare necessities! There were tables covered with white oilcloth, heavy dishes and iron-like silverware which constituted our coarse, pioneer eating-equipment.

Fresh milk, we never saw—just the canned, liquid kind, and it was always put right on the table in the tin containers. There was very little variety in the menu, and most of it was made from canned goods, or dried foods—except for caribou, or a little fresh fish which, they told us, was grayling and had been caught back at Lake LeBarge.

Of course our beverages were always tea and coffee—our dessert— mostly stewed dried prunes. Then too, beans were served quite regularly. And so, we were certainly getting an idea of what Klondike fare would be like! Already, we were half-starved for fresh foods!

In the staterooms there were drinking glasses, water pitchers and washpans (placed on small stands) for our daily water needs, including sponge baths. There was only one small tin bathtub on the steamer, and for this we had to make reservations hours or even days in advance. Those who'd had baths said the water was riled and gritty because it was drawn right up out of the Yukon as the steamer glided along.

At four a.m. one morning, I arose to keep an appointment with the bathtub. It was a dark, chilly morning, the water was barely warm, but oh, what a luxury that gritty bath was!

Constantly, the swish of the stern-wheeler was a steady reminder that we were going farther and farther north—farther away from civilization, and mile by mile getting closer to the Klondike—and to dear Edward.

We passed the mouth of the Big Salmon River, coming in from the East, and there, we saw a small settlement of Indians and a trading post. It was easy to spot the trading posts, as they were usually near the Mounted Police Barracks over which flew the colorful Canadian flag.

Beyond the Big Salmon, about 36 miles, we came to the mouth of the Little Salmon River. It, also, came in from the east. Across from the Little Salmon's mouth was located a large, picturesque Indian village. (Left bank.) The purser said that this particular settlement, with its well-built log cabins, was almost entirely free from white settlers. Only a missionary lived there. The village was supposed to be the finest example in the Territory of pure Yukon-Indian culture and primitive living.

The Flora landed at this village, and as usual, Clemy played with the Indian children. When we were ready to leave, he told the captain that he wished he could stay longer with Tooya because Tooya said he'd show him how to make bows and arrows and how to build a canoe; said they could even go fishing. It was with sad regrets that the two children parted and waved to each other, as our boat pulled away. Little did any of us dream that the village, in 1917, would be almost wiped out during the devastating influenza epidemic that swept the States, and somehow reached this remote village.

Each day as we progressed farther North, we felt the weather grow colder. Large chunks of ice were forming in the river as the temperature always went below zero at night. Darkness came earlier each night. Most of the trees along the river had already lost their leaves of vivid autumn colors. They now lay on the ground mixed with winter-white as a few quick snow-flurries had already come. It was a warning that winter was just around the corner.

At times we passed boats and barges packed with men who looked weather-beaten, gaunt, and blue from the cold. All faces bore that same imprint of anguished suffering, and the same gold-fevered expression!

Tensions mounted aboard our ship. It was hurry, hurry, faster; beat the ice! Gradually, and silently, it was surely closing in on us. But the land itself was appealingly beautiful, a beckoning wilderness—grippingly peaceful. Caribou, bear, moose and deer sprang up from the bushes whenever our steamer would pass too close to shore. Now and then, we passed a few trapper's cabins.

"Ah yes, this country is surely beautiful, and a trapper's paradise," said the purser. "there's an abundance of bear, beaver, ermine, martin, wolverine, muskrat, lynx, fox (red, black and silver) and also the lowly snowshoe-rabbit. Yes, they are very plentiful, too, and are widely used for food. Then, there're red squirrel and Yukon ground squirrel; and of course brown and white lemmings, but as you can see, it's a very lonely

---

*Birds that remain in the North during winter are ptarmigan, starling and the raven. Trees found in the North are pine, spruce, cottonwood, juniper, and willow.

life for these trappers."

"And look," said the purser, pointing to a black hole in a side-hill, on the left bank. "That's a real, honest to goodness coal mine! It belongs to George Carmack, the Klondike King. You bet! Lady Luck sure smiled on him. Imagine—a fortune in coal on the Yukon, and a fabulous gold mine in the Klondike!"

At Carmack's Landing, our steamer pulled in and tied up. The Captain said that stopping for the night was very necessary, since ice-floes were presenting a real problem. (In summer, boat-travel continued day and night.)

"Oh, Mother, hurry, wake up!" cried Clemy excitedly, early the next morning. "The Captain says, 'We're coming to the Five Fingers!' "

I was up and dressed in a minute and out on deck. Even in the Five Fingers, many of the early Argonauts had perished.

Soon, we swung around a very wide bend in the river and right ahead of us, standing in mid-stream, like black monsters, were four, huge, ominous, triangular-shaped rocks. They rose at least forty-five feet above the river, and there, the river spurted through five different channels. A formidable sight!

Our Captain steered his course to the extreme right-hand channel, to the one nearest shore.

"My God, he's going to hit the rocks," screamed a woman passenger, hysterically.

"Aw, no, just watch," said Jack Diehl calmly. "The Captain always steers for that rock-wall, first. He knows what he's doing. There's a cross-current which will swing us right through the center of that channel just when we think we're going to crack up. But a great many early stampeders didn't know about the direction of that current, and so they took the safest looking channel—the one nearest midstream. Consequently, they never got through alive—poor devils!"

Our steamer headed for the dangerous rock, but hitting the cross-current, it bounced through the channel safely, just as Jack Diehl had said it would.

"Yep, he's a good Captain!" exclaimed the miner, with admiration. "But now, in a few minutes we'll reach Rink Rapids.* They're not so bad—just fairly dangerous! Strangely enough, though, some of the stam-

---

*Rink Rapids were named after Dr. Henry Rink of Christiana, Sweden, by Schawtka. Dr. Rink was an authority on Greenland.

peders were wrecked there, also. Just guess they musta' got careless after reaching that point safely. At any rate, the Canadian Government has been blasting out the bad spots in Rink Rapids, just as they did back at Thirty-Mile River last spring."

Again, I thought of my husband. No doubt he had been told of the safest Five Finger channel.

After the Flora had whizzed through Rink Rapids successfully, I gave tremendous sighs of relief. They told us on ship that now we would have no more frightening water to navigate, and that it ought to be clear sailing to Dawson, that is—if we weren't held up by the ice!

Finally, we came to Minto, a small settlement nestled on the east bank of the river. It was just about sixty miles below Yukon Crossing. The purser told us that the place had an attractive roadhouse, some freight-sheds and a few trapper's cabins. (Little did any of us dream that tragedy awaited near this spot, in only a few short months, and that it would vitally affect the life of one of our youngest passengers.) In mid-afternoon of that day we approached Ft. Selkirk, on the west bank of the river. Here, we pulled ashore to let off a missionary, a trapper, a trader and freight.

The busy looking settlement stretched along the Yukon for perhaps a half-mile. Dozens of cabins crowded the water's edge and many more were scattered back among the trees.

"Ah yes, old Ft. Selkirk* surely has a colorful history," said the purser, as we walked along the bank for exercise, while the deck hands gathered wood, and while Clemy, as usual, played with the children. "Originally, this was an old Hudson's Bay Trading Post. But sometimes it's called 'Harper's Landing.' You see Arthur Harper was an early trader, who ran the place for a number of years, or until he went out to Arizona for his health. There, in Arizona in 1897, he died of consumption. The Indians in this area adored him perhaps as much as they do old Bishop Bompas. Harper and the famous missionary have surely wielded a tremendous influence on the lives of these Indians.

"See that attractive little Anglican log-church near the schoolhouse, only about fifty feet back from the river? Well, it, and all its equipment, including the fine pipe-organ, were bought with gold, given by George Carmack. In '98 he sent Bishop Bompas a very large sack of

_____
*Fort Selkirk was named after Lord Selkirk, by Robert Campbell.

The Flora taking on wood, Yukon River. (Courtesy Mary Vogel)

Stampeders on their long, cold, hazardous trip to the Klondike
... at least 500 miles.

Yukon Indians in front of a North American trading post.
About 1898. (Courtesy of Paul Mizony)

Steamer Flora, on the mighty Yukon, going through the "Five Fingers."
Some people walked around the rapids.

nuggets from his famous Bonanza discovery claim for these Indians. Now the church stands as a monument to Carmack's generosity. You bet! The names, Bompas and Carmack will always be remembered at Selkirk. And when you come to think of it, those early pioneers have changed the course of Yukon history. Probably none of us would be here in the North were it not for Carmack's chance discovery of gold!"

"You're right!" agreed Jack Diehl and several others.

"But say, now, aren't there lots of half-breeds at this place?" remarked someone in our crowd as he pointed to a group of children.

"Sure! It's part Indian and part White man's outfitting center. Miners and trappers stop here when they go up the Pelly River, or out over the Dalton Trail to Haine's Landing on Lynn Canal. But first I must say that these Indians have always been quite friendly with the whites and because of this, some years ago they suffered a terrible raid. It all happened like this:

"Back in 1852, the Chilkat Indians from the Alaskan Coast, without any warning, swept in here and pillaged and burned the Trading Post and Fort. Most of the trouble was over valuable furs. The fierce Chilkats sought vengeance on the Dene natives, often called 'Knife Indians,' because those Indians were selling furs and meats to the Hudson's Bay Company. Previously, the Chilkats had traded with the Denes for these very same products. Well, it was a mighty bloody raid!

"Now if only there had been a hundred Red Coat Mounties stationed at Selkirk in those days as there are at this date, the Fort and village would never have been destroyed. It seems that there was just a small handful of soldiers here in 1852."

"Yes, it's a fact," said a Mountie, who had joined our group, "the barracks that you see over there by the river, with the Canadian flag flying high, houses about one hundred Mounties. We were stationed here, in '98, to guard large shipments of gold. That first year, gold worth millions went out over the ice to Skagway. One shipment alone amounted to $170,000! It belonged to Joseph Ladue, the Sawmill, Sawdust King of Dawson.

"And not only are valuable shipments going Outside, they're coming

*(Rev. R. McDonald, a co-worker of Bishop Bompas, was the first white man to discover gold in the Territory. His discovery occurred at Birch Creek in 1863. He sent some of the gold to England but very little attention was paid. When the 1896 Klondike discovery electrified the world, the London Times published an article on the Rev. McDonald discovery thirty-three years before.)

in all winter long. The Yukon has several well-known freighters and mail-carriers. One famous veteran is Ben Atwater. He's perhaps the most famous in this country and his territory extends from the Arctic Circle clear to Juneau—a thousand miles! Not only does he carry letters, he carries legal papers and sometimes obliges the miners and hauls gold shipments, too.

"Jake Kline is another of Dawson's intrepid freighters. He has a beautiful string of powerful malemutes and makes record trips for the Klondike Kings. Often he delivers merchandise to the numerous dance-hall girls and wealthy prostitutes—brings diamonds, silks, expensive perfumes; all sorts of luxuries—even very expensive gowns imported straight from Paris! You'll be surprised to know that Dawson sports the largest diamonds in the country; all of them bought with virgin gold!

"In the first gold-rush year, there was hardly any crime on the Yukon, but now, it's a different story. Why, a little over a year ago (in '98) not far from here, on the Dalton trail, two prospectors, A. H. Frazer of Snoqualmie, Washington, and E. F. Follner of Seattle, were going along with their pack-horses, carrying sacks of gold which represented a hard year's work in the Klondike. Follner's poke was worth $1,800.00; Frazer's, $3,000.

"It was drizzling that night. Suddenly, two men with black handkerchiefs across their faces rose up from the bushes. They had guns and commanded Frazer and Follner to halt and hand over their gold. The two robbers grabbed it and backed off into the bushes and quickly disappeared.

"Next morning, only four miles beyond that spot, Frazer and Follner found a dead man in the trail. It was Ike Martin, a trader. His throat had been cut. Then it was discovered that he had been robbed of $4,000, in gold-dust. The poor man had been murdered on his way to the Outside.

"Well, of course, everyone was shocked over the news at Selkirk and the Indians were in great fear. They were afraid they would be blamed for the awful crime. However, there was little doubt that it was the work of white men. Many thought Soapy's men had been responsible, but as yet, the crime has been unsolved. (Soapy Smith and gang went over the ice in winter of '98 but were turned back by the Mounties.)"

"Look, Clemy," said a young deck-hand, pointing to a spot directly across the Yukon from Selkirk as the steamer got underway. "See them big round holes in the bluff? Well, many, many years ago the soldiers here used that bluff for target practice; or, maybe it was just to scare away them savage Chilkat Injuns! But anyway, the soldiers shot at the bluff! People who dig over there can find rusty old cannon balls that are exciting relics!"

"Gee, I'll bet the cannons made a loud noise," exclaimed Clemy.

"Worse!" said the deck-hand. "They roared and shook the earth, and you can surely bet your boots the Injuns ran for the hills! Yep, them surely was the wild old days 'round here!" said the deck-hand, as he began sweeping the decks.

"Passengers," said the purser, leaning at the rail, "look ahead to the bend of the river, on the right-hand bank. Notice that huge rock, jutting out from the bluff? Well, that's the famous Victoria Rock. Now, we Canadians think it looks just like out good old Queen Vic's face?"

"Why, you're right!" all of the passengers agreed in astonishment. "She's facing West; watching over the Yukon." someone said.

"Sure," replied the purser, looking very pleased. "She, no doubt, will remain there for many centuries! Nature certainly did a remarkable job of sculpturing our good Queen Victoria's features. The Indians revere the rock and bow to it. In summer, they put flowers at her feet, especially on the Queen's birthday, May 24th. Travelers salute Her Majesty as they go riding by."

Next day, late in the afternoon, we passed the mouth of Thistle Creek which was beginning to be clogged with anchor-ice. Already, it showed signs of freezing over. There were countless false channels and numerous islands where ice was beginning to pile up. Several times in one day we ran aground and it took much skillful maneuvering by the captain and crew to get us off. Of course this delayed us many nerve-wracking hours and it added to the danger of the ice which was running faster and jamming many places in the river.

Yes, the Indians had certainly been right about an early winter along the Yukon! A good part of the time, we passengers huddled in the small lounge, close to the wood stove. There was almost no promenading, now. Clemy spent most of his time drawing and painting scenes of mountains, rivers and Indian villages which he had observed along the way. Some of these he expected to send to his Grandmother. Already, he was being called "The little Cheechako Artist" by the passengers, whose cabins were now decorated with Clemy's colorful versions of

Yukon scenes.

Whenever we would pass a particular place of interest, the miner was always there at our elbow, to point it out and explain its significance:

"Say, now, Folks, if you'll look to the east, or right of the boat, you'll see the settlement of Ogilvie; it's opposite the mouth of the Sixty-Mile river. They named it in honor of Major William Ogilvie* who is Canada's famous explorer and surveyor. He, with a group of surveyors, marked the Canadian-American Boundary Line. He and his men walked thousands of miles charting the hitherto unmarked Line—even blazing it with axes on trees when there was no other way to mark it. But what chaos Ogilvie's work has saved! Previously, people weren't sure whether they were on American or Canadian Territory. When the Boundary Line was actually established, the authorities discovered that Fort Yukon was really on American Territory! What a shock that must have been to the Canadians!"

"And look! There's the mouth of Ensley Creek, and right in the middle of the Yukon stands famous Monte Cristo Island. That spot was the scene of a mighty exciting stampede back in 1898. Confidence men secretly planted gold nuggets there and then sold claims to several newly arrived cheechakos. Of course finding gold on the island caused a wild stampede. But a smart miner soon discovered the hoax. Now, the crooks are in jail in Dawson. They'll be cutting wood for the Mounties for the next four years! They tell me Sergeant Corby is keeping that gang mighty busy and he's just the one who can do it, too! But, now we're passing Swede Creek, to the west. It's had its share of stampedes and excitement, too, but it's never yielded any startling quantities of the yeller-stuff!"

"What's Dawson really like?" I asked eagerly.

"Well, Lady, it's pretty hard to describe! It's drab, yet it glitters! It's fascinating! But Dawson is a strange contradiction in many ways. It's a place where fortunes can be won, or lost in one night—at the turn of a wheel, or the shift of a card; where a saint often and unexpectedly becomes a terrible sinner, and where a sinner just as unexpectedly becomes a revered saint. Unusual happenings often take place, like the extremely silly act of a well-known character, Swiftwater Bill, the Daw-

---

*The first Governor of Yukon Territory was William Ogilvie (1900), altho' Major Walsh served for two months previously. Governor Ogilvie spent most of his time at Dawson, the capital of Yukon territory at that date.

son dude and confidence man, the great gambler and dubious Klondike King.

"To show you what I mean, when Dawson was starved for fresh eggs, back in '98, Swiftwater Bill Gates bought up every last egg in town, 5,000 to be exact, just so a hated rival, a rich mine owner, wouldn't have eggs to present to his 'Lady Love,' actress Gussie La Moore. And would you believe it? Gussie and Swiftwater Bill ate ham and eggs every morning while Dawson people drooled and went hungry for the 'hen-fruit-delicacy.'

"And now Lady, here's another example of what I mean. Not long ago, all of Dawson turned out to mourn at the funeral of a little prostitute who had become a Saint through her acts of sacrifice in helping save the lives of many of Dawson's typhoid victims. It finally took her life in the end. She was a pretty, dark-eyed little woman; apparently from a good family. What had happened in her life to drive her to the world's oldest profession? Well, no one knows. All we do know is that in our eyes, she died a Saint!

"And here's another puzzler," continued the miner. "What would you think of a fat, lazy Priest, chewing tobacco and spitting the brown, juicy-stuff all over the floor and letting a sweet, patient, uncomplaining Sister of his own religion crawl on her hands and knees to mop it up? No, it isn't a pretty picture, is it? Yet I saw it happen with my own eyes!

"Well now, I'll describe how Dawson really looks to the eye when first you see it.

"The store-buildings and music halls and other places of business have tin roofs and are mostly built of rough logs with false fronts. There are many shacks and people still living in tents. Perhaps there are forty-five thousand people crammed into Dawson. Unfortunately, the city is built on low, swampy land, at the confluence of the Klondike and Yukon Rivers. It's very muddy during the rainy season. That's why you'll see so many high, boardwalks. I've seen horses get stuck and mire down in the mud, clear to their knees, and have even helped pull 'em out!

"But now, Lady, let me tell you about the golden glitter. You'll see Klondike Kings, . . . pockets heavy with gold-dust, just throwing their wealth around! And you'll see dozens of dance-halls and painted girls; gambling joints and gambling men, and saloons wherever you turn. And you'll see some real fashion in Dawson too—straight from Paris! Yes, and gorgeous, feathered, flowered hats to match! Madame Trembley's Dress Shop has the latest styles from Paris.

"I'll say there are plenty of the wrong kind of women in town too, but the good ones are greatly appreciated and respected. Somehow, Lady, you don't seem the rugged type, but I'm saying this, once you're at Dominion Creek never turn back, 'cause that would be far worse on your husband than if you had never come at all!

"Why, I know a miner whose wife came to Dawson last year. She took one look at him and at the cabin he'd built, and turned 'round and left on the next boat. It was a terrible blow to her man. It nearly broke his heart! And to think, he had even planted flowers 'round the cabin door. The whole town felt sorry for him!"

"Get all baggage ready to take ashore, Dawson is next," called the purser.

"Here, little Clem," said a gambler, who was one of the passengers, "here is an extra silver watch that I won at Black Jack coming down the Yukon. Keep it—maybe it'll help you learn to tell time."

"And here, little Clem," said a girl passenger, who was obviously an actress, "here is a woolly stuffed brown bear. It's very much like the ones you'll see up here.

"Do you mind, Mrs. Lung?" she asked, nervously, as she hugged Clemy, and then thrust the wooly bear into his hands as a parting gift.

"Of course not," I told her. "It's nice of you. He doesn't have any toys."

"Oh thank you, Miss ——, exclaimed Clemy with childish delight. "It's just like a real, live bear. Thank you, thank you."

"Don't mention it, my dear little friend," said the actress dance-hall girl, with a hint of a tear in her eye. "Always be a good little fellow, Clem, and keep painting pretty pictures. Maybe someday you'll be a fine artist. Someday I'll see you in Dawson. I hope so, for you've made my trip down the Yukon more enjoyable."

"Aren't you gonna meet your husband in Dawson, like my mother?"

---

*The luxury steamer, Hamilton, in spring of 1898, was stuck on a sand bar. She was rammed by the ice and broke in half.

*Old Fort Reliance was just six miles below Dawson. Jack McQuesten, called "The Father of the Yukon," ran a trading post there as well as at Forty Mile, and Circle City.

asked Clemy innocently.

"No, little man," said the girl, with a strange quiver in her voice. "No, I sing and dance and dress up pretty every night. It's my job to entertain the miners—to make them whistle, laugh and sing! Goodbye little Clem, and God keep you!"

As we rounded the last bend in the river, there was a great commotion and a wild scramble on deck. The captain was lustily tooting the whistle. "It's Dawson! Dawson!" everyone cried. "We've made it! We've beat the ice!"

"Yep, it's the old town, all right," said the miner, leaning at the rail, shading his eyes from the glare of the cool, September sun. "Yea, it's the same old glittering city of gold. But golly, how it's grown!"

Chapter 7

GLITTERING DAWSON

From the decks of the "Flora" Dawson appeared drab, a miscellaneous hodge-podge of log cabins, warehouses and shacks. High hills shut off the fabulous country to the east, where we knew the famous Bonanza and Eldorado poured forth their tons of rich gold. But as for Dawson-glitter, I saw none!

I had been told that the hills directly back of the "City of Gold" were covered with wild delphinium and bluebells in spring and early summer, giving off a lovely bluish haze when viewed from the Yukon. But now, there were just a few autumn colors showing. Somehow, I felt a wave of disappointment. Was this scene, almost devoid of beauty, truly the place that was so much in the limelight of the world?

At the first toot of the ship's whistle it seemed that all Dawson rushed to the river-front to welcome us: miners, traders, Indians, riffraff, gamblers, Klondike Kings, and a few Mounties, with their bright red jackets standing out like, scarlet dots. Also there were a few gaudily dressed women scattered among that multitude of men. All nationalities seemed well represented in that strange, frontier patch-quilt of humanity.

A great wave of excitement surged through me. Eagerly, I scanned the host of upturned faces, trying to locate Ed's among them. Of course there were many loud "hello's" and other salutations called across the water, and back, from the steamer.

Quickly, the gangplank was lowered, and the passengers flocked ashore, however, I decided to hang back a little so that my husband could more readily spot me. But suddenly, I became alarmed. The crowd was thinning out!

Oh, where was Edward? Surely something dreadful had happened to him! Were Clemy and I all alone in the far North? It seemed that I lived many panicky years in those few, uncertain minutes!

With fear gripping my heart, and tears blinding my eyes, I took Clemy's hand, and together, we walked slowly down the gangplank. When we stepped ashore I felt a friendly hand on my shoulder, and a man's voice inquired:

"Lady, are you Mrs. Lung, and is this little Clem?"

"Oh yes," I replied, eagerly. Brushing the tears aside, I turned and looked into the bronzed face of a jovial little miner. "Please, please, sir, where is my husband? Oh, tell me!"

"Now, don't worry Lady, he's safe, but he's been working like a slave day and night, trying to get the cabin ready. No one could tell, exactly just when the steamer would arrive, so Ed asked me to watch for you. He'll come to Dawson in a day or so. In the meantime you are to make yourselves comfortable in a little log cabin* offered by a friend.

"I'm Joe Latshaw, Ed's partner," continued the pleasant little man, "and may I welcome you and your small son to the Klondike? A lady and a little boy are certainly a rare sight up here! You can't know how eagerly Ed has been awaiting your arrival."

"Oh, Mr Latshaw, I thank you for taking us under your wing," I told him, gratefully and in relief.

Mr. Latshaw beamed a smile, and replied that it was a pleasure to be of service to us then he escorted us to a cabin, near the Klondike River. He carried our things inside and patiently showed us how to build a fire in the little stove. Before he took his departure, he warned that it might

---

*Cabins in Dawson rented from $75 to $150 a month.

Dawson City, Y.T., at an early date. Photographed from the Moosehide slide. (By Adams & Larkin)

Dawson City, with Moosehide slide in rear. Yukon River is in foreground, 1902. Indian Village around left bend.

Dawson City people eagerly awaited the steamers.

Front street of Dawson, Y.T., in '99.

be several days, yet, before Ed would be in town, and that he would have to walk every step of the way, forty-five miles, from Dominion Creek.

Of course Clemy and I were forlorn at being alone in Dawson, but I told him we would look up Nelly Daly, that nice young lady who had come on the trip with us from Tacoma. In parting, she had urged us to drop by her mother's restaurant, on Third Street, and have a cup of tea. (Mrs. Daly's Cafe was a homey little place where she served home-cooked meals. She had gone North in '98 on the Steamer Portland.) I assured Clemy the time would pass quickly, and before we would know it, his father would be in Dawson!

* * *

The next morning, when Clemy was playing near the cabin, suddenly, I heard my husband's voice booming:

"Well, well, so this is Clemy!" In answer, there was a spontaneous shout from the throat of a very, very, happy child!

My heart jumped and leaped, and almost stood still. I rushed to the door, and was quickly caught up in Ed's strong arms, in a tremendous bear hug!

"Oh Edward," I cried, "it's so good to see you, so very good." For answer, he just laughed happily, and hugged Clemy and me closer.

My husband had changed considerably! He had grown a thick Van Dyke beard and his clothes were obviously several sizes too large for him. He was wearing black corduroy trousers, tucked into high-top boots, a heavy black shirt and a miner's cap.

Before the gold-rush he had always been so well groomed. And when I had first met him seven years earlier, he had worn tailor-made suits, stiff shirts, and derby hats. He had even carried a jaunty little cane in true, New York fashion. (This, of course, was when he had first come to Tacoma from the East, when he spoke in those broad-voweled, soft, accents.) Now, he looked, and talked like a rugged Westerner, with that resonant boom to his voice. Tired lines of severe hardships had etched themselves around his sensitive mouth. Yes, it was evident Ed had done

---

*Nelly Daly brought to the Klondike the first Smith Premier Typewriter (double keyboard).

hard battle with the North. His face showed it. A little sadly, I noted, too, that his light, wavy blonde hair had thinned at the temples. There was even a tinge of grey showing. Edward was only thirty, yet he appeared much older.

All at once, I saw a malemute perched in the doorway, watching us quizzically, its head cocked to one side. Clemy bounded from his father's embrace to pet the dog.

"Clemy," said Ed, "I bought this young malemute for you, son. You name her."

"Oh Daddy, Daddy," cried Clemy, throwing his arms around the shaggy dog's neck, "if she's mine, her name is Nelly. Follow me, Nelly."

Nelly bounded after Clemy and it was evident that boy and dog would be the best of pals. Of course Clemy was supremely happy with his new pal and Nelly slept at the foot of his cot that night.

Words are inadequate to describe the emotion of true love. Our joy was boundless—like the ecstasy of the stars! To me, my husband was Polaris, the magnetic one—My North Star. And he was the 'Great One' to Clemy—the ideal Sourdough, who knew all, and was all.

It proved to be an interesting, exciting week in Dawson. Nelly faithfully trotted at Clemy's heels, wherever we went, and as Joe Latshaw had said, a lady and a little boy were a rare sight in Dawson.

Edward was proud and pleased to show us off to his friends. First of all, there was Paul Hebb, whom we visited at his cabin. Then, as we began walking through the business section, we met Charles Debney, Elmer Chamberlain, Mr. John Mead, Mr. Thompson, also Ed Simpson and Frank Morrison; and there was Captain Breeze, a blonde giant, who owned a claim on Little Skookum Gulch. All made a fuss over us and told Ed how lucky he was to have his family come North. All wanted to know the latest news of home.

Of course Clemy and I were all eyes and ears as we explored Dawson. The air was invigorating and crisp, and as we walked the streets, loud honky-tonk music greeted us on every side—from dance halls, saloons, and other spots of pleasure.

As we came down Front Street, out in front of one saloon, a huge ship's bell was raucously clanging. A rush of men made for the entrance

---

*Harry Ash's famous Northern Saloon was the most famous and well-known. Bill McPhee's Saloon was also well-known. He was an old pioneer from Circle City. Dawson saloons were said to take in three and four thousand dollars a day.

GLITTERING DAWSON 67

of the saloon. Ed explained that the raucous clang of the bell was a signal that a Klondike King had thrown down a full poke of gold at the bar and there would be free drinks for all who could crowd in.

Everywhere there was almost that circus, carnival-like atmosphere. Nasal-toned singers—some with tinny voices, screeched from gramophones, "The Last Rose Of Summer," "Tell me with Your Eyes," "After The Ball Was Over," "Home Sweet Home," "Break The News To Mother," and many others.

Sometimes the records had developed annoying cracks. But cracks or not, the records were played anyway, with the bright big horn placed in front of the machine, amplifying every single sound coming from those precious records.

Curiously, we paused to listen to this recent invention by Thomas Edison*; he had won fame for his marvelous electric light bulbs which were now replacing gas lights on some city streets in the States. Even some "Flickers" were being shown in Dawson, another wonderful invention by Thomas Edison. They were called, "Edison's Projectoscopes," and we got some rapid-moving, last-scenes of the Battle of Manila and the destruction of the Main, and the fall of the Morro Castle.

United States Consul, Mr. J. C. McCook*, welcomed me to Dawson when I visited him at his quarters. He had known my father, the late Horatio C. Clement of Tacoma, formerly from Montreal (many years before).

"Mrs. Lung," Mr. McCook said, "I think you'll notice that they're no social* barriers here, and it's a good thing. Everyone is judged on his own merit. How long this will last, I cannot tell. If ever I can be of service to you, let me know. However, I may soon be leaving the North." (McCook left Dawson in late '99.)

With a feeling of high adventure, I mingled with the Dawson people. They were of all descriptions, truly a melting pot, and no social boundaries seemed evident, as McCook had pointed out. In daytime the

---

*It was said that Thomas Edison, as a boy, was such a slow learner that his teachers had despaired. One of them told his parents that Edison never would amount to anything, and that he might as well not go to school.

*U. S. Consul McCook arrived in Dawson July 26, 1898. (Note in diary.)

*In 1900, Dawson became the capital of Yukon Territory. About that time it began to be more socially conscious.

business streets were pack-jammed with humanity, (the streets were hardly wide enough.) The strange, almost swampy smell of Yukon water, mixed with dust and liquor seemed to permeate the atmosphere, also that vague, exciting, metallic smell of gold-dust! The whole town seemed aglitter, and revolved around, and under an aura of light-hearted music and gaiety. Gold was the keynote and eventually the main topic of every conversation. Everyone paid for purchases with gold-dust except newcomers, like myself. Quickly, I learned that a quarter was the smallest coin used in the North, and that I could expect no change back from it, no matter how small the purchase. Pennies simply weren't seen or used. Of course five and ten-dollar gold pieces were very common.

It seemed that next to food and clothing, wood was the most important commodity. Everywhere we looked, we saw stacks of firewood. "Any day now," Ed told us, "there could be a big snow storm."

While walking along the riverfront, we noticed ice running thicker in the Yukon, also that late steamers and small river-craft arriving, were encrusted with icicles. Then, word came that the steamer Stratton and the Willie Irwin had both been wrecked in the Yukon, near the Selwyn Creek Mounted Police Barracks, and that the Irwin had gone under the anchor ice. The reports were that all passengers were saved on both steamers. This was heartwarming news. There had been a troupe of actresses aboard the Irwin, the reports said, including Diamond Tooth Gertie's sister, May Field. All Dawson thanked God for the good news of "no loss of life." But to lose these steamers was bad news!

On one excursion through Dawson, Clemy, Ed and I, with Nelly walked briskly along the waterfront, towards the north end of town, where the city abruptly ended at the Moosehide slide. Here, we saw Ladue's Lumber Yard, a very important spot in Dawson life.

"Yes," said Ed, "that little sawmill is really making history. And over yonder, is the Catholic Mission and hospital. They're both in the tract called "Ladue." It was named in honor of Joe Ladue, the late Klondike-Sawdust King. Ladue was among the first to reach this spot soon after the big gold discovery. He realized that a new gold camp would quickly develop, so he hustled up to Sixty Mile and dismantled

---

*The City of Dawson was named after George Mercer Dawson. He was the Director of Canada's Geographical Survey.

*There were several other sawmills in the Klondike besides Ladue's, but Ladue's was the first one in Dawson.

GLITTERING DAWSON

his little sawmill there. Floating it to this spot, he hurriedly set it up. Then, he and Arthur Harper, another old-timer, got an exclusive land grant from the Canadian gόvernment, naming this town Dawson. But poor Ladue! He died a few months after going outside in '98 to marry a childhood sweetheart, who had for many years, waited for him to come back to her. Well, it was a sad love story. Anyway, before they died, Harper and Ladue established "The Harper and Ladue Milling and Mining Company, now a very rich company through its many holdings. Kirkpatrick is president and lives in Dawson. Ladue was right about this place—it's the biggest boom-town in the world. Maybe as big as Seattle or Vancouver, B.C. (1899)

"Little Clem," said his father, "look at the mountain back of Ladue's Sawmill. See that white slide which extends almost from the mountain-top to the shore of the Yukon? Well, that white chalky stuff is asbestos. They use it to make things fireproof. But back in '97 there was a real gold stampede to that spot. Stacey and I climbed up there, but found absolutely no trace of gold. Some one who had started the stampede had staked a claim. It was later reported that it was just the prank of a practical joker. Well, anyway that stampede did bring to light something startling—human skeletons! An Indian legend was then told.

"Well, it seems that a very long time ago, a band of fierce Yukon Indians landed on this shore and made camp. They had come a great distance to force the Princess of the Moosehide Indians to marry their ugly Chief, but the princess wouldn't consent to marry the ugly Chief and leave her people, who lived on the other side of the mountain. The enemy Indians became very angry and were about to make war on the Moosehides and carry off the lovely princess, when she implored the Medicine Man to do something quick to save her, and her people.

"Suddenly, the earth shook and the mountain split wide open, raining hot-stone, and white-earth down upon the enemy Indians encamped at the base of this mountain. When the earth stopped shaking, all of the enemy Indians were gone, buried under an avalanche of hot asbestos! Yes, and that's the story of how all those skeletons got buried in the asbestos slide! Of course the Moosehide Indians were saved, and the princess married a warrior of her own choice.

*About fifty skeletons were found in the asbestos slide.

"Some day, Clemy, we'll get a boat and row around the bend of the river and see the Moosehide Village. I know Chief Isaac and he is friendly to Dawson people. We might even see, 'The Hiyu-Skookum Girl', the Indian Princess who often comes to town decked in all of her finery; lots of jewels, gold rings, and bracelets, and in winter, mink and leopard-skin-parkas. She's the wealthiest Indian girl in the North, as she has gone on many stampedes and has located rich ground."

"And now, let me tell you another Indian legend; it says that a long time ago the sun looked at Alaska and loved her dearly. He showered her with warm, summer-kisses; made plants, flowers, and forests bloom profusely to cover her naked bossom. And he wooed her and wanted her to be his Queen. But she spurned his love, and turned to the North Star. For him, she dressed herself in sparkling, bridal-white, crystal-array. But the sun still loved her dearly, and he filled her lap with rich yellow-gold, and made her lakes sparkle like gems. But she spurned the warmth of the sun's great love, and kept her eyes fastened on the North Star. And she hid her gold from the sun, locked deep in her heart. But in spite of this, the sun could not forget his dear Alaska, so he returned a few months each year to see her, and woo her again, for he still loved her and wanted her to be his Queen.

"Clemy, that's the beautiful Indian Legend of winter and summer in Alaska, and it's a very poetic explanation of how gold came to the North."

As the three of us walked back towards the center of Dawson, Ed told us some colorful anecdotes concerning well-known characters of town:

"Dawson surely has had some colorful people," he said. "It would take a book to list them. I have known many of them, like Joaquin Miller, the poet gold-rush reporter, Frank Slavin, the heavyweight champion of the world, Judge McGuire, Sam Wall, the famous news-paperman; Thomas O'Bien, also a very well-known newspaperman. I've known Swift Water Bill*, Bill Gates; The Oatly Sisters, who sang the "Star Spangled Banner" at the last Dawson Fourth of July celebration, a thrilling occasion! Then too, there is Nigger Jim. Maybe we'll see him in Dawson, for he is one of our interesting celebrities. Everybody wants to know about him, so I'll describe how he looks.

*At the "Combination Theater" a show was called, "Swift Water Willie," a caricature of Swift Water Bill (1898).

Street scene, Dawson, Y.T., showing Palace Grand Theater, built by Arizona Charlie Meadows in 1899 (July). Theater is 4th building from right. (Courtesy George O. Shaw of Dawson, Nugget Shop)

Arizona Charley Meadows, famous Wild West showman. Came to Dawson in 1897; became wealthy and built the famous Palace Grand Theater in 1899.

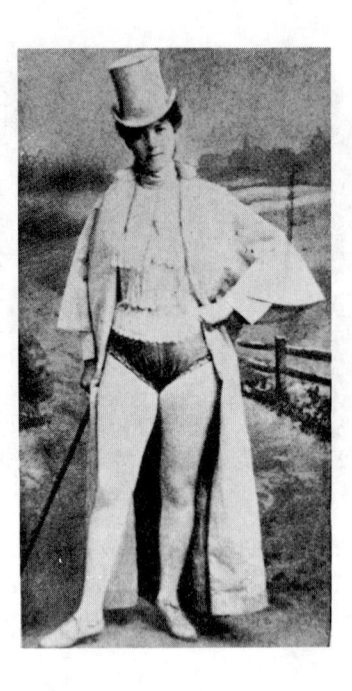

"Klondike Kate," actress, queen of the bright lights and toast of Dawson.

Weighing gold dust and sacking it in a cabin in the Klondike. Notice the gold brick held by man on the right. Mrs. Collins, second from left. (Courtesy Mary Vogel)

"If you see a tall, lanky, young fellow wearing a big cowboy hat and fancy high-top boots, more than likely it will be Nigger Jim, the friendly, likeable, dynamic cowboy-singer from Alabama. He struts around Dawson with his guitar and a pocketful of gold, for he recently sold his claim up on the Upper Bonanza to one of the trading companies for $300,000. No, he is not a colored man, but got his nickname because he sings southern songs so well. He loves to be in the limelight and after he sold his claim he celebrated for a week, getting himself roaring drunk, and he was host to all who gathered 'round. During his pleasure-binges, he would announce:

"Pretty soon I'm going Outside and get supplies and start the biggest saloon in Dawson. You'll see." He told everybody that, and he meant it.

Jim always brought a thick sack of gold-dust to town for his lavish entertaining. One night he gave it to the bartender for safe keeping. It contained $8,000. This happened to be in Kerry's Saloon. That night there was also another sack of gold placed in the same drawer, $11,000 worth, and it was owned by the proprietor. The next morning all of the gold was missing, a very unusual occurance, for honesty is the keynote, even among saloonkeepers.

When Nigger Jim* sobered up, he began watching the barkeeper and saw that the fellow was beginning to deck himself out in diamonds and was plunging wildly at the faro tables. This infuriated the Alabama cowboy. Sticking a gun under the chin of the barkeeper, in a dark ally, one night, Nigger Jim threatend to spirit the barkeeper away into the woods and tie him to a tree, and leave him, if he didn't tell where he had hidden the two pokes of gold. Fearful that Nigger Jim meant to carry out his threat, the barkeeper quickly confessed to the theft and revealed that he had hidden the gold under the Alaska Commercial Company's warehouse. Result was, Jim got back what was left in his sack of gold and so did the proprietor.

"Yes," continued Ed, as we walked back to the cabin, "Dawson has had some rip-snorting, wild, hectic, times lately and we've had some terrible fires. The last one was on April 26, (of '99.) I have good reason to remember it, for I had been on a stampede to Last Chance Creek,

---
*The famous Oatly Sisters owned the Pavilion Theatre, built by Pete McDonald. The popular Hueston Orchestra was one of its main features. Often Nigger Jim sang at this and other theatres.

Sulphur, and Little Brimestone and had just come in to Dawson, exhausted from a sixty-mile-trek.

"That night, at 8 p.m., while some of us fellows were recuperating and finishing a late supper in Paul Hebb's cabin, suddenly fire bells began clanging.

"We jumped from the table and ran outside. Something was burning like a torch at the waterfront. We rushed down to Front Street and witnessed the first stages of that terrible holocaust!

"From the Bodega Saloon, where the fire first started, it quickly caught onto the Tivoli Theater. Scantily-clad, terrified girls in flimsy butterfly gowns came screeching from the place, followed by Fred Tracey, the owner. Then we saw the fire leap with unbelievable malignant speed to the Northern Saloon, and on, and on it went, taking the three-story McDonald building, the Monte Carlo Casino, The Aurora Saloon and Tremons, and others. They couldn't stop the fire's devilish glee!

"Well, we could see that a big part of town was doomed to go up in smoke. A stiff wind was blowing and there was very little water available as the Yukon was still frozen over. But anyway, we fellows joined hundreds of others, quickly forming bucket brigades, working like demons back and forth from the waterhole, cut in the ice. But our efforts were useless as the buildings were as dry as tinder.

"Finally, the Mounties gave orders to 'let 'er burn' rather than risk life. In a few cases dynamite was used to raze the buildings. A section of the fire reached a powder magazine, and you should have seen it go up! I tell you all hell broke loose. Exploding bullets popped and whizzed in all directions. Everybody scattered like crazy. Some fellows were injured, including a Mountie, and it was only by the grace of God that no one was killed. Half of Dawson* burned that night. Nothing was insured. None of us slept for at least forty-eight hours. George Cant-

---

*Fred Tracey was a well- known singer and often sang in his own theater. He was having financial difficulties and the fire wiped him out. In an earlier Dawson fire, in 1897, Pete McDonald's pleasure palace, "The Pavilion," was burned to the ground as was the famous La-na-na, owned by William R. Loyed, James V. Harrison and Thomas J. Nash. They were both later rebuilt.

*In the small Feb. 13, 1899, fire there had been two fire engines available. The April 26, 1899, fire was the worst in the history of Dawson to date. Many people have confused the two fires. The first fire just took a row of shacks along the waterfront. The latter took about half of Dawson, but by July 2, 1899, the city was almost entirely rebuilt.

GLITTERING DAWSON 73

well, Dawson's City Photographer, was running around like mad, snapping fire scenes. Joe Latshaw and I happened to be out on the ice in front of Dawson and Cantwell caught us in one of his pictures. But, oh, it was a crime that there was only one fire engine that was working, and it proved completely inadequate as the water froze in its hose, and the thing burst.

"Of course," laughed Ed, "liquor was free to all that night and there were many drunks wobbling about. Hardly had the coals cooled before fellows were digging like fury through the ashes. Why, there was almost a stampede to certain burnt areas. Some of the fellows actually recovered hundreds of dollars in gold, just as others had done in the 1897 and '98 fires."

"Do you know what started the April 26, '99* fire?" I asked, with keen interest.

"No one knows, for sure," said Ed, "but there's persistent rumor that Belle Michell, the evil-tempered dance hall girl, started the April fire, just as she had the others. But as yet, no one has actually been able to pin the blame for this last one on her. However, she was definitely responsible for the worst 1897 and '98 fires. Both times she threw lighted lamps at rivals while quarreling in hotel rooms with other girls over mutual lovers. These are unsavory stories, tragic in consequence, and why that particular girl has been permitted to remain in Dawson, is more than any of us can fathom!

"Yes, as a flash-back, I remember the terrible 1898 fire, too. I had just come to Dawson from the Bonanza to wait for the little steamer, Ora, as she was scheduled to come down-river with the last mail* of the season. While waiting around for the boat to put in its appearance, I worked a part-time job at the Alaska Commercial Company, as I had done before, to supplement my diminishing funds. But let's let my diary tell it:

> Dawson — Oct. 4, 1898
> Cashed in my time at A. C. Company — $120.00. Am now working as a part-time accountant. Bought outfit with money.

---

*A week before the last fire a blaze broke out in the Presbyterian Church during church service. Twenty people in a second story barely escaped.

*Carrier pigeon mail service was tried in '98, but it was not too successful owing to the extreme weather and very long distances.

Dawson — Oct. 5, 1898

El Wright, Wincroft and I went to combination theater to see Cad Wilson, the new variety star. Quite good, but not rest of the show——very poor! Audience did not like it and showed disapproval by howling like a pack of malemutes!

(Cad Wilson, the popular star, was given a belt made up of matched nuggets, held together with a diamond clasp, from one of the Klondike Kings. It was on display in Dawson in one of the jewelry stores, a truly beautiful work of art.)

Dawson — Oct. 6, 1898

Learned to play the new game, "Solo." Fair game. Got into post office, but no mail for me. El, Mead, Warden and I went up to Hebb's cabin. Simpson brought his Gramophone and we spent a musical evening.

Dawson — Oct. 7, 1898

Stayed at cabin all day. Fixed my window and cache. Bought 19 lbs. of honey at 40c — $7.60 (Arizona honey) brought in by one of the owners of the Gold Star in which Mr. Rogers is interested. Formerly he was a contractor in the Union Pac. R.R., Portland extension. Randolph Kahlenborn is in from Skagway.

Dawson — Oct. 8, 1898

Str. Ora is due from White Horse. Looks quite wintry now, but hardly look for colder weather until the 15th. Wonder what dear Velma is doing today. Got permit to cut wood—3 cords—cost $2.00. 50c a cord—one free.

Dawson — Oct. 9, 1898

Mead, Wynkoop and I start tomorrow to get raft of wood. In eve, went up to Hebb's cabin. Mr. & Mrs. Morrison and a Mrs. West from Seattle came up. Ed Simpson entertained us with the Gramophone and also some delicacies he brought in. 25 lb. fruit cake is fast melting away!

Dawson — Oct. 10, 1898

Started for wood up Yukon. Took (Ezra) Meeker's boat. Wynkoop is not in good shape. He rode in boat nearly all the way. After inspecting several places finally stopped ½ mile above

---

*Ezra Meeker was of Oregon Trail fame. He crossed the plains in a covered wagon. During the Klondike gold rush he brought produce to Dawson to sell from his farm near Tacoma, Washington. In the fall of 1898 he went Outside by way of the Dalton Trail, carrying mail.

A lady and a little boy were a rare sight in Dawson, Y.T., in 1899.

Two of the first places of business in Dawson. The Dawson Town Site Co. and Harper & Ladue Mill Co., 1897.

The Canadian Bank of Commerce, on right, and stampeders standing in line in front of Dawson Gold Recorder's office, 1898.

A Fourth of July parade in Dawson, 1898. The Hotel Northern is second building from left, and the Regina Hotel is the last building in view on the left.

Swede Creek. Located dry wood on hill. No one has ever been here. I started to cut ½ cord of wood before dark. (Ezra Meeker, the famous pioneer of Oregon Trail days was from Oregon and Washington. He made regular trips to Dawson bringing in mail and produce in his boat during the open-river season.)

Swede Creek — Oct. 11, 1898
Had breakfast and took our lunch up on the hill. Wynkoop is not much account. I worked hard all day!

Swede Creek — Oct. 11, 1898
Cutting wood. Wynkoop can't work. Will let him take boat tomorrow and go to Dawson.

Swede Creek — Oct. 13, 1898
Wynkoop went back to town. Mead and I got in good day's work. Hardly look for El. Although we sent word for him to come up by Wynkoop. Started a fine trail and put skids on (wood box).

Swede Creek — Oct. 14, 1898
Cutting wood 7 miles up Yukon. Worked hard all day on raft. Got our last wood down at 11 A.M. Three men came up river and said Dawson was burning down. Will leave tomorrow. No floating ice yet. 10 below, and ice is liable to run any day. Out of grub. Living on coffee and pancakes. No baking powder. (Well, Dawson was burning down and what could we do?)

Swede Creek and Dawson — Oct. 15, 1898
Woke up to find river full of ice. Worked hard until 3:30. Broke ice and launched raft. Exciting 7 mile ride! Three scows had gone past during the early afternoon. Last one stuck on a bar above Louse Town. Ice was pounding her to pieces! We worked like fiends and landed raft just below the Mounted Police Barracks. Saw where the fire had eaten a big hole in Dawson!

"Yes," said Ed, closing his diary, "when I viewed the smoldering ruins that day from the raft, I said to Mead, 'Well, Dawson's flim-flam shacks are gone! It's a terrible loss, yet from the ashes will surely arise better buildings, if that's any consolation.' Of course, my first thought was of the Alaska Commercial Company. I was fearful it had been burned in that half-million dollar fire, but when we landed I was glad to see that it had been spared. Perhaps the most disheartening loss of all was the new post office with a lot of mail. Many important restaurants, clothing stores, food stores, and hotels had been lost in the fire. The Warden Hotel, a $40,000 building, was one. Also, The Greentree, and Alexander McDonald's hotel were lost, and many other places of business. But the worst loss of all was The Bank of British North America. Three days after the fire, October 17th, the weather had turned as cold as 'Helen-Blazes!' Luckily, Paul Hebb's cabin had escaped the flames, and so about a dozen of us fellows temporarily crowded in with him. Others had to double up too. Newcomers had to find shelter mostly in tents. Perhaps they suffered the worst hardship.

But to get back to Wyncook: He was now dangerously ill. In fact, all of the time that I had thought him lazy, while gathering wood, he had been coming down with typhoid fever. When next I saw him, he lay in the Catholic Hospital. I tell you, I felt remorse, and I was plenty afraid of the disease, too! Oh, I had good reason to be afraid! Good old Stacey was lying in the cemetery because of it, and so was Fenwick Williams, Bill McPhee's young nephew; and also Captain Barrington was in the cemetery, and the young Goodwin boy, and many others. Some of the poor Sisters had died too, and even the much-esteemed Catholic priest, Father William Judge, had finally succumbed.

Happily though, Wyncoop recovered and was so well the following spring that he took off for Nome in that historic stampede!

Edward was rapidly getting us acquainted with rambunctious Dawson and its colorful history. And, too, he hoped that Clemy and I would become used to walking long distances, for we had almost a fifty-mile trek ahead of us in order to reach our new home on Dominion Creek. (There was no stage as yet to upper Dominion Creek.)

That week we ate most of our meals in the Dawson cabin. Ed was chief cook and I was grateful for this. Several times, however, we dined at restaurants, but food was dreadfully expensive. Here are a few food items and prices as they were:

Stewed fruit—one serving, $1.25. Pie or sandwich with coffee, $1.25. Beans, coffee and bread, $2.00. One piece of pie, 75c. Beef steak, $5 to $10. One dish of canned corn, $1.25. One serving of canned tomatoes, $2.00. Bowl of soup, $1.00. Mush and milk (canned), $1.25.

The Klondike Meat Market specialized in all kinds of wild game in

---

*It is believed that Wyncoop of Dawson was the same man who became sheriff of Nome at a later date. The Bank of British North America was on Queen Street.

season—moose, caribou, bear, deer, wild Rock Mountain sheep and rabbits. Also, wild ducks dangled on display. But it was difficult to relish the strange gamey taste even though Ed went to great pains cooking it.

My husband wished me to see Dawson in all of its many phases, even its night life! "Vel," he said, "it's hard telling when we'll ever get back to town again. Joe Latshaw will stay with Clemy and Nelly while we take in the 'bright lights'."

On our first night out, we went to the Palace Grand Theater. (A year later, in 1900, it was renamed the "Savoy" and in 1901 it became the "Auditorium." Still later, in 1930, it was the "Nugget Dance Hall.") It was in the Palace Grand that Klondike Kate soon became so famous. Arizona Charlie had just built this new plush theater. Here it was that Klondike Kate did the exciting "cake-walk," wearing a crown of lighted candles; and here she performed the breath-taking "flame act" while she danced with spectacular fury to fast-moving music, swirling hundreds of yards of filmy gauze up and down and across the stage, illuminated under very fiery, flame-colored spotlights (coal oil carbon). And it was in this same theater that she reached the peak of her brilliant career and became known as the "Queen of the Klondike." It was reported that Kate made $200 a week for her flame dance, but at the floor dances she often cleared $500 a night as a percentage-girl on champagne sales. She had the plush Star's Room upstairs over the theater, trimmed in red and gold.

That night we did not see the "Queen of the Klondike." It was a rather nondescript show, but the miners seemed to appreciate it, and did not howl like a pack of malemutes as they so often did when displeased. Perhaps it was because "Diamond Tooth Gertie" saved the show with her cryptic remarks and humorous songs while all the while a diamond flashed in the filling of her lovely front tooth! And from her bare shoulder to her wrist she wore a fascinating snake bracelet studded with diamonds. Somehow, she seemed to almost hypnotize her audience by that long, silver-snake shimmering on her arm!

The gay "cancan" girls and Gertie kicked their silken legs high and sang and danced in the usual eye-opening way, and to wind up the act, threw their lace garters at the audience. Then they eagerly gathered up the loot, or offerings of the miners in the form of loose nuggets* and little sacks of gold-dust tossed* at them. Of course, a few notes were attached "to meet the admirers after the show." This, I understood, was standard procedure as there was to be dancing and drinking after the performance.

Red cloth curtains divided the boxes for privacy where all evening Klondike Kings could be seen entertaining lavishly their Lady Loves, spending perhaps a small fortune on liquor!

A fine, hand-painted mural ran around the outside railing of the first balcony, depicting many beautiful Yukon scenes. We learned it had been done by the New Klondike Nugget cartoonist and artist, Art Buel, recently arrived in the Klondike from Puyallup, Washington.

On our second evening, sightseeing, Edward and I dropped in at the Flora Dora (later called the Royal Alexandra Hotel.) On the first floor was a small lounge, a large bar, and a sizable dance floor. Edward and I did a few whirls, but the crowd became too much of a free-for-all.

As we sat watching the dancers my eyes were drawn to a spot just above the bar, where reclined several girls in the nude. At first I was startled, for the figures gave the illusion of real flesh and blood! I was fascinated, yet shocked, as these paintings were quite brazenly displayed. Edward saw my disapproval and exclaimed, "Now, my dear, you'll have to excuse this scene. Those nudes are a part of Dawson life."

"Who are the beautiful girls?" I asked, as I saw two old derelicts come staggering to the bar. They looked up at the girls, smirked and nudged each other, then raised their whiskey glasses in a very suggestive salute.

"Well," said Ed, "it's impossible to learn the girls' true identity. It's said Murray Eads*, the owner of the Flora Dora, had the pictures packed in by Indians over the Chilkoot Pass in early '98. The Nudes were supposed to've come from the Barbary Coast near San Francisco, originally. They say they were painted by a very well-known artist who refused to sign his name to the paintings. Maybe the artist's identity will always remain a mystery. If Eads knows, he isn't telling. Neither is he telling who the models were, tho' many have tried to pry it from him."

*It was said that many times after a show the actresses' legs were bruised from nuggets hitting them!

*Art Buel's son, years later, became cartoonist for The Examiner newspaper of San Francisco.

*Murray Eads was drowned when the Princess Sophia was wrecked in 1918. He was on his way to the States. The ship went down near Juneau.

"Oh, it's a shame to have those lovely oil paintings in these rough surroundings," I told Edward. "Why, in a good art gallery, The Nudes would be recognized as very fine works of art!"

"Yes, I guess you're right," agreed Ed.

There were other hotels, too, that we visited that night, where we saw many similar nightlife scenes, except, of course, for those special nudes. There was the plush, four-story Regina Hotel, the three-story Dominion, and the three-story Klondike. Also, there was the new three-story 22-room Fairview, supposed to be the most plush hotel in Dawson, but Ed said the walls were a combination of canvas and wallpaper and that you could almost hear people breathe in the next room.

Of course we went into a few of the gambling casinos. There was the rebuilt Monte Carlo and the Standard—where young Alexander Pantages and Tex Rickard (both were later to become famous) tended bar, where Klondike Kings, the near-rich and the poor, pitted wits and skills for yellow gold, and where it seemed that gold was as common as bags of peanuts! During the night hours numerous pokes of nuggets and dust were rapidly changing hands* as feverishly, miners played roulette, faro, black jack, and even the shell-game, against hard-eyed nimble-fingered professional gamblers.

And, as always, hovering over the men were Dawson's painted girls, the Percentage Women, playing their own special little game of counterfeit love while watching with calculating smiles, and fondling soft fingers, the gambling strategies of their prey!

However, I was truly amazed to find that the city was surprisingly orderly. Seldom did the police have to use the bobby-cart to pick up derelict drunks. Civilians weren't allowed to carry firearms in Dawson. No liquor was sold between the hours of midnight and dawn. Stern-faced Mounties regularly patrolled the streets from their barracks near the Klondike River. To say they ruled Dawson with an iron hand is putting it mildly. It was obvious that the vices of gambling and immorality were tolerated. Like all new frontier towns, these sins were not legally condoned—neither were they legally prosecuted unless per-

---

*Alexander Pantages started his career in the North with the help of Klondike Kate. Later he established a syndicate of theatres in the States.

*"The Portuguese Prince," said to be a retired bootblack, paid a certain dancehall girl $100 a day on condition that she wouldn't speak or dance with a rival Klondike King.

sistent complaints were filed.

But now, after a hectic weekend and an enjoyable one too, I was ready and eager to leave glittering Dawson—to shake my skirts free of the sawdust and gold-dust. I wanted to go to Dominion Creek and live in that dear little log cabin which Edward had so painstakingly built with his own hands—our snug little home! Yes, I had had enough of the gaudy, honky-tonk, irresistible City of Gold—enough to last me many, many months!

*Often, when people would become separated from one another they would tack letters up on the outside walls of hotels. The Fairview had such a wall.

*One of the Flora Dora or Royal Alexander nudes found its way to the Dawson Museum in 1959. The next year the picture was destroyed in the museum fire, a terrible loss!

*Street plan of Dawson City (City of Gold). Front Street ran parallel with the Yukon River. The numbers followed in sequence from one to ten. Tenth Street ended against the hill, to the east. Other streets numbering to fifteen, climbed part of the hill back of Dawson. But these were only half-streets and ran through the Catholic and Public cemeteries which made them mostly for the deceased.

*First Street ran parallel to the Klondike River. Then, at right angles to the Yukon River these streets followed in sequence: Second Street, Dugan Turner, Grant, Hanson, Church, Harner, Princess, Queen, King, York, Duke, Albert, Edward, George, Judge. Judge St. was at Moosehide Slide which bordered Dawson, on north end of town. The Klondike River bordered the south end (it was too bad that no street or landmark was named for George Carmack or Robert Henderson, both discoverers of Klondike gold.)

*In 1897 and '98, several enterprising stampeders who got the first newspapers to come in from the outside, hired halls and publicly read the late news to packed audiences. The charge of admission was 2 pennyweights of gold, equal to about $1.75. The first accounts of the Spanish-American War were read publicly in this manner. Dawson's young playboy, Wilson Mizner, bought a paper from newsboy, young Sid Grauman, for $25. He then rented a hall and read the war news. From this venture Mizner cleared $150.

Chapter 8

THE FAMOUS BONANZA AND ELDORADO

If it had been winter, little Clemy and I could have ridden in a sleigh to our new log-cabin-home on Dominion Creek. But it was still early fall, with only a light peppering of snow showing on the frosty foothills.

Ed had made final arrangements for my heavy trunk to be hauled to Dominion Creek after the first big snowstorm, when the trails would be hard-packed enough for sledge-freighting.

The morning we were to leave Dawson, I put on my new high-top boots, a short khaki skirt, a warm blouse with green felt jacket, and a knitted wool-tam, to match. Clemy wore heavy shoes, corduroy knee-pants, red flannel shirt, a sweater and red stocking cap. Ed, of course, was dressed in his usual miner's garb. While getting ready to vacate the Dawson cabin, Ed packed a small bundle for each of us to carry of personal things for the long, forty-five mile journey.

"And we'll start training Nelly right," said Ed. "Alaska dogs, even young ones, must bear their share of the burden." Ed fastened a leather harness on Nelly, part of which encircled her neck, the other section wound around her middle, forming kind of a belly-band.

"High on this contraption, near the middle of the malemute's back," explained Ed, "we strap pack-bags. These hang down on both sides of the animal's flank, but the trick to good dog-packing is to have bundles of equal weight. It's really pitiful to see a dog staggering along under sloppy packs." As Ed had predicted, Nelly, at first fought the small packs, but soon became resigned to her new role of pack-animal. Now we were ready to leave Dawson.

It was a frosty morning with a real snap to the air—"A perfect day for hiking," said Ed as we headed for the Klondike River where a small ferry was moored. Ed decided it would be quicker to cross the river here, by boat, rather than walk the distance of several blocks more to reach the small foot-bridge spanning the mouth of the Klondike River.

In no time the boat landed on the opposite shore, at "Louse

---
*"Louse Town" was really Klondike City. The Klondike River was only about 100 feet wide.

Town,"* a real shacky place, built on low, swampy ground. Although I had been in Dawson a full week, it was the first time I had set foot in this ugly suburb, where it seemed that the malemutes howled at the slightest pretext, and on this particular morning they set up a wild chorus.

Nelly, in her excitement, tried to break loose from her harness, but Ed held her firmly, saying, "No Nelly, you must stick to the trail. This is another lesson you must learn."

Immediately, we began following a swampy trail which headed east, closely following the bank of the Klondike river. The trail skirted most of Louse Town, which, I had been told, sheltered a host of painted women, the "alley girls," who lived on a notorious roadway, "The White Chapel," as it was called. Here, about sixty girls were housed in a half-hundred tiny cabins of prostitution.

Mrs. Daly had described the place like this: "It's a scandalous thing, but 'Hell's Half Acre' is supposed to be one of the sights of the town! Over the door of each hutch is the Christian name of the occupant. When the girls are not otherwise engaged, usually the blinds will be up and there they'll be, on full display, on silken divans scantily clad in chiffon, using every enticing blandishment of the profession to lure their male spectators into their hutches. There is one well-known girl of particular beauty who usually has a queue of customers! As many as six have been seen waiting outside her door. Some of these girls get a great deal of gold and pay their Dawson landlords very high rents, as much as $800 a month! Oddly, most of these young women are of French or Belgian nationality, but some are half-castes.

"I must say life is unpredictable up here," Mrs. Daly continued. "Some of these girls have gotten themselves very good husbands. Some have taken sizable fortunes Outside and have become respectable—even society leaders! Yes, the rugged North seems to pull out of kilter many of civilization's strictest moral codes."

After scanning the place at closer range I could see that the White Chapel was easily accessible to Dawson and designed to catch the miners, both going and coming from the gold fields.

Mrs. Daly had mentioned that the foot-bridge (spanning the Klondike), and its pedestrians were always a matter of sly speculations, especially on dark nights when many a shadowy form could be seen slinking across the bridge from Dawson, headed for the White Chapel.

One of the markets of Dawson which carried wild meats in season, 1899.

Bird's-eye view of the mouth of the Klondike River, looking up the river towards the Bonanza and Eldorado. Dawson is to the left, Louse Town to the right. Yukon River in foreground, 1899.

"Gay girls" of the White Chapel, or red-light district, at Louse Town, across the Klondike River from Dawson, 1899.

Mary's Hotel at No. 20 Below Discovery on the Bonanza.

Well, perhaps because of the bridge's reputation, Ed preferred crossing the river by ferry. Many did!

Now, as our little family-caravan stepped gingerly along, leaving Louse Town behind, often we had to jump onto nigger-heads to avoid the mud. A nigger-head, I quickly learned, was a large mass of long, stringy, wiry, dark-green leaves, growing on a round, head-shaped plant. Each head was supported on a long, tough, rubbery stem. These unusual weeds had little stability and could be very tipsy. If a hiker managed to jump onto the exact centers, the bunches would hold him, but just let him miscalculate, even a little, and the nigger-heads would quite venomously throw him—as sure as fate!

After many leaps and misses, my boots and clothing were muddy, and by the time we reached the confluence of the Klondike and Bonanza Rivers (about two miles above Louse Town), I was really a dishevelled sight! Of course Clemy and Nelly fared much better than me, and Ed proved to be quite an "expert jumper!"

"But I haven't always been this expert," he laughed. "The first time I tackled this trail, I had plenty of spills. But notice, Vel, this is where the Bonanza comes into the Klondike River. We have a choice here of two trails—one follows the banks of the Klondike, to the left, up past rich Hunker and Gold Bottom Creeks, the other, the Bonanza, is straight ahead. Even tho' it's a little farther to Dominion Creek by way of the Bonanza, we'll take that trail. It's an easier grade to the mountains and besides, you'll see the famous Bonanza and Eldorado where there's a settlement called the Grand Forks. It's at the confluence of the Bonanza and Eldorado Rivers. We'll stay there for the night. Fifteen miles is quite enough for one day."

"Fifteen miles! Oh! Merciful goodness!" I groaned. "I wonder if my aching feet will carry me."

"Of course they will," encouraged Ed. "We've gone two of those miles already. But we'll take a quick rest and snacks at Mrs. Prichard's Coffee Stand at the junction of the Louse Town Trail, then, we'll be on our way."

After having hot coffee and doughnuts and a brief visit with likable Mrs. Pritchard, a real pioneer woman, we were on our way, ready for the panorama ahead. At last we came within view of miles and miles of sluice boxes, crossing and criss-crossing the great Bonanza Valley. And there were mounds and mounds of grey gravel, heaped high, everywhere we looked, with tents and shacks wedged in between all these.

Edward hastened to explain that the gravel-mounds contained pay-dirt of glittering gold and nuggets.

To my great surprise, the Bonanza Valley wasn't wide at all—only about three or four hundred feet across from rim-rock to rim-rock. High hills followed along on either side of the valley, completely hemming it in from higher hills and mountains beyond.

The winding trail led past many groups of hard-working miners and interesting, exciting claims. We paused to watch a miner emerge from a gopher-like hole. He was dragging a bucket of pay-dirt which he had just dug in a deep shaft. Eagerly, he ran to the creek's edge and with a battered old skillet, which obviously served two purposes, went through the process of testing the gold-run. It showed rich, coarse gold, like small kernels of yellow corn.

This was my very first glimpse of gold in the raw, and I found myself exclaiming, "How beautiful! Oh, how very, very beautiful! Why, the nuggets seem to dance for joy to be freed from the earth! It's incredible how very bright each nugget is!"

"And now let me give you your first lesson in gold mining," said Ed, as we strolled along. "Gold is found mostly concentrated on bedrock. Now it's evident that in previous centuries, way back in the dim, dark past, long before the North became a frozen land, quantities of top-gold gradually washed downward through the gravels and sands to bedrock. (Bedrock ranges from fifteen to forty feet below the surface.) Sometimes gold has even worked its way into the crevices of bedrock, itself. These crevices will often go down three or four feet into the rotted rock.

"The operation of gold-mining means digging a shaft to bedrock to remove the ground (all the way down) and then, to get the accumulated rich sediment at bedrock and also in the cracks below that, if any. If the ground proves to be very auriferous, naturally, it brings great joy to the miners. The pay-dirt with black sand is hauled up to the surface in buckets by attaching the buckets to a rope that is wound up on a windlass (a large, spool-like contraption). The buckets are then emptied at the surface, right near the shaft. During the big clean-up process, which always starts in late spring, the pay-dirt is usually run through rockers and then sluice boxes. (Rockers are large boxes with heavy coarse screens at the top.)

THE FAMOUS BONANZA AND ELDORADO 85

"But everyone must admit that getting gold out of the ground in the North means much more effort than elsewhere. It's well-known that in winter the earth is frozen solid and in summer it's frozen up to eighteen inches of the surface. To overcome this permafrost, we literally melt our way to bedrock. The common method is to use bonfires. Once we reach bedrock we drift-in, or cross-cut, which means melting the earth in a horizontal direction in tunnels. Often we make a number of 'drift-ins,' so many, in fact, that if you were to see them from above ground they would resemble a large wheel with numerous spokes.

"An underground wheel of gold," I mused.

"How right you are!" said Ed. "Yes, that's the kind every miner dreams of, and they're many in the Klondike."

The miners along the Bonanza stopped work and watched Clemy and me and hailed Ed. Proudly, they showed us their gold. It seemed that gold was everywhere—just for the asking—and some of the mine owners were eager to give away their choicest nuggets. Consequently, Clemy and I became the proud, new owners of a few beautiful specimens.

"And now we've reached the Tacoma Hotel!" Ed announced gaily, as he bounded forward to a very weather-beaten looking tent pitched near the river.

"Hello, is anyone inside?" he called jovially. There was no response, so Ed ushered us into the tent. "We'll make ourselves at home and build a fire in the little stove and soon have coffee." said Ed. "Sure," he laughed, when he saw me looking around inquiringly, "the furniture is homemade—mostly from wooden boxes—but what a haven this tent with its furnishings has been, especially when the fellows and I have barely reached it from strenuous stampedes in blizzardy weather. This happens to be No. 60, below Discovery. The owner let some of us Tacoma Fellows pitch our tent here. What a good scout he is—a real 'Skookum'* fellow!"

"Oh, Ed, please tell us about the stampedes," I begged. "Now that we're here, on the spot, we can really appreciate hearing about them. And tell us all about that Bonanza claim, too. You sent a letter by William Rogers, saying that it's among the rich producers."

"And it is," said Ed, "so while we munch sandwiches, I'll give you a

*The expression "Skookum" was widely used in the Klondike and in the States. It meant, "The greatest!"

run down on it. Yes, pretty soon, about eight miles up the Bonanza, we'll be coming to my hillside Bench-claim, No. 7. I staked it in September of 1897. It's the cussed ground that I sacrificed all other mining rights for, here, on the Bonanza. It's just 100 feet up from the floor of the great Bonanza. Yet, while I've had title to this ground, only a few tantalizing colors have shown up. In all of those shafts, at the bottom, there's been nothing—nothing but seeping icewater and hard, unyielding bedrock!

"During the past two years, I've had to have a constant string of laymen and I've let some of the Tacoma boys take a crack at that claim, too, but there's been nothing in it for anybody but hard work. Yet, I've persisted in my hopes for that claim. And why shouldn't I have high hopes? By late summer of '98 miners were reaping unbelievable quantities of gold on the Ancient Channel Hills, on the other side of the Bonanza.

"Of course, by summer of '98 all hills of the Bonanza were staked. Even my hillside was showing some signs of gold. Oscar Fisher's bench, just 500 feet downstream from me, yielded $15,000 in one season. VanZant had a lay there and sold it. And Cook's Bench, just a few hundred feet upstream from me, had yielded $1,000 in gold, in one clean-up.

"So, through the summer and fall of '98 I kept digging in my hillside, spurred by the sight of the gold around me, and of those fabulous hill-claims across the valley in which they were getting $50, $100, and $500 to the pan. Think of it! One pan! Ah, I could have wept—my claim only yielded a few glints of flour gold, just a stone's throw from those glittering claims about 300 feet away!

"Well, at last I was beginning to think, maybe, I had drawn a blank—that I was losing very valuable opportunities elsewhere, so, together, Poole and I bought a Lay on No. 37 Gay Hill (my side of the valley) and we worked it intermittantly with my Bench claim, but with no results. Neither claim was yielding a tinker's damn! I was getting disgusted, and very poor too, so around the first of October of '98, I resolved to go on stampedes to other creeks outside the Bonanza area where I could legally stake a new claim. No, I couldn't stake another one in the Bonanza Klondike area according to law. A miner can buy as many claims as he wishes, but I hadn't enough money to branch out any further than Gay Hill.

"Then too, it was necessary that I stay within easy walking distance of Dawson, as I had to rely on temporary jobs at the Alaska Commercial Company, working as Expert Accountant, in order to have pocket money, and to be able to buy grub to stay alive. Of course, this was a terrible handicap, but it was the only way that I could remain in the Klondike.

"Near the end of July (1898), there had been stampedes over beyond Queen Dome to Sulphur and Little Blanche (on the hills), sixty-five miles away. A man by the name of Andy stopped at my tent on the way back and gave me the details. Several nights before that, at midnight, I had suspected something was up, as a group of dancehall girls and miners went by, cat-footing it. 'Well, there goes one of those mixed stampedes,' I had said to myself, half amused. I could have followed that crowd, but I had no idea where they were going and besides, I had no time for a wild-goose, sneak-stampede.

"Then, there was another stampede I heard about, right after it had taken place: A fellow named Shaw came along the Bonanza and spilled the beans—said the whole mountain side near Gold Bottom Creek had been staked—said that fifteen 'roaring drunk' Australians had started the rush off, said it was a wild affair. Well, I kept thinking, 'Here am I, chained to this Bonanza claim. What a blankety-blankety chump I am, hanging onto this cussed ground, "Old Brutus." ' (I was beginning to call it by that name.)"

"And, oh, why did you?" I asked seriously.

"Well," said Ed, "it was because, first of all, I was on the great and glittering Bonanza, and secondly, because the Canadian laws are very strict. Once a fellow starts digging in ground that he's staked, come hell or high water, that claim must be steadily worked by someone, and if there occurs a lapse of more than five days, without an acceptable excuse, OK'd by the Gold Commissioner, a fellow can forfeit his claim.

"During my absence from the Klondike, Captain Breeze and his crew of laymen had seen to it that my claim was represented and worked. And now, after all that effort, I certainly wasn't willing to forfeit that claim, where, with the next turn of the shovel I could become a wealthy mine owner. Yes, you bet! I was still gambling on cussed 'Old Brutus,' even though it had been a betrayer of high hopes to fortune thus far. Gradually Poole was taking over the Lay on No. 37, Gay Hill and I approved. I just couldn't continue to exspend my energies in both claims, and also work at Dawson at the A.C.C. Company, at intervals, in order to survive.

"Gold Commissioner Fawcett, at Dawson, was not an easy man to reason with, or even to get into his office to interview. Such an obstinate, severe person, I've seldom met. His word was absolute law, and Major Walsh, the shrewd Northwest Mounted Police Commissioner, stood firmly behind him. (Major W. L. Walsh, called 'Foxy Grandpa' by the miners, was a hero in the Indian Wars and had helped capture Sitting Bull.) Fawcett's secretary had special orders; they called her 'The Tigress.' Indeed, she stood guard over Fawcett like a snarling feline.

"Some folks accused the Gold Commissioner of being plain dishonest. Well, let's say he, at least, played favorites, favoring his own Canadian countrymen above others, for it was well known that we Americans made up 90% of the Dawson-Klondike population. But with all of his faults, the Commissioner was a faithful Presbyterian Churchman, singing in the choir every Sunday, looking quite sanctimonious, and I have to say that the few times I heard him sing, I had enjoyed his fine voice. However, on weekdays his personality and even his speaking voice underwent an unpleasant change—and no wonder—his life was full of turmoil. Almost every day, irate miners' meetings were held protesting the high-handed way that Fawcett was running things. It didn't do any good to appeal to our U.S. Consul, McCook, either. As I said before, Fawcett's word was law! Where great fortunes are concerned, that kind of law is quite often corruptible.

"Well, to get back to the Stampedes—in the latter part of October, of '98, I had my travel-pack all ready to take off at a moment's notice. I had decided that I could risk leaving my hillside for five days. Any longer than that, and I could lose 'Old Brutus,' as the Gold Commissioner would be quickly informed of the claim being idle. But it was becoming increasingly difficult to learn of any promising, new goldstrikes. In fact, news of stampedes was always available after they were over. I had watched scores of fellows depart, half-cocked, for remote streams, God only knew where, and later, had seen them return, path-

―――――――――――
*Special friends of the Gold Commissioner were often seen going through a back door to his office. Major Walsh was Yukon Commissioner for two months.

*Corrupt officials actually stole ground by saying the claims were already staked. Capt. Constantine, the Mountie Commissioner, was honest, but poor. His name shines as a light in Yukon History.

etic, human wrecks, frostbitten and starved. A hundred miles in subzero weather! That's a very long trail of suffering, especially if unrewarded.

"By the first of November of '98, the Stampedes were occuring closer to Dawson. In early fall, there had been a rush to Sulphur Creek, and I had stampeded over there for several days only to be disappointed with worthless ground. Then, on November 14th, there was still another one much closer to Dawson. This one was to Swede Creek. I happened to be in town when I heard the good news.

"Immediately, I bought a permit. Yes, it's actually necessary to have a permit for each special area—another sly trick of the gold Commissioner's! Imagine being in stampede-territory and finding you're not eligible to stake, simply because you haven't a permit at the proper moment and for the proper section! They never issued a general permit. Sometimes we walked fifty miles for those darned permits!

"Well, so I bought my permit for Swede Creek. I was all set. Now, all I had to do was go there and get myself a fine prospect.

"The temperature on November 14 was 10 degrees below zero. It was cold, but not as cold as I knew it was going to be. With luck, I figured I could run up there and be back at Dawson in two days, for Swede Creek was only about ten miles from town and, praise the Lord, it was out of the Bonanza mining zone. Well, I took off on the run.

"But when I reached Swede Creek I found the place bristling with stakes; that is, all except No. 72 which was in among the boulders. It was either that or nothing, so I drove my four stakes with name and number on the boundaries of that claim, then I looked around a bit. It was then I noticed No. 78. Obviously, someone had been there doing a lot of digging. This caught my eye. I wondered if someone had abandoned that claim. Well, I would soon find out!

"I rushed back to Dawson as fast as I could, and registered the No. 72 claim. Then, I inquired of 'The Tigress' about No. 78. Disdainfully, she looked it up and informed me that it belonged to a man named John Caim, who by the way, was an acquaintance of mine, a man who had been in Circle City.

"I hurried to see him. He was doubtful about the 'Swede' and said he would sell it for a low figure, but I told him I couldn't buy. Then he said, 'All right, Ed, you're welcome to work it as a layman, but that ground is chuck full of big rocks. If there's any gold, whoever gets it out will surely pay a heavy price in back aches.'

"Well, I reminded Kain of how Alex McDonald, the Klondike King, had put down three shafts in one of his first Bonanza claims before he finally struck it rich.

" 'Of course, Ed,' said Kain, 'you just might be lucky, too, like Alex. But it will be a colossal task, especially if you try to work No. 78 and No. 72 at the same time. Certainly, you'll need a very good partner—one who's not afraid of hard labor!'

"Well, the long and short of it was that later that same day, I ran into Joe Latshaw in Dawson and altho' I knew him only casually, I took a chance and invited him to go to Swede Creek as my partner. He was pleased and consented. Later, I discovered that if I'd searched the North over, I couldn't have found a more reliable partner.

"So, that day I was really jubilant! I had acquired a partner and a new claim, and possible a good lay from Kain. Swede Creek had a special appeal. It was fairly close to Dawson. Now I was really in business! Best of all I could still keep track of 'Old Brutus,' too, because that same day, I had been able to make arrangements with three enthusiastic, newly-arrived cheechakos—Lester, Leibling and Leitel—who would go up on the Bonanza and work 'Old Brutus' as my laymen for 50% of the gold. This was a perfect deal. They would hold the claim and possibly hit that elusive pay-streak. Who could tell? Yes, I was beginning to believe my stinkin' luck had finally changed."

"Listen to what my diary has to tell about it," said Ed, as he produced his little red leather-bound book from his vest pocket. Flipping its pages back to a well-worn section, he began to read:

> Nov. 17, 1898   Dawson and Swede Creek — 45 degrees below zero!
> Joe and I started from Dawson at 11 A.M. Very cold. Found trail a little wet. Had 300 lbs. Took Wyncoop's sled. Camped 1 mile up Swede Creek. Have my thermometer, so can keep track of the weather. Our beds are good and warm and have plenty to eat—so am not worrying on that score. (Sleep in large sleeping bags on Yukon feathers—spruce boughs.)
>
> Nov. 18, 1898   Swede Creek — 52½ degrees below
> Broke camp 10 A.M. Cold as hell! Good trail—but sled pulls as if it weighed a ton. Reached No. 72 at 3 P.M. Made camp and am

George W. Carmack, left, discoverer of Bonanza gold, and the great "Klondike King," Alexander McDonald.

Stampeders' consultation on the Klondike trail.

Looking down Bonanza valley from Cheechako Hill, 1898. (Winter)
(Photo by Adams & Larkin)

Skookum Jim, one of the richest Indians in the North; was
co-discoverer of the Bonanza gold.

now quite comfortable. There are five cabins between here & the mouth of the creek & there must be a good many people up the creek, to judge from the trail.

Nov. 19, 1898   Swede Creek — 55 degrees below
  Kept fire all night as it was so very cold! Fixed up camp & made tent smaller, now 10 x 10 instead of 10 x 12. Started hole on the line between No. 71 and No. 72. Several parties passed. One fellow stopped; his feet were nearly frozen. Have frozen my two toes on right foot.

Nov. 20, 1898   Swede Creek — 50 degrees below
  Another cold night. Kept fire all night. Joe took his turn. Started another hole on No. 72, more in middle of gulch. The cabin nearest is on No. 67. Put in fire in first hole, only thawed 3 inches. We are both in good health & spirits. Worked all day in spite of cold. Joe was formerly in Real Estate business in Tacoma. Forgot today was Sunday. Wonder what dear Velma is doing.

Nov. 21, 1898   Monday. Swede Creek — 50½ degrees below
  Put big fire in upper hole. Have taken an awful cold. My back & neck are ready to break. Cold weather hangs on. Ther. seems to be frozen at 50 degrees below.

Nov. 22, 1898   Swede Creek — 50 degrees below
  Have stayed in bed all day. Am feeling awful—every bone in my body aches—and as sore as a boil. Managed to keep warm. Joe has worked like a trooper all day. Could hear him slashing down the timber. Just had strength enough to get meals for him. Will take some of his Carter's Liver Pills.

Nov. 23, 1898   Swede Creek — 50 degrees below
  Did not get up until noon. Am feeling 100% better. Pills seemed to take all the poison out of my system. Am putting all of the time on lower hole which is beginning to look deep now—4½ feet down. Man stopped on his way down creek. Looked like a ghost, all covered with frost! Beautiful moonlight.

Nov. 24, 1898   30 Below at 8 A.M. 50 degrees at 9 P.M.
  Have put in good day's work. Started hole on Kain's claim, No. 78 Below Discovery. Sinking hole in old creek-bed, right in the gravel which saves going through the muck. Joe made drum for windlass. Hole on No. 72 is now 6 feet deep. Two fires today. Am putting her down in good shape. Snowed hard all day. Cold weather has broken, glad of it.

Nov. 25, 1898   Swede Creek — 10 degrees Below
　　Party stopped & had supper with us. Said he was on No. 493 Above Dis.—had done no work—heard they had only got 20c to the pan just above him. Am feeling better. Joe is working windlass. The change in temperature is agreeable.

Nov. 26, 1898   Swede Creek — 10 degrees Below
　　Worked hard all day. Hole on No. 78 is going down fast, now 3 feet—no colors yet. Beautiful looking quartz. My heel is sore from being frostbitten.

Nov. 27, 1898   Swede Cr. — 8 degrees Below
　　Did not get up until 7 A.M. Worked all day, but did not contemplate doing so. Our fire did not burn last night, on No. 78, so put in fire this A.M. which thawed down 2 ft. & water is now troubling us. Could not pan satisfactorily, but think we are near bedrock & colors are showing up. Wonder what dear Velma is doing tonight.

Nov. 28, 1898   Swede Cr. — 10 degrees Below
　　Upper hole No. 78 full of water this A.M. Will not try to do anything with it until a day or so. Put all time on lower hole.

Tues. Nov. 29, 1898   Swede Cr.
　　Am not feeling first class. My cold is getting worse. Snowed a little last night. Bailed out No. 78 hole—will see if it fills again.

Nov. 30, 1898   Swede
　　Am feeling awfully mean. Full of cold and can hardly breathe. Joe is a good fellow to be with—makes no difference, he will keep on working whether I have to stop or not.

Dec. 2, 1898   Swede — 10 degrees B.
　　Did not sleep at all last night. A gathering is in my right ear & is playing hell with me. Reached bedrock on No. 72 & then I collapsed. Couldn't do any more work if there were millions in it! We'll go to Dawson tomorrow.

Dec. 3, 1898   Swede — 10 degrees Below
　　Left No. 72 at 10 A.M. Feeling horrible. Could hardly walk—let alone help to mush the sled—which is a hard-running one. Stopped for lunch at mouth of creek. Made Dawson 6:30 P.M., almost knocked out. My head is aching to split itself with pain

from my ear. Earl and Bertram are in from Sulphur Cr.

Sun. Dec. 4, 1898   Dawson
Stayed in bed all day long & damn glad to be here. Have a slight fever, my ear is playing hell. Did not sleep last night.

Dec. 5, 1898   Dawson — 10 degrees Below
Did not sleep more than two hours last night. My ear is gathering again. All the boys have gone out. Kahlenborn & Wynkoop were in, former, has brought me some morphine tablets to ease the pain so I can sleep. Joe got letter out of P.O. from Velma dated July 25—sent in with some acquaintance of Dr. Misner, so Joe says.

Dec. 6   Dawson (Zero)
Went up to G. Com. office twice to see Fawcett, could not catch him. Am feeling a little better. It is getting very warm. Wind blowing hard, regular Chinook. Hear that Hebb is going Outside. Will send letters. Nothing yet known of bench, (of my Bonanza claim). Usual luck, suppose. I was not born under the lucky stars, my life so far shows.

Dec. 7   Dawson (30 degrees Above)
This is dangerously warm on account of sickness. Half the people have colds & are looking bad. Am all O.K. except my ear & neuralgia. Spencer died while I was up at Swede Cr.

Dec. 8   Dawson (22 degrees Above)
Got an extension of time on Swede Cr. until Jan. 1, '99. Will try to sell Swede Cr. if possible. Swanson & Poole were down.

Dec. 9, 1898   Dawson (22 degrees Above)
Went up town for Swanson's bench-claim trial. Was postponed until P.M. Did not go in P.M. Am feeling better, but head is still out of joint.

Dec. 10, 1898   Dawson — 15 degrees Above
Have not left cabin all day. Have been feeling blue—discouraged—fearful that my bench-claim No. 7 Bonanza is N.G. What else can I expect? My luck is always rotten! Who cares? Life is short anyway. Hebb goes out the 15th. Bob Walker was in. Invited me to New Years' banquet on Stampede Gulch. (What would fellows do without friends? I can use a good dinner!)

Dec. 11, 1898   Dawson — 10 degrees Above.
Joe, Bert & Al & I went to Methodist Church in P.M. Am deaf as a bat—still.

M. Dec. 12.   Dawson
The boys all went on a wild tear. Jim McGrath came near getting a jagg on. Makes me more disgusted with this Dawson life we are living.

Dec. 13, 1898   Dawson
Joe went up to the gulch. Looking after my Bonanza bench claim, "Old Brutus." My star of fortune is well below the horizon. Wonder if it will ever turn up!

"Yes, by December 10th my impatient, gold-hungry laymen had thrown down the Bonanza claim. 'Old Brutus' was still playing its usual abominable tricks, throwing a little flour gold. Well, I really couldn't blame the fellows. No one could live on a few pennies a day! So I stood to lose the claim, but good old Joe rushed up there to do some work to hold it. On that date, I believed my star of fortune had permanently sunk below the horizon.

"On December 31, ('98) I sent a letter Outside by Will Rogers* telling my family that I had been under the weather, but that I was going to hang onto my Bonanza claim. Also, that Will Rogers had promised me a shipment of honey next trip in. I had had several before, and had sold the honey to the miners, for $1.00 a pound. Yes, not only was I a poor mine-owner and part-time accountant, but I was also a honey-salesman in my 'Spare Time,' tho' I wasn't too anxious for the latter to be generally known.

"Now, more about the Swede claim, No. 72: By January 10, I had forfeited it. I had been too ill to work it, and I couldn't find anyone to buy it. It was too early in the game to get anyone to go in there with machinery. John Cain's No. 78 was in the same category, and he agreed. So once again, I pinned my hopes to 'Old Brutus,' thinking, 'Yes, at the next turn of the shovel I could strike it rich, then it would be hi, ho, for Tacoma!' But from the start, that Bonanza Brute has had a very strong influence on my destiny. It's maddening! It's been almost like dictating my future in the Klondike. And, I still have the 'Old Brute' to deal with!" sighed Ed.

"Vel," said Ed a little later as we trudged the trail, "we are now coming to the richest placer ground in the world. The miners are taking out gold that is making mining history. Now look at the claims to the right of us, on the hills, bordering the Bonanza. These are the hills that I was telling you about. They set the Klondike agog when gold was discovered in early spring of '98. As luck would have it, I was out of the region for a time, but when I returned, I heard the amazing story from everyone's lips, so here it is:

"On March 2, 1898, three Swedes, who were out after wood, climbed a hill above the forks of the Bonanza and Eldorado. Their cabin happened to be just below, in the valley.

"After cutting logs and hauling them down the hillside for most of the afternoon, they decided to make one more last trip up. On their way down, Ole, one of the Swedes, spied a nugget sticking up out of the moss and snow where their logs had cut into the ground. Thinking that a miner must have dropped the nugget, Ole gratefully pocketed it.

"That evening, while the Swedes were having supper, a friend, Bill Seating dropped in. Naturally, the conversation swung to gold, and it was then that Ole remembered that bright yellow nugget in his pocket. He pulled it forth and briefly told where he had found it. The friend closely examined the glittering gold, and admired it. Soon after that, he excused himself and left.

"Along about mid-night, there was a soft knock at the Swedes' door, and the friend called in a hurried, muffled voice, 'Ole, let me in. Quick! It's very important.'

"Ole was awakened out of a sound slumber, but being very good-natured, he hopped out of bed, and let the late-comer in.

" 'Hurry, light your lantern,' ordered Bill. 'I've got something mighty important, a handful of nuggets and they came from the hill just about where you found yours. No, Ole, a miner didn't drop that nugget! You see, I climbed up the hill about 400 feet, right after I left your cabin. I was curious. I had an exciting hunch. By lantern-light I found the exact spot that you described. With a small spade, I dug around, tearing off pieces of moss. Just under the surface, I found these nuggets—a handful of beauties! Man, I've staked a claim! Now I'm on my way to Dawson to record it. So you Swedes get dressed. Get up the hill and stake. Then beat it to town. Between us we've made a tremendous discovery. We're rich. Hurry!, and keep it secret!'

"Well, it was a colossal discovery, and the four men meant to keep it secret. But next day, somehow, the news leaked out. Hundreds of people came running to the hills like crazy, staking everything in sight. They even came after dark, staking by lantern and candlelight. They said it was the maddest gold-rush that had ever taken place in the Klondike; hordes of wild-eyed people came. After they had staked the left limit, they rushed to the right limit—on my side of the Bonanza.*

"Right afterwards, the experts tried to explain this new gold field, and how the gold got up on the hill-top. Then, at last, when it became apparent that the streak of gold continued in great richness for miles and miles along the hills on the left limit, or the Southwest Bonanza, William Ogilvie and Alexander McDonald finally came up with a startling theory. They said it must be an ancient channel of the Bonanza, or maybe the Klondike River. They said that many centuries ago the old river channel had been upped, forming these hills. Anyway, the gold had been right there under the moss all the time, just crying to be discovered!

"Great Scott!" sighed Ed. "Many's the time I climbed those hills, back in 1897, especially that extremely rich one which they named 'Gold Hill.' Why, oh why, couldn't I have stubbed my toe on a bunch of nuggets before the Swedes came? Instead, I climbed a slope on the almost barren side of the Bonanza and got No. 7—Old Brutus! Well, to go on with the story:

"The first hill in the high chain of Bonanza gold (as we go up-stream, right hand side) is Sourdough Hill, the second is Sherry, then comes Boulder. King Solomon Hill is next, fifth is Monte Cristo, the sixth one is Orifero, and the seventh hill is known as American. Magnet comes next. Then Adams is next. Cheechako Hill is above Adams. Then comes famous Gold Hill. Just above Gold Hill is French Hill, the last on the high, ancient channel. The pay-streak runs in great richness on French Hill, for at least 300 feet long and 200 feet wide. No one knows exactly how deep it extends. There is something very interesting about this particular hill, too. The experts surmise that once it was an old, old sand-bar. It's difficult to imagine a sand-bar way up there on that hill, but it's true because there is evidence.

"There's something very significant too, about French Hill. Beyond

---

*Left limit," mining term, means the left-hand side, facing down stream. "Right Limit"—also facing down stream.

it, the Ancient Channel abruptly disappears.* But just about at this point, down in the valley, the Eldorado River pours forth some of its biggest nuggets—its most dazzling wealth!

"The well-known Berry claims at this spot, are producing $5,000 to the box-length (a box-length is 12 feet). These fabulous claims are just a little bit beyond the confluence of the Bonanza and Eldorado, or Grand Forks.

"The Berry brothers, Frank and Clarence, with their silent partner, Antone Standar, own Eldorado No. 4, No. 5, and No. 6. Of course these men are very prominent Klondike Kings. But only three years ago, in '96, they were unknown. In fact Clarence was just about down to his last dollar when he and his bride came in over the ice to Forty Mile in the spring of '96. Then George Carmack made the big Bonanza Discovery (Aug. 17, 1896). Clarence Berry and his two partners were close at hand—so close that they could rush to the new diggings with little trouble. (forty-five miles away)"

Our family caravan continued to plod onward, always keeping the famous hills with all of their "Ancient Channel Wonder-Claims" in view, while our feet trod over untold wealth in the valley.

"Why was it," I asked myself as we hiked along, "that the yellow metal, bright as the sun, had always been fascinating to humanity—had always had a magnetic influence—was always fatally irresistible?" And now I was beginning to confess to myself that I, too, was falling under its hypnotic spell. All of the way up the valley I had been surrounded by gold and had heard the names of many famous mine owners; had met some, and had seen their fabulous claims.

There was the young lawyer, S. O. Morford, and his partners, on No. 50 Below Discovery. He was associated with the Kirkpatrick, Harper and Ladue Land and Mining Company. There was Col. McKinnis, at No. 34; Harry C. Ashe at No. 32; Paul Hebb owned No. 29; James Morrison at No. 27; Jack Donovan at No. 18; David McKay and Henry Waugh owned No. 16, No. 15, and No. 14, all Below Discovery; No. 12 belonged to Jack Dalton, of Dalton-Trail fame; The Morford, Kirkpatrick, Harper and Ladue Company again, at No. 11.

*Clam shells were found on several hills which would indicate that the ocean was once there.

*In 1898 Clarence J. Berry discovered that steam could be forced through the barrel of a rifle and that when the rifle was driven into the frozen earth, it melted the muck. Thus, was invented the first steam-points used underground.

Most amazing of all was that in between these scattered numbers, the fabulous Klondike King's glittering name, "Alexander McDonald," appeared. There was one, however, that he didn't own as yet, and it was No. 10, held by a French Canadian, Alphonse Lapierre. His story made glad the hearts of all who heard it.

Lapierre had been a discouraged miner in despair. He had prospected the Salmon River, the Stewart River, the Forty Mile, and he was about to leave the country in August, '96, when he and his partner chanced to meet George Carmack, who was on his way to Forty Mile to record his Discovery Claim. Carmack generously showed Lapierre and his friend samples of his gold and told them how to get to the Bonanza to stake. The two partners got up to the Bonanza ahead of most of the Fortymile-crowd and chose No. 9 and No. 10, Below Discovery. Both turned out to be very rich claims. Now, the two Frenchmen were in Paris enjoying their tremendous success and owing a lot of it to George Carmack. Yes, such were the dazzling stories of some, who had been among the lucky ones, those who had had a big part in a gold-rush that had electrified the world!

Later in the afternoon we reached Euly Gaisford's rich No. 7 claim (below Discovery in the valley). I had heard about it and its owner. Euly had been a poor barber from Tacoma before he went to the Klondike. Then, he had struck it rich. In '98 he had gone Outside to buy a large cattle ranch in Northern Washington and was the envy of all his friends. Little did any of us dream that his future years were numbered. (On June 5, 1902, he was swept to his death while crossing the swollen Methow River with a herd of cattle. His horse became frightened and threw him.)

Jovially, all the miners at Euly's claim greeted Ed, for it was evident they were all very good friends, and they were pleased to see Clemy and me. After salutations, Ed, Clemy and I climbed the hill to reach "Old Brutus"—a steep 100 feet above Euly's valley claim. Somehow the cold, deserted shafts of "Brutus" seemed to stare up at us with defiant, insolent, mockery. How I pitied Ed for all of the slavery, sacrifice and worry he had put into this desolate place!

"'Say, now, do any of you fellows down there want a good miner's lay?" called Ed to the claim below.

"Hell, no!" exclaimed an old miner as he thrust his shovel into the sluice-box and spat a wad of tobacco. "No sir, Ed, 'tain't nary a nugget up there—just a little flour gold. Your last laymen proved it—Benton and Stickney. They took off for far more profitable fields, over in them Skookum Hills. Said there's a solid rock slide deep under your bench. Even tried a little blasting, but couldn't move the rock. Tough luck, Ed. It's just too doggone bad the old river-bed didn't touch your claim with a chunk a' gold. Why, across this valley they're picking big nuggets out of the hills like they was raisins in a plum puddin'! And even on your side some of the Benchers are gittin' somethin' fer their efforts."

"Sure," said Ed with a bitter smile, "It's pretty ironic, isn't it? Just makes a fellow sick to come so close and yet end up so very, very far from the goal!"

As we left Euly's claim, several nuggets were pressed into our hands, as souvenir, friendship-esteem-tokens.

At the next claim, which was No. 6 Below Discovery, we met a long pack-train of mules headed for Dawson. The poor animals were staggering under the weight of tremendously heavy bags of Something! Stamped on each, in black letters was the name, "Alexander McDonald."

"Yes, that's Alex's gold, all right, perhaps a half million dollar's worth!" exclaimed Ed, with an odd catch to his voice.

"Yep, you're absolutely right, partner," echoed the mule-driver, as he stopped to adjust a strap on one of the mules. It 'tain't no wonder Alex's the biggest Klondike King of 'em all. He owns dozens of claims up and down the Bonanza and Eldorado, some on Hunker, and even over on Dominion Creek. But most of this here gold comes from 'The Banner Claim' on Gold Hill. You should see them nuggets! Alex owns half of that hill, too! Wow! He's actually been getting $1,000 and more, to the pan! You bet, he's the richest feller in the Klondike, maybe the world! And in Dawson he's snatching up real estate like mad."

"Yes," sighed Ed, "everything Alex touches turns to gold. He has the Midas Touch, all right. How can a man be that lucky?"

After the pack train had swung by, Ed remarked half-playfully and a little sadly, too, "Vel, if 'Old Brutus' had only yielded the equivalent of just one sack of Alex's nuggets, you and Clemy wouldn't be trudging up to Dominion Creek like this."

*Ed sold his bench claim for a song. The new owners carefully blasted the rock ledge away and took out $40,000 in gold. Stickney and Benton tried the same method, but had no success.

"Oh, Ed," I assured him, "I wouldn't be missing this wonderful adventure for anything in the world. It's quite evident that the good Lord didn't wish us to have any of this bright Bonanza gold or He would have arranged things differently."

"Sure, I guess you're right," agreed Ed, thoughtfully. "But Vel, this claim that we are now standing on, No. 6 Below Discovery*, has a pay-streak that is running a million dollars, or more. It's owned, half-interest, by Ezekiel Ogilvie, who came to the Bonanza in '96 from Miller Creek, where he had labored long and hard and unsuccessfully. But surely Lady Luck was with him, here in the Klondike. This claim is the richest on the Bonanza and is called 'The Million Dollar Claim.' Must be that a good part of the Mother Lode was spilled over here. They get $600 to the pan and the pay-streak runs up onto those Ancient Channel hills. So you see Vel, my hillside claim, No. 7, is really in the company of tons of big nuggets and yellow dust.

"And now we're coming to the famous Discovery Claim," said Ed, as we continued our hike. "It's the custom for the Discoverer of gold on a new creek to legally stake two claims, so George Carmack* staked Discovery and also, took No. 1 Below Discovery, Tagish Charlie staked No. 2 Below Discovery, and Skookum Jim took No. 1 Above Discovery. These claims are near the mouth of the small gulch called 'Little Skookum.' Just above these claims is Cheechako Hill. Of course Carmack and his two Indians didn't dream of the vast treasure up above them, The Ancient Channel! No, nor did anyone else."

By the time we had reached the Discovery Claim I had grown weary and footsore and Clemy and Nelly were lagging behind.

"Oh, come little Clem," called Ed tenderly, as he encouraged Clemy to catch up, "climb up on your Dad's shoulder and go piggy-back. It's only a short distance to the Grand Forks. What a long trek it's been for a cheechako lady, a very small boy, and a puppy!"

In a few minutes the bedraggled Lung family rounded the last bend of the river. There, before our eyes, loomed the confluence of the two rivers—the Bonanza and the Eldorado.

"Yes, this is the Grand Forks," said Ed. "Some folks call it, 'Forks

---

*Alexander McDonald owned half interest in No. 6 Below Discovery. The biggest nuggets found on the Bonanza were in this area. One weighed 64½ ounces. Carmack's gold ran from $250 to $280 to the pan. By 1911, Alexander McDonald, the "Klondike King," had lost his immense fortune. He died on Slough Creek about sixty miles from Dawson, forgotten and alone.

of Gold,' but the popular name is 'Grand Forks.' It's right here that those dazzling big nuggets have been found. One weighing nearly a pound was dug up in the Berry No. 5 Eldorado claim, just a few months ago. But farther up-river the famous 'Knutson,' a pear-shaped nugget, was found in 1897. It was on display in Dawson. That nugget was a beautiful sight, a pale yellow gold, and it weighed nearly two pounds. It came from Michael Knutson's Eldorado No. 36 (half-interest). He was with the lucky Forty-Mile group, of '96. And he was a passenger on the Steamer, Portland, when it went to Seattle in '97 with its 'ton of gold.' Other early Klondikers on that ship were: Clarence Berry, Frank Phiscator, Dick McNutty, Thomas Lippy, William Stanley, Frank Keller, Mr. Gage and Mr. Warden.

"But now, Vel, see that peculiar round-shaped hill to the right of us with all those earth-scars and sluice boxes? Well, that's Gold Hill, and the gulch that seems to slice off part of the hill on the upper side, is Big Skookum Gulch. Someday you can tell our grandchildren that you slept this night in the shadow of tons of nuggets and yellow dust."

Night was falling rapidly and it was a sign to hurry. Crossing a small bridge, we reached the two-story Mulrooney Roadhouse just as a supper of moose-steak was being served.

To say we were dog-tired is putting it mildly. While we had supper, I listened to many thrilling "Sourdough Tales" told by Captain Breeze, Jim McKay and Dan McRae—three friends of Ed's—having dinner at the Inn. (Captain Breeze had a lay on Little Skookum Gulch.) One story that caught my ear was about Belinda Mulrooney, the owner of this Inn. First, I learned that she was the daughter of a coal miner. She had joined the early stampedes and had crossed Chilkoot in early 1897. An intrepid woman! Arriving in the Klondike, she had set herself up in business here, at the Forks. She had also managed to acquire interests in several rich Bonanza and Eldorado claims. She was also the proud owner of the most plush hotel in Dawson, "The Fairview," and gossip had it that in a few months she was going to marry Count Carboneaux, and that they would tour Europe on their honeymoon.

Then, too, Belinda Mulrooney was a director of the Eldorado Bonanza Quartz And Placer Mining Company, which had been formed a few weeks after the Ancient Channel had come to light (spring of '98). The richest Bonanza and Eldorado Kings formed the nucleus of this syndicate—Alexander McDonald, Frank and Clarence Berry, Dr. C. C.

Savage, M. J. Neil, P. D. Carper, W. T. Posey, J. D. Seitz, C. W. Clapp, W. L. Stocking (lawyer), and Jimo J. Rieger (a capitalist), and of course, Belinda Mulrooney. The syndicate now held some of the richest placer and quartz ground in the Klondike. Its mines—Victoria, Regina, Globe, Anaconda, Aetna, and Plunger—extended from the Westside, left limit of the Eldorado, from the Berry claims, on through the mountain to the Big Skookum Gulch-side, and on into the "Skookum Hills," and were producing glittering returns. Also, they had acquired a hill on the eastside of the upper Eldorado, and owned No. 44 through No. 47. Here, they said, was a rich vein of blue quartz, which speared down into the Gulch. Already they had started work on The Last Dollar, The Eureka, and The Eldorado Queen. Of course, the company had its eyes on all good auriferous ground in the area, and was acquiring it, little by little.

Besides "Syndicate-Talk," there was an exciting account of how Dick Lowe, a mule-skinner, had gotten a small fraction of extra ground that had shown up after persistant surveys by William Ogilvie at the mouth of Big Skookum Gulch before the richness of the area was fully realized. There being no other ground available, Lowe took the fraction with reluctance, feeling that he would sacrifice his rights if a bigger fraction should show up in the surveys. He tried to sell the small, pie-shaped fraction for $800, but no one wanted such an insignificant claim, so Dick Lowe put down a second shaft and in eight hours took out gold worth $45,000! He had acquired what amounted to be the richest strip of ground in the world, and his little claim was worth at least one half-million dollars.

Well, naturally, hearing all these stories was terribly exciting, but I, quite early in the evening, was beginning to feel that I would have to listen another day—I had absolutely reached the saturation point, and

*It was reported that Dick Lowe took out over a half-million dollars in gold from his small pie-shaped fraction which was 86 feet at one end and 40 feet at the other. It is reported that Dick Lowe was a wild spender and in a few years had dissipated his wealth. He was reported to be in a continual state of drunkenness and would gamble $10,000 in one throw. He married a dancehall girl. He died a pauper in San Francisco in 1907.

*In 1898 Charlie Anderson paid $800 for claim No. 29, Eldorado, while he was intoxicated. When he sobered up he tried to get his money back, thinking he had a worthless claim on his hands. The sellers thought they had got rid of a blank claim, but a few weeks later Charlie Anderson was treating the "boys" in Dawson. He had hit the pay-streak and had a million dollar claim.

Adams Hill, rich with gold. Not far from the Grand Forks and the Bonanza Discovery claim. (Right across the Bonanza from Ed Lung's bench claim.)

Gold Hill - 1899. It was not uncommon for miners to get $1,000 to the pan. Grand Forks is in middle, right-hand side of photo. (Courtesy of Frank Clark)

The Mulrooney Roadhouse at the Grand Forks on the Bonanza and Eldorado.

Looking up the Eldorado from the Grand Forks. Exceedingly rich claims in foreground, the Berry No. 4 and No. 5 produced $5,000 to the box-length. Very large nuggets found here.

was reeling with fatigue.

As I almost collapsed onto my bunk, to my dismay, I discovered that it had no coil springs. It was the crudest kind of arrangement, made of peeled sapling poles, placed horizontally across the narrow bunk frames. Only a thin pad served as a mattress. That night I put in the worst hours of my life. It was necessary to keep turning every few minutes in order to keep the sharp edges of the poles from cutting my flesh. Clemy and Edward, somehow, slept soundly. Perhaps I, too, would have slept, just a little, had I not been so dog-tired and keyed-up over all I had seen this day in the Fabulous Valley of Gold!

At last I crawled to the little one-paned window and looked out over the Bonanza Valley where cabins and sluice boxes dominated the scene. Under a bright, starry sky, the Bonanza appeared almost beautiful despite the earth-scarred shafts and ugly dumps which were everywhere. Instinctively, I searched the heavens for the Dipper and the North Star—the Guide Star—wonderful Polaris!

"Vel, Vel," it seemed to twinkle, "you must not be dismayed or doubtful. Dominion Creek is a good place, a very beautiful valley—trust—trust. And there's gold—there's gold—there is gold!"

"Oh, but poor Edward," I inwardly wept, "what a heart-break of disappointment he has experienced!" Everywhere there had been great quantities of gold; around him, below him, and across from him—just within a stone's throw; on the hills and under the hills—everywhere—so close, and yet, yet, so awfully far!

---

*The Eldorado Bonanza Quartz and Placer Mining Company also had six claims on Henderson Creek, number sixty through sixty-five; placer claims, one through four above Discovery, and one through three below Discovery on Reindeer Creek. In 1898 the company was incorporated under the laws of the State of Missouri with $3,000,000 as capital stock, at $50 a share. The main office building was at 216 Sheidly Building, Kansas City. Phone number, 2830.

*In 1906 The Klondike Mines Railway was completed, having been started in 1903. The Railway ran from Dawson to Sulphur Springs, following the Bonanza to its source, 32 miles. It was the only railway that far North. Passengers could ride, but it was mainly for hauling ore.

Chapter 9

DEEP VALLEY AND LITTLE LOG-CABIN

Early next morning we were on our way to Dominion Creek. We began following the upper Bonanza, which veered abruptly to the left of the Grand Forks, passing many rich mines along the way. High hills bordered both sides of the narrowing valley. Ed pointed out Dick Lowe's "luxurious" cabin up on the hillside at No. 6 Above Discovery—"a mecca for rich-living and successful Sourdoughs," he said. "Yes, Dick Lowe's living 'high on the hog' now, and his door is always open to his numerous friends. When he needs gold, it's only a short walk to his Fraction Claim at the mouth of Big Skookum Gulch."

We paused a moment to look at No. II Above Discovery, where Ed said there was a seven foot pay-streak showing up. The lucky owners were John Hartwell, Web Lampkins and Thomas Ashly. We stopped to catch our breath at No.14, another amazing claim owned by Wilfred Gauvin, a young man from Quebec. This mine was doing extremely well and the miners were bringing up much gold. Next, we stopped at No. 15. It was pouring out its wealth to its owner, Frank Conrad, and giving the miners much joy. Another exciting claim belonged to L. P. Oksvig, at No. 17. It was pouring out its treasure to this Norwegian immigrant who had come to America without a dime. Now he was wealthy! At No. 19, we paused to see exciting nuggets washed out of a claim that would make its owner, John Wick, independent for life. At No. 22, a phenomenally rich claim, owned by James Monroe, W. M. Crowly and W. E. Ayers, we stopped to catch our breath and see a washtub full of yellow gold waiting to be sacked for shipment. I learned that No. 20 and 26 belonged to the Gauvin brothers, Wilfred and Alfred, both in partnership with Mr. Pichon. "And one of these days," said Ed, "they'll return to Quebec wealthy beyond their wildest dreams!"

As we continued along the upper Bonanza, we learned that Charles Lamb and James McNamee owned rich No. 26-B and No. 32. What lucky fellows they were! Both very well liked in Dawson. Charles Lamb and McNamee also owned No. 8, Eldorado. "And they claim to have found the the largest nugget on the Eldorado," said Ed.

"And now we've reached No. 34 Above Discovery," said Ed. "This

DEEP VALLEY AND LITTLE LOG CABIN 105

one belongs to two famous Klondike Kings, Alex McDonald and Pat Galvin. Galvin is fabulously wealthy through his many mining holdings, and 'The British American Commercial Company' of which he is president. He also owns 'The Banner Line' of steamboats of which he is president. And his latest boat-building achievement is a coalburning stern-wheeler, The Mary Ellen Galvin. That boat is the most elaborate and palatial ever to ply the Yukon and has accommodations for 435 passengers. Because of their many holdings together, the friendship is very close between McDonald and Galvin. Among the numerous rich claims they hold are No. 40 and No. 41 Above Discovery, on the Eldorado. Yes," concluded Ed, "these two men have the 'Midas Touch' and neither one was born with a silver spoon in his mouth."

Continuing along our way, we passed claims No. 37 and No. 38. These were of special interest as they belonged to two former Mounties. Both had been fortunate. In '96 John Brothers rushed to No. 37, and Evertt J. Ward rushed to No. 38. Everyone was glad that these Mounties had been so lucky. (Evertt Ward also had an interest in No. 42 Above Discovery, just beyond Thomas Pelky's No. 41 where the miners were getting $68 to the pan.)

Hurrying on, we passed Famous No. 40. In '96 Antone Standar had traded half-interest of this No. 40 to Clarence Berry for a little grub to get himself through the winter. It would have been a terribly uneven exchange had not Standar ended up with half-interest in the fabulous No. 4, No. 5, and No. 6, Eldorado Claims. Such was the astonishing luck of these men, these early Bonanza-Eldorado Kings!

About noon our little caravan reached the place called McCormack's Forks. Here, there was a roadhouse and a group of miner's cabins. We took a brief pause for lunch, then we were ready to tackle the rough trail again. We began following McCormack's Creek which flowed down from the mountains to the east. (The Bonanza had veered off to the southeast.) Soon, Ed pointed to two peaks jutting up from the ridge. They seemed to stand about fifteen miles apart. "These are very well-known landmarks," he said. "The smaller one is Queen Dome and the larger one is King Solomon's Dome. The view is breathtaking from King Dome, and there's a roadhouse there where we'll spend the night."

I looked up at King Solomon's Dome with extreme misgivings, wondering if we could possibly get there before dark. In fact, I wondered if we could make it at all! As we began climbing higher and higher, King and Queen Domes appeared to be on the very top of the world. They seemed to face each other proudly, above subjects of mountains, valleys, forests and streams.

"Yes," said Ed, "there has been so much gold found in all the streams below the Domes that the old timers speculate a great Mother Lode must be located somewhere in the vicinity. But where?

"Gold in numerous quartz ledges could be deep under the surface of the ridge and Domes, then, again, it could be fairly near the surface. Last May, I met Tom O'Shea up on the ridge. He indicated that he was under contract to Alexander McDonald (the Klondike King) to work on the ridge, but O'Shea wouldn't give the location. It would mean, of course, sinking shafts, or burrowing tunnels into the quartz-strata—of perhaps solid rock, a colossal undertaking—but the results could be staggering! Many sourdoughs and cheechakoos, including myself, have dug in the ridges around King and Queen Domes, yet none of us have ever found any gold.

"But there's something mighty exciting about Dominion Creek. Its headwaters rise on the eastern slope of King Solomon's Dome. No one can tell in what location the next strike will take place. It's a matter of chance and gamble, a whim of Lady Luck. And, yes, later, the whim of the Gold Commissioner!

"A year ago, July 8, 1898, a thousand men rushed over to Dominion Creek to stake, when late in the afternoon, Gold Commissioner Fawcett suddenly posted a sign in Dawson declaring the Dominion Creek District legally open to location. We miners knew the creek would be open sometime, as the surveyors had completed their job, but we had been given to understand the time would be later. I happened to be on the Bonanza and didn't get the news of what Fawcett had done until it was too late to run to Dawson for a permit. Fawcett, of course, had tipped off his own special friends. They say some of those men ran until they fainted; some already had rich claims on other creeks. Anyway, the creek was staked clear to the Indian River. Joe Beck got No. 1 Above Upper Discovery and Swiftwater Bill No. 21 and No. 21 Fraction. Well, it turned out to be the climax in Fawcett's career. A great furor of protest reached Ottawa. It was too much for the officials to ignore, and so Fawcett was removed from office of Gold Commissioner about six months or so later."

As the three of us, with Nelly, reached a higher altitude, Ed light-

Dick Lowe, said to have staked the richest Fraction Claim in the world, Klondike, 1898.

The Bartlett Brothers made their fortune in freighting. Scene shows them in the gold fields.

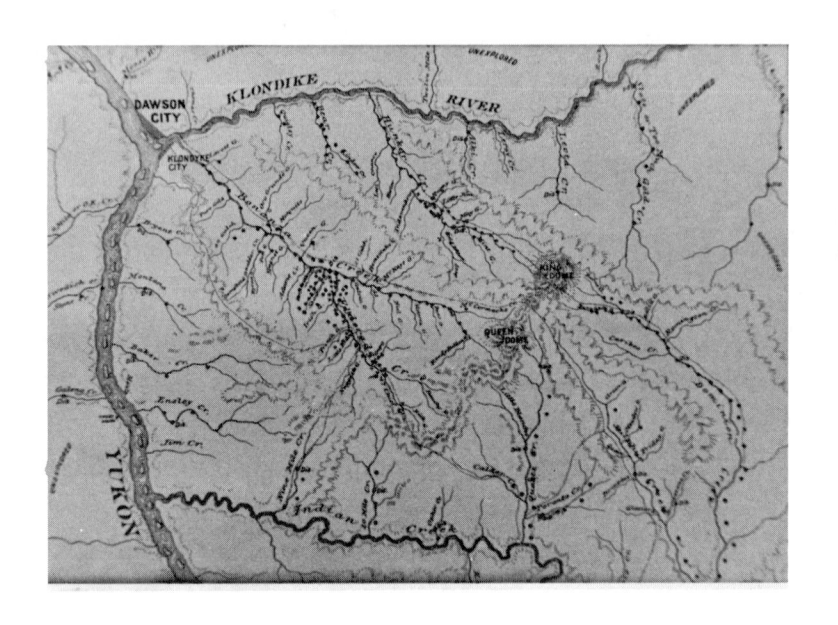

Map of the great Klondike gold fields about 1899. Dots show claims.

Looking up the Eldorado valley from the Grand Forks, fifteen miles from Dawson City, 1898.

ened Clemy's pack. He also shouldered some of mine. He was now carrying about forty pounds. Nelly trudged along, proudly carrying her own small load.

Once we saw a black bear. It had already caught our human scent and went crashing through the bushes.

"He's just as much afraid of us as we are of him," said Ed, calling a halt, "but if that bear is ever cornered--look out! He'll be the fiercest enemy in the woods! It's a sad thing to see a man who's been ripped to pieces.

"I remember a particular day in early spring when I was on my way back from stampedes to Sulphur Creek and Little Brimstone. I was hiking along on the ridge at a fast clip. I was all alone. Suddenly, I rounded a bend and there was a huge brown bear, right in the middle of the trail!

"He snarled and rared up on his hind legs, towering above me, not fifteen feet away. What a terrifying giant he was—at least nine feet high! Most folks think there are no Brownies in the Klondike, but they're wrong. There are a few of the Grizzly Bear species, and, of course, it was my bad luck to meet one.

"For a few split seconds I stood frozen to the spot, with more terror than I can describe. One swipe of his enormous claws and he could have torn me to pieces. Somehow, I regained my senses and control of my legs. I backed off, turned, and bolted back towards Little Brimstone, yelling like a Comanche Indian. Yes, you bet I was terrified. I waited on the ridge for some time, but after a while I said to myself, 'Ed Lung, you're a coward. You can't sit here all day. You must get past that spot!'

"But I had no weapon, so I cut the limb of a stout scrub tree to use as a club. Then, cautiously, I tackled the trail. When I came to the spot where I had met the bear, I began whooping and waving the club, fully expecting him to lunge from the bushes and strike me down. Well, nothing happened, and, believe me, I was anxious to get out of the vicinity. So I started running along that narrow trail and didn't stop for at least a mile.

"Later on, I met an old Sourdough with a couple of dogs. When I told him of my hair-raising experience with the Brownie he exclaimed, 'Man alive! Apparently the wind was blowing towards you and the bear didn't get your scent. It was all that saved you. Holy Mackerel! You sure did have a mighty close call!' "

As our caravan journeyed upward, Ed told us other interesting anecdotes which helped pass the time: One, for Clemy's benefit, was about the time Ed was out hunting moose on the hills towards the ridge. After following tracks half the afternoon he found he'd been trailing 'Wise Mike,' the pet burro of Dawson, the burro that liked to sip whiskey with the 'boys.' The little burro had come from Colorado with some unknown stampeders, and, after reaching Dawson, had decided that his was not going to be a life of toil. So he had taken to the hills, only coming to Dawson when he wished companionship, food and whiskey. Everybody called him "Wise Mike,* the loveable cuss."

Then Ed told an anecdote for my special benefit. "Yes, the year '98 was the big one of the gold-rush. But it was also the big year of turmoil and much disillusionment, too. Ten thousand frenzied men had fought their way North, only to find that gold was not so easily found. As everyone knows, the first wave of 1896 men had gobbled up the rich ground within easy reach of Dawson. Then, too, the fellows who managed to get cheap claims found that the gold tax, which was ten to twenty percent, depending on the Gold Commissioner, took all incentive from that body-killing effort of wresting the gold from the icy ground!

"In '98, ten thousand irate men walked the streets of Dawson, or sat on the banks of the river and talked of nothing else but high taxes, their bad luck and this 'cussed country.' Many of them forgot why they had come North—that part about pitting their strength and wits against a hostile country in order to find security for themselves and families.

"The fellows who had come over the passes—many of them—had spent their stamina, and were in poor health. The fellows coming in by the water route, many of them, labored under a strange inertia. Some of them had been a whole year en route, frozen-in at different points down the Yukon, above St. Michaels.

"One of these fellows was young, colorful Thomas Wiedemann. I happened to meet him for the first time on the ridge near King Dome, in the spring of '99. He was on his way back to Dawson from Dominion Creek where he had a lay to claim No. 11½ Above Lower Discovery. Naturally, he and I stopped to 'chew the fat.' I had heard of him in Dawson, as he had been on the famous Eliza Anderson Expedition

*See "Black Sand and Gold" for more about 'Wise Mike.'

Ed Lung's brother, George A. Lung, Lt. Commander in the Spanish-American War. After World War I, he became Rear Admiral.

A large Dawson crowd celebrating Admiral Dewey's victory in Manila, Spanish-American War. Notice the pictures of Dewey and President McKinley, with American and Cuban flags.

Discouraging ruins after the terrible April 26, 1899, fire at Dawson. Scene looking down Yukon River. Half of Dawson burned.

Gold Bottom Creek about 1900. It was in this creek that Robert Henderson, the Canadian, first found a few colors, in 1896.

which had left the States in the spring of '97, about the same time that I had. Only, of course, my travel route had been by way of Chilkoot Pass.

"While Wiedemann and I were visiting up there on the ridge, he told me some of his exciting adventures: Of how his party had been almost shipwrecked near Unalaska; of how a mysterious phantom-pilot had suddenly appeared out of the storm, and how he had steered the ship to safety; of how Wiedemann's party had finally reached the lower Yukon in fall of '97 in time to catch a late boat to Dawson only to get blocked by the ice and end up frozen in at a remote Eskimo-Indian village. He told of his chagrin at being stalled for the winter, and then how he had made the best of it and learned the Eskimo language and customs. He had put his time to such good use that the U.S. Government had heard about him, and when he reached Dawson in late summer of '98, he was offered a job as interpreter for Alice Rollins Crane, who was making studies of the Eskimos and their customs and wanted to go to that village. She had been waiting for Wiedemann in Dawson. He told me he had declined the interpreter offer, but had let Miss Crane read his diary. Wiedemann said he had laughed at a very mistaken idea she had; it was that Eskimos were sun worshippers. He said that the Eskimos did a lot of peculiar dancing and worshipping, but they certainly weren't sun worshippers!

"Wiedemann and I discovered, too, that we had several things in common. We both had come from the Puget Sound area. We both had kept gold-rush diaries, and we were now inhabitants of Dominion Creek, members of the 'Miners' Fraternity,' a group of hard working Sourdoughs and Cheechakos. Yes," concluded Ed, "you meet some mighty interesting people up here in the Klondike."

It was late afternoon when Edward, Clemy, Nelly, and I finally reached the King Solomon roadhouse. As we trudged into the cozy, one-story log house, a fat colored cook poked his head through the low kitchen doorway and exclaimed in a startled voice, "Lawsy me, if it ain't a Lady and a little boy! Awh knows youse awful hungry, and I's 'll have ya' suppah ready in a jiffy."

Hurriedly, he set to work broiling luscious chunks of moose steak, also desicated potatoes. When the food was ready, we sat down to supper. The steak was tender and juicy, cooked to perfection, but I couldn't relish the peculiar flavor of the dried potatoes. While we were eating, the cook kept his eyes fastened on Clemy and me and kept repeating incredulously,

"Lawsy me, a lady and a little boy!"

After we had completed our meal, which, by the way, was $2 apiece, we went outdoors to see the sunset. Ed was right. It was a scene that was to imprint its beauty upon my memory forever—a great mural of the Klondike region—my future home.

Magnificent mountain ranges, row after row, far across the Yukon, marched off to purple-blue horizons. And to the east, the giant snow-clad Canadian Rockies stood out clearly against the deepening colors of the sky, spotlighted by the burnished sun. From our perch on this mountain-top, we could see part of the mighty Yukon trailing off to the far northwest, like a strip of satiny ribbon. There, to the west, far below us in the valley were rich Hunker Creek and Gold Bottom, and the upper reaches of the Bonanza and McCormack's Creek, the tributary that we had followed the latter part of the afternoon.

Ed quickly pointed to the southeast, to Gold Run, Sulphur, Quartz Creek, Little Blanche and Little Brimestone, and to the big Indian River trailing to the south, and then he pointed to Dominion Creek and to a dozen other smaller streams on the Klondike Wheel of Gold. "But they're nearly all staked," said Ed. "No doubt Robert Henderson wondered in 1895 which stream to choose, in his quest for gold, when he stood on this mountain-top and surveyed the beckoning scene below. Yes, any of it could have been his—claims on the Eldorado or Bonanza—but he ended up with a claim on Gold Bottom which was not of the richest auriferous pay-dirt. Even at that, he never legally owned the claim, for he had neglected to register his discovery. McDonald found it out. He staked it, and registered it, and the claim became his, another of the Klondike King's holdings! (The Canadian Government pensioned Robert Henderson for life after he lost his Gold Bottom claim.)

Ed pointed to the huge amounts of snow in the upper regions and said it was due to some very late, freak snow storms which had hit the country; one May 4th, one May 6th, and another June 3d (1899). It had even snowed in Dawson on the June date.

As we drank in the glorious country, our "Promised Land," Ed's strong arms were around me, and mine around Clemy.

"Yes, Vel," said Ed, softly, "you'll grow to love the Dominion Valley as much as I have. Under starlight, sunlight, and moonlight, it's an enchanting valley. And there's gold there, maybe not as much as on the Bonanza or Eldorado, but there is gold!"

After a restful night at the comfortable King Dome Roadhouse, and a good breakfast of sourdough pancakes, we said goodbye to the amiable innkeeper, Joe Cook. Then we were on our way down the steep mountainside to Dominion Creek. Often we had to stop and rest as there was a terrific drop in altitude. It was at one of these rests that Ed began telling me more about the richest section of Dominion Creek, and as a flashback, how he had gotten a foothold there.

"Vel, it happened like this," he said. "Soon after the last Dawson fire, Paul Hebb looked me up. Of course, he knew that my Bonanza claim, 'Old Brutus,' wasn't panning out. So he offered me a job as manager of No. 12 Below Discovery on Dominion Creek. He wanted me to go there immediately.

"So, on May 2, 1899, I left 'Old Brutus' and headed for Dominion Creek. I was jubilant. Everybody was celebrating, like the Fourth of July, Dewey's Victory in Manila, the surrender of the Spanish in Cuba, followed by the Treaty of Paris* and its acceptance by Congress. (The Spanish American War) I was thankful for this news. I knew that my brother, George, who was a high ranking naval officer, would soon be coming home to the States. I was elated too, because of my change in fortune. Shortly after starting on the trail to Dominion Creek, I met Al Chamberlain, a friend. He was going to his claim on Dominion Creek and knew all the fellows, so I was glad to travel with him.

"When Al and I reached No. 12 Below Upper Discovery and I announced that I had come to take charge of the claim, Mr. Currie, who had been serving as manager, didn't take kindly to the news. He became quite angry and promptly went on a 'bender.' Of course, I did not wish to forcibly take command as I had known Currie in Dawson the year before, and he had helped me get started in temporary jobs at the Alaska Commercial Company when I so desperately needed funds. Luckily, Paul Hebb arrived on the scene and helped ease the very awkward situation. He quietly urged me to go back to my Bonanza hillside claim and get a miner on the next bench, a Mr. Cook, to work 'Old

---

*The United States won possession of Puerto Rico, Guam, the Philippines, Hawaii, and independence for Cuba in the Spanish American War.

*Dominion Creek has the distinction of two Discovery claims. Claims running down valley from Upper Discovery run to No. 13. Claims running up valley from Lower Discovery run to No. 11½, inclusive.

brutus' for wages, to hold the claim. Then I was to pack my belongings and return to Dominion Creek to my job. Hebb indicated that he would fix things up with Currie.

"I did everything as Hebb instructed, then I started back to Dominion Creek. It was on the summit near King Dome, on May 4th, that I met Tom O'Shea when he spilled the beans about the Klondike King, Alex McDonald, hunting for the Mother Lode around King Dome. It was on the summit, too, the same day, that I met Thomas Wiedemann. To continue Wiedemann's conversation: He told me that his Lay on No. 11½ was a fairly rich one; however, he said that Dominion Creek was very erratic; that the pay streak wig-wagged this way and that, especially around the area of No. 10, No. 11, and No. 11½ Above Lower Discovery; also around No. 13 and No. 12 Below Upper Discovery, which was right in the same area where his claim was located, and where I was to have charge of that claim.

"It was then that Wiedemann told me about a sensational discovery made by a miner whom I was shortly to meet on Dominion: Joe Barrett had pitched his tent on unstaked ground, on a hill slightly above Wiedemann's shack. Then for several days Barrett was not seen by anyone, but he was really prospecting! In digging out a space to level the ground for his tent he had hit some gold nuggets only a few inches down under the sod. Barrett had actually hit the big, illusive pay-streak which had zagged up onto the hill! It was very much like Gold Hill all over again. When Barrett picked up those nuggets he was destined to become a rich man—later his claim was valued at nearly $100,000. Realizing that he had made a significant find, he quietly went to Dawson and recorded his mine as Bench Claim No. 12 Above Lower Discovery. Weidemann and Bill Hinkley were only a few feet below Barrett's tent, and the tent was only a stone's throw from the valley claims, No. 12 and No. 13 Below Upper Discovery. Nevertheless, Wiedemann* and Hinkley weren't doing so badly as some of the pay-streak from centuries ago had spilled over into their No. 11½ Fraction Claim in the valley.

"Well," continued Ed, "I went on over to Dominion Creek a lot wiser. I only stayed on No. 12 about two weeks. Currie was gone and I had to face the bitter truth—Father Swanson's dump on the claim No. 12 only yielded 9½ ounces of gold and McFarland's dump, on his half

---

*See "The Klondike Kid," by Thomas Weidemann, published by Binfords & Mort, for further details.

of the claim, barely yielded 3½ ounces. It certainly was a bad showing for a claim which had been valued at $40,000 and mortgaged by the bank! There certainly was no use staying there any longer, and I began casting around for other openings. It was then, on the evening of May 17, 1899, that Paul Hebb came from Dawson and offered me the job as manager of No. 2-B Below Discovery, and No. 5, with the promise of a Lay, later, if I wished it.

"I was having supper with Joe Barrett on No. 27 Above Discovery (he had an interest there) when Hebb found me and offered me the new prospect. Barrett urged me to accept, and I did. It was a few days later, Vel, that I wrote that letter urging you and Clem to come North, and that I was building a little log-cabin. Yes, future prospects on Dominion Creek looked very bright, as I had seen forty-three ounces of gold come from the first sluicing on No. 2-B and No. 5 Below Discovery in just one day.

"Mining Inspector Cantly, from Caribou, was there that day giving good advice, as was George Hill and N. H. Bertram, and then Billy Moore showed up. It was wonderful having these friends of the Circle City Crowd on the spot to share in my good fortune, and we had a jolly-good meeting right there in the little No. 2-B cabin. Alex Cammeron, one of the fellows who had been frozen in at Circle City, came too. (Hill, Bertram and Moore had interests on Dominion and up on Sulphur Creek.)

"Funny how good old friends have all seemed to gravitate to Dominion Creek—really our last chance for Klondike riches. Yes," continued Ed, "all nationalities are represented at Dominion, and there's a number of Frenchmen, too. We call the two places where they are thickest, 'Little Paris,' and 'Little Quebec.' Most of these Frenchmen belong to, or work for, the French Syndicate called 'Le Syndicat Lyonnais du Klondike.' Of course, some of them will be our neighbors and they are very colorful, interesting fellows. There is obviously a race between them and the bank to gain control of the richest claims on the creek."

The rough mountain trail took us on a strenuous quick descent towards the beautiful green valley below, past the Upper Discovery claims at the headwaters of Dominion Creek. Ed pointed out Paul Hebb's No. 24 and No. 25 claims and cabin, then to Swiftwater Bill's No. 21 and No. 21-Fraction.* In no time we were at Joe Beck's No. 1

*Swiftwater Bill also owned No. 13, Eldorado.

Above Discovery claim where Ed said the miners had recently found a huge pocket of gold amounting to $60,000. Continuing on the winding trail, following the river for about two miles, we reached Caribou. Ed informed me that the Northwest Mounted Police had barracks here, and I would have to register. (Dominion Creek is only three or four hundred feet across, at the upper end of the valley.)

"These men keep a very close watch and strict records of all newcomers," said Ed. "This village has recently grown up around police headquarters—a few miners' cabins, several officials' offices, a roadhouse (owned by Joe Barrett) and—I regret to say—several houses of prostitution."

Corporal Hilliard welcomed me cordially to Dominion Creek and said that there were few children and women in the section and that he hoped Clemy and I wouldn't be too lonely. After his solicitous remark, I hastened to assure the good Corporal that I expected to be far too busy to get homesick or lonely. He also told me that there was to be a small school at Caribou where Clemy could attend, then added, "There's a Mrs. Webster here who sometimes does practical nursing should you ever need her." Gratefully, I thanked the thoughtful Mountie for the information and our caravan was on its way, following a rather indefinite trail along the river. Soon, we began meeting some of Ed's friends, a Mr. Kershaw and several miners on No. 7 Below Upper Discovery, and a Mr. Longwell at No. 10 Below Upper Discovery.

Here, at No. 10 we paused to catch our breath while Ed told us that this claim had been staked in that wild stampede a year ago, in '98, by James V. Harrison, who had also succeeded in staking a rich Bench Claim on the lower Eldorado, in that Ancient-Channel Stampede. (Spring of '98). Harrison not only owned other mining interests, but he was part owner of a Dawson hotel and casino called "Lo-Ha-Na," a plush new palace of pleasure. Harrison's well-known partners were William R. Loyd and Thomas J. Nash—all likeable, wealthy fellows!

Next, we stopped to talk to miners on No. 12 Below Upper Discovery, the claim that had lured my husband to Dominion Creek where Father Swanson and McFarland held half-interest apiece. The miners were still working there, hoping for another gold streak in the future spring cleanups. After visiting a bit, we hurried on, passing Jack Stewart's No. 13 Below Upper Discovery. Apparently, he was not superstitious about his number and was determined to prove that his claim

Robert Henderson, Canadian, discoverer of gold at Gold Bottom Creek, 1896. (He never struck it rich.)

The Dome Roadhouse on the ridge above Upper Bonanza and Dominion creeks was always open to weary summer and winter travelers.

Claim No. 2-B Below Lower Discovery, Dominion Creek. Clemy on top of pay-dirt. Joe Latshaw left, Ed Lung second from left, with miners.

Log cabin at Claim 2-B Below Lower Discovery, Dominion Creek—"Pink Flannel Heaven," 1899. Velma, Ed Lung and little Clem and dogs.

was as good as any! Then Ed pointed out Joe Barrett's startling No. 12 hillside bench claim.

"What a quirk of fate that was, to strike it rich through pitching a tent!" he exclaimed half enviously.

Next, Ed pointed out the No. 11½ Fraction Above Lower Discovery. The place seemed deserted, and Ed explained that Wiedemann and his partner, Hinkley, had hit the pay in their spring cleanup and that Wiedemann was on his way back to Seattle with a fat poke of Dominion gold to dazzle his young friends. (Wiedemann was only about 21 years of age.) "Yes, it's too bad that you couldn't have met him, too," said Ed, "for he is certainly a colorful fellow!"

"And now we're at No. 11 Above Lower Discovery," said Ed. "This fine claim belongs to Hans Starke. Everybody calls him 'the German.' The next is No. 10. It's a rich one and is said to belong to Joe Long. Several of the claims below him, towards Lower Discovery, belong to the French Syndicate, and several to the bank, the Canadian Bank of Commerce. Tommy Riggs and a fellow named Cushman are working No. 3, No. 4 and No. 5 for Hebb." (Above Lower Discovery)

All along the way into Dominion Creek we had met dozens of mineowners and many crews of hard-working but good natured sourdoughs. It almost seemed that they had all been watching for us. Little Clemy was in seventh heaven from all the attention that he drew from these "family-hungry" men. And, of course, he was intrigued by all he saw. For a small boy, he had gained an elementary knowledge of the process of mining just from his long walk through the gold fields since leaving Dawson, and I, too, had gained a feminine smattering of it!

Before we had reached the Lower Discovery Claim, we had met Father Swanson, Charles Debney, Al Chamberlain and Mr. Barbier. And, of course, we'd met Tommy Riggs and Cushman. Then too, there was Mr. Louis, who helped out on No. 5, and there was Mr. Kyle, who seemed to have an interest in several Lower Discovery claims and was representing H. T. Wills on Nos. 2, 4 and 6 Below Upper Discovery. At one spot we met McKinsie, Slaven, and Cantly. They were having some kind of a miner's powwow, and, lo and behold, Al Portlock[*], our former gardener in Tacoma, was with them! He seemed very glad to see me, and said that he was doing extremely well on Dominion Creek. He

---

[*] Al Portlock was called the "biggest liar of Dominion Creek." He spun yarns as fast as he could talk.

also said that Ed was pretty fortunate to have us with him. Naturally, he wanted to hear all the latest Tacoma news.

Ed introduced Alex Cammeron, and a Mr. Latham, who were on claims just below Lower Discovery; they would be our close neighbors. "Yes," I told Ed, as we continued on our way, "they are all a fine group of hard-working Sourdoughs, the very best that I've met since coming into the Klondike." (Many of them and other miners, whom we hadn't met as yet, were to be our close companions for the next five or six years.)

Already we had walked about three miles since leaving Caribou and I was bursting with a great eagerness to see our new home. We had passed the Lower Discovery Claim and I knew it couldn't be very much farther. All at once, Ed told us to look down the trail; said that we were now at Claim No. 2-B Below Lower Discovery. Clemy went wild with excitement; I felt a happy thrill of anticipation.

The dear little cabin was picturesque and would have made a very pleasing subject for an artist. It was nestled in among low, bright evergreen trees, its logs weathered to a deep rich brown. Only a few feet away, a tiny brook wound its way merrily down the hillside and passed the cabin.

My husband hurried to open the cabin door; Clemy rushed inside and I followed. Momentarily, the sudden change of light blinded me, but when I could see clearly, I was shocked and sick at heart—the 'dear little cabin' was nothing but a very small, dingy, one-room shack! When I could find my voice, I asked weakly, "Oh, Ed, is this going to be our home?"

"This is it, Vel," he answered solemnly. "If you're going to be a miner's wife, you'll have to get used to this kind of living."

Well, I must confess I was very much taken back at the sight of that cabin! It was certainly a dark, ugly hovel with only whiskey bottles for a window! Quickly, I observed several torturous looking pole-bunk-beds. They appeared to be even more uncomfortable than those at the Grand Forks. My heart sank very deep—I had expected a comfortable, cozy little place. However, I tried to hide my chagrin and disappointment.

The usual Klondike stove stood in a corner; a small oil drum was fastened to the chimney about two feet up, hanging at a precarious angle, and serving as an oven. A greasy grub-box with a cover over it for a table was placed by the whiskey-bottle window, and there were several rickety, homemade chairs placed about the room. Also, I observed a homemade broom, fashioned of twigs, leaning in a corner, twig-side up.

Yes, living in this place would certainly be primitive all right, more primitive than anything I had ever imagined! However, I laughed to myself when I spied that broom, for Ed had casually mentioned on our way to Dominion Creek that it was always the sign of a good housekeeper if he, or she, kept the broom placed upside down, when it was not in use. Also, that a teakettle should be turned upside down, too, when not in use. This peculiar custom, of course, was to make the articles last that much longer. Naturally, lasting that much longer was a "necessary must" in frontier living!

There, on the stove, was the teakettle, upside-down, being well-drained. And when my eyes became more accustomed to the dim light, I observed a number of very ugly grease-spots all around the stove.

"My dear Edward," I said compassionately, "it's quite evident that you very badly need a wife to keep house. Yes, somehow, I'll try to brighten up this place— somehow!"

For answer, Ed just gave me a great big bearhug, and a tremendous pat of affection. "Vel, Vel, this isn't our real home," he said, tenderly, "I'm building it on the hillside. No matter how hard I tried, I just couldn't get it finished before your arrival. Oh—I just couldn't resist seeing your reactions to this cabin," he laughed merrily, "and, I must say, you came through like a champion!"

"Oh, Bamba, Bamba!" exclaimed Clemy enthusiastically, as he quickly tried each homemade chair, then darted around the room examining everything, "this place sure looks like Buffalo Bill's hut! Wow! Aren't we gonna have fun living here? Wish dear grandmother in Tacoma could see us!"

"Heaven forbid," I laughed, "She'd never understand how we could like such a dark little place. But, I'm wondering who previously lived here?"

"Oh, it was a lonely old sourdough, named Ed Lung. Yes, Vel," said Ed, "I've lived here since May 17th and I've dreamed of your coming

---

*Whiskey bottles grouped together, chinked with moss, were the common kind of windows used by miners. Real windows were very expensive and hard to get.

North ever since. And, to make my dream come true, I started cutting logs for a nice, cozy little log-cabin on the hillside, our first home!"

DIARY FOOTNOTES, 1899

April 26, 1899–DAWSON FIRE. First alarm, 8 P.M. Fire caught Bodega Saloon, soon caught the Tivoli Theater, and then the Northern Saloon. Did not go to bed. One half of Dawson burned.

DAWSON, April 28, 1899. Hebb wants me to go over and take charge of No. 12 Below Upper Discovery, on Dominion Creek during clean up. Will go as it will be a good job.

DAWSON, April 30, 1899. Start for Dominion Creek tomorrow. Will have to pack my stuff, as I cannot get anything packed until ice in Klondike goes out. Wrote to Dear Velma and sent her three views of the Dawson fire, taken by Cantwell, also pictures of the gang bidding goodbye to Rob. Walker and Mrs. Henningain who were going outside.

BONANZA & Dominion, May 2, 1899. Packed 55 lbs. We (Al Chamberlain and I) left No. 7 Bonanza at 6:40 A.M. Stopped at Grand Forks an hour. Jim Mckay is running the Butler Hotel there. Saw Stickney who had been on a "jag." Had a big blowout here last night in celebration of Dewey's victory at Manila. Trail fairly good, very windy on Divide. Made No. 12 Below Upper Discovery at 5:45 P.M. Al went on down to his Bench Claim. Bartlett Bros. had opening of new saloon & road house. Good supper. Kirshaw was there.

DOMINION & Bonanza, May 3, 1899. (22 miles) Hebb came up in A.M. Slept with Alex. Cammeron, whom I met last winter at Circle. I left for No. 7 Bonanza at 1:30 P.M. Made Bonanza at 8:30 P.M., footsore and stiff. Will sleep in Morrison's bunk.

BONANZA & DOMINION CREEK, May 4, 1899. Left Bonanza No. 7 at 8:30 A.M. Pack weighs 40 lbs. Met Tom O'Shea who is going to work for Alex McDonald on the Summit. Met young fellow by name of Wiedemann who spent last winter among the Indians below Minook Creek. Learned the language. Says Miss Crane who is sent in by U.S. Gov., to write up the country, wants him to go with her next winter & help her in her work under pay of U.S. Gov. Made No. 12 at 5:30 P.M. Found Hebb in Currie's cabin. (Snowed hard on the summit, & wind, cold.)

DOMINION CREEK, May 5, 1899. Feel stiff & sore. My feet are covered with blisters. My shoes are very heavy & too large & they are continually hurting my feet. Currie & Mullen were "full" last night. Hebb came up this A.M.

DOMINION CREEK, May 6, 1899. Hebb told Currie this A.M. that I now had charge of the claim. Currie got on a grand drunk. I cannot begin to sluice until No. 11 gets their lower dump shovelled in. Have two men cleaning the brush off of claim. Very cold wind is blowing, not freezing though. Heavy snow storm on summit. Can see the Dome very plainly from here.

DOMINION CREEK, May 11, 1899. Beautiful day! Did my washing in early A.M. Currie moved his sluice boxes. Poor clean up—only 9½ oz. 15 gr. Rather a poor showing for a $40,000 claim! Scales did not come over from town. Hear ice has not yet gone out of Yukon R.

DOMINION CREEK No. 12 below Upper Discovery, May 14, 1899. Had cleanup of McFarland's dump. Very, very poor—3½ oz.—Did not pay to shovel-in!

DOMINION CREEK, Monday, May 15, 1899. Went up to Upper Discovery. Scales did not come over. Will not be here before Wed. P.M. Father Swanson is here, part owner of No. 12 Below Upper Discovery. Saw Chas. Debney & Kirshaw. Have caught cold & settled in the cords of my neck & shoulders. Paid Cook in full. Am out of debt.

DOMINION, May 17, 1899. Hebb came over. Wants me to take charge of 2B Below Lower Discovery and No. 5. We went down creek. Father Swanson went with us. Took dinner with Joe Barrett at No. 27—who is rich mine owner. Has Bench claim opposite No. 12. Report Yukon opened today.

DOMINION CREEK, May 24, 1899. (Queen Victoria's Birthday) Hebb came over this A.M. He seemed pleased with my work so far. He stayed with Tommy Riggs & Cushman on No. 3 all night. The Bank is going to buy No. 36 Above Upper Discovery.

DOMINION CREEK, May 25, 1899. Hebb went to town this P.M. Wrote to Velma & he will mail it. She will be surprised to read that I want her to come in. Dear girl, how I would love to have her with me. I left all those I loved best, my dear wife, and baby boy. Little do we know how the time passes & where fate drifts us! Things look brighter in here for me now than ever before. I have full charge & am fully competent to run the claims, I know!

DAWSON, July 2, 1899. Hardly knew the place as the burned district was all built up!

Chapter 10

ALIVE, WARM, AND BUBBLIN'

The following day Edward took Clemy and me, with Nelly at our heels, on a grand tour of No. 2B and No. 5 Below Discovery. One by one, we met the miners. Some were sluicing; some running the engine at the boiler house; some at the hoist or windlass near the hill of pay dirt. There was Charles Burnett, Mather, Bud Liker, Fricks, Mike Johnson and Mr. Emery. All stopped work to say "Howdy," to the boss's wife.

Even Joe Latshaw poked his head out of a tunnel to say with a smile, "Hello, and greetings, and a big welcome to our Dominion Creek!"

"Yes," said Ed, proudly, as we walked back towards our cabin, "we are making deep tunnels and are going to cross-cut in a half-dozen different directions. That way we're bound to hit pockets of gold, maybe find that big, illusive pay-streak that wiggles along this valley. Joe Barrett surely hit it on the hill, but it's funny about that gold! Beyond Joe Barrett's hillside, the pay-streak almost vanishes. Fellows with Bench claims other than Barrett have nothing much to show for their pains."

* * *

Ed had promised that the new cabin would be finished by the last of October, or the first of November. He certainly was working like a Trojan, and sometimes far into the night! I could hear him hammering and sawing—sometimes a snatch of song mixed in—or whistling. Yes, great happiness seemed to radiate from that partially-finished little log-cabin up on the hill, and how I looked forward to moving in!

But Ed had exacted a promise that I wouldn't go near the new cabin until it was finished. He wished it to be, as much as possible, a "big surprise!" But many, many times I was sorely tempted. I felt like Bluebeard's wife, it was all I could do to refrain from peeking just a wee, tiny bit!

Clemy often went to the hillside to hand nails and lumber to his father. From these trips he would always come home looking very important. "Bamba," he would say, eyes wide with excitement, "me and Dad are building you a real fine cabin! It's gonna be the prettiest, the best you've ever seen!" Of course, in response I would always give Clemy a big hug of appreciation.

From the little path where I often walked afternoons by the hillside creek, I could see that at least the log-structure had a roof and four sturdy walls and a door! How I hoped that the new cabin would be an improvement over the ugly, inconvenient shack that we now occupied. My biggest problem, so far, had been the day-to-day cooking. It was difficult for me to learn to fix even the simplest of meals. It seemed I was not cut out for this kind of work. Oh yes, Mother had been right about my domestic abilities!

Ed was now putting in such long, strenuous hours, both in the mine and at the cabin, that I certainly wished to do my part. Usually, at meal time he would come rushing home a little early in order to see that things were going well and to assist me, if need be. It was really all very confusing. Frankly, and sometimes tearfully, I admitted that I didn't know beans about cooking! Ed would nearly always find me in a horrible muddle of something stewing on the stove—pots and pans—and all kinds of miscellaneous ingredients strewn about the worktable, from which I didn't seem able to bring order out of chaos, or to concoct a palatable dish!

Why, just keeping that greedy, choking, smoky little Klondike stove stoked and hot seemed a full-time job, and a losing battle. Baking sourdough bread, "the staff of life," was a horribly messy ordeal, a major problem! I wondered if I would ever really master the art of bread making, and many times I was on the verge of tears.

My first batches of sourdough bread were a dismal failure. The stuff looked like hard, uneven chunks of sun-baked muck. As a result, Ed ate odd-tasting, yellow- looking bread. For many weeks, I suffered from swollen, burned, smudged hands, and bruised, frustrated spirits.

"Look," said Ed, finally in desperation one day, "Making good bread is really very simple when you catch onto it. Vel, you do it like this:

"Into a pail of sourdough starter (which, by the way, you are supposed to always keep at a warm, even temperature behind the stove, ready for action) you stir two cups of warm water and a half cup of flour, and then you let it stand overnight. In the morning you pour most of this mixture into a big pan and add a small pinch of soda and a pinch of salt. The small amount of batter you saved out is to be for your next starter! Now, add enough flour to the mixture in the big pan to make it thick and doughy, then you knead it and mold into loaves. Put the loaves into a greased pan and set in a warm corner. Let rise slowly, and when the loaves are up to the top of the pan, bake in a moderate oven to a golden brown. Some folks push the dough down and let it come up a second time, but that isn't necessary.

"Now if you wish to have sourdough pancakes," continued Ed, "just make your sourdough mixture the same way, only this time make the batter a lot thinner. It can be made immediately from the sourdough starter which you must always remember to save and keep warm, and stored behind the stove, ready for the next time. I can't stress this enough," said Ed desperately, after I had completely used up several starters. "Vel, you'll surely learn the importance of saving a starter as winter comes on! Alaskans always have starters ready to use at a moment's notice, and enough to give newcomers some, too. The main idea is to keep it (the starter) warm, and the bubbles working. Yes, even if you have to cover the pail with warm, woolen blankets!

"And," laughed Ed, "it's no joke when the old-timers smoke their pipes, wink their eyes, wag their heads and tell you tales of how they've even taken their precious sourdough starter to bed with them when the mercury hits 50 degrees below zero. Up here in the North, you just can't be too particular. It's survival, plain, simple survival that counts!"

* * *

Now the weather was becoming more bitterly cold, its breath like the sharp edge of a dagger. I felt the severe change of season keenly, but Clemy didn't seem to mind the withering blasts of Old King Winter. He spent long hours playing outside in the snow with Nelly, or down in the mine with his father. Sometimes Clemy wore two sets of underwear and two sweaters under his parka, which gave him the overstuffed appearance of a bulging poke of gold. The miners began teasing him and affectionately called him their "Fat Little Poke."

Often, I could see Clemy's red stocking cap bobbing up and down among the sluice-boxes, or I could see him climbing up the gravel dumps. Of course Nelly, his dog, was always with him, and I knew that Clemy was safely within range of an affectionate eye.

By the first of October a big snowstorm had come and gone. Then my trunk with other valuable luggage arrived from Dawson by sledge-freight.* How glad I was for the extra supply of warm clothing, and I appreciated and prized the "odds and ends" that I had managed to stuff into the trunk.

My new otter fur coat, with cap, looked more beautiful and stylish than ever, but somehow it seemed a little too stylish for Dominion Creek! Anyway, it would be a real inducement to persuade Ed to take me on my first sleigh-ride. This, he had been promising for several weeks.

But more than a sleigh ride, I hoped to get settled in that dear little

---

*The Michael Bartlett Freighting Company did most of the heavy hauling for Klondike people. They had sledges and horses; also teams of malemutes.

log cabin before winter would set in with a bang, for already our beautiful green valley was covered with a feathery blanket of white snow. I could just barely make out a small dot way up on top of King Dome where stood the snug little roadhouse. I knew that high drifts of snow would soon be covering its low doors and windows. Also, travel would soon become precarious, might even be cut off for awhile.

Oh yes, it was too late to turn back to civilization now, or go "Outside," as old-timers liked to call it.

"No," I told myself fiercely, as I watched the mountaintops pile higher with snow, "I wouldn't go back to Tacoma if I could! No! I wasn't homesick at all!"

But, as the severe cold settled down, tightly gripping the valley, and more snow fell, and as the wail of the wolf reached my ears, I did have some sinking feelings! Truly, I was extremely grateful for the shelter of that ugly little brown shack. And I was more than grateful too, for the dry logs and boxes of kindling which Ed kept piled in one corner of the cabin ready for that obstinate, snorting, greedy little Klondike stove!

And, as I listened to the wind screech and wail through the valley, like a dozen Banshees, I thanked God many times, over and over, for the presence of Ed and my little son. Yes, we were safely together! And I was grateful too, for that pail of sourdough starter, which hung significantly on a nail behind the stove, warm and "ready to go."

Rapidly I was adjusting to the rugged, austere ways of the North and man's sturdy methods of survival. It was my job to keep the home fires burning, a kettle of soup brewing, a pot of beans stewing, the cabin cozy, warm, and the sourdough starter bubblin' and bubblin'. And bubblin'.

Chapter 11

PINK FLANNEL HEAVEN

Almost every day, in October (1899), unless it was bad weather, I could see Ed, and sometimes Joe Latshaw, up on the hillside about 600 feet away. No, the two weren't hunting gold, but were doing something, which, at the moment was far more important. They had to finish our little log cabin before winter would set in with a bang! I could see them, working like beavers, chinking and sealing the cabin's outside cracks with mud and moss. Yes, almost like two father birds building a nest!

Little Clemy was nearly always in evidence, maybe getting in his father's way, or helping, whichever the case might be.

At last, Ed announced that the cabin stood ready and waiting. It was the morning of the First of November, and I had not, as yet, laid eyes on the interior of that little cabin, although I had watched its exterior change and grow these many days. But a promise was a promise and had to be kept! I had solemnly given my word to Ed that I wouldn't peek inside even a tiny bit!

Yes, so this was the big day! Clemy and Ed with Nelly at their heels escorted me up the hill to inspect the cabin. For many weeks I had tried to picture what its interior would be like. Well, I would soon find out. I was bursting with curiosity and expectation.

As we approached the door, Ed said half apologetically, "Vel, the cabin certainly isn't luxurious, but it's the very best I could do. Anyway, it will be our home for the next few years, and it's a big improvement, I hope, over the old shack in which we've been camping."

"Oh Edward," I told him, enthusiastically, "it will be a wonderful improvement, no matter what!"

As we reached the cabin door, suddenly I was swept off my feet. Ed held me in his steel-like arms.

"Vel," he laughed, "close your eyes. I'm going to carry you across the threshhold, as all brides should be."

"My goodness," I chuckled, "Clemy will be five next birthday! It's a little late for that ritual, isn't it?"

"It sure isn't," laughed Ed, "because this is our very first home.

Clemy, you'll have the special honor of opening the door for your Mother."

Of course Clemy jubilantly hastened to do his father's bidding. I closed my eyes very tight, as Ed whisked me through the doorway. When I opened them I was in the middle of heaven. I thought it was the most beautiful little place I had ever seen!

"Oh Edward, Edward," I gasped, "it's a dream! It's beautiful! All rosy pink! Why, the cabin is all lined with pink outing flannel! How did you manage to do it?"

Ed looked immensely pleased, tears of joy stood in the corners of his eyes.

"Vel," he said, "I knew you wouldn't like the ugly, knotty logs with moss and mud showing, so I decided to cover it all up with something soft and pretty. Pink flannel seemed the answer, so I ordered it from Dawson and the freighter brought it out, yards and yards of it, when he delivered your steamer trunk. Yes, this is your big surprise," he laughed, "and I didn't want you to discover it before it was time to move in."

"Oh Edward," I told him, "this is truly a sweet, dear little pink doll-house! I'm going to love every minute of living here and keeping house."

Clemy, of course, was delighted with my joyous response, and he and Nelly pranced around the one-room cabin in happy glee. Nelly obviously understood that something important was going on.

The cabin was about 20x18 feet. A brand new Klondike stove stood just to the right of the door. Near the stove was a nice new worktable. Next to it was a combination storage cabinet and dish cupboard. Beyond it was a dining table, under the window.

At the rear of the cabin was a large double bed with a ticking bulging with thick stuffing of wild hay, which Ed hastened to say he had gathered in late summer from the hills. The smell of the hay was aromatic and sweet in the cabin, like the fresh breath of spring.

In another corner of the cabin was a small cot for Clemy, also with a fragrant mattress of wild hay, and there was a large clothes closet, too. Then there were several comfortable-looking homemade chairs. To the left of the cabin door stood a wash stand and basin with a big dipper and water pail, all ready for use.

"Oh, Ed," I exclaimed again and again, "you didn't forget a thing!

It's so complete. And too, there's a real glass window. And, look at the floor! It's almost chalk white."

"Sure," said Ed, "it's made of cottonwood, real cottonwood. It was a job cutting the wood, planing it, and smoothing it down. I even tried to polish it. Vel, I thought you'd like that, too, altho' it may be quite difficult to keep it always white and clean."

"No matter! I love its whiteness! And I'll keep it 'spanking' clean. But, Ed, when can we move in?"

"Today," said Ed, looking supremely happy. "Yes, Joe is stopping by early to help us get settled before leaving for Little Chief Gulch for several weeks. He has a Lay over there."

"Good old Joe!" I said with much appreciation, as I thought of the round, jovial-faced little miner with swarthy complexion, merry black eyes, and dark wavy hair. Somehow, he had appointed himself as our special guardian angel and he seemed to be bringing us luck! "Joe's a wonderful friend, the best in the Klondike," I told Ed.

That evening the miners gathered in our new cabin to admire it. It turned into a real housewarming. A cozy, warm fire glowed in the stove. Several candles burned on the table, casting a rosy cheerfulness into every corner of the dear little cabin.

"Say, she's a honey! A mighty sturdy little cabin," exclaimed Mike Johnson enthusiastically. "And, Wow! Pink flannel, too! Lordy, if it ain't real purty! Bless my soul, but I'll bet there ain't another cabin like it in the Klondike—maybe the whole wide world!"

"And, man alive, there's a real window that ya' kin actually see out of," said Mather enviously. "I shore do get tired of tryin' to see through that whiskey bottle window in the bunk house! Yes, I shore do envy ya'all! You know, Ed, our bunk house is as cold as hades. We've pasted newspapers all over them blasted cracks, but the wind still whistles through like Banshees!"

"Yes, I know," said Ed, "and I'm sorry, but all of you are certainly welcome to come here any evening. Yes, you bet you're welcome!"

Well, as a result of having the new, warm cabin and a rosy pink atmosphere, and Ed's cordial invitation, the miners began coming quite regularly.

Soon, I decided it was necessary to have a little more privacy, so I handstitched a cretonne curtain and had Ed stretch it across the end of the cabin where our bed was located. Also, I made ruffles of the same

PINK FLANNEL HEAVEN

pink flowered material to put around the lower part of the bed to hide the boxes and crates of supplies stored there. This, of course, gave the big bed a sort of pretty pink "skirted" appearance.

* * *

Contentment in a little log cabin! Yes, I'm sure we three were happier than if we had dwelt in a palace. In 1899, I sang as I worked, baking bread, preparing meals, sewing, washing, ironing, and doing numerous other cabin tasks. I accepted the cares and and hardships of the North with a smile, for I was truly happy—probably the happiest woman on earth, or at least—in the Klondike. It seemed that our cozy pink-lined cabin radiated everything that makes life good and worthwhile—peace, joy, tranquility, love, good humor, and human understanding.

On cold winter nights when the thermometer hit many degrees below zero, often we would bundle up and go outside to stand by our cabin to watch the amazing Aurora Borealis, almost always called the "Northern Lights."

It seemed that these mysterious lights would usually start early in the evening (during the darkest nights), appearing on the horizon in the form of a broad arc. From this, there would come great beams of light, like huge searchlights. They would cross and recross the heavens, as tho' looking for something unknown in the universe. Often, the lights would appear in beautiful pastel colors of rose, violet, lavender and pale blue, and also in various irregular shapes. Many times they would be rich in red and green and gold; then again, the Aurora Borealis would flash on in just a plain, steady glow of brilliant white, or misty light—"angel light"—as Clemy liked to call it.

Always, it gave me a strange feeling to watch the display of the northern lights—to hear them hiss and crackle overhead, and also to hear the malemutes howl.

When the lights would flash on, the dogs would throw back their heads and howl and howl, almost continuously, giving forth that peculiar, wild, wolf-like wail that is absolutely blood-curdling!

In the cold, still air, that was almost electric, we could hear the dogs for miles and miles up and down the creek! Of course, our dogs would add their voices to that weird, mad chorus!

Even Nelly would wail loud and wolfish—no matter if she was in the cabin with Clemy, or standing outside in the snow with us. This peculiar habit of the malemutes and huskies always made me shudder ... gave me a certain eerie, uneasy feeling. Nevertheless, I was extremely fascinated by the lights, and watched in awe, as they would play, and sweep, and swing across the heavens.

At such times I couldn't help but wonder what primitive man must have thought of them long ago, and I wondered too, how present day Indians and Eskimos explained them, and what their superstitions and fantasies were. I could see that under the spell of the Aurora Borealis it would be very easy to believe almost any unusual, supernatural story.

"Yes, little Clemy," Ed said lightly, one night, "I'll bet there're tons of gold and treasures of diamonds, rubies, emeralds, and blue sapphires planted far to the North, and that the ghosts of the dead prospectors are trying to point the way. Maybe they dance and change shape and color and crackle to get our attention!"

"But why don't we go after that big treasure?" Clemy asked innocently and excitedly.

"Because, little son, the treasure is buried too deep under the earth —maybe the polar ice cap—right under the magnetic pole. Why, it would take a great stampede of giants to find that treasure and they would have to have gigantic picks and shovels, maybe as high as these mountains, maybe as high as the moon!

"But, just maybe, Clemy—yes, maybe—some of that treasure is buried right here under our feet, too! Some of it must be here, and you can bet your boots, if it is, we'll find it!"

* * *

Sometimes Ed would come rushing home after checking on the mine at night and would say, "Vel and Clemy, how would you like to take a sleighride? It's a fine moonlight night, the air is invigorating, and we could have an enjoyable time."

Almost before Ed could finish the sentence, Clemy would be off in his corner putting on extra stockings, dry moccasins, his heavy flannel shirt and warm sweater. Over his sweater he'd pull his parka, and of course he'd put on his red stocking cap.

I, too, would hurry and bundle up in my warmest clothing—several wool petticoats, a blouse, sweater and an extra heavy woolen skirt. Then I'd put on my beautiful short otter fur coat (which Ed had said was certainly very stylish, but not very practical for the North). While I would be fitting on my perky little furcap, at a jaunty angle, and pinning my curls into place, Ed would bring the sleigh around to the door. Then he'd go after the sled-dogs which were always staked near the cabin.

They were Boris, Rover, Queen, Pat and Fritz. Each one had an important place in the team, and I was beginning to realize how very valuable each dog was. Also, I was learning that each animal had his own distinct personality. On the coldest nights Edward would bring the dogs into the cabin to get them lined up in the harness. Always, they would become greatly excited when anticipating a fine run in the moonlight, and it seemed to make them impatient and difficult to handle and as a result, they would quarrel at the drop of a hat. They were naturally very jealous of each other. Sometimes fierce battles would develop, which would delay our sleigh rides.

Ed, of course, showed no favoritism, but he usually tried to harness Boris, the leader, last. This dog would snarl at the others if they didn't behave and stand still. Always, Boris tried to help Edward bring order out of chaos. Somehow, the sleigh bells and their jingle would excite the dogs when not in harness, but once in line the bells meant a fine run.

Already, Nelly, Clemy's pet, was breaking in as a sled-dog, but she preferred running loose by the sleigh, near Clemy. Obviously, she was pretty spoiled and wished special consideration and privileges. Yes, she was certainly a pampered animal!

When the dogs would be harnessed securely, Ed (who always dressed appropriately for the cold in heavy reindeer parka, gloves and hood) would take the dogs outside and fasten them to the sleigh and then Clemy and I would climb aboard and snuggle down among the deep folds of the warm sleigh-robe. Then, Ed would carefully tuck us in and secure the robe under us. When we were comfortable and ready, he would grasp the handle at the back of the sled, crack the whip and yell, "Mush on!"

Away we would go, in a cloud of loose snow, down the Dominion Creek Valley Trail, or up towards Caribou. Usually, Ed would run behind the sled, but on the downgrades would jump on the backrunners and ride.

The clear, crisp air was always exhilarating and invigorating. The dogs never looked back once they started and Ed at times had difficulty keeping them in check.

Our sleigh bells jingled merrily as we sped along. On these nights it was usually too cold to talk much. It was safer to keep the cold air from our lungs and just drink in the scenery. The predominating sounds would be the sleigh bells and the squeak, squeak and crunch of the runners on the hard-packed snow.

No one "outside" could possibly imagine how beautiful the Yukon hills and valleys appear under bright moonlight. It was like a northern fairyland—just like an old fashioned Christmas card scene.

The frozen snow on the ground scintillated like jewels, often in star patterns. The ice-draped trees wore hundreds of crystallized eardrops, like myriads of blue-white diamonds, all sparkling at once under the bright moonlight!

"Ah yes," I would say to myself on these occasions, "this is the life ... something I would never, never have known if I hadn't come North."

"Oh Edward," I would say as he would lift me from the sleigh at our little cabin door, "The ride wasn't quite long enough!"

"Great Scott," he would laugh, "ten o'clock is far too late for an old fellow like me! You know I must dig for gold in the morning. And, sometimes it seems the devil himself looks over my shoulder when I'm thirty feet down under ground! But it's always gotta be 'mush on with a smile' for you, Dear Vel. It will be like that for as long as I live."

"Oh Edward," I said (on a particularly glorious night, after he had unharnessed the dogs and after little Clemy had gone off to bed and while my husband and I were drinking our last cup of hot chocolate, made of snow water, canned milk and chocolate), "Oh Edward, what spot on earth could be sweeter than right here in this dear little log cabin—our wonderful world of candlelight, pink flannel, and heaven."

"Pink flannel——heaven!" Ed echoed in a surprised, pleased tone as a soft look crept into his eyes.

"Yes, Vel, this truly is heaven," he said gently, as he slowly blew out the candles.

Chapter 12

THE TWO CHAMPS

Now it was becoming a favorite pastime for Joe Latshaw and Edward to reminisce about what they called "the good old days" while they would smoke their pipes in the evening and relax, after a hard day's work.

"Dawson is slowly changing," they agreed. "It's simmering down and becoming a typical town. Much of the wild-west, woolly spirit is going away."

"Remember when there was excitement galore? The noisy crowds, the amateur shows and even big celebrities who came to entertain us in '98?" asked Joe nostalgically."

"Yes, Joe, I surely do remember," said Ed, one evening, "and I remember, too, how I first met you. I believe you had just come up the Yukon from Candle, that small mining town on Cape Nome."

"You're right," laughed Joe, "and I remember the first time I ever saw you, Ed. It was in that big log cabin in Dawson in the summer of '98 when you fought the Champ!"

"The Champ!" I exclaimed. "Why, Edward, you never told me about fighting a real champion!"

"No," laughed Ed, "you see, Vel, it was all a joke and a mistake."

"Golly, it didn't look like it to me," said Joe, with a chuckle.

"Well, it all happened like this," said Edward, as he tapped the ashes from his pipe:

"One night in Dawson, in '98, I decided to visit some of 'the boys.' They were staying at quite a large cabin, and when I pushed open the door, I was surprised to see, not a small group of fellows, but a large crowd sitting around the sides of the room with the floor all cleared as if they were waiting to put on some sort of entertainment."

" 'Hey Ed, come on in, we're having a party,' Bert Bass called.

"Thanks," I said. "Looks like I'm just in time."

" 'Yes, you sure are,' said a tall, slim fellow, whom I had never seen before, and as he spoke, he thrust some boxing gloves into my hands.

" 'Come on,' he said, 'put 'em on. Let's box a few rounds.'

"Not I. I'm no boxer!" I exclaimed in surprise.

" 'Oh, come on Ed, be a good sport,' called Bert and the boys.

"But I'm not a boxer. I've only had gloves on a few times in my life, that was when I was a boy at school, years ago.

" 'Well, be a good sport Ed, anyway, and try your luck,' the tall fellow challenged smilingly.

"O.K." I said, so wanting to be a good sport, I took off my heavy shirt and stripped to the waist, put on the gloves, then, stepped to the middle of the room. The tall fellow had done likewise.

"Well, here goes!" I yelled and plunged straight at him with both fists flying. I hit him in the chest with a terrific thud. He grunted and backed off a pace with a look of startled surprise.

" 'Say, fellow,' he said, 'you must wait for the bell!'

"What bell?"

" 'There it is now, hear it? So—come on,' he yelled, as he danced toward me, both fists up.

"This time, he hit me a jolt on the shoulder and I swiftly thrust back, hitting him on the head, then, on the shoulder. He looked surprised again. Then we danced around the ring together, I punching and hitting wherever I could reach him. The boys all cheered and yelled, 'Come on, Ed, give it to him! Come on, Ed, punch him in the solar plexis!'

"The wild cheering spurred me on to greater efforts and I danced and punched, punched and dodged some blows and received some. But every time I hit that tall fellow he managed to hit me back. I seemed to be making good headway tho' as my muscles were just like steel. I had recently come over the stampede trail from Skagway and I rather prided myself on my stamina and toughened condition.

"Soon the bell sounded and each of us went to opposite sides of the cabin for a breather amid the howling cheers of the men.

" 'You're all right, Ed, Keep it up' they called. 'Keep it up, boy!'

"One of the fellows wiped the perspiration from my face with a towel and hastily rubbed me down. Then, the bell clanged and I was up in the middle of the floor, punching and pounding at the tall fellow with all of my might. I was pleased at the number of times I was able to sock him—and each time, he socked me back, I felt a blinding rage and a desire to punch him more fiercely, again and again—harder and harder!

THE TWO CHAMPS

" 'Come on, Ed, get him! Punch him in the eye!' yelled the boys.

"One of the fellow's fists caught me on the nose. I saw stars and teetered on my heels. Luckily, the bell sounded and I staggered to my side of the room. One of the boys grabbed a wet towel and sponged some blood off my face, while another fellow rubbed me down. Great Scott! How I hated to be punched in the nose, my very weakest spot, the spot where it had been frost-bitten so many times! Well, I decided I would fix that big Blubber!

"The men in the cabin kept yelling, 'Come on, Ed, you'll knock him out this time. Get mad! Come on, you'll do it this time. Get good and mad!'

"Again the bell sounded, and I was in the middle of the floor; the tall fellow and I met head on, like two bulls in an arena. We punched viciously, tangled and separated, danced, clinched and punched again. In the mad scuffle the man managed to hit me in the nose again, a stinging blow! It started to bleed badly. I must say the sight of my blood spurting all over the place and dripping to the floor maddened me beyond all reason. I saw red—very red! In a wild rage, I charged at the fellow with a superhuman strength that I didn't dream I possessed.

"Suddenly, I had the strength of ten mad bulls! My hard, right fist sprang at him like a solid iron trip-hammer, catching him squarely between his blazing eyes.

"He staggered, hesitated, then caught himself and danced to a safer position.

"I charged after him with all the fury in me, yelling and whooping like a wild Indian. He tried to evade me, but I caught him. This time I poked him right in the left eye!

"The boys yelled wildly, 'You're doing it, Ed. Now come on, hit him in the solar plexis—come on Ed!'

"The tall fellow wiped his eye and started towards me, knock-out determination in his expression, but then, the bell sounded at just that crucial moment!

" 'You're the Champ, Ed! You're the Champ!' the crowd howled in glee.

"Now to my great surprise, the tall fellow came over to my corner. He patted me on the back, and in a very friendly way said, 'Thanks, Ed Lung. You did a terrific job. Let's say we've had enough for one night. We fought three good rounds and gave the boys here, a good show!'

"O.K." I said. "It suits me just fine because I must be on my way as I have another engagement."

"As I left the cabin, the crowd enthusiastically cheered me again. I think you could have heard them all over Dawson.

"The next day in the barber shop, while I was having a haircut, the barber said, 'Ed Lung, I hear you gave the Champ a black eye last night!'

"The Champ?" I asked in surprise. "Oh yes, I did fight a fellow last night, but he was just one of the boys."

" 'The hell he was!' roared the barber. 'Didn't you know he was the Champion from San Francisco? He was looking for a sparring partner, but none of the fellows would risk fighting him—then you came along. You gave him a black eye and he's got to fight in two nights at the Combination Theater. All Dawson has tickets! Ha, ha, ha! What a joke that is!'

"From the next chair, in the barber shop, I heard a merry chuckle, and turning, I saw the friendly face of a dark-haired stranger, whom I thought I had never seen before, and yet there was something vaguely familiar about him, too!

" 'I believe you were the real champion, Fellow,' the stranger laughed. 'I was in that cabin last night. You were sensational!'

"Then he added, 'My name is Joe Latshaw, I'm new here, from Candle. Just got in town yesterday. Will you have lunch with me at Mrs. Daly's restaurant?'

"Thanks, I'll be mighty glad to, Joe Latshaw," I said. "My name is Ed—Ed Lung."

"Yes, Eddy," laughed Joe from his chair in our cabin, "that was over a year ago," then adding a finishing sentence to the story, he said, "and we've grown to be the best of Sourdough Partners!"

"You bet we have," agreed Ed, with a smile of enthusiasm, as he refilled his pipe, and then leaned back with complete contentment.

---

*Green, of San Francisco, and another Pacific Coast pugilist fought in Dawson, July 30, 1898. Frank Slavin arranged the big bout. Joseph Boyle was Frank Slavin's sparring partner. Boyle, also was in Dawson in 1898.

Chapter 13

THE LITTLE PREACHER

By stern necessity we lived very austere lives in our secluded valley, where we were a scattered group of miners, traders and several women. Also, there were about six Mounties, who ruled the Dominion Creek area with an iron hand.

Almost pathetically we depended on each other for companionship even though we had obviously come from different walks of life. There was no room for snobbishness in our valley. Everyone was important, every item that helped sustain life was precious, too. Absolutely nothing was wasted, even tin cans were saved and put to various uses.

Many times we joked about our rugged existence and our perpetual sourdough, bacon and bean table-fare, and often pretended we were in luxurious surroundings and dining on sumptuous meals. Good humor, with imagination, was part of making life bearable and staying alive. A trip to Dawson meant a somewhat change of diet and environment, a welcome break in our grinding routine, but it had its limitations too. It was a rugged oasis of civilization dropped into a frozen wilderness, only open to boat-travel through summer months (a little over three months). The only other way* to reach the coast after winter came was to go over the ice, (walk, or ride by dog team). Many people reached the coast safely, but whole dogteams had vanished through the ice! Even if all went well, it was bound to be a rugged trip of perhaps a month or more.

Often, as I worked in our little cabin, my mind would take me back over that long, uninhabited route, and I would shiver a little at our isolation should a real emergency develop. Well, I decided, it behooved us to stay in good health!

It had been many months now, since I had had any news from my mother and sister in Tacoma, or relatives in Oregon. How I longed to hear from them! I knew that sometimes it took six or even eight months to get a letter through. It was four months already since I had

---

*The first overland stage did not run until mid-winter of 1903. After freeze-up, it ran from Dawson to the City of Whithorse, and was a large sleigh, drawn by horses.

left home. When I had first arrived in the Klondike Ed had mailed to Ena, a few tiny nuggets for a brooch. He knew how pleased she would be, for Klondike nugget-jewelry was all the rage in the States.

Now, as the months wore on, I was beginning to fall into the pattern of a miner's wife. My hands were getting hardened and calloused, and my back ached much less. Often I would say to myself, "Wouldn't Mother be surprised if she could see me now!" But was I happy? Oh yes, very happy!

Many evenings, after I had done the dishes, Ed and I would start testing the pay-dirt from the day's diggings. We would sit at the small table, side by side, near the lamp, and with powerful magnets, draw off the black sand from the sample pans of pay-dirt. While we would be evaluating the clean-up, often I would say, "Oh Ed, is the mine really going to pay us? Is it *all* going to be just black sand?"

"No, darling, just you wait," Ed said one night. "From the looks of this last batch we'll be getting at least 25c to the pan—could run even higher. That's not bad! It's only a pittance to the rich claims on the Bonanza, but we can eventually make a small nest-egg by grinding away steadily like this."

Every Sunday now, unless a severe snowstorm was in progress, we were having informal church services.

At first, the lonely miners had come to our cabin just to visit and talk nostalgically of home. But gradually we began reading Bible verses and singing a few hymns from memory. Then we decided to rotate to the different cabins. Always the miners were well scrubbed, combed and shined in their "Sunday's best."

Edward, being a minister's son, knew the Holy Scriptures* much better than I, and so he proved to be almost a religious encyclopedia. Consequently, he was of real help in suggesting religious topics, also where to find the needed verses in the little white Bible that Mother had given me. Not only did Ed know the Bible, he lived by the Golden Rule himself.

"Thankfulness and appreciation for everything are the deep roots of real happiness and contentment," he told Clemy and me. "We must be sure to remember that even in these humble surroundings."

---

*By spring of 1902 Rev. John Pringle of Dawson made trips to Hunker and Dominion Creek (occasionally) to hold church services. He was serving the Presbyterian Church.

When Sunday morning rolled around, we would dress in our very best clothes and go, either by dog-team or walk, to the designated cabin. Usually, we would find the place crowded with miners—sitting on boxes or standing along the walls, if the supply of homemade chairs had given out.

Somehow, the leadership fell to me to plan and conduct these informal services and from the start, the men began calling me, "Little Lady Preacher." At first I was somewhat embarrassed over this new title, but gradually grew used to it.

It was especially touching to see how hard the men tried to have their cabins spruced up. And they were trying their best to be refined! No spittoons would be in sight! No red flannel underwear drying around the Klondike stove. The last items mentioned usually meant that our host, whoever he was, might have to wear his socks and red flannels an extra day longer!

"Little Preacher," said the proprietor of the new Dominion Creek roadhouse, after he'd attended a particularly overcrowded cabin service, "how would you like to hold church in my roadhouse? It's obvious that you need a bigger, more comfortable place. These cabins are far too cramped, and ill smelling."

"Oh," I said, "your offer is so appreciated! Twenty miners squeezed into a tiny cabin are almost too many miners!"

"You're right," laughed the roadhouse owner. "Young woman," he added, 'you're doing a splendid thing for the miners. They're talking about it even in Dawson, and did you know that Alex Adams, the well-known actor of the Palace Grand Theatre, dropped in last Sunday? No, of course you wouldn't know him—he was dressed like a miner; came with several other actors from Dawson. Why, I'll bet those old reprobates haven't been inside a church since they were christened!" laughed the proprietor.

"And here's something else," he continued, hesitating a little, "not long ago a badly crippled miner came to a Sunday-meeting. The poor man had previously been injured in a tunnel cave-in. He limped badly and suffered a great deal of pain. Do you remember what you said when he was leaving the service? You said, 'Never mind, my friend, there'll be no cripples in heaven.'

"Do you know where that man is now? He's in Dawson, and he's walking normally! His recovery is almost miraculous."

One evening, after Clemy had gone to bed and while Ed and I were sitting at the table, and, as usual, drawing off the sand from the gold with magnets, Ed said a surprising thing: "Look! This sand is very black, hard and glittery—kinda reminds me of Lucifer—the Evil One! Notice that when all of the sand is finally drawn away there sparkles only pure gold, bright like the sun. But just drop one pinch of this black stuff into the golden heap and you get the impure combination again. Well, and so it's pretty much with life. Wherever there is gold, often you are likely to find old Lucifer mixed in, trying to control it! These powerful magnets can be likened to the good forces of life. The drawing, pulling quality of the highly magnetized magnet is much stronger than that of the black-sand-particles, which are really black iron and have a tremendous strength all of their own."

"Oh, it's a startling thought," I said. "It would make an effective illustration for the miners. We know how sorely tempted they are when they go to Dawson with their hard-earned gold."

The following week I thought a great deal about Lucifer, the Fallen Angel, and how the Bible said he had been cast out of Heaven for his dark deeds. But Lucifer had wasted no time in setting up his own special kingdom and powerful forces on earth, and he had quickly decided that gold would be a useful commodity.

The following Sunday I delivered the talk on Almighty God and Lucifer, using the process of cleaning the gold as an example. The miners sat in surprised attention on the new wooden benches (which the Innkeeper had so thoughtfully provided). A heavy curtain had been draped discreetly over the roadhouse supply of whiskey.

After I had presented my sermonette with all of the zeal I could muster, I asked the miners if they could think of words that would describe Lucifer's list of temptations. They scratched their heads, thought hard, and came up with,

"Loot," "Lure," "Lies," "Lucre," "Lust," "Licentiousness," even "Lazy," and others. Oddly enough, all these words, which are so descriptive of undesirable-ways-of-life, begin with the letter L, as did Lucifer's name. Was this a strange coincidence, or was it significant?

Often, I had read a comforting verse in the Bible and so I read it to the miners. It was the 103rd Psalm, the 12th verse:

"As far as the east is from the west, so far hath He removed our transgressions from us.

THE LITTLE PREACHER

13. "Like as a father pitieth his children, so the Lord pitieth them that fear Him.

14. "For He knoweth our frame; he remembereth that we are dust."

Yes, I was truly concerned about the welfare of the miners. They were homesick and far from home. In Dawson, Lucifer was King. He had many lures to take away the miner's hard-earned gold and he knew how to lead them astray.

"Blessed are the pure in heart," I reminded the miners, earnestly, "for they shall see God."

That first Sunday in the roadhouse, I was delighted to find a portable organ placed there by the thoughtful Innkeeper. However, it was apparent that I was the only one who could play the instrument, so I became the organist and choir-director all in that one day.

As I pumped the bellows of the melodious little organ, I listened with a great deal of gladness and sentiment to the untrained voices of the miners while they sang some of the beloved old gospel hymns— "Onward Christian Soldiers," "The Old Rugged Cross," "Jesus, Savior, Pilot Me," and "He Lifted Me." Edward and Joe led the tenor and bass and even little Clemy's voice chimed in, sweet and high—a tiny bit off key, maybe, but it did have an angelic quality.

If we found that we had some extra time, the miners liked to tell, as sort of testimonials, some of their religious experiences in conquering, or mastering old Lucifer. Often, they would come forth with some rather odd and startling accounts, sometimes humorous, sometimes plain scandalous!

A miner volunteered one Sunday: "By Jimminy, we miners try to give them 'Licentious wimmin' of Dawson a wide range! We sure try to keep out of reach of that big gal they call, 'The Grizzly Bear.' She's a great big hulk of a woman, and a pretty tough one—nearly breaks a fellow's bones when she squeezes him during them lively two-steps and polkas! Then, there's 'Bertha, the Adder'—the 'Loot-Money-Mad-gal,' who ran through the streets one night a-chasin' the other woman who had ripped the Adder's clothes right off her back in one of them fierce, female quarrels over one of them rich fellers!

"Then, there's another hussy, too! 'Nellie, the Pig,' they calls her. She's got awfully sharp teeth, and a mean, quick temper—actually bit the ear right off one of the fellers in an awful brawl. By golly, the miners give her a wide range when they see she's on one of them mad, ear-biting sprees!

"Man! oh man! how those wild, licentious women needs convertin'! Don't take much figurin' to see they're Lucifer's own hellcats.

"Well, now, there's another gal—'Susie Blue-Nose,' they calls her—a real different kind. She's a wild-eyed, religious reformer; spouts hell-fire and brimstone all over the place—after both men and women—homely as a mud fence! Last time I was in Dawson I collided with her. I'll never forgit it! It was when my thirst got the best of me. Yep, the old urge got me, I confess! And so, by golly, I sneaked into McPhee's saloon. Oh! I had a turrible, guilty feelin', all the way in. Well, there I was a leanin' against the bar, a tryin' my best to fight off old Lucifer, when suddenly, I heerd an awful commotion out in the street, and who do ya' suppose it was? Sure, you guessed it! 'Twas old Susie Blue-Nose!

"She came a-bustin' into the saloon and she was a-carryin' a big, long club! Man! oh man, did the fellers try to git out of her way! Old 'Blue-Nose' jumps onto a chair and then ups onto the bar, and with eyes a-flashin' wild blazes she started screaming bloody-murder that we was all a-goin' ta' hell and that we'd better clear out of that saloon real quick! By golly, I feared' it! I was right there between the bar and some chairs. I tell you 'Blue-Nose' started swingin' that club with a vengeance, like a mad one—just barely missed my head once by inches! Then, she turned 'round and commenced smashing glasses and everything breakable at the bar. Say! liquor spattered all over the place, and by Jimminy! if she didn't end up by breakin' that beautiful $500 mirror. Well, before anyone could stop her, out Blue-Nose flew like a typhoon—tornado, a-runnin' and screamin' down the street and headed for the Aurora saloon! And as she tore away, she yelled back at us that she was a-doin' us all a big favor—was cleanin' up the town, and savin' our souls from hell-fire and damnation! In several spots she stopped just long enough to deliver quick, fiery sermons—speeches about the awful power of Satan and such, then, on and on she went! Well, by golly, that night she pretty nigh demolished all bars in town!

"So now, when fellers drink in Dawson, they tells me, they keeps a weather eye on the door. Most of 'em think the 'saloon wrecker' is quite funny—say old 'Blue-Nose' sort of livens up the place! But by golly, I guess that that long-nosed gal is really a-tryin' ta' save* souls and do good in her own special way. Anyhow, she sure goes after the prostitutes, and here in this kind o' meetin', I daren't say just how!"

On another occasion a miner told about a recent wedding held at a place on Dominion Creek:

"Yes, folks," he began in a rather shy voice, but quickly warmed up to his subject, "as ya' all know, holy matrimony is sure mighty fine, but 'sceerce' around these parts! And ya' know too, that they say marriages are made in Heaven! Well, now let me tell ya' about this one. Not long ago there came to the Mounted Police Barracks at Caribou a young French Canadian who couldn't speak or understand very much English.

"Young Frank Corby happened to be on duty as Sergeant Hilliard was away at Dawson. From a few broken sentences uttered by Frenchie, Corby got the idea that the Frenchman wanted a mining license. So Corby reached for one of the mining forms, saying the charge would be $10. Then, he asked the usual routine questions before issuing the permit.

"In broken English, the young Frenchman gave his mine location as No. 4 Below Discovery, on Caribou Pup. He seemed to answer all of the questions satisfactorily enough, while Corby wrote down the information. Then, 'Frenchie' paid the required ten dollars and left with the license in his pocket. But little did Corby dream of what was soon to follow.

"The next Sunday the Mounties were all invited to a weddin' which was to take place at Little Quebec. Well, because holy matrimony is such a mighty interesting affair, several of the Mounties decided they would attend. One of them was Corby.

"When they arrived at the log cabin they found the place crammed to overflowing, but anyway, the Mounties managed to squeeze inside. In fact, they got seated just in time to hear the priest say, 'My son, have you got the license?'

" 'Oui,' said the young Frenchman, 'right here—ici, in my pockette.'

"The good priest took the license, examined it closely in a very puzzled way, then, shook his head emphatically and said,

" 'Oh, no, my son, this is a prospector's license! You have to have a Marriage License! Who sold you this?'

"Well, as you can imagine, the mill blew up. There was a lot of snickering and commotion! The young Frenchman grew highly excited. Waving his arms, he exclaimed,

" 'Sac a papier! She should be good. Zee Mountie, Corby, he charge ten dollaire for eet! Mon Dieu. Mon Dieu! Now what I do?'

"Just at that moment 'Frenchie' happened to spy Corby in the front row. Well, you should have seen how fast Corby tore out of there! Suddenly, he remembered he had some very important business back at Caribou. He practically climbed over everyone's shoulders to reach the door.

"But anyway, the good priest took pity on the poor humiliated Frenchman . . . he performed exactly half the ceremony, then stopped with the agreement that the half-married bridegroom leave the church immediately for Dawson to get the real Marriage License—and—alone!

"Two days later, Frenchie waded through a snowstorm to reach Little Quebec with the license. The rest of the ceremony was performed and he claimed his bride. But poor Corby! It's hard telling what will happen if the two men should meet!"

* * *

One day when the valley was stark-white and still shrouded in a late spring snow, a miner came to our door. He asked that I come quickly to a cabin not far away. He said it was urgent. A man was very ill, and he thought—dying.

Hurriedly, I bundled up in my parka and started out with my small white Bible tucked under my arm. A half-hour later I was in a dingy little cabin standing by the cot of a man who plainly had the stamp of death on his face.

Life was quickly ebbing away.

"Little Preacher," he gasped, as he groped for my hand, "I'm dying. Please lean closer," he whispered, "I . . . I . . . accidentally killed a man . . . a long time . . . ago. It . . . it wasn't my fault, but I . . . I . . . never told. The police . . . they never . . . caught . . . me. I came way up here. I can't die without telling a preacher."

Quickly I soothed the dying man—asked the name. Then, as I held the emaciated, quivering hand, I slowly recited the 12th verse of the 103rd Psalm, a verse that we had used often in church service: "As far as the east is from the west, so far hath He removed our transgressions from us."

"Yes . . . yes . . . go on, Little Preacher," he begged. Please . . . please."

I laid my hand gently on the man's forehead and softly said the 23rd

Psalm:

"The Lord is my shepherd, I shall not want. He maketh me to lie down in green pastures; He leadeth me . . . "

The man painfully repeated a few of the words. Then, before I could finish the Psalm, there was a great sigh of relief. The labored breathing stopped. The fevered brow grew cold. His hand still. But over the tortured features there had come an expression of absolute peace. His soul had fled to its Maker.

"Yes, He remembers that we are dust," I whispered sadly, as my tears dropped to the snow, and as I walked slowly homeward.

* * *

On one particular Sabbath morn my subject was "Elijah." My little son, Clemy, who had a very vivid imagination, sat on the front bench, never taking his eyes from my face as I recounted the Bible story of the ancient prophet, and how he was finally transported to Heaven in a cloud of glory.

"Of course it is one of the great mysteries of the Bible," I told them, and as I repeated the story, I dramatized it. When I came to the climax I told of how old Elijah stood on the mountaintop; how he raised his arms to Jehovah and prayed, and then, how suddenly, a great cloud descended and whisked him off to Heaven.

"Yes, folks, it happened quickly," I said. "Maybe it was a beautiful white cloud, or a pink one, or maybe it was a golden one, but anyway it took Elijah up–up–up, into the Heavens, and he was never seen again after that day.

"And so, dear friends, the Bible records that in the last days, the Devout will be caught up to Heaven. Perhaps it will be in like manner, as Elijah . . . in a huge Cloud of Glory."

I closed the talk with a short prayer, and as I'd had a request for a solo, I went to the organ and played and sang, "Sweet Chariot" (my favorite). The miners softly joined in, in the chorus, and Max Lange, our mail-carrier, who had come with his violin, played a beautiful obligato.

That same afternoon Clemy took his sled to a nearby hillside to cut willows for a bow and arrow set which he wanted to make. While he was up on the hillside I had an urgent request to visit a miner's wife who had become ill. (It seemed that now, I was being called upon to perform the duties of a minister, except marrying and burying folks.)

And so, as a result of the long walk and visit, I was gone much longer than I had anticipated. It was quite late when I reached our cabin, and when I opened the door, I saw a sight that wrenched my heart.

Little Clemy was down on his knees by his cot, praying aloud. There was a pitiful look to his small, bent figure and his half upturned, profiled-face.

"Oh Lord," he was saying, "I know that you've taken my dear mother up to heaven, just like you did old Elijah. But please, oh please, Lord, if you'll only bring her back, I promise I'll be a real good little boy. I won't gather no more willows on Sunday for bows and arrows and I won't swear no more like the miners, or tell no more of them big, Lucifer lies, neither! Oh Lord, please bring my dear mother back, please—please—."

His imploring words broke off into choked sobs of utter despair. I stood in the doorway listening, my eyes swimming in tears. Then I called,

"Clemy, my darling, I'm back. I'm here, little son. Don't cry! Look, I'm here!"

Clemy jumped from the floor in astonishment and throwing his arms around me, he cried hysterically, "Oh, mother, mother! You did come back. Oh, you did come back! What was it like way up there in heaven?"

When Clemy had calmed somewhat I tried to explain where I'd been, but he just wouldn't accept my explanation. He insisted that I had been taken up to heaven in a "Cloud of Glory" and that his prayers had been suddenly answered. The following day he told the miners that he was sure he had seen the "Big Cloud" from the hillside while he was out cutting willows. He even drew a picture of the "Cloud of Glory"—his version.

"Velma," said Ed, with a bothered little smile, a few days later, "you must give some kind of talk about heaven. Clemy has invited all of the miners to come next Sunday and hear his mother describe what heaven really looks like."

"But how shall I do that?" I asked desperately.

"Well, there's only one description in the New Testament that I know of," said Ed, "and I'll try to find it for you."

THE LITTLE PREACHER 145

As could be expected, the roadhouse was packed to the doors the following Sunday and I sensed that the miners had come with an air of amused expectancy. Clemy was sitting in the front row with his father. His eyes were big, his face—beaming. He was very excited! All of his friends had come to church at his invitation.

"Folks," I said, "no living mortal has ever gone to heaven and returned to earth to tell about it, that I know of. Of course, I've never been there either, but it is my hope that I shall make that wonderful journey some day. If I go in a "Cloud of Glory," I'll be happy to travel that way, or if I reach heaven through Paradise I shall rejoice to go that way, too. The main thing is that we live each day so that we will be ready to go when we are called to eternity.

"Now, if you really want to know what heaven looks like, let's read how St. John described it many centuries ago, after he saw it in a vision. (I opened my Bible and slowly began reading Revelations 21.)

"And I saw a new heaven and a new earth, for the first heaven and the first earth were passed away; and there was no more sea.

"And I, John, saw the Holy City, the new Jerusalem, coming down from God, out of heaven, prepared as a bride adorned for her husband."

(I carefully read the third and fourth verses and continued to the fifth.) I read it:

"And He that sat upon the throne said, 'Behold, I make all things new.' And He said unto me, 'Write, for these words are true and faithful.' "

Then, I continued reading until I had finished the 16th, the 17th and 18th verses, in which the exact measurements of the City of Heaven were specifically given. Then came the 19th verse which described the beautiful walls of the Holy City. The Bible said the walls were garnished with all manner of precious stones, including jasper, sapphires,, topaz and amethyst. The gates were all pearls and the streets of pure gold, like unto clear glass!

The 23rd verse proclaimed that the City had no need of the sun, nor the moon, for the great glory of God lighted it.

The 27th stated no one could enter the heavenly place if he "defileth or worketh abomination, or maketh a lie . . . only they which were written in the Lamb's Book of Life could enter the Holy City!

"And so, my dear Sourdough friends," I said in conclusion, "this is a true description of what is to come. The 22nd chapter of Revelations goes on to elaborate further on the dazzling splendor of that heavenly place."

When the service was over, Clemy seemed quite satisfied, and happy. The miners were wistful and quiet, and unusually thoughtful. Clemy's face was radiant, like a cherub's.

Little did I dream that he had but a few brief years left on this earth.

Star Flowers

Snow-flakes, falling, falling to the earth,
Like white petals from distant star-flowers—
Blooming in heaven's sweetest, celestial bowers.

Snow-flakes, soft snow-flakes of many lacy patterns,
Fragile petals of a million, billion star-flowers—
Gently falling through winter's hushed, and silent hours.

By Ella L. Martinsen

Chapter 14

TALKING DOG

Alaska malemutes and huskies are faithful to their masters, but they are not very affectionate or companionable, like dogs on the Outside. Their real mission in life seems to be to assist humans with their heavy burdens; and these dogs are content if they are but rewarded with one good meal a day, a little kindness and a place to curl up at night, be it in the snow with blizzards blowing.

Rover was Ed's favorite sled-dog. This animal was of mixed breed and had been sent in to us from the States. He showed great affection for the family, especially for Edward.

"I tell you, Vel," said my husband one day when he was playing

TALKING DOG

with Rover, "this dog is exceptionally smart. He intrigues me! I only have to tell him something once, and he always catches right on. Someone once said that a very intelligent dog has the mentality of a twelve year old child. Well, I sincerely believe it."

Ed had discovered how really intelligent Rover was when one day he was showing him how to shake hands. The dog responded by immediately putting up his paw for another hand-shake. Then, Ed threw back his head and laughed long and loud.

To Ed's amazement, Rover threw back his head also, and tried to make similar sounds.

"Well, I'll be jiggered," laughed Ed. "Rover is certainly trying his best to imitate me."

For several evenings afterward, Ed trained Rover, or I should say, "coached" him.

"Come on boy, show your teeth." said Ed. "Draw your lips back, like this," he encouraged, while he showed the dog the way he wanted him to grin, and in no time Rover was grinning back at Ed almost like a human. "Now laugh like this, Boy, ha, ha, ha!" encouraged Ed with relish, as the dog copied him again and again, each time giving a better performance.

While Ed was teaching Rover, the animal would keep his big intelligent eyes fastened on Ed's face. Rover seemed so very eager to please his master that it was almost pathetic.

Then, one day, Ed said, "If Rover can laugh, he certainly can talk, so we'll try it. He's a lot smarter than a parrot."

So Ed began showing Rover how to open and close his mouth, preparing him to say two-syllable words such as "mam-ma," "pa-pa," "Clem-y," "Yum-yum," "hun-gry," and also putting simple words together like "good-boy," and "go-home."

When the dog would begin his "talking lesson" he would start with a low, peculiar, almost weird rumbling sound in his throat, quickly increasing the pitch and volume and steadiness of his voice, while he clicked his mouth and teeth open and shut, which gave a very good imitation of human speech. Not only that, he seemed to know what each word meant.

"I tell you Vel," this dog is a wonder!" exclaimed Ed, with a lot of enthusiasm. "Why, if we were in the States, he could be a real show-dog!"

Not only did Ed teach Rover to laugh and talk, he taught him how to stand up on his hind legs and walk around the interior of the cabin. The dog had unusually strong hind-leg muscles, and with little effort could easily stand erect for many minutes. Just for fun, one night, Ed placed a miner's cap on Rover and also put Clemy's little red jacket on him. To our surprise, and much to Clemy's delight, Rover objected not the slightest, and, as he pranced about the cabin he seemed to thoroughly enjoy the scene he was creating. Of course when we laughed hilariously, Rover loved it and acted very pleased with himself and strutted all the more.

The next step in Rover's education was to teach him to do a sort of waltz while Ed whistled a merry tune, usually The Blue Danube. Also, the dog did a jig dance to the tune of "A Hot Time in the Old Town Tonight." Rover took a special delight in making up his own dancing steps, too, and he seemed to have a natural sense of rhythm. Of course Ed usually rewarded Rover with some coveted morsel.

One morning a miner, who lived down the creek a few miles from us, came to our cabin and asked if he might borrow Rover for three or four days so that the dog could help him haul some heavy equipment to "Little Paris," which was a settlement of Frenchmen on middle Dominion Creek. Even tho' Ed wasn't very eager to let Rover go, he consented, for this particular miner, once had done Ed a big favor.

The following morning, however, when Ed happened to be away, the miner came down our path leading Rover at the end of a long rope. The man kept yelling, "Stay back, Rover, don't you dare come near me! Rover, keep away, I tell you. Stay back."

Poor Rover! He had a very unhappy, dejected, hang-dog look and seemed utterly bewildered at the unfriendly treatment he was receiving.

"What on earth is the matter?" I asked, as I ran forward to meet the miner. "Did Rover bite you or something?"

"Oh no, Lady," answered the miner, with a strange quaver to his voice. "No, Rover didn't bite me. But please, please take him off my hands. I don't want him near me and I don't ever want to see him again!"

"Tell me what in heaven's name happened?" I asked, with a feeling of apprehension.

"Well, I hate to say it, Lady," said the man, as he cast furtive glances at Rover who was now cowering more dejectedly than ever, "but that

TALKING DOG

dog is hexed!"

"Hexed!" I exclaimed in amazement. "Why, whatever do you mean? Ed says that Rover is the best sled-dog he's ever had."

"That may be, Lady, but just wait 'til I tell you something:

"As you know, I'm a lonely man, so last night after Rover had done a good day's work I took him inside my cabin for company. Well, he seemed contented enough; laid by the stove while I smoked my pipe and read. Then I got pretty sleepy, so I went to bed, leaving him right there by the fire.

"But, in the middle of the night, suddenly, I was awakened out of a sound sleep by a peculiar noise. I wasn't sure, but I thought I heard someone laugh like a crazy maniac, right outside my cabin door!

"Well, of course it startled me. So, I got up, got dressed and went outside to have a look around, but I saw no one around the place.

" 'Oh, maybe I just imagined it.' I said to myself. 'Maybe I was only dreaming!'

"So I climbed back into bed and was just dropping off when I heard that strange laugh again! This time I knew I'd heard it! It was sort of a horrible, weird, unearthly laugh. It made my hair stand straight up on end. Now, maybe you don't think I was scared—and puzzled, too! I asked myself, 'Who in tarnation would want to come prowling around my cabin in the middle of the night, and who would laugh like that?'

"So I got up and cautiously searched the premises, but it was the same story—no one in sight! Well—I went to bed a second time, feeling mighty uneasy, and was just pulling the covers up over my head when I heard that same, awful, blood-chilling laugh again. It sounded like it was right in the cabin this time—almost at my elbow—yes, almost in my ear!

"Say, I nearly jumped outa my skin—but—instead—I jumped right outa bed! Quickly, I lit the candle and what do you think I saw? No, you can never imagine it!

"'Twas Rover, your dog! He was there in the middle of the floor—standing straight up on his hind legs, staring right at me, and mind you, he was laughing, laughing, laughing loud, I tell you! Yes, it's absolutely true. His lips were moving and were drawn back into a hideous grin, showing those sharp, white teeth. Lordy, I was glued to the spot—scared stiff!

"Then, as I watched, Rover began talking. I'll swear I recognized some of the words he said. After that, he gave some more of those fiendish laughs, then he began moving across to the opposite side of the room. From there he danced slowly back towards me. It seemed he was keeping time to some sort of queer, rhythmic, demonic music. He repeated the act several times, then as if that wasn't enough, he began prancing around and around the room in a very odd manner.

"Finally, he stopped dead still, right in front of me and in that awful voice started asking questions. Yes, imagine it—a dog asking questions! Under the flickering light his eyes glistened like I've never seen any other dog's eyes glisten before. Why, that dog looked half-mad-beast, and half-mad-human!

"Well, I tell you, I was rooted to the spot, scared out of my wits! I wondered, what next? And if the dog would tear me to pieces! But, just at that moment, Rover drew back his lips, clicked his teeth and said in a wild, fierce voice that he wanted to go home—wanted his "ma-ma," wanted his "pa-pa." Well—that was the climax! So I, having once been a cowboy, and fast with a rope, decided there was only one thing to do—lasso him.

"So, Lady, here is your dog. Take it from me, he's hexed! And tell Ed, never, never again will I borrow him!"

When my husband returned home and after I had told him of the horrible scare Rover had given the superstitious miner, Ed became nearly convulsed with mirth.

"Well, I'll be darned," he grinned. "I certainly am proud of Rover's accomplishments. I never tried to keep them secret, but neither did I talk about them to the miners! I guess I had, in the back of my mind, a plan to show him off on some special occasion, but I never thought that Rover would beat me to it and put on his own special act for that fellow. Holy Mackerel, the man must have been frightened to death, and I can hardly blame him.

"But poor Rover! No doubt he couldn't sleep and so decided it was a good time to show what he'd learned. Or, perhaps it was just plain hunger or homesickness that prompted him to perform so well. Anyway, whatever it was, he expected something in return for his tricks. Yes, that's why the poor dog was so bewildered at his bad treatment. Good old Rover," laughed Ed, affectionately.

After that particular episode, Rover's fame spread rapidly. Soon he became known as the "Talking, Laughing, Dancing Dog of Dominion

Creek." And on many a cold, wintery night, when other sled-dogs were curled up outside in the snow, Rover would be enjoying a nice, warm cabin, entertaining groups who had come especially to see Ed's "wonder" dog.

Chapter 15

THREE MEN IN A CASKET OF ICE

It was a very chilly day in spring of 1900 when Max Lange, our mailman, rapped at our cabin. As I opened the door, right away, I noticed a strained expression of deep anxiety written across his usually jolly face.

"Come in and have a cup of coffee," I invited.

"Thanks," said Max, gratefully, as he thumped the slush-ice from his mucklucks. "Yes, I could use a good cup of coffee. It's been a very long, strenuous trip this time from Dawson."

"You do have some mail?" I asked hopefully, "We've waited many weeks."

"Yes, Mrs. Lung, I know! You people on Dominion Creek have been pretty much cut off from town this spring due to these very late snow-storms and mushy thaws. But, at last, here's your mail," he said, wearily, as he handed me a bundle of letters. "Here's your Dawson paper, too," he added. "I'm afraid you'll see some mighty disturbing news. There's been a terrible ferment of indignation going on in town lately, and some furious wild-talk of lynchings!"

"Lynchings!" I exclaimed, in startled surprise.

"Yes, it's true, and because of this, I almost brought you a visitor, your friend Nelly Daly. It surely would have done her good to get out of town, and she did start out with me on the mail route from Dawson as a passenger, but we only got as far as the Grand Forks, then my dogs got into a fierce fight. Well, then she suddenly decided to return to Dawson. Poor Nelly! She's in a highly nervous state. It would have done her good to be at Dominion Creek with you for a while. You know, they've caught George O'Brien, the most vicious of the two murderers. They're now combing the countryside for Thomas Graves, the other criminal."

"A murderer at large?" I asked in shocked alarm, for our cabin was quite isolated and the thought of a desperate criminal in the vicinity was terrifying.

"Oh I guess you needn't fear," replied Max. ' It's thought that Graves went up the Yukon towards Skagway. But the alarm has been spread in all directions. Everyone is saying the murder of Fred Clayson and his two companions is the most fiendish crime ever committed in the North!"

"You don't mean Fred Clayson was murdered?" I exclaimed in horrified astonishment. "Not that fine young man from Skagway?"

"Yes, it's true," said Max sympathetically, "and such a nice chap he was. Nelly is now saying she wishes she'd never met Fred Clayson on the Rosalie, coming North, eight months ago. Maybe, then, this awful thing wouldn't have happened!"

Immediately, my thoughts flashed back to the ocean voyage from Tacoma to Skagway on the freighter Rosalie, where I had first met Fred Clayson and Nelly Daly—she, coming alone, to meet her mother, Mrs. Daly, who owned a cafe on Third Street in Dawson, Clemy and I, to meet Edward.

Like a flash I could see the crowds of eager would-be miners on the Rosalie's crowded decks, their equipment piled high, could hear the excited talk of gold, gold, and see the mixed assortment of passengers milling about. Also, I could see Clemy, my little son, running back and forth from the deck to the engine room, and could see his perspiring little face as he threw off his blue reefer-coat and red stocking cap.

Also, I could hear the rowdy laughter of the stampeders as they made jokes and teased Clemy, especially when he became excited over a whale spouting in the distance. I could hear, once more, the sweet-toned voice of a young woman in a deckchair nearby who intervened, rescuing Clemy from the uncouth glee of the men. She was Nelly Daly from Tacoma, a fair-skinned, pretty, blue-eyed blonde-brownette, a girl of winning personality and unusual charm. She only appeared to be about nineteen.

"Mrs. Lung, it seems that Nelly meeting Fred Clayson on her way North turned out to be a tragic thing!" said Max Lange, breaking into

"The little preacher," Velma D. Lung, second from left, at the Dominion Creek roadhouse, after Sunday services. Clemy, second from right. Ed Lung, third from right.

Salvation Army people at Dawson City, 1898.

Nelly Daly with a malemute puppy, Dawson, 1899.

Mounted Police officials, July 1900. Superintendent of Mounted Police Z. T. Woods is second from left; Dr. A. Thompson is first, right. Both figured prominently in the Fred Clayson case.

THREE MEN IN A CASKET OF ICE

my flash-back reverie. "But I guess it was pure fate!" he added, as he slowly sipped his cup of coffee.

"Yes," I agreed, "it must have been, but why, why?"

Again, my thoughts flashed to the Rosalie which Dr. Misner of Tacoma had advised me to take. I recalled how I had hurried to get the doctor's advice right after I had received an urgent letter from Edward in early August of 1899, begging Clemy and me to come to Dawson.

Yes, once more, I was chatting with Nelly Daly on the steamer, and a short distance away sat two very attractive young people, whom I later learned were Fred Clayson and his lovely sister, Anne. Anne had a book and was reading aloud. From where I sat I could plainly see the name on the cover, "David Harum," printed in big gold letters! I could also see that, although the book was a best seller, the tall handsome brother, Fred Clayson, wasn't concentrating on the story, for I noticed him casting his laughing blue eyes engagingly in our direction, obviously smiling straight at Nelly Daly!

Of course she pretended not to notice, but it wasn't many minutes before he made an excuse to come over to pick up a bit of sewing which Nelly had somehow dropped! It was a gallant gesture—a charming way to get acquainted with Nelly, I thought.

From that time on the two were pretty much together, although the sister did succeed several times in coaxing her handsome brother to listen to David Harum. But, I rather doubted that Clayson could have given a clear synopsis of what he'd heard.

As we neared the end of our voyage most of us were better acquainted and knew a little bit concerning the circumstances surrounding each one on this freighter headed North. It proved that Fred Clayson and Anne were returning to Skagway after a fine vacation in Seattle, and a very profitable buying trip for their general merchandise store in which, it seemed, their entire family was engaged.

When the Rosalie docked at Skagway I recalled how Fred and Anne had gone hurriedly down the gangplank to meet a happy group of good-looking people gathered there to greet them, including their mother and other members of the family. I recalled, too, how Fred and Anne had told us goodbye, saying they hoped we'd all meet again sometime! How meloncholy Nelly had seemed after that last farewell!

Yes, the whole trip flashed back in great detail. Nelly had been with Clemy and me all the way to Dawson and we had become good friends.

"Ah yes, poor Nelly feels dreadful about Fred Clayson!" (Max Lange's voice jerked me back.) "But, she is still very young, and in time will get over it—I think!"

"Please, please, Max," I implored, "tell me all that happened! I haven't laid eyes on Nelly, nor heard from her since that last day we said goodbye in Dawson."

"Well, if you want the full story, here it is. First, Nelly's version," said Max, "then what I've heard myself."

"A few weeks after Nelly arrived in Dawson, she got a job at the Washington Mercantile Company on King Street, as clerk and bookkeeper. Then, one day not long after that, she looked up from her books at the tinkle of the bell over the door, and to her surprise, saw Fred Clayson, grinning down at her with his engaging smile.

" 'Why, Fred Clayson! I never expected to see you in Dawson,' Nelly told him. " 'How did you ever manage to get here before the big freeze, and so late in the season?' "

" 'Oh,' Clayson laughed, obviously pleased with his surprise visit, 'I brought a scow down the Yukon loaded with food and merchandise. Thought you people in Dawson would welcome me and my stuff! My folks urged me to wait until spring, but I couldn't contain myself. They predicted a hazardous trip through the anchor-ice, because, after all, it is October! But, here I am, safe and sound, although we did have a wild ride, and in places some pretty close calls. I didn't come alone, though. Have another fellow with me and we brought bicycles on which to travel around later.

" 'Nelly,' Clayson told her, 'while I'm in Dawson, let's get better acquainted.'

"Well, to make a long story short, Fred and Nelly did get better acquainted. He disposed of all of his merchandise and stayed around the vicinity of Dawson until the middle of December. Then, he told Nelly and other friends that he had to be heading back to Skagway—back up the Yukon. Everybody knew he would be carrying a great deal of gold and bank drafts of large denominations. But that didn't worry him. He said he'd make the trip safely and would return in the spring.

"My! My! How very significant that remark has proven to be! Yes, Fred Clayson has returned to Dawson, but as a ghastly corpse, a *bullet hole in his head and one in his side* and with mouldering features!"

"Oh, merciful heavens! How dreadful, how very dreadful!" I

shivered, feeling ill, and ready to swoon. "But please, Max, I'll be all right. Tell me all that happened."

"Well, the 17th day of December—the day Fred Clayson and Lynne Relfe, his companion, age twenty-five, a gold weigher of the Monte Carlo Casino, left Dawson—it was very cold, but they said they didn't mind. They were warmly clad. Said they could make good time on the smooth ice of the river on their bikes. (A very novel way to travel.) And, too, they expected to stay at roadhouses all along the Yukon. Fred said he'd write, and Nelly should hear from him soon after Christmas.

"Time went on—Christmas and the big snowstorms and heavy freeze. There was absolutely no word from Clayson. Even after the calendar said, 'the middle of January'— still there was no message! Then, suddenly, the Mounted Police began checking, for word had come down the Yukon from Minto that three men, Clayson, Relfe, and another fellow named Olson, a young telegraph operator, had all mysteriously disappeared on Christmas Day. They had vanished somewhere between the little settlement of Minto and Hootchikoo. (Hootchikoo is a tiny outpost fifteen miles above Minto where is located a Mounted Police barracks. A Corporal Ryan is in charge of the telegraph station there, and he's also in charge of a group of woodchoppers.) Well, it seems that on December 23rd Corporal Ryan sent Olson downriver to repair a very sudden break in the telegraph wires near Minto.

"But before starting out, Olson had promised to get back to Hootchikoo by Christmas night, as the woodchoppers and Corporal Ryan had planned a dinner-celebration.

"Now, when Olson didn't show up at Hootchikoo by Christmas night, Ryan put it down as just one of those things. No doubt Ole had changed his mind and had stayed over Christmas at the very comfortable Minto Roadhouse, run by Captain and Mrs. Fussel.

"But two days later, Corporal Ryan faced a very stern, fellow Mounted Policeman, a Constable Bacon, who was looking for Olson, as he desperately needed him to repair fresh breaks in the telegraph wires farther upriver, not far from the Five Fingers Police Barracks. "When Bacon heard that Olson had not come back to Hootchikoo, he was worried because Olson, while making repairs on the lines near Minto on December 24th had tapped out a message to a Mountie at Five Fingers stating that he would definitely be at Hootchikoo Christmas night.

Since there had been no further word from Olson, Bacon felt sure that Olson had met with serious mishap, as the telegraph operator was known to be extremely dependable!

"Now, Corporal Ryan was truly alarmed! Quickly he set off down-river towards Minto. He had only covered a few miles when he met several miners coming up the Yukon. Ryan questioned them and learned that they had seen Olson the night before Christmas at the Minto Roadhouse, and that he was in the company of two very congenial fellows who were traveling to Skagway, a Fred Clayson and Lynn Relfe. These miners had even overheard Ole Olson invite Clayson and Relfe to a special Hootchikoo Christmas dinner and heard them accept the invitation. The plan was to leave the roadhouse very early Christmas morning.

"Of course, this information was very bad news, and it confirmed Ryan's growing fears. Now, he knew he'd have to make a very careful search of the route above Minto. It was over three days since any of the men had been seen!

"Well, of course, Ryan knew it was going to be a difficult search. He was on snowshoes, but by watching the trail closely he came to a spot, about six and a half miles above Minto (up the Yukon) where he saw faint sled-tracks leading off the ice of the river. He followed these tracks for about 700 yards, through brush and thick timber and then he came to a well-concealed, hidden tent. It was set up on a log foundation and Ryan soon discovered that it was full of all kinds of valuable equipment—a stove, an axe, and many other useful tools; also a good supply of canned goods. Most amazing of all was a Winchester 40-82 calibre, an 1866 model, showing that whoever had camped there had certainly left in a hurry!

"Now Ryan felt sure that this tent, in some way, had a real bearing on the mysterious disappearance of Olson and his two companions.

"He left everything intact and hurried by dogteam to the Five Fingers Police Barracks so that he could get an urgent telegraph message through from there to Tagish Post, to Captain A. Pennycuick (known as 'the Pinkerton' of the Yukon).

"When Pennycuick arrived at Hootchikoo, he informed Corporal Ryan that a confidential report had come from Skagway that Fred Clayson had been on the Secret Vigilante Committee which had broken up and driven out the powerful Soapy Smith gang from Skagway during mid-summer of '98. He also said there were people who were suggesting that if Clayson had disappeared, it could have been a kidnap act of revenge. Pennycuick said that this might be possible too.

"When he examined the deserted tent, he then decided it was the hideout of George O'Brien, the notorious sneak thief, who had been released from the Dawson jail just a few days before Clayson and Lynne Relfe left town. Now it had come to light that O'Brien had been seen with a companion in the area of Minto House the 19th of December. The day following, the Arctic Express Company's storage cabins on the river bank had been robbed of a number of things, including a tent and canned goods.

"Pennycuick was sure now, that the tent had been O'Brien's hiding place because O'Brien's stove was there. He was sure of this because of a telltale mark, resembling a figure-eight which, by mistake, had been punched in the handle of the damper of the stove by C. J. Apple, the tinsmith at Dawson. O'Brien had purchased the stove in Dawson right after coming out of jail.

"Now, the chase was on in real earnest. From that moment on, O'Brien was Number One Fugitive of the Yukon! Then, the police decided that Thomas Graves, the dreaded cache-robber, was the Number Two Fugitive, for he was the man who had been seen with George O'Brien the day before those express robberies!

"Right away all villages and trading posts were alerted, also, a number of Indian scouts as far downriver as Forty Mile. Twenty-two Mounties on the Yukon went into action. But Pennycuick felt almost sure that the two criminals had fled up the river to escape the country. He sent a swift messenger to the Five Fingers telegraph station to get an urgent message through to Lake Tagish Military Post to advise them to arrest O'Brien and Graves and hold them on robbery charges should they come that route.

"Word flashed back immediately from Superintendent of Mounted Police, Zachery T. Woods of Lake Tagish Post, that they had already detained O'Brien. O'Brien had been observed traveling alone and acting mighty queer. Something about him had aroused sharp-eyed Constable Dickson's suspicions. He had spotted the end of a Mountie's blanket sticking out from a pack on O'Brien's sled. So the Mountie had had an excuse to hold O'Brien for questioning. But immediately O'Brien produced a note signed by a prison guard at Dawson, stating he was giving

O'Brien the blanket. Woods was just about to free O'Brien when Pennycuick's message arrived. It was then the Mounties searched O'Brien and found two very small pistols on him. Then they searched every inch of his sled, even the runners, and on them found traces of blood. They questioned O'Brien but he swore the blood was from animals which he had shot for food. It was after finding that blood that the Mounties tore every inch of the sled apart and found considerable amounts of gold hidden in the hollow handlebars of the sled.

"They also discovered that O'Brien was carrying on his person a great deal of cash and bank drafts of high denominations. Then, too, he had a large diamond ring which looked like the one Clayson was wearing when he left Dawson. Also, there were many small personal items which the police were sure had belonged to Lynne Relfe and Ole Olson.

"Of course they questioned O'Brien about these valuables, especially the diamond ring, but O'Brien wouldn't say where he had gotten it, or any of the other things. Angrily, he denied any knowledge of the Clayson party, nor would he admit camping with Thomas Graves in the tent near Minto, or of any warehouse thefts.

"From the sled runners, the police carefully removed the frozen blood and sent it posthaste to McGill University at Montreal to be analyzed by the chemists. A heavy guard was then placed around O'Brien's cell to make sure he couldn't escape.

"Now, the police, with eagle eyes, watched all trails for Thomas Graves. With fading hope that any of the three fine young men could still be alive, they kept sending out their descriptions, but there was no response. Apparently, no one had seen the men alive after they had left the Minto Roadhouse Christmas morning.

"In the meantime Pennycuick and the Mounties kept up an intensive search centered around that deserted tent. It was a difficult search handicapped by snow and freezing weather, but from the tent they fanned out, examining everything within a mile for clues. Finally, after many days, they uncovered, under the snow, and not far from the tent, the remains of what had been a huge rubbish fire, and in the ashes they found bits of charred men's clothing. Also, they dug up buttons, belt buckles, keys and parts of a broken bottle which had once contained electric oil for bicycles. In the ashes they found a pearl-handled pocket-knife which had once been Clayson's, and also a medicine bottle which had been his.

"The Mounties were now certain that Clayson and his two friends had met death in the close vicinity. Pennycuick was determined to locate the bodies. Like bloodhounds, they searched the fifteen-mile zone along the Yukon between Hootchikoo and Minto House.

"Everyone in that area was questioned. Finally, someone came forward and reported that right after Christmas two men who had been hauling freight up the Yukon had mentioned, in passing, that they had seen three pools of frozen blood back in among the bushes, near a small sidepath, quite close to the Yukon River. This report was indefinite, with no real location to go by, except that the men had said it was in the stretch between Minto House and Hootchikoo. The unidentified freighters had remarked that perhaps the blood was from wounded animals.

"With only this vague information to go by, the police began checking all small trails and paths which are always near a main route of travel. Immediately, their attention was focused on a short cutoff trail leading away from the main Yukon River route. This trail began about six miles above Minto. It was sometimes called the 'Pork Trail,' and was only about a mile long, but travelers could save considerable time by taking it.

"While looking over the area, the police found a place where someone had recently gone to a great deal of trouble to cut down a number of small trees at a bend in the river, just about 950 feet south of the entrance to the Pork Trail.

"Immediately, Pennycuick was curious and puzzled. Then he stood behind a bush at the south edge of the clearing and looked north, down the Yukon, towards Minto. Ah, yes, that *was* it! As plain as day!

"Anyone concealed where he was could easily see travelers coming up the Yukon; he could watch every move they made, and should they choose the Pork Trail cutoff—well, this same man in hiding could then quickly rush through the bushes to the Pork Trail, at a spot where it swings close to the Yukon. He could easily make it in time to conceal himself there in the bushes, and be ready to pounce on his victims! Then, too, if he had field glasses, which the police discovered O'Brien had bought shortly before leaving Dawson, he could see just who had decided to come up that trail!

*Tom Hebert of Dawson, with his brother, were the men hauling freight, it was later discovered.

"Now Pennycuick was sure the three young men had been waylaid and killed near this spot and that the pools of frozen blood, mentioned by the freighters, were human and belonged to young Clayson and his two companions.

"After many weeks of search in the area, sure enough, they found the three pools of frozen blood under several layers of snow and about two hundred feet back from the river, just as Pennycuick had figured. Close to the blood was a white linen handkerchief with the initial 'C,' It was mute testimony that Clayson had been there and one of the pools of blood was his!

"So now, as the Mounties reconstruct the story: Clayson, Relfe and Olson took the Pork Trail. It would shorten their trip.

"When they were going along, suddenly O'Brien stepped out of the bushes in front of them, and the Clayson party found themselves looking into the barrel of his rifle! 'Hold up!' They must have cried. Then, no doubt they looked hastily back over their shoulders to see if there was any escape only to discover that Thomas Graves, the other bandit, had them covered from the rear. Well, of course, Clayson and his friends must have realized they were hopelessly trapped!

"No one knows exactly what happened, but the police picture it this way: Held at gun's point, the three men were marched along the Pork Trail for just a short distance, then they were ordered to step aside onto a much smaller footpath which turns toward the river through thick bushes. Probably without any warning, O'Brien and Graves opened fire, shooting the three men down in cold blood.

"The poor fellows put up a desperate battle! The police say there is still evidence of it in the trampled bushes! They have found bullet holes in the trees and some flattened out in the ground, directly under the frozen blood. Of course, Pennycuick took samples of the three kinds of blood to send to the experts at McGill University, just as Superintendent Woods at Tagish Post had done when he found the blood on O'Brien's sled runners.

"Well, to go on with the tale: Now that the police had located the exact scene of the crime, it was their grim job to find the bodies. They always went back to a certain airhole in the ice as it showed evidence of having been chopped out by an axe. Certainly the murderers had had one, for there it was in the hidden tent. Also, there was the rifle that had fired some of those bullets.

"The police dragged the river, through the airhole and others too, which they made in the ice. They kept it up many days. They even brought dynamite and carefully blasted out sections of ice. Then, they used a waterglass to survey the bottom of the river, but they found absolutely nothing!

"Bill Clayson, Fred's brother, came from Skagway with a long line of grappling hooks, and after dragging the river many times, at different points, he finally gave up the work as futile.

"Of course, Anne Clayson and the family were broken-hearted. They hired Private Detective Walsh of Skagway to help solve the case. Then the family offered a large reward for Fred's body.

"O'Brien, in the meantime, had been brought to Dawson. He became angry when told that a report had come from Montreal saying the blood samples on the runners of his sled and those of the three pools of frozen blood found in the bushes near the Pork Trail, were human and matched. Then, he grew silent. Finally, he said, 'Aw, you can't convict a man without the real evidence—the bodies!'

" 'We'll find them,' the police told him sternly.

"Yes, scores of people were watching when the Yukon ice began thawing recently," said Max.

"And," he continued, as he handed me the Dawson News, "it seems that even though he was dead and couldn't speak, Fred tried to help the police wwhen the ice started going out. Anyway, he rose part way out of the Yukon to condemn O'Brien.

"When the ice broke up, Clayson's body was seen in shallow water just a short distance above Ft. Selkirk.

"One hand protruded above water and pointed upriver towards Minto. John Kehoe and his partner saw the 'ghastly hand' as they were passing in a rowboat. The very next day Relfe and Olson were found floating in the Yukon, not very far from where Clayson's body was lodged on the shallow sand bar. Yes, at last the ice had given up the three men!"

"Oh, it's too terrible to think about!" I shuddered. "Poor Nelly, and poor Anne Clayson and her family, and the families of the other men too. But Max! I'm concerned more than ever about Thomas Graves still being at large."

"Well," said Max a little nervously, as he gathered up his mailbag, "if I know these Mounties they'll find him too. The whole territory is up in arms, and so are the authorities on the American side of Alaska."

After the mailman had gone, I bolted the cabin door and sat pondering over the tragedy. It was too awful to contemplate—Clayson's life and the others wantonly snuffed out—just for gold!

And if the three young men had just accepted Captain and Mrs. Fussel's Christmas dinner invitation at Minto House (as I later found out, they had been urged to), they might have escaped that terrible fate on the cutoff trail. But who really knows?

For many, many days the Mounties searched the trails, checking and re-checking all deserted mines and cabins. Their presence was comforting. We could see the flash of brass buttons on scarlet coats when they would go galloping past our cabin.

But Thomas Graves simply couldn't be found any place in the Territory. It was as though the earth had opened and swallowed him up!

But, at last news came by mid-summer that a horribly water-worn body had been pulled out of the Yukon by the Mounties at Island Post (below Dawson). Then word came that the dreadfully disintegrated body had been identified as Thomas Graves.

While this was shuddering news, still it was also good news! Now, once more we could roam the hills and walk the trails and take that long desired trip to Dawson without fear. A spirit of trust and peace had been once more restored to the Yukon.

"It is very apparent," said the Mounties, "that this man (whom we recently pulled from the river) died from drowning, because there isn't a single bullet hole on him.

"Did you kill your criminal partner as well as murder Clayson, Relfe and Olson?" the police kept asking O'Brien in an effort to make him confess at the jail in Dawson.

"Well, you can just be sure that I fixed it so that no one will ever give me away! That's the way to be!" O'Brien snarled at the police when the fourth body was discovered.

Later, a friend of Ed's, Jack Kline, a well-known merchant and freighter of Dawson, told Edward and me with deep emotion shaking his voice:

"If O'Brien and Graves hadn't waylaid the Clayson group, it would have been me. I'm sure of it! You see, I was coming just two hours behind the ill-fated Clayson trio. I was traveling alone and was mushing a dog-team. My sled was loaded with a valuable shipment of gold. I,

The beginning of spring break-up on the Yukon River, usually around the first of April.

"Little Sourdough," Clemy, with malemute pups. Claim 2-B Below Lower Discovery, Dominion Creek, 1900.

Jefet Lindeberg with a pan full of gold from his famous "Million Dollar a Month" claim on Anvil Creek in the Nome District. It was a rich Discovery Claim.

Thousands of stampeders camped on the beach at Nome in July, 1900, before the devastating September storm. Afterwards, epidemics of disease, plunder and murder were rampant. (Snake River at upper left.)

too, chose the Pork Trail cutoff. Yes," he added, with tears in his eyes, "and I had a sick wife waiting for me in Seattle."

A few days after Clayson's body was found, Nelly Daly suddenly decided to leave the Klondike on the Steamer Syble, its first trip for the season, upriver. It wasn't until the steamer was well out in midstream that Nelly discovered, to her sorrow, that there was a black casket aboard containing the pitiful remains of Fred Clayson!

All of the way up the Yukon, never could she forget that black casket in the baggage room! Finally, one of her friends tried to console her by saying, "Never mind, Nelly, when you reach Skagway and board the steamer for home, you'll begin to forget this awful episode!"

But when Nelly reached Skagway she learned that after a very brief funeral service, which most of the passengers wished to attend, Fred Clayson was scheduled to go to Seattle on the freighter Rosalie!

Nellie's ticket also called for the Rosalie! It called for a certain cabin often used as the bridal suite! What diabolical humor was this? The two tickets were identical— Clayson going from Seattle by train to his former home in Portland for burial, she, also going by train to the same city to visit relatives.

When Nelly saw that fate* was still grimly weaving their paths together, she could no longer endure the cruel, unusual chain of events. Hastily, she cancelled her reservation and let Clayson go on ahead of her. Finally, she got a ticket on the old steamer Alki.

After Nelly left Dawson her friends wondered if she would ever care to return to the Klondike. If not, she certainly had good reason. However, before very long, the call of the North became strong enough to draw her back to the City of Gold. (Always, while in the North she was called Nelly, which was her nickname. Her true, given name was Mary.)

"Why, oh why, did it have to happen?" Nelly had wistfully asked, before she left Dawson.

"What price gold?" the spirits of the three men must whisper to the icy winds as they swirl around that tragic place near Minto, on the Yukon!

---

*"It was a planned and premeditated crime—thought up while George O'Brien was serving his year's term at Dawson," so say the police records at Dawson and Ottawa.

Kid West, the petty thief, who had also been in the Dawson prison at the time prior to the crime, confessed later that O'Brien formulated the plan and method of robbery while still in his cell. He said O'Brien had tried to persuade him (Kid West) to go into partnership. O'Brien had outlined just how to stage the holdups on the winter trail; then, how to cleverly dispose of the bodies. He had tempted Kid West, reminding him how easy it would be "to get rich quick." He had pointed out that all winter long there would be great quantities of gold hauled Outside by miners, traders, and travelers.

"We will ambush them, rob them, and put their bodies in the ice," he had told the Kid. "The Yukon will do the rest. Then we'll divide up the spoils and skip the country."

It was proven, however, that Kid West had had nothing to do with this crime as he was in the States in the Walla Walla penitentiary when it was committed. However, the Kid was brought back to Dawson to testify at O'Brien's trial which began in early summer of 1901.

At the most sensational murder trial ever held in Dawson's history, when the courtroom was packjammed to the doors with miners and others, Kid West, who was brought in as a main witness, wept when he was forced to view some of the documentary evidence used to convict O'Brien. And when he had to see the gruesome pictures of O'Brien's victims, he cried out: "No, No, No! I'm not a murderer!"

"'No, you're not a murderer," retorted the prosecuting attorney, "but you could have stopped this sickening, shocking, cold-blooded, premeditated crime—this crime which will forever be a dark blot on Yukon history!"

Four hundred carefully prepared, documented pieces of evidence were used at this trial. They were the most minute and conclusive circumstantial evidence ever assembled by the Mounted Police in Yukon Territory to convict a murderer. It cost the Canadian Government $150,000 to get all of the evidence.

All through the trial O'Brien sat with sealed lips—with a certain set bravado and nonchalance which infuriated the people in the courtroom. Prosecutor for The Crown was Attorney S. C. Wade. O'Brien's defense attorneys were Donaghy and Bleeker. Of course, their plea for their client was that all of the evidence was purely circumstantial. But all of this tremendous evidence was so overwhelming that there was absolutely no doubt of O'Brien's guilt in anyone's mind. So, on June 10, 1901, Judge Dugas passed sentence and George O'Brien was executed at 8:30 a.m. on August 23, 1901. To the very end he appeared to be unremorseful, seemingly more concerned about the quality and quantity of his food. (O'Brien was hanged at the Police Barracks in Dawson.)

Following the execution it was revealed that George O'Brien had shown blood mania tendencies way back in England in the 1880's. He had served a 7-year prison term for intent to kill and had been in the Dartmoor prison at Stafford, England. When he had been released in 1894, he had been given a ticket of leave to get out of England. When he was next heard from, he had turned up in Dawson, having come in with the stampeders of 1898.

For some years after O'Brien's execution, and as though his evil, rebellious spirit was still stalking the land taking sadistic delight in heckling the police, persistent rumors of Thomas Graves still being alive were reported from different parts of the Yukon. First, reports came from Whitehorse, next from Forty Mile, then from St. Michael on Bering Sea, and last, from the fabulous new gold boom town of Nome. But, of course, they all proved false!

In Yukon Territory today, George O'Brien and Thomas Graves are still remembered with extreme loathing and horror, and in the fading glory of Dawson and Skagway, Fred Clayson and the two other fine young men are still remembered with sorrow and sympathy.

It is noteworthy to add that the Clayson murder case was conducted and carried out to its end in the best tradition of the famous Northwest Mounted Police!

The two doctors who performed the autopsies on Fred Clayson, Lynne Relfe and Ole Olson and also on Thomas Graves, were W. E. Thompson and H. H. Hurdman—both of Dawson.

Chapter 16

RAINBOW-GOLD, FRENCHIE AND NELLY

In North country, around the first of March, the mercury begins its slow upward crawl and, almost simultaneously, the sun which has sulked below the horizon all winter long sends its first golden rays horizontally across the frozen land, hitting the highest mountain peaks first.

Each day it was exciting to speculate where the sun's rays would next strike. Down in the valley, how we craved warmth and sunlight! Then, came that momentous day when the sun's brightness reached us, almost searching us out, accompanied by thaws and the gentle spring rains, followed by beautiful rainbows spanning our valley.

Now, almost every day, through my cabin window, I could see little Clemy searching, searching on the hills for the exciting pot of gold. His father had told him there was sure to be gold up there, a pot of it, because the rainbows always seemed to bend down and touch our hillside and linger until the rains were over.

Of course, during all spring showers, Clemy eagerly watched the rainbows, and then one day we marked off a likely spot with stakes. This would be his "Rainbow Claim" and here he would find the ancient Channel of Gold!

Through my cabin window I could watch Clemy with his dog Nelly usually beside him, digging, digging into the hill. Ed had helped Clemy set up a small sluice-box, patterned exactly like the real ones. The tiny spring flowing down the hill from melting snows helped Clemy sluice his pay-dirt. It was a perfect setup for a little miner.

After several weeks of "mining operations" Clemy's pile of pay-dirt grew until it was a small mound and when he wasn't present Ed slipped some real pay-dirt into the claim.

Late one day Clemy came rushing home from his mining operations tired and wet. He had been guiding water through his tiny sluice box, and washing the pay-dirt on the small riffles. Triumphantly, he held up a miner's panful of black sand.

"Oh Mother! Look, look!" he cried in excitement, "Look at the specks of yellow gold! I'm rich! It's rainbow gold, yes, real rainbow gold!"

That evening as I was preparing supper, Clemy's pan of black sand held a prominent spot on the stove while he hovered near, stirring the damp mixture with a big spoon.

"Sure," exclaimed Ed, who had come home early to watch Clemy's efforts. "Sure, little son, you've really struck it rich! Just look at that kettle of gold! Why, there're lots of tiny yellow nuggets showing up! Who knows, maybe you've hit the big treasure that we're all looking so hard for—the big pot o' gold!"

"Oh! How much do ya' think I'm gonna get to the pan?" asked Clemy eagerly, as he stirred his mixture vigorously, trembling with happy anticipation.

"Oh about a dollar's worth," said Ed slowly, "but we really can't tell until we've drawn off all the black sand with a magnet, and then carefully blown away all remaining particles of black dust."

Our supper waited and grew cold that night, but I didn't mind. It was Clemy's long-to-be-remembered first clean-up, a child's dazzling dream of wealth and achievement.

"Yes, you bet," said Ed as he carefully dropped the small particles of gold onto the delicate scales and weighed them. "Yes, Clemy, you have here exactly a dollar's worth. Keep it up, son, you'll soon have a little poke full of this bright yellow stuff! Now you're a real miner—just like Joe and me and all the rest of the old Sourdoughs."

Clemy's enthusiasm reached the stars. At last he belonged to the Sourdough fraternity, and not only that, he was learning the process of real gold mining and also an appreciation of the hard work connected with it. And, best of all, he was contented!

"Next time we go to Dawson, little man, you should buy something you really want with that hard-earned gold," his father told him one day. "But always remember this, Clem, that if you take good care of what the earth yields, the earth will always take care of you. It seems to be a natural law."

* * *

A likeable Frenchman who often got his English slightly confused and who lived on a rich claim on Upper Dominion near Little Quebec, took great pride in his expensive horses. One day he visited us. Right away he began bragging in his pleasing French accent about the speed of his horses. One, especially, he was proud of and he had just ridden her over to our claim on this particular day.

"Look eet her," he said admiringly, "I tell you she is zee one, fine leedle race horse! She go to Dawseen in one, two, three ah-weres—and if she no go in one, two, three ah-weres—I—geeve you to her!"

"Wow, let's hope she makes it!" chuckled one of the miners.

This same Frenchman liked to hunt rabbits with his prize dogs. In summer the rabbits took on a dark brown coat which blended with the bushes, but in winter they turned pure white so that they were almost impossible to detect in the snow.

However, the dogs could usually find them and would always give wild chase. In their terrible fright, the poor rabbits would run and jump, making excellent targets for the Frenchman. In telling of his exciting rabbit-hunting episodes the Frenchman would boast:

"I tell you, folks, I all-wees get one, two, three rabeets every day," and then there would be a long pause, "—and sometimes—one!"

Well, of course everybody would laugh in amusement. Frenchie never seemed to catch on why the men were so amused at his stories. Part of it was that everyone liked to hear his pleasing accent and they loved the way he told the hunting stories, too, even though they recognized that he was an incurable bragger. He had the reputation of starting his story with the truth, then building up with colorful imaginary embellishments and, at the very end, retreating again to the absolute truth.

But one day he did prove that he was an expert hunter. He brought Edward at least a dozen rabbits and they were supposed to be a surprise for me. When I opened the door to the food cache there they were, hanging from the ceiling by their hind legs—stark white, glassy eyed, and frozen stiff! I had never eaten rabbit and the thought of doing so now made me ill, even though I was very hungry for fresh meat. I only consented to cook the poor things if I wasn't expected to eat them.

If I knew we were going to have company I always tried to have cake, which I made with powdered dried eggs and other necessary ingredients. However, my cakes were usually badly flaked with the dried egg, no matter how many hours I soaked them or how hard I beat them. But, lumpy or not, the men seemed to think the cakes were wonderful! Sometimes, I made a special filling of thickened Eagle Brand condensed milk, and that made the cake extra fine, they thought.

Well, I never began making a cake that I didn't have very good reason to think of Nelly, Clemy's dog. In fact, I always tried to check on her whereabouts as part of the cake-making procedure. It was sad but true, Nelly was becoming an incurable thief and certainly had to be watched!

And it was uncanny the way she seemed to know just when I was about to make one of my cakes! She would either sneak into the cabin slightly ahead of time and crawl under the bed and lie in wait, or else keep close watch outside from some hidden, secluded spot which she alone knew.

One day I put a dozen granulated eggs to soak in a bowl for a cake and left the bowl on the table. I planned to stir up my cake in late afternoon, as I was expecting company that evening. Then, I walked to the mine to see Edward about something. Before leaving, I made sure Nelly wasn't in the cabin and as I went out I latched the door good and tight!

Evidently Nelly had been watching from her favorite haunt, for as as soon as I was out of sight, she proceeded to paw at the latch until she had swung the door open. Later, when I returned there she was in the yard with my cake-bowl between her paws, vigorously lapping up the very last drops of the foamy egg-mixture. When she became aware of my presence she raised her head, her mouth still dripping with egg.

"Nelly!" I cried, "You bad foxy thief! You stole my eggs!" Nelly didn't move an inch. She just crouched there looking defiant, a wolfish expression written all over her face which plainly said, "Just give me another chance and I'll do it again! I mean to have all the goodies I can get!"

Well, even tho' I punished her this time and many times afterwards, I knew that she would never stop stealing. She had acquired a taste for different kinds of food and was determined to have them. It was too bad because it spoiled her value. She was now an incurable thief, a real catastrophe for us and to the neighborhood. Everybody began calling her "Long Nose Snoopy Nelly," and even though she was Clemy's loving pet, her habit of stealing valuable food was a constant problem. She was becoming almost too expensive to keep. For, in less than a year, she had eaten a great deal of our precious food, and some of our neighbors' too, costing us many ounces of gold!

Chapter 17

GREAT NOME STAMPEDE

One winter-like day, late in the fall of 1900, Edward came rushing to the cabin with an astonishing announcement.

"Vel, there's been some mighty exciting news!" he exclaimed, "Just heard it from a passing fellow on the trail. Said there's been a gold stampede in Dawson. If I thought there was any chance to stake a claim, I'd hurry off to town.

"Yes, you bet I knew there was gold in town," continued Ed, "because Stacey and I saw tiny glints of it along the river when we were camped on the sand bar in 1897. We asked if we could stake, but the Mounties wouldn't permit it, either there or up in town. Seems now they've changed their minds. Wish someone would come from Dawson so we could get full particulars. No doubt every inch of Dawson is now staked!"

Suddenly, our ears caught the merry jingle of sleigh bells. "Why, that's Max Lange, the mail carrier," exclaimed Ed eagerly. Presently, there was a knock at our cabin door. "Max, you're just in time for lunch," said Ed, as he flung open the door.

"Please do come in," I smiled, "We have wild blueberry pie. Ella McGillacuddy sent the frozen berries from the roadhouse and we're glad to share our pie with you."

"Who could refuse such a tempting treat?" said Max, as he knocked the snow from his boots. "But I already knew about the pie," he laughed, "I met little Clem running up the trail with Nelly. First thing

*Bear Creek nuggets were at first the envy of the Klondike miners because these nuggets were a very bright yellow. Eldorado miners often traded their nuggets for the Bear Creek ones. Later, it was learned that the Bear Creek nuggets had a copper mixture.

he told me was about the pie, so I hurried to the cabin hoping you'd invite me in. And by the way," he added, as he seated himself, "Clem sent word that he'd be back in a few minutes for his pie. He was rolling snowballs. Had already placed a snow man at the head of the trail. You should see it! It looks almost like a real miner perched there. And," laughed Max, "I'm sure little Clem has his father's best cap on that snow man!"

"Oh, it hardly matters!" exclaimed Ed, half impatiently, and with unconcealed eagerness to press a question, "Max, please, tell us about the Dawson stampede."

"Well, folks, there was a lot of excitement in Dawson yesterday! I've never seen such a wild, perspiring lot of overheated people. They came running from all directions, driving stakes in every vacant lot, even in little open spaces between cabins. Just anyplace where they could squeeze in—then running like crazy to the Recorder's office! Why Dawson hasn't seen that much commotion for over a year! But imagine it! Right IN Dawson this time!"

"What touched the whole thing off?" asked Ed eagerly, leaning forward with glistening eyes.

"Well, sir," said Max, "the whole darned thing started when some fellows at the end of Third Street, kinda up on the hill, began digging a well near their cabin. They'd only gone down a few feet when all at once—whammo! They come across some real wash-gravel. They tested it and, lo and behold, there was real gold in it!* Well, the news was out quicker than a flash! I tell you it was like the big gold-rush all over again. You should have been there for the fun."

"How much are they getting to the pan?" Ed asked, with keen interest.

"Oh," laughed Max, "not much. I guess seven or eight cents, in most places. Certainly not worth the $250 each 'city prospector' has to put up as security against possible cave-in damage to adjacent buildings. But, Ed, near the waterfront behind the Alaska Commercial Company's warehouse—would you believe it—they're getting 67c to the pan! Not bad, eh?"

"By George, I'll say that's not bad!" exclaimed Ed, jumping to his

---

*In 1898 a miner accidentally spilled $300 worth of gold-dust in Louse Town. The following year it caused a cheechako stampede. Many of the greenhorns staked the area!

feet. "I'm only getting 25c to the pan. But tell me more about the Dawson stampede."

"Well," laughed Max, "it was just a flash in the pan stampede; that's all. At least so nearly everyone thinks. But the old Sourdoughs are now saying that Dawson is built over an old river bed—maybe two river beds, probably the Yukon and Klondike, or maybe it was the tail end of the Bonanza. At any rate, they say if Dawson hadn't been put where it is, probably there'd be some kinda gold field right there on the spot. And, did you know that deep under all that gravel and muck, they say there's an ancient glacier that shifts and moves a little each year? No doubt the glacier was formed millions of years ago and will remain frozen like that 'till Doomsday!"

"Say now, maybe that's why it's so blasted chilly in winter," laughed Ed. "But seriously now, the thought that Dawson could be sitting over heaps of the yellow stuff is an exciting conjecture!"

"You bet it is," agreed Max. "But now, Ed, since you're a true Sourdough do you think there's likely to be any more real big gold discoveries in the Klondike?" he asked eagerly.

"Probably not," said Ed. "I think this Dawson stampede maybe is the tapering off. But who really knows? However, I'm sure that great rewards are bound to come to hardworking mine owners and Lay-men, like myself, when we delve deeper underground.

"Oh it's difficult to describe the feverish exultation that hits a fellow when he makes a real gold strike!" exclaimed Ed with fervor. "A fellow wants to throw back his head and shout and howl to the stars. He wants to laugh and cry and get down on his knees and thank God. He wants to grab up all of that gold and hug it to him, and squeeze it tight in his hands!

"Suddenly, he's a king, a ruler of the universe. Everything is his . . . his! Everything he's ever wanted, hoped for, or dreamed about. Gold fever madness sweeps over him in a flash. It's overpowering! Then, after that, it's like a burning, consuming, hot yellow flame. Ask anyone who has ever found gold.

"But listen, while I tell you about the very last big stampede to hit the North. It took place far down the Yukon—on Bering Sea—and it was in American Alaska this time."

"Ah yes, I know about that one," sighed Max. "It was the big Nome Stampede!"

"You bet," said Ed, "and this was my situation and predicament just before it struck . . .

"A few weeks prior to the Nome Stampede, in 1899, I had signed a contract for this very mine—Claim 2-B Below Lower Discovery, issued by Paul Hebb who had the legal authority to grant it for the Canadian Bank of Commerce.

"Well, my second cleanup was quite disappointing, considering the many weeks of back-breaking work which the miners and I had put in. The pay-dirt only yielded $90! It wasn't enough to even pay meager wages. Naturally, I was mightily discouraged. But I decided to try my luck in another spot.

"I had noticed a peculiar rock standing out in midstream. It was fairly large and protruded above the water level several feet. Suddenly I got an idea. I was curious to know what lay beneath that rock, as it seemed to beckon to me in the warm June sunlight. So I went to work damming up the river just above the spot.

"When that was accomplished I was able to turn the course of the stream sufficiently so that the rock stood only in wet sand. When I pushed the rock over, I gave a shout of joy.

"Lo and behold! There was gold—almost pure gold—a pothole of it! There was coarse gold, fine gold, and nuggets galore! Man alive, I was excited! Gold seemed all over the place. It was the first pot of gold I had ever found. I scooped it all up in a bare twenty minutes—$206.60 worth! Yes, that gold-flame swept over me with a bang!

"Of course I was elated! No doubt there would be many, many more like it, and I would be rich! The date was the 21st of June, 1899. I could scarcely wait for Paul Hebb to come to Dominion Creek so that I could tell him of my good fortune.

"But next day I got some very jolting, upsetting news. To a miner who casually stopped by, I told of my exciting gold-strike. Much to my chagrin, he replied:

" 'Ed, you may not be working this claim much longer. They say in Dawson that Hebb has been let out of the bank and all his contracts go with him, and of course that means you, too!'

"Well, no one will ever know how my elated spirits dropped to bedrock. The news was like a bombshell. If this were true I knew my goose was cooked. Some other lucky fellow would get this promising Lay. News travels rapidly. I had unwisely let the cat out of the bag

GREAT NOME STAMPEDE 173

about that pothole of gold!

"Naturally, I was greatly agitated. Finally, I decided not to wait for bad news. I would go to Dawson and meet it head on. I would see Hebb and find out where I stood. Of course, it meant a two-day hike, each way. A whole week or more would be wasted. Nevertheless, I was anxious to make the journey. And so, on June 23rd, I left Dominion Creek with a pack on my back. I reached the summit of King Solomon's Dome late in the afternoon.

"As I made camp I could see dark clouds forming over the mountains and I knew we were in for a big rain sometime during the next twenty-four hours. However, the deluge held off until the following morning. Before daybreak I broke camp and then almost ran down the mountainside in order to reach Dawson before the summer storm would break. But my haste was useless. As I hurried along Hunker Creek the rain caught up with me. It was a summer storm all right, with loud crashes of thunder and vivid sheet lightning. The heavens opened and it poured buckets! Finally, I reached Dawson, drenched to the skin.

"Before I could look for Hebb it was necessary to dry off so I darted into a dance hall and stood by the big round stove warming myself, watching the dancers and listening to the music which was rather good and entertaining.

"Yes, I guess I was destined to be in Dawson on this particular day.

"Suddenly, the music stopped. Someone nearby whispered, 'Gold, Gold! Big gold stampede to Cape Nome. Hurry! Hurry down the Yukon.'

"Immediately the dance was over. You should have seen the crowd tear out of that hall!

"I ran out into the street with the rest of them. Everybody was oblivious to the rain!

"Great Scott! A big stampede to Cape Nome on Bering Sea? My God, who would have guessed it?

"Already the news was spreading through Dawson like wildfire. People were running like crazy through the streets to the stores, grabbing outfits, talking excitedly, bartering, and borrowing. Some even stealing equipment. In one short hectic hour, gold fever had swept over Dawson like a yellow flame! Fellows jumped onto any kind of small boat that would float and, in the rain, shoved off half-cocked for Cape Nome—two thousand miles away. Man! You should have seen them go, a dishevelled, wild exodus, a great motley scramble of people, worked to a high fever pitch, all with hysterical expectations. All were potential millionaires!

"But there was a little pathos, too! Of course, we on the bank who were a little thoughtful—knew, and some of them, too, I suspect—that there would be those who would never reach Nome. The Yukon can be extremely treacherous at times, and so can Bering Sea. Although it was late spring some ice was still running in the Yukon. But away those gold-bitten people went, headed for the glittering strand. As I stood watching them my little pothole of gold on Dominion Creek was all but forgotten.

"I witnessed the departure of the little steamer 'Rideout.' She was the first to go——loaded to the guards! And the huge scow she was pushing was black with people! Think of it! There were almost five-hundred gold-crazed stampeders, some in small boats, clinging to that one flotilla!

"Should I go with the next flotilla? The awful urge to join that crowd was terrifyingly strong! Should I allow that all-consuming 'yellow flame' to sweep me off to the golden shore? But I was held, half slave and half prisoner, to that pot of yellow-gold which I had so recently found on Dominion Creek. Curses! Curses and damn that gold!

"Yes, I was chained to it as a Lay-man in spite of the uncertain legalities surrounding it. And then too, I had only—just four weeks previously—mailed a letter to my dear wife, begging her and little Clemy to join me in the Klondike. I had already started to build the little log cabin!

"Well, I stayed on in Dawson a few days longer, watching others depart, still weighing all of these matters heavily in my mind. Nome! Nome! Nome! It was all people could talk or think about. Again and again I fiercely wrestled with my very soul, and all the time I kept a sharp eye out for Paul Hebb. Like a caged lion, I paced the muddy banks of the Yukon, watching scores and scores of friends and strangers depart for the most astonishing stampede to ever occur in Alaskan-American territory!

"Paul Hebb was nowhere to be found, and I had just about decided that he, too, had taken off for Nome, when I met a friend who said that Hebb was away on a business trip; said that he had gone to Gold Bottom and Sulphur Creeks, and expected to stop over at Dominion on the round trip.

"Well, I flipped a coin, and it helped me decide to take a chance and go back to Dominion Creek and wait for Hebb there. But, naturally, I was on edge. It was one of the hardest decisions of my life!

"Before I left Dawson, of course, I began to hear full details of just how the first gold at Nome had been found. Here is the story:

"Some explorers, while scouting along the coast of Bering Sea in summer of 1898, were caught in a bad storm and shipwrecked, but all managed to reach shore safely. They found they were at the mouth of the Snake River, about seventy-five miles northwest of Golovin Bay, where there is a small settlement.

"Just as a matter of curiosity these man panned for gold at the Snake River and found good colors. They were excited about their find, but decided to make their way to Golovin Bay, to report the shipwreck. At Golovin, they showed the gold specimens around to an assortment of traders and fishermen and persuaded a group to return with them to the scene of the shipwreck. These men found more gold near the mouth of the Snake River and also in several small streams nearby. Among the men were three young fellows named Jafet Lindberg*, Erick O. Lindshom and John Byrnteson.* The trio found some very big nuggets in Anvil Creek, a tributary of the Snake River. Others found gold in small creeks named Dexter, Center, Snow, Newton and Little Moonlight.

"These discoveries were made in late fall and early winter of 1898. But the exciting news didn't reach St. Michaels until early December. When the news broke there was a wild stampede from there.

" 'It's a brand new gold field; a big wonderful gold field on American Territory!' friends and acquaintances shouted as they passed the word along.

"In only a few hours everyone who had dogs and outfits was on his way from St. Michaels to the new gold field. The excitement continued through December and on into spring of '99.

"But with all of this excitement there was still a great treasure yet unknown, the fabulous deposits of loose gold in the red sands of the Cape Nome beaches which stretched for miles—in fact, for fifty miles—

---

*Jefet Lindberg, Erick O. Lindshom and John Byrnteson were destined to be called, "The fathers of the Nome District." Later, their claim was known as the "Million Dollar a Month."

along the shore.

"In Dawson, we heard several stories of how this unusual beach gold was accidentally discovered, but there is only one accepted version, and it goes like this:

"Late in May of 1899, a miner working at Little Moonlight fell ill from scurvy. He was advised to go to the beach to absorb some good sunlight and salt air, which is a well-known cure for scurvy among seagoing men. While he was recuperating on the beach, aimlessly, he began making pan-testings, using his frying pan to wash the beach sand with salt water. He had noticed a peculiar red sand* and some black sand too, and wondered about it.

"After he had gone through the panning process, suddenly his washpan revealed tiny particles of fine gold! Forgetting his scurvy he ran to other locations along the beach, trying the sand at different spots. He could hardly believe what he saw! Each testpan of sand came up with gold, and more gold!

"Well, of course, news of this tremendous and unusual discovery couldn't be kept. It traveled rapidly along the coast of Alaska and simultaneously on up the Yukon to Dawson, and to the Outside. Soon, thousands of eager, gold-hungry men were on their way from all parts of the world—all anxious for a share of the Cape's yellow treasure. There was a first, second, and third wave of stampeders from Dawson. But we in the Klondike learned that a discouraging situation had quickly developed. Many of the very first stampeders to reach Nome had gotten power of attorney which enabled them to stake numerous claims for relatives and friends, many who weren't even in the Territory.

"This same kind of abuse also took place in the early days of the Klondike gold rush, in 1896 and '97.

"Well, to get back to the great Nome excitement—while I waited anxiously for Paul Hebb—we men of the Klondike kept hearing more and more glittering tales of Cape Nome, as more steamers arrived from downriver. The reports were:

"Gold, gold everywhere! Gold in the tundra! Gold along the beaches! Gold for many, many miles, from a point below Cape Rodney! Gold back from the beaches for many miles! Gold, gold everywhere! It just sounded unbelievable, incredible! But if only a tenth of it

*The red sand was called "Ruby Sand."

was actually true, it certainly was a mighty big gold strike—the biggest ever! And, best of all, for United States citizens it was on American territory. Well, to get back to my story:

"When I got back to Dominion Creek Paul Hebb was there waiting. Immediately, he assured me my Lay was secure and that he still was in good graces with the bank. Said that the gossip about him had just been a vicious rumor. Said that I'd be a fool to start off for distant Nome when the future was so promising here on Dominion Creek. Reminded me of all the rich producers in other parts of the Klondike, too. However, I must confess that the luring glitter still emanating from Cape Nome was almost overpowering! Made me feel that that small pothole of gold which I had so recently found was nothing at all. Yes, that gold seemed almost a curse and hindrance."

"My friend," said Max solemnly, "I'm mighty glad you didn't go to Cape Nome because just before I left Dawson reports came that Nome has suffered the worst storm catastrophe in North coastal history! It all started September 12th. They say the giant storm roared across the Cape like a furious hurricane, lasting two full days. Fellows panning gold along the beaches were swept out to sea. Small boats and barges that were trying to land capsized while hundreds of miners watched helplessly from shore.

"But the reports also say that tremendous waves surged up into town, covering wide areas, especially in the lower section of Nome. People who had climbed on rooftops were thrown into the deluge when structures collapsed. Cabins even beyond River Street—with occupants —were washed out to sea! The force of the storm was so great, they said, that ocean water swept up the Snake River for many miles, taking out dozens of miners' cabins.

"Lucky were the ships that reached 'Port Safety,' twenty-five miles away, and Golovin Bay, seventy-five miles away. But the mammoth barge, 'Skookum,' which had previously hauled the narrow gauge coaches for the White Pass Yukon Railroad* (to Skagway from Seattle) was not so lucky! She caught on a reef and cracked up right in front of Nome, spilling out a thousand screaming passengers! Many thousands of feet of lumber, and tons and tons of provisions, were swept into the

---

*In July, of 1898, the Ajax and the Bjax, of the Pacific Clipper Line, hauled two White Pass narrow gauge locomotives to Skagway for the railroad, the White Pass Yukon Railroad.

sea. The water, they said, was full of hysterical people, flying lumber and battering logs."

"Yes," said Max, "you should be thankful, Vel and Ed, that you're here in the Klondike, although at the very peak of the great Nome stampedes, I suppose, Ed, it seemed that you should have moved heaven and earth to go with the others. But it really must have been the watchful care of Providence the way things turned out. An epidemic of typhoid is sure to break out in Nome. How little do we know what is best for us, and——"

Suddenly, the air was rent by a long anguished howl. There was a brief pause, then a series of sharp similar cries followed.

"Oh!" I exclaimed in alarm, "that's Nelly, Clemy's malemute!"

The cabin door flew open and there stood Clemy, red-faced and puffing, hanging onto Nelly's collar.

"Now what in blazes is wrong with that dog?" asked Edward.

"Well," explained Clemy, half apologetically, "Nelly got hurt!"

"How?" asked Ed, briskly. "How could she get hurt in the snow?"

"Well," said Clemy, "she just happened to go runnin' past the roadhouse and a big black cinder came flying out o' the chimney, and it came down and hit poor Nelly right on the head, causing her to howl and howl! See, it hit her right there," Clemy said, pointing at Nelly's head for emphasis.

"Now that's a walloping good story," I said sternly, "and tell me, Clemy, what was Nelly doing up there at the roadhouse, anyway?"

"Oh, she was just runnin' away!" said Clemy, with a sudden mischievous look in his expressive grey eyes, while Nelly rolled hers in anguish.

"From what was she running?" I asked suspiciously.

"Oh," said Clemy, "Oh, well——then——I'll tell you; she was runnin' away from my snowman. Nelly was awfully scared! The snowman got right up outa the trail and chased her up the hill to the roadhouse—and the snowman was waving a big, thick club!"

"And did he catch her?" asked Max, suppressing his laughter.

"Well——yeah," answered Clemy, eyeing us uneasily. "Yea, he did, and he hit poor Nelly pretty hard, too!"

"Now Clemy," I said, "that's another big whopper about the snowman. Besides, you know Nelly's always had a black spot on her forehead. Now Clemy, tell us the truth, son!"

"Oh Bamba, I give up. I'll tell you all about it, then," said Clemy. "Ella McGillacuddy did beat Nelly, and it was because Nelly stole a ham. You see, Nellie saw the kitchen door of the roadhouse standin' wide open and there was a nice big ham sitting on the table. So Nelly just sneaked in and began eating that ham up, fast! But, all at once Ella McGillacuddy came into the kitchen and saw Nelly, and so she grabbed a big club and chased her all around the kitchen and then outside and on down the hill waving that big club. Oh my! Miss McGillacuddy was awfully angry! You should have seen her. She walloped poor Nelly several times too, when she got close enough. Oh, poor Nelly!"

"A ham!" exclaimed Ed, aghast. "Now we've got the real story!"

"Come here, Nelly," he commanded. Nelly came whimpering and crawling over to Ed, while Max nearly rolled with laughter! Nelly's stomach was bulging, and she limped quite badly.

"Well," said Ed, "it's plain Nelly got a good thumping right on her rump where she deserved it!"

"Ah ha—just wait 'til I tell the miners at the roadhouse why they're not having ham tonight," laughed Max, slapping his sides. "It's a mighty good story: A ham! A snowman! A club and a big black cinder! Ha, ha! No, I can't keep this one. Ella McGillacuddy surely swings a mighty wicked club when she's angry!"

"Vel," said Ed, looking quite serious, "we've got to pay for the ham. It proves again that we must sell that malemute."

"No, no, no!" cried Clemy, "she's my dog, and I'll pay for her! I've got a little gold-dust and I'll work for more. I'll do anything. I'll haul water, sweep snow and gather wood. I'll do anything—anything!"

"My son, you'll have to do all of those things," said Ed, half tenderly, half severely. "But how would you like to pan for gold right in front of Dawson, on the sand bar? Yes, sir, there's been gold found in town recently, and a stampede followed. I know where we can find gold in a hurry, and we can get in on a little Dawson fun and excitement too. Perhaps we can find enough gold to help buy the roadhouse another ham. I know where we'll buy that ham, too—at the little Dawson store owned by Nelly Cashman*."

"Why, I think that's a splendid idea," said Max eagerly, between mouthfuls of juicy blueberry pie.

"Tomorrow," said Ed with a soft look in his eyes, "Yes, tomorrow we'll go to Dawson because we do need supplies. But from now on, son, you must keep a sharp eye on your malemute. She's been raiding too many kitchens and grub boxes lately!"

After Max had gone, Ed reached to a high shelf and drew down his little red, leather-bound diary. Flipping its pages, he read:

> Dawson, June 24, 1899
> Cleaned up $206.00. Struck a pothole. Could see gold all over the place! Suppose Hebb will be along in a day or so. Will then know what is up. Big stampede out from Dawson to Cape Nome Country, on coast north of St. Michael. Just got in town. Rained hard, and creek is booming. The dance started the rush off!

"Yes, Vel," said Ed, with a sigh and pained look, "yes, I wrote that diary a year and a half ago. Much has happened since then. Of the thousands who rushed up to Nome, hundreds of them from Dawson, I'm wondering just what percentage really found fortune. And I'm wondering too, what percentage found death. I'm sure all of us will long remember the awful storm at Nome September 12th and 13th of this year, 1900."

"And so, Vel, it makes a miner seriously wonder. Where next? And what sacrifice—gold?"

---

*Miss Nelly Cashman, who had lived at Tombstone during its gold-rush boom days and who was called, "the Angel of the Gold Camps," came to Dawson in '98. She had been to Wrangell and next to the Cassier district. From there she mushed with her dog team to Dawson along the ice of the Yukon. In Dawson she established a small store and boardinghouse, continuing her charitable work of helping destitute miners. At the height of the Nome stampedes Nelly Cashman took off for Nome. Fame followed her wherever she went and she continued her work. Finally, as a frail little lady, she was forced to return to civilization where she died at the age of seventy, at Victoria, B.C.

*Beach gold of Nome was very fine; some of it actually floated out of the gold-pan. It was found in large quantities on false bedrock of blue clay. There were from one to three pay streaks. Each gold streak was mixed with ruby sand and it varied from one to four inches in thickness. Bedrock was from two to six feet deep. The best of the beach gold was taken out by late 1901. However, great riches remained in among the hills, and much of it remains to this day. Gold in paying quantities didn't exist below the beach waterline.

Eskimo boat (oumiak) and a group of natives near Nome on Bering Sea, 1899.

Famous actresses in Dawson, "Diamond Tooth" Gertie, left, and Cad Wilson, right, 1899. They saved many a show from the "howls of malemutes" in the audience!

The Lung family, as photographed by a roving photographer, in their cabin on Dominion Creek. Left to right: Ed Lung, Clemy, Velma D. Lung, and baby Ella (Lung Martinsen).

Velma D. Lung, baby Ella and Clemy, in Dawson, 1901.

Chapter 18

FIRE IN THE CABIN

Selma and Miss Magillacuddy, two of the likable girls working at the new Dominion Creek roadhouse had kindly taught me how to make better sourdough bread by using Hudson Bay flour. It was a special blend of very hard wheat, grown in Canada, and it always made a delicious, fine-grained bread, which was soft and flaky.

One day when I was stirring up the fire, trying to get the oven piping hot, in order to bake a batch of bread, a spark flew out and caught in the fuzzy nap of the pink outing-flannel-covering of the wall. The spark must have been lodged there only a few seconds, when suddenly, like an explosion, the whole cabin was flushed in flames!

Fortunately, Clemy happened to be home. We both grabbed towels, frantically beating at the flames, first on one side of the cabin, and then on the other.

Finally, we succeeded in smothering the blaze. But it was a terrifying experience! There was absolutely no time to call for help.

Oh, I was sick at heart! I hated to have Edward come home and see what had happened. Now, our pretty pink outing-flannel-covering, which Ed had worked so hard to line the cabin with, was reduced to a scorched, ugly brown and a large black hole, about the size of a basketball, showed by the stove.

Of course, Ed was terribly shocked when he walked in the door and saw what had happened, but hastened to say that he was so thankful that Clemy and I were not hurt, and that we were pretty brave to stay and fight the blaze. But he also said that if we hadn't fought the fire, in no time the whole cabin would have burned to the ground! Well, it made all of us a little ill just to think of it!

When the miners heard of our accident, they came crowding into the cabin, and when they saw that nothing was actually destroyed, just the nap of the flannel singed and gone—they said it was really a miracle, as a flash fire can become a roaring inferno in seconds. Of course they complimented us on our courage and presence of mind, but all of their fine compliments couldn't compensate for the loss of that cozy, rosy-pink-look to the interior of our cabin which I had loved so dearly!

"Never mind, Vel," said Ed consolingly, while I was sweeping up the powder-like cinders, "we'll reline the cabin, some day. Maybe a coat of pink wallpaper would do the trick. But it'll be a big job, I'm afraid!"

For many days I was unhappy and miserable about the catastrophe. Now the inside of our cabin had a gloomy, ordinary look, and the odor of burnt cloth was strong in the air. Was it a bad omen that our "Pink Flannel Heaven" had vanished so quickly? I hoped not! I reminded myself that if we had been burned-out, we would have lost everything, and in the coldest months of winter! Yes, there was truly a great deal to be thankful for!

* * *

My husband certainly did try to do things to make me comfortable and happy, and he was extremely handy at small jobs. Once I was completely out of hairpins, which was a real calamity!

"Well, we'll soon fix that," he said with assurance. "We'll just make some!" He found some bailing wire and cut short pieces into the proper lengths, then, he bent them double. He finished the job by carefully filing and smoothing the ends so that they wouldn't be scratchy. However, my hair was so very fine and curly that Ed's coarse, homemade hairpins just wouldn't stay in place. They kept flying out from the bun, at the nape of my neck, almost every time I bobbed my head, or leaned over.

Clemy made it his special task, when home, to crawl around the cabin floor, picking up hairpins, and by nightfall he would usually have most of them in his pocket, ready to return to me.

"My goodness, Vel," said Ed, one night at supper, looking quite ill, "guess that after all we'd better send to Dawson for some real, store hairpins. Clemy and I just found three that I made, in the soup!"

Answering a rap at our cabin one day, I found one of our miners at the door with a buck skin bag tucked under his arm.

"Mrs. Lung, I have something important to show you," he said, mysteriously. "May I come in?"

"Of course," I answered cordially.

The miner stepped inside, then walked to the table and pulled open the leather sack. Quickly he poured its contents out onto the table.

My eyes stood still! Bright rays of sunlight, coming through the window, focused on several of the rocky pellets which flashed and gleamed rich red and lavender lights with surprising brilliance.

"Look, Mrs. Lung," said the miner, "aren't they beauties? They're real garnets and rubies! Have you ever seen such large garnets? They're as big as walnuts! And the small, reddish-lavender stones are rubies—real little rubies! Maybe they're too small for commercial purposes, but nevertheless they're rubies!"

"Rubies and garnets!" I gasped. "Why, I had no idea they could be found on Dominion Creek!"

"Not many know it," said the miner, "but this is proof that they are here—that is, if you know just where to look for 'em. Now you take a few for yourself," he invited generously. "Yes, I'm giving 'em to you as a gift. Soon I'll be leaving the North and I want to show my appreciation for all you've done for me and the miners."

"Oh no, I musn'. take any of your stones," I told him firmly, "but I appreciate your letting me see them. They truly are very beautiful, especially the big, dark red garnets!"

Later, Ed also discovered garnets on claim No. 2B, Below Lower Discovery, but thought nothing of them as he was only interested in gold. Then, he found a pale, silvery colored metal which the miners impatiently called "that hard, pesky, platinum stuff!" Ed, like the others, attached no particular value to this strange, hard, new metal. It was only gold Ed and all the others were after; and so in the course of our hectic lives the little sacks of platinum were spilled out and lost.

Chapter 19

GODDESS OF THE GOLD-RUSH–KLONDIKE KATE

"Yes, you bet, time has surely flown quickly!" said Ed to Joe Latshaw, one evening when they were both talking and smoking their pipes in our cabin.

"Sure, that's right," said Joe. "Do you remember the time, Ed, when we got a ride to Hunker by stage? That was back in early summer of '99 and do you remember us meeting Klondike Kate and the other showgirls?"

"Showgirls!" I gasped. "Why Edward!"

"Great Scott, Vel, it was only a chance meeting," said Ed, coloring a bit and looking sheepish. "Believe me, it was innocent fun, and it all happened like this:

"One morning Joe and I waited at the confluence of the Klondike and Bonanza Rivers for the little stage that ran to Hunker. (During that summer a stage was running for a few months.) Hunker was a small mining settlement, eighteen miles from Dawson. Getting a ride meant a big lift in our forty-five mile hike to Dominion Creek.

"Well, it was a bright sunny morning, the kind that it's good to be alive! As we stood waiting for the stage, we heard voices coming in the distance. Then, short snatches of song, followed by pleasing, lilting laughter.

"Singers!" I said.

"Girls!" said Joe.

"Just for the fun of it, let's answer," I said. Joe grinned and said, "Sure!" So we both threw back our heads, opened our mouths wide, and imitated in ridiculous, high, falsetto tones, the feminine soprano voices.

"We listened—there was a short pause—then came the answer.

" 'Ooo, la, la, there. Ooo, la, la!' Then, another pause, and 'Yoo, hoo, there,' and 'You? who, who?'

"In a few seconds we could hear the quick beat of horses' hoofs.

"The stage!" said Joe.

"The stage rounded a bend in the road, and immediately we saw the girls perched high on the front bench—two actresses from the Palace Grand Theatre of Dawson. Joe and I recognized them right away, as any fellow would, who'd been in town.

"The girls spied us and waved gaily, merrily singing out:

" 'Why, hello, hello, boys! So it was you playing Echo?'

"Well, of course, they made a very pretty picture, sitting there in long silk dresses of pink and blue. In their laps were large bouquets of wild flowers—blue bells, wild roses and delphinium.

"One of the girls was Kathleen Rockwell (Klondike Kate), the most popular, and highest paid singer and dancer in Dawson—the bright star of the footlights.

"The stage stopped and Joe and I threw our packs aboard, then hopped on. There were only three other passengers on the stage besides the two girls and they happened to be old men sprawled in the back seats.

"Joe and I took places in the middle of the coach and then, away we went up the road, following the Klondike River.

"It wasn't many minutes however, before the girls began singing popular songs from their show, and of course we were pleased to join in as we knew most of the tunes. I took the tenor and Joe the bass.

"After a while, the girls called back, 'Come, sit up front, boys. There's plenty of room!"

"Well, you can be sure, we didn't need any urging! I took the seat next to Kate and Joe sat by the other pretty girl.

"I'm Ed Lung," I said, "and this is Joe Latshaw."

" 'I'm Kathleen Rockwell,' said the beautiful actress. 'And this is Cad Wilson. Say, we're awfully glad you boys are traveling our way. We were afraid it was going to be a very dull ride. Have you ever seen us at the Opera House?' asked Kate curiously.

"Sure," we replied, "a few times."

" 'Listen, Cad, you know we could use a good tenor and bass in our show,' smilingly suggested Kate, Looking Joe and me over approvingly.

" 'Let's sing,' said Joe. "And in a few minutes we were singing with real gusto many numbers, including the famous Rigoletto quartet.

"Occasionally, the old men on the back seat would pipe in whenever they knew the tune. Even the driver chimed in!

"And as we passed the claims along Hunker Creek, Kate and Cad pelted flowers at some of the miners and called them by name; of course, the hills echoed to their vivacious laughter, and our hilarious songs.

"The girls had playfully pinned flowers to our coats and caps, and even the men on the back seat were not forgotten. Well, as you can imagine, we presented a very gay, festive appearance as the horses went trotting along, and I think we were the envy of all of the fellows who saw us!

"When our voices grew tired, we talked and visited. I had heard a great deal about Kathleen Rockwell. It was rumored that she had evaded the Mounties at Miles Canyon when she jumped aboard a scow that was heading through the rapids. Of course the Mounties were trying to keep all women away from danger. Kate had been a determined lass. She had dressed like a boy to fool the Mounties, but they had discovered the hoax, just as the scow was pulling out. As the barge hit the rapids the Mounties yelled, 'In the name of the Queen, stop! But the swift river had settled the argument, whisking Kathleen far out of reach. And so she had landed in Dawson a whole year ahead of the other show-people who followed.

"Well, of course, I had never been this close to 'Klondike Kate,' though in Dawson I had seen her from the audience of the Theatre. Now, I had the rare opportunity to study her at close-range.

"She was certainly very young! Couldn't have been more than nineteen or twenty. She had an appeal and winsomeness that was truly captivating. It was an alluring, intangible-something, yes, difficult to describe.

"She was just a bit taller than average; hair, reddish-gold; eyes, blue; complexion like peaches and cream; her voice ranged from velvety-soft, to musical-bells; and yes, she was as sweet as honey!

"Oh, she was a charmer! She exuded youthful loveliness! It was easy to see why she was the "Queen of Hearts," darling of the footlights—sweetheart of the dance-hall—the belle of Dawson. Already, she had had a hundred proposals.

"Well, impulsively, I reached into my hip pocket and drew out my small poke of nuggets. How very hard I had worked for that poke of gold!

"Look at these yellow babies," I said eagerly, as I spread the nuggets out in the palm of my hand, so that each shiny, golden particle would show off to its best advantage in the bright sunlight.

" 'Oh,' Kate exclaimed, 'they're beautiful! Real gorgeous! Why, I've never seen such rare beauties! Say, did you get them all from your claim on Dominion Creek?'

"Sure," I replied, "do you like them, Miss Rockwell?"

" 'Do I!' she exclaimed, enthusiastically. 'I just love them!!'

"Then pick one out," I invited, "and you may keep it."

" 'Oh, thank you, thank you,' she exclaimed. Her lovely hands grasped, fondled, and almost weighed each nugget. And then, she chose my biggest one!

" 'This piece of gold will always remind me of you, Ed Lung,' she said, sweetly, as she quickly opened her purse and dropped the shiny gold in with a collection of many other nuggets. 'Yes, I think the one you gave me is the prettiest, yet!'

"Well, her smile was so bright, and her manner so very sweet and pleasing, I swear, I could have given her my whole bag-full of gold that day if she'd asked it!

"And Great Scott! Before I knew it we were at Hunker, the end of the line, and it was time to tell Kate and Cad Wilson good-bye. You see the actresses were giving a vaudeville show that night at the little Hunker Theater. It was going to be a good one too, as 'Diamond Tooth Gertie' and the new girl, 'The Oregon Mare,' were there with the troupe. These actresses, with chorus, had gone up to the place the day before with their trappings, so, were waiting with the musicians for our stage to arrive.

"Well, of course, Joe and I were sorely tempted to stay over for the show, but decided against it, as I had to be back at Dominion Creek by dawn. Even to make it by then, I knew we would have to 'step on it' and walk all night. However, it being summer, we could count on daylight lasting almost all night."

"But gosh!" said Joe, taking up the story, "it was kinda' hard to tear ourselves away from Hunker that night, 'cause we knew the fellows were in for a 'Jim Dandy' performance.

"Yes, you bet, we knew how Kate would come out in those pretty, pink silk tights and dazzle the miners, and how she would dance right into their dreams, and maybe their pocketbooks.

"Yep, she's a peach all right—a real, beautiful, luscious peach!" sighed Joe. "To see and hear her is to let her sweep your cares away. And she has a lot of funny, sly wit, too. And she knows how to be a lady—real genteel-like! They say she came from a very good family in Spokane, Washington."

"Sure! It was gonna be a 'cracker-jack' of a show!" added Ed. "Cad Wilson, the baby-face-girl, is no slouch, either. As a comedian, she holds up her end and is very popular.

"Then there's Diamond-Tooth-Girtie with her famous smile. That diamond always flashes when she quips:

" 'Hey there, boys! Ain't it pretty? This diamond, I mean. Why, it's like real money in the bank, the family jewels! You know someday, I may have to dig it from my tooth to keep the wolves away from the door. Now, what was that I just heard, boys? Aha! The wail of a wolf!" (Wolf calls come from the wings.)

"Well, and then, Gertie frolics some, dances a jig while chattering the common gossip about some of the well-known Klondike Kings and also of the new people, recently arrived in town. Often, she makes ridiculous cracks about Swiftwater Bill's many escapades and his latest amours while that diamond flashes and glitters with almost malignant glee. 'Folks, Dawson would be dull without him—dull I tell ya! Why almost any day our 'Diamond Jim Brady' can be seen chasing a new petticoat through town. But girls, don't ever go boat ridin' with our Swiftwater Bill, 'cause ya' might have to swim home. He's really sc-e-r-r-ed of swift water!' "

"Ah yes," laughed Ed, "and there was the handsome 'Oregon Mare,' the fourth girl in the troupe. She's the talk of Dawson, and wherever she goes. Some say she's a cowgirl from Oregon, others say Montana. Anyway, she surely knows horses. And she must be a ventriloquist, too, the way she throws her voice.

"Sometimes she wears a horse-mask. She hoofs it, kicks, cavorts and horseplays all over the stage. Sometimes even gallops like mad around the audience. Her imitations of a pony are a rollicking scream!

"Often, she stops in her wild antics to give those long, drawn-out horselaughs which you would swear are real. Then, back to the stage she gallops. There are imaginary horse-races, horse-fights and silly, moon-eyed love-making accompanied by lots of significant whinnying, neighing, and kicking.

"Well, to tell about it seems nothing at all, but to see her is something special! Anyway, she surely makes a hit with the fellows. Just seems to tickle their funny bones!

"They throw nuggets at the 'Oregon Mare.' And as she romps off the stage they slap their sides and exclaim between fits of laughter, 'By George! She's earned 'em. By George! Haven't had so much fun in a coon's age!'

"Well, as I was saying," continued Ed, "we did not stay for the show

---

*"Diamond-Tooth-Gertie," whose real name was Hornora Ornstien, has also become a legend of Klondike days. She lived to be 90 and had to use the diamond in her front tooth and other diamonds that she acquired in the Klondike.

that night, but we did eat supper at the little restaurant near the Hunker Theater. That gave us an opportunity to visit with the others in the cast and to see a little more of fascinating Klondike Kate. And, By George, I do admit it, we left Hunker regretfully! And as we slowly started up the steep mountain trail towards King Dome, with our packs strapped to our backs, the girls waved and trilled a sweet, alluring farewell:

" 'Goodbys, boys. Don't forget. Come see our new act the next time you're in Dawson. Will you?'

"Oh sure, you bet we will!" Joe and I called enthusiastically.

Now, while Ed was telling his story, his face had taken on a faraway, dreamy expression. With half-closed eyes, he had leaned back, and as he talked, blew smoke rings towards the ceiling. It was obvious that he was living over every pleasant moment of that stagecoach episode, and had completely forgotten my presence in the cabin. Joe also had a rapt, distant look in his handsome brown eyes.

"Ed! Edward!" I called briskly. "Where was I when this actress-episode took place?"

"Why, Velma, you were in Tacoma," Edward gasped in a startled voice as the smoke rings abruptly vanished. "Yes, that was it! Just a month before I met Kate on the stage coach, I sent you a letter from Dawson asking you to come North. Yes, Vel, I had to get back to Dominion Creek that night to cut logs for our new cabin, and I had to work like a beaver, too. Sure! Believe me, that's it!"

"Oh, Vel, now don't worry," laughed Joe. "It was the last time Ed ever talked to Klondike Kate. I know, because he worked the rest of the summer building your little cabin. Remember that you arrived in early fall."

"Yes, I remember, Joe," I smiled, "but I wish to know something else," I said slowly.

"What?" asked my husband, looking a bit worried.

"Ed, did you ever throw gold at Klondike Kate when she performed in Dawson?"

"Well," said Ed, clearing his throat and knocking the ashes from his pipe while he considered a moment, "Well, yes! Yes, Vel. One nugget, maybe two, but they didn't amount to much. All of the fellows were throwing gold, and so did I. I was just having a little fun, like the rest of them. It got to be a game among the fellows to see who could come the closest to hitting Kate's silver slippers."

"So," I chuckled, as Ed looked extremely uncomfortable, "so Klondike Kate has three of the Lung-nuggets!"

"Aw, that's nothin'," said Joe gallantly. "Why, I'll bet she has at least a dozen of mine. Nope, you don't need to worry about your Eddy throwing much gold away. He just isn't that kind, Vel.

"But Kate is really quite a gal!" laughed Joe. "She surely is a clever actress, and is expert at collecting gold. She works it from all angles—even wears an unfinished link-bracelet of twenty-dollar gold pieces. Most of the miners count it a rare privilege to add to that bracelet. They say when one bracelet is completed she just starts another. Great Scott! It's no wonder she's rapidly amassing a fortune! Surely, Kate has Dawson at her beautiful feet. But now, there's Alexander Pantages—that little Greek. Must have been love at first sight! Sometimes Pantages works at the Monte Carlo Casino as a waiter and bartender, but after the shows, on moonlight nights, he and Kathleen go sleighing, pulled by a string of handsome malemutes.

"By golly, it's strange," sighed Joe, "and she could have married any one of a dozen Klondike Kings! Diamond Tooth Gertie says, 'Kate's plumb crazy to fall so hard for a foreign "patent leather kid" who will love her, take her gold and maybe some day leave her!' "

*The little waiter and bartender who distressed so many of Klondike Kate's admirers, was destined to become the famous "Theater King." In 1901 and '02 he borrowed all of the gold Klondike Kate had and went to Seattle and bought a theater, naming it "The Crystal." From this venture he expanded and created his chain of vaudeville theaters, which spread throughout the country and made him a multi-millionaire. However, family troubles seemed to dog his footsteps. It is said he never paid Kate her full share in their business ventures. And when, years later, she was without funds he doled out five dollar bills, grudgingly. He further broke her heart by never marrying her, but married a young violinist in his orchestra in Seattle.

By 1906, Klondike Kate had met heartbreak and loss of zest for the theater. Her fortune was dwindling and so was her first bloom of youth. By 1910, she was living in the States.

Years later, in 1933, she married John Matson, an old admirer, a Sourdough who had watched her dance to fame in Dawson and had secretly loved her through the years. When he learned of her altered fortunes he got up courage and proposed by letter, and she accepted him. She went back to Dawson and they were married.

In 1946 Kate's husband died in a blizzard in an effort to get a letter Outside to her. He had insisted that Kate live Outside during the severe winters. A few years later Kate married W. L. VanDuren, a former acquaintance in Oregon. They lived in "Sweet Home," at Bend, Oregon, until Kate's death in Feb. 21, 1957. (She was 80.) In her community in Oregon, she was respected and admired by her many friends and neighbors. To old Sourdoughs of the gold-rush era, mention of her name brings glittering memories of the glories of the fabled and fabulous North. With the passing of years, "Klondike Kate" has become a golden legend of Americana.

"Well, whatever happens," said Ed, "I wish Kate well as do all of the miners. I hope none of Diamond Tooth Gertie's dire predictions ever come true. Kathleen Rockwell is really just a very gay girl who loves the bright footlights and gold, and . . . gold-rush excitement, and has the great talent, beauty and youth to add to the glitter of Dawson. Let's hope Dame Fortune is very kind to our Goddess of Golden Charm, the 'Queen of Hearts—Klondike Kate!' "

Chapter 20

THE ALASKA STORK or THE EXPECTED GUEST

It was in late summer of 1900 when I suddenly realized, with a start, that the stork was planning a visit about Christmas-time.

What should I do? There wasn't a doctor within forty-five miles! The closest was Dawson.

Should I tell Ed? If I did, I knew he would give up the claim and make a dash for the Outside. I couldn't let him do that! No, not when we were so near success!

Yes, I would keep my secret a little while longer, or until the ice closed in, then it would be too late to leave the Klondike. I would trust in God and Nature to carry me through the ordeal ahead.

Secretly, I set about making baby clothes from odds and ends that I had around the cabin. It was amazing what one could make from sugar and flour sacks, and how nice they looked after the letters were bleached out! Several times when the miners made trips to Dawson I had them bring me pink outing flannel. Of course no one suspected why I wanted the outing flannel, as it had so many uses in the North.

One day in late September, Ed came in early from the mine. It had been snowing during the day, after a heavy freeze the night before. Now, I knew it was safe to tell my husband the momentous news.

Ed stamped the snow from his boots and shook his coat, then closed the door quickly against the blustery gusts of wind and snow.

"B-r-r-r," he said, "winter's here with a bang! And do you know, Vel, today I've discovered a lady's secret." His voice was playful and his eyes danced and twinkled.

"What?" I asked, with a catch in my voice and the feeling of blood rushing to my cheeks. "Is it . . . is it important?"

"Well, yes, of course, you bet it is!" he said. "It means an increase in our family. That's a big event!"

I felt my face grow hot, my heart pound furiously. So Edward knew! But before I could answer, he went on.

"Yes, we're going to have a 'blessed event' around here. Queen is going to have pups, and from the looks of things they'll probably come around early November. She's been awfully cross lately, snapping at all the dogs."

"Pups!" shouted Clemy, who was sitting at the table making drawings and paper cut-outs from a Sears & Roebuck catalog. "Did you say pups, Dad?" For months Clemy had been wishing for a small pet. Nelly who had been his companion, was now full grown and had taken her place with the dog-team. Clemy had no children to play with, except when the weather allowed him to go to Caribou, to school. My husband and I had realized that he was leading a lonely life for a child.

"Yes, Clemy, Queen will have pups, and you may have one for your very own," his father assured him.

Clemy's expressive face lighted up with joy and excitement as he dropped his pencil, clapping his hands with glee, tears of happiness welling in his eyes. With a tug at my heart, I realized more fully just how lonely my little son had been for companionship lately. I had tried to fill his need, but I had been busier than usual with my own secret affairs.

That evening after Clemy had gone to sleep I told Edward the momentous news. He looked shocked, and I could read extreme apprehension in his face.

"Oh Velma, you should have told me sooner! It would have made such a difference. Yes, I could have taken you Outside in time."

"No," I told him, "I couldn't let you do that. Besides, I'm not really afraid. I can get Mrs. Webster, the practical nurse in Caribou. I've sent word and she's promised to come if you'll go after her when the time comes."

THE ALASKA STORK or THE EXPECTED GUEST 193

Now, the tempo of our lives increased. I was very busy with my tasks, and Clemy was happy in the knowledge that he would soon have a puppy to play with. As the days sped by, Edward and I felt the bonds of affection grow even stronger. We agreed not to tell Clemy about the Big Event until sometime close to Christmas.

The miners were worried about me when they heard the news, and I could read real concern in their shy, respectful glances.

In his spare time Edward made a baby-bed of fresh pine lumber, and I took fresh hay from our mattress and made a tiny pad from it. Then, I collected the finest white rabbit furs from our storehouse. Sewing them together, I made a snug, warm, cozy nest for my little one.

One day, early in November, Queenie had her puppies. Clemy came rushing into the cabin in great excitement.

"Oh Mother, come quick! Queenie has two beautiful puppies, and she's in the deserted cabin!"

We found Queen, the proud mother of two of the softest, tiniest little pups that were ever born! They were like little puff-balls, one dark gray, the other black. Perfect little malemutes—they would be worth many ounces of gold.

During the days that followed, Clemy spent most of his time with Queen and the pups. I always knew just where to find him. The little black one was to be his. He had chosen it because he said that "Blackie" winked at him and kissed him the day he opened his eyes.

Time passed quickly. The pups were growing, and Clemy often brought them inside our cabin to play on the floor.

Then, one day, the little gray malemute became sick, and several days later we found him dead. Clemy cried and Queen howled, and there was extreme sadness in our cabin. We tried to console our child by pointing out that he still had Blackie. But Blackie began to droop. Apparently there was nothing physically wrong with him, but he just wouldn't eat. He seemed to be grieving for his twin.

"We must try to get him to eat something," Edward said, in desperation, but the puppy refused all food, and in a few days Blackie, too, was dead.

"I'm sure he died of a broken heart," my husband said, "because there was absolutely nothing physically wrong with that pup! But sometimes animals will grieve until they die."

Clemy's grief was inconsolable. Nothing we could say would cheer him. I was deeply concerned.

"Now is the time to tell him, Edward," I said. "In a week it will be Christmas."

"Yes, I suppose we'd better," Edward agreed.

"Clemy, come here." I said gently, putting my arm around him. "Don't be sad any more. You're going to have a real playmate soon. Yes, a little baby brother or sister, maybe during the next week or so. Maybe for Christmas. Look in the corner under the gray blanket, and there you'll see a new baby-bed and little clothes."

Clemy broke from my arms to inspect the corner, then he ran back to me.

"Oh Mother, God has answered my prayers! Oh! I've prayed so hard for a sister! Will she be here for Christmas?"

"We must wait and see, dear. I hope she'll be here for Christmas."

In a few minutes Clemy, bursting with the joyful news, rushed to find his friends at the mine. The miners, of course, acted surprised and pretended they hadn't known.

"Velma, how do you feel?" Edward would ask anxiously a dozen times a day. "Shall I get the nurse? The weather's getting so cold and the snow so deep, I worry all the time about getting through to the nurse. I tell you I wouldn't know what to do if the nurse couldn't come."

"Don't worry, dear," I would tell him. "Selma at the roadhouse will come to help if we need her, and she's not too far away. She said she'd come any hour of the day or night."

Each passing hour added to the mounting tension. Even the miners were anxious.

Two days before Christmas, Edward and Clemy waded through the snow to find a small spruce tree on the hillside. They shook the snow from its branches, brought it into the cabin, set it up and decorated it with little candles and colored paper. What a beautiful little Christmas tree it made! Clemy drew pictures of angels and babies and tied them all over the tree. He was bursting with excitement and importance. Several times I found him standing by the baby's bed looking tenderly at the tiny clothes stored there.

"I hope my little sister will come for Christmas," he would say a dozen times a day.

December 25 dawned cold and bleak, but in our log-cabin there was warmth and excitement. Under the fragrant tree Clemy found boots and snowshoes from his father, and new mittens and a bright red stocking cap from me, and a brand new red sled from the miners. I found a pretty dress with pink roses all over it, from Edward, and a little bonnet to match.

"Oh Edward," I asked, "when will I ever wear such a lovely dress and bonnet?"

"In the spring when we go to Dawson, my dear. I want my lady to look beautiful."

Fastened to a limb of the tree was a small leather poke of gold-dust labeled "For a new little cheechako and future Sourdough." The gift was from the miners to the new baby.

Early Christmas evening, Ed lit the candles, and the miners gathered to celebrate the birth of Christ and the coming of the first white child to be born on Dominion Creek. Happily, and in the Christmas spirit, we sang all the dearly loved Christmas carols while I played the accompaniments on my tiny portable organ which Mother had sent in to me as a gift. Then we had canned plum pudding and coffee for refreshments.

Yes, I was quite relieved that the stork had passed us by on Christmas! The six days following were uneventful, but filled with intense anxiety. I had many things yet to do, and kept busy. Clemy, sensing the mounting anxiety, assumed new responsibilities and I could see unusual seriousness on his expressive face.

New Year's day came, and still no sign of the stork! A severe storm raged all that day, and everyone remained indoors. In the evening only Joe came to our cabin. As he entered, he knocked the snow from his boots and closed the door quickly behind him.

"Sufferin' cats, what a night!" he remarked as he began peeling off extra layers of shirts and trousers until he reached "bedrock," or the first layer. "Do you know, Ed, the thermometer is dropping steadily. It's forty-eight degrees below zero and freezing the clothes right on a fellow!"

Ed and Joe smoked and talked, and I slipped behind the curtain, to bed. The two men talked on and on in low tones.

"The Indians have predicted a very cold spell," Joe was saying. "Maybe the coldest in history!"

Suddenly I felt strangely ill and began to tremble. I pulled the blankets closely about me, shivering in fear. I glanced over at Clemy's sweet, upturned face resting there on his pillow only a few feet away. The sight of the child gave me a new surge of inward strength and calmness. Soon, I fell asleep.

January 2 was extremely cold, with snow deep and white. It was now fifty degrees below zero and too cold to work outside. Only Joe and Edward ventured to the mine.

Edward's face was now beginning to take on deep, drawn lines, and I knew his cheerfulness was forced. January 3 dawned clear and colder, and the thermometer showed a new low of fifty-five below! That day a terrific storm raged, abating a little toward evening, then a deadly cold settled down over the valley. The spirit thermometer showed another big drop. It was now sixty-six below zero!

"Vel, do you have everything ready?" Edward asked nervously.

"Yes, dear. Clean sheets, cotton and everything else. You'll find them all in the upper compartment of the trunk. If you have to, I know you can deliver the baby." And I told him all I knew about the process.

"Vel," groaned Edward, with an anxious shake of his head, "I've climbed Chilkoot and White Pass, and shot the Whitehorse Rapids. I've faced a thousand other dangers and haven't been afraid. But this, I cannot do. I just can't! The nurse has got to be here!"

By next morning the storm had passed, but snowdrifts were piled against the cabin and the thermometer still slid downward. Joe came to the cabin, early in the morning, and inquired anxiously about me. He appeared almost laughable! Thickly-bundled, he looked like an overstuffed bear, being of stocky build anyway. Over what amounted to almost his entire wardrobe, he wore his parka. Across his face was tied a red silk hankerchief, and the wolverine ruff of the hood of his parka was turned down low over his forehead so that only his eyes showed.

"The thermometer's gone down another two points," he announced, incredulously. "It's the coldest I've ever seen. Colder than the winter I spent in Candle! It's colder than hell outside!"

For a moment I had a queer, sick, sinking feeling, but a small voice within me counselled: "Courage! Everything will be all right. Don't fear."

We waited all that day. But each hour dragged by more slowly than the last. That same evening Joe returned. He stamped his feet at the door, knocked off the snow and frost from his clothes, then began the well-known ceremony of peeling off his many layers of clothing.

"Man alive," he exclaimed, "I hope the stork stays home tonight! The thermometer's hit seventy-two below, and it's colder than you can ever imagine outside! Why, the mercury in ordinary thermometers has frozen stiff, and if it weren't for our spirit-thermometer we wouldn't even know how cold it is."

Evidently the two men were preparing to spend the evening together, in a sort of "stork-watch." Edward and Joe had a deep friendship for each other and it seemed only natural that Joe should be with us now.

Joe held Clemy affectionately on his lap. "Clemy," he said, "as soon as we know for sure about this stork-fellow, I'm going to take you to my cabin."

"How will we know he's coming?" asked Clemy, curiously.

"Oh, your mother will know," laughed Joe. "He always knocks a little before he comes into the cabin."

A thousand thoughts rushed through my mind. I shivered in fright and panic. I knew it would be extremely dangerous for Ed to be out in such terribly cold weather. Was the North playing a cruel, cruel trick? Yes, oh yes, I should have gone back to Tacoma!

Too late, now! I was utterly trapped and helpless. There was no escape. What if something dreadful went wrong? Suppose I needed instruments? Could Edward get through such beastly weather to reach the nurse in Caribou and bring her back in time? I said a silent, fervent prayer as a thousand disorganized thoughts raced through my mind.

"Say, is that signal bell outside the door, working?" Joe was asking Ed. "Have you pulled the rope to test it today?"

"You bet I have!" replied Ed. "And I'll pull that rope so hard when I signal you, that all Dominion Creek will hear it, and you'd better come running as fast as you can!"

"Don't worry," said Joe. "I'll get here fast!"

After a while Clemy told the men goodnight and went to bed and so did I. I had a strange feeling of fatigue and longed for rest. Clemy said his prayers and was soon fast asleep. I lay drowsing and half-listening to the men on the other side of the curtain as their voices droned on. Occasionally I could hear Edward stir up the fire and chop a little kindling.

* * *

Suddenly, something awakened me about midnight. The cabin was very dark and Edward was sleeping beside me.

The stork was knocking!

"Oh Edward, Edward, wake up! This is it!" I cried.

Edward sprang from the bed, pulled on his clothes and rushed to the door. "Clang, clang, clang!" boomed the signal-bell. "Clang, clang," it cut the cold air.

"Vel, Vel, are you all right?" Ed cried, running back to me.

"Yes, dear," I gasped between spasms of blinding pain, "but hurry, hurry!"

Clemy had crawled from his bed. "I . . . I know, the stork is coming," he chattered. Poor little Clemy! He was shivering with cold and fright, and his small hands shook as he tried to dress.

Minutes later Joe came dashing into the cabin, wearing only half the usual layers of clothes.

"Joe," cried Ed, "stay here while I run up the trail to the roadhouse for Selma. Stoke up the fire, put more snow in the pails and get them on the stove and then harness the dogs and have them ready and . . . "

"Run," Joe shouted. "I know what to do!"

In no time Ed was back with Selma. Both were out of breath.

"Velma, hold on!" Ed called, as he flung open the door.

"Hurry, get the nurse," I gasped. "Hurry!"

"I'll be back in no time," Ed called as he dashed out into the night again. I could hear him frantically mushing the dogs and could hear the quick jingle of sleigh-bells mingled with the sharp yapping of excited malemutes. Then, all sounds faded in the distance. Joe wrapped Clemy in a warm blanket and carried him tenderly away, while young Selma nervously held my writhing hands. She, being very young (about nineteen), knew absolutely nothing about delivering babies and was as frightened as I, if not more so!

There are some hours in the lives of all of us that seem like an eternity. Each minute seemed endless as I waited and waited, pain-racked, gritting my teeth and praying.

Edward sped up the hill trail as fast as he could, through the snow towards Caribou, three miles away. That night it was pitch-black, with not a single star showing. Halfway to Caribou the oil in the lantern froze and congealed and the light died. In only a few minutes Ed was completely lost in the snow. (He described it later.)

"Rover," he called frantically, "it's all yours, Boy! Find the trail!

Please Boy, find the trail!"

Rover understood Edward's plea. In a few minutes Rover had the dog-team back on the trail. Ed hung onto the sled and ran behind, jumping on only when they hit the down grade. Finally he reached Caribou and drew up before a large cabin. It was completely dark, but Edward banged on the door and shouted in great excitement, "Nurse, nurse, it's Ed Lung. Get up! I'm in an awful hurry! Let me in!"

"Aw, go away!" a woman's shrill voice answered. "You miners can think up the damnedest ways to try to get in here! I'm not open for business on a night like this, and you oughta know it. Go away, I tell you!"

"Where's the nurse?" Ed cried. "For God's sake, woman, where's the nurse? I'm going to have a baby!"

"Miner, now that's a good one!" the shrill voice laughed. "Well, if you're really going to have a baby there's a nurse across the road, and if this is a bad joke I hope you freeze to death!"

Back in the cabin, I wondered desperately if Edward could possibly, possibly make it in time! It was such a black night—so bitterly cold! Birth pains were coming faster and harder—pains unlike any others. I writhed in terrible agony.

Selma now had quantities of boiling water and had made a pot of strong coffee. Everything I would need was out of the trunk and waiting. I strained my ears and listened. Oh, if only the nurse and Ed would come! At last I caught a faint tinkling of sleigh bells. Then I heard Edward's frantic voice call, "Rover, Rover, Mush! mush! Hurry! Hurry!"

In a few minutes Ed and the nurse stood by my bed. Both were covered with frost and the nurse was wrapped to her ears in furs. Edward was out of breath from running behind the sleigh, but Mrs. Webster was composed, having ridden in the sleigh.

"Thank God," I sobbed, "oh Thank God, you're here!"

Quickly Mrs. Webster went to work, while Edward paced the floor and drank cup after cup of black coffee. I was now in a continuous and terrible blur of pain. Finally the nurse said to Ed, "Mr. Lung, why don't you go to Joe's cabin? Selma and I can manage nicely and I'll ring the bell when the baby comes."

"Please go," I begged, "Try to get some rest."

Very early the next morning, before five o'clock, the stork visited me, and then left our cabin. From the dimness of the shadows into which I had sunk, I heard the nurse speak softly, "It's a girl, Mrs Lung." Then, faintly, I could hear the bell clanging and clanging and the muffled cry of a new-born child.

Some time later I was gently awakened by a soft kiss on the cheek.

"Mother, wake up!" Clemy was saying happily, "My baby sister's here!"

Beside Clemy stood Edward, big tears of joy streaming down his tired face, and there was good old Joe beside Edward, tears in his eyes too, his kind face showing marks of strain.

"Velma! Oh, thank God, you're safe," Edward cried, fervently. And Joe repeated, "Yes, thank God!"

Mrs. Webster smiled and brought the baby and laid her in my arms.

"We'll call her Ella," I said, as I gazed at her tiny pink face. "Yes, in honor of my younger sister who died when she was a very small child. Oh yes, this poor little thing did have a strenuous time getting here!"

There was great rejoicing in our cabin on Dominion Creek. Edward hung out the American flag in jubilant celebration, and in a few days the miners came to see the new baby. She was still asleep when the nurse brought her from her cradle, but soon she opened her eyes and smiled at them. Of course they were delighted!

"She's beautiful!" exclaimed Mr. Olson.

He picked her up tenderly and cuddled her in his big arms. Ella smiled again, straight up at her admirer, and from that time on, Mr. Olson was her willing slave. Many times after that he would come to the cabin just to see Ella and to hold her and softly croon lullabies. One day he gave me a slip of paper on which he had written a verse, "Sweet Ella Lung." He wrote affectionately of her and her smile. (Yes, I have kept the poem all these years.)

Mr. Olson was a well-educated man and an ordained minister. For some reason, which I never knew, he had given up the ministry and had come North, like so many others in the gold-rush. But he seemed utterly out of place in the role of an ordinary miner, and in these rough frontier surroundings. After a while he left our claim and the Klondike. (Years later we met him again in Tacoma.)

* * *

After Ella was born our lives moved along in deep channels already

THE ALASKA STORK or THE EXPECTED GUEST

cut out for us. Clemy loved Ella and when she grew big enough to toddle about from place to place, she became his adoring shadow.

As a leap ahead in the story, almost exactly two years later the stork visited our cabin again, and this time left us our little son, Paul. Almost the same episodes were reenacted as when Ella came into the world. It was in January when Paul made his debut in the Klondike and again the temperature hovered at seventy-two degrees below zero! This time, however, Edward did not disturb the scarlet woman at Caribou when he went to get Mrs. Webster.

Ella grew into a chubby, healthy baby with blue eyes and light golden, curly hair. On cold winter nights we would wrap her securely in heavy blankets and then tuck her into her own downy white bed, with more heavy blankets and a fur robe over her, as the temperature inside our cabin would often drop to many degrees below zero. Mornings we would find frost on the nail heads in our cabin.

I fed Ella Eagle Brand condensed milk, as it was the only kind of milk I could get. But it seemed to agree with her and she certainly thrived! I just followed the directions on the can.

SWEET ELLA LUNG

She is the loveliest flower in the North,
    There's none so fair or sweet,
As the little Klondike baby-girl,
    Heaven sent for us to greet.

Her eyes are blue, like summer skies,
    Of fine spun gold, her hair,
Her face is soft, and smile so sweet,
    Her baby laughter fills the air.

Sweet Ella has come to bless us
    In this frozen land of treasure;
The radiance of her smile has cheered us,
    Brought joy and happiness beyond measure.

Of all the flowers in the Klondike
    She's the fairest of the fair,
And if we searched this wond'rous land . . . far-flung . . .
    We'd never find a sweeter one, than little Ella Lung.

By Rev. Olson
Dominion Creek, 1901

Chapter 21

AUNTY FANNY AND A GALAXY OF STARS

Mrs. M——, Aunty Fanny, as Clemy was beginning to affectionately call her, lived down the creek from us, about a mile. She was Spanish and her husband whom she called "Pappy" was an American. They owned a small very unattractive log cabin on a Fraction Claim close to the river. Whoever had built their cabin had not bothered to scrape the logs smooth, even though they had been badly charred by fire. Consequently, poor Aunty Fanny, with very little soap, was always trying frantically to keep the interior of her place clean. But it was a losing battle, for every time the wind blew, or someone slammed the door, down would come cinders and ashes!

Aunty Fanny was not especially fond of dogs either, but her husband had bought an immense dog of unknown breed. This dog, Bob, called "The Snarler," was a very vicious and horrible fighter. So, between the dog and cabin cinders, Aunty Fanny's life was rather unhappy and full of turmoil. However, in spite of the dog hazard, Clemy adored going to visit the couple and he certainly didn't mind the cinders!

One day Clemy insisted on a visit to Aunty Fanny's, and while he hitched up the dog team, I bundled Ella, then a small baby, in the fur robe, and the three of us took off for the visit.

When we arrived at Fanny's, we found her in one of her daily housecleaning sprees. She was glad to see us and hastened to assure us that Bob was away with Pappy on a hunting trip and that the afternoon should be peaceful.

After the usual greetings, I noticed that our dogs had curled up in the snow, heads on tails, reluctantly resigned to a nap. Apparently they were bored and disappointed not to find Bob at home, eager for the usual dog fight.

Comfortably settled in the cabin (with Ella asleep), soon our conversation swung from dogs to a bit of Dawson gossip, and then to any snatch of available news of the outside world. Fanny said she had something very interesting to show me. Almost reverently she lifted down from a shelf a magazine called "Munsey's," which was slightly larger than regular book size (1899 edition). Soon Fanny and I were seated side by side browsing through its glossy pages.

The first article to catch our eye was an account of America's recent war with Spain, centered in Cuba. There was an artist's conception of how the United States Fleet must have looked as it steamed into the Santiago Harbor, where it had won a decisive victory. There were several fine pictures accompanying the story including one of General Russel Alger, and one of Admiral Sampson, Commander of the Fleet.

But our feminine interest really caught fire when we turned more pages and found photographs of the country's most prominent social set. Among the beautiful women depicted, were regal Mrs. Clarence McKay taken in a formal garden; Mrs. Burke Roche in a handsome white satin gown, her curls caught up in bows and feathers; an exquisite profile view of Lady Montagne, daughter of the Duchess of Manchester. And then there was a lovely view of Mrs. Oliver Iselin, formerly Miss Goddard of Providence.

Fanny and I stared long and wistfully at these glamorous women, their portraits having been taken by Aime Dupont, she herself a prominent young woman from a wealthy family. Then, to climax all these intriguing pictures, there was a handsome photograph of stately Lady Randolph Churchill of Briton. How regal and queenly she looked!

Among the male scions there was a splendid view of Howard Gould, third son of Jay Gould, multi-millionaire. The caption praised Howard's many philanthropies such as giving large sums to the little slum children of New York. His wife, too, was doing her bit, by sending a relief ship to Dawson to aid the destitute miners. (This very good news, we had heard before and appreciated.)

Turning more pages, we were in the Grand Opera Hall of Fame. Lillian Nordica looked out at us as if she expected an adoring burst of applause. But poor Nordica! In spite of her fame as a great Metropolitan opera star, she could not escape deep sorrow. The magazine told us that her young electrician husband, whom she had so recently met in France and married, had gone up in a balloon of his own invention, never to be seen again!

Turning another page, beautiful Madame Sembrick smiled out at us, enshrined in a halo of musical glory. Sembrick, Munsey's informed us, had come from a humble Polish family. In fact, there had been so many children the poor distraught father, a violin teacher, had barely kept the wolf from the door. "But oh, what a voice!" the critics raved on and on.

Turning more pages, we found ourselves staring at famous Nellie Melba. Seemed that across the miles we could almost hear the pure silver tones of that great Australian soprano in her thrilling Jewel Song from Faust. Surely, she was adding her luster to the bright firmament of the operatic world! Then the rich, velvety voice of handsome Emma Eams, the popular diva from Baltimore, seemed to reach us in Aunty Fanny's humble, blackened log cabin in the Klondike.

Flipping more pages, we came upon Marie Barna and gorgeous, dark-eyed Anna Held, the current toasts of New York, both very beautiful of voice, face and figure; both in great demand, names very high on the musical-theatrical ladder.

But now, what was this amazine news about Adelina Patti, the great—greatest diva of them all—leaving Grand Opera for a season to wed handsome Baron Relf Cederstron, the Swedish nobleman and noted athlete, thirty years younger than Patti? Diplomatically, Munsey's glossed over the glaring difference in age and told how exceedingly youthful Patti was and that the couple should be unusually happy in the Great Diva's castle in southern Wales.

"Oh, I hope this marriage won't hinder Patti's brilliant career," I told Fanny apprehensively. "To say one has heard Patti is almost like saying one has heard Jenny Lind."

"Jenny Lind!" exclaimed Fanny, almost in awe. "Oh, do you suppose there's an Edison talking-machine record of her beautiful voice?"

"Oh, I'm sure not, and it's a great pity. Jenny Lind died long before Edison's wonderful invention. Now all we have is the legend of her phenomenal voice. They called her, "The Swedish Nightingale." She's supposed to have possessed the most perfect voice ever known to man."

"It must have been like an angel's," said Fanny, with a trace of tears in her eyes.

Now, Munsey's shiny white pages urged us rapidly toward the exciting male stars—New York's wonderful theatrical world—brilliant actors, Joseph Sparks, Harry Woodruff, Nat Goodwin and talented James Powers. John Sheehan smiled gaily at us. Very handsome Denis O'Sullivan wore a broad smile, and John Blair too, both sophisticated leading men of the celebrated actress, Julia Marlow.

Reluctantly passing the male stars, we applauded a cluster of beautiful young women—dazzling actresses; truly a part of the great galaxy of golden talent that glittered across the country. Lovely Rhoda Cameron, Mary Manning, Marie Dickerson and Blanche Duffield. But there was one great star that shone above all others: Sarah Bernhardt! Surely her brilliance would never fade and she would become a legend like Jenny Lind.

But now, Aunty Fanny and I were eagerly turning pages faster, towards the classified section, when suddenly the picture of Burton Holmes* came into view.

"Look, Fanny, this young globetrotter is to fall heir to John Stoddard's lecture-travel platform. Holmes is drawing large crowds in New York, showing colored jack-o-lantern slides of the Mikado's kingdom."

"Where is the Mikado's Kingdom?" suddenly asked Clemy from his spot at Fanny's table where he had been quietly copying pictures from a Sears Roebuck catalogue.

"Oh, it's far away across the Pacific Ocean, on an island, I think," said Fanny vaguely. While she was telling Clemy all she knew about Japan, her stubby fingers were turning pages hurriedly to the shopping section.

Eagerly, Fanny and I scanned pictures of many miscellaneous items —dresses, hats, coats, corsets—one designed for plump dowagers. Aunty Fanny jotted down the dowager number. After that, a parade of ladies' buttoned high-top shoes, $3.50; a group of men's woolen suits, $4.95. Boys' woolen suits, $1.90. These all caught our attention.

Other things cried for our consideration: Beeman's Chewing Gum, Mennen's Talcum Powder, Capitol Hair Tonic, Dixon's Pencils, Great Western Champagne, Dollar Ingersoll Watches, Blue Label Tomato Catsup, Liebig's Extract of Beef, Columbia Canned Soups by Armour Packing Company, Rogers' 1847 Silverware. It was all pretty bewildering, almost like being turned loose in a department store!

Intriguing things like Eastman's Kodaks, $5.00 to $35.00; Victor Sewing Machines at $9.50; Victor Talking Machines, $15.00, and up. Wonderful Edison Talking Machines at $20.00 and up! We gazed longingly at pictures of these desirable items. Then our attention was dis-

---

*Burton Holmes visited Yukon Territory and Alaska in 1908, taking pictures. He called his trip, "A Summer's Delight," giving a glowing account of the magnificent scenery: "a warm, dry climate . . . a rich Yukon dream . . . wild flowers, breathtaking!"

tracted to "Unusual Services Offered for Home Treatment... The Drink Habit Cured... The Tobacco Habit Cured." A health, strength and grace exercisor, $2.00. The thing had long heavy pulleys to manipulate. It made both of us groan just to look at it! Another contraption followed, "A remover of wrinkles—The Venus Massager." Another ad caught our attention, "A Rheumatism and Dyspepsia Cure."

We hurried on to "The Rock of Gibralter" ad, by the Prudential Insurance Company, a "solid company."

Now, hurrying faster along Munsey's trail of ads, our eyes found, "The Rambler and Columbia," beautiful bicycle! To get a bicycle without paying money for it, a person could actually do so, by selling a hundred pounds of tea. "But," I asked Fanny, "how on earth could a person dispose of one hundred pounds of tea, and for that matter as much as seventy?" We were debating that subject when our eyes came to rest on pictures of that fascinating new invention, "typewriters—the marvel of the business world," Smith's Premier, The Blickensderfer, The Densmore, The New Century, and The Franklin. They ranged in price from $35 to $50.

Oh, there were so many wonderful things to see in Munsey's it "made our heads swim." Next, the pictures showed us all kinds of pianos. "The Weber" and a player called, "The Aeolian." It had the finest selections, both instrumental and song. Words were printed right on the cylinder-scrolls that revolved 'round and 'round, as the piano played the marvelous selections.

"My goodness, if it ain't all pretty wonderful," sighed Fanny. "We sure live in a wonderful age; what more could a body ask for? And look," exclaimed Fanny, "McCall's magazine is giving away a free dress pattern with a year's subscription—50c. Hope they have size 42."

"I'll order that style too, in a 36," I said.

"Say, now," said Fanny, "here's a real meat grinder, 'The Enterprise.' Next time Pappy brings home an old tough bear, a grinder will be just the thing! Oh, yes," said Fanny, with a doleful sigh, "I'll skip the Lowery's Chocolates, but I'll surely order that nice box of Sparkling Knox Gelatine—the pink kind. It makes such pretty desserts. All you have to do is add sugar, water, and flavoring."

Ah, the mention of food! The subject was fatal, and she knew it! Almost automatically, Aunty Fanny reached for her precious cookbook. After that, we were lost in the agony and delight of thumbing through the cookbook's apetizing pages. We read and re-read, and looked at pictures of special recipes, which were utterly impossible to duplicate, until our mouths literally drooled and our tummies ached for the good food.

Finally, Fanny herself broke the painful, hypnotic spell by saying, "This is a crime! I have no refreshments to offer company. I've been too busy cleaning up cinders and ashes. But next time I'll have pink gelatine and sugar cookies. It's a promise, Clemy. I must say," she added, with a twinkle in her expressive brown eyes, "we've had a mighty interesting afternoon of opera, concerts, the theater, and shopping, and good, imaginary meals, haven't we? Please do come again, and let it be soon."

Well, of course we were more than normally hungry after spending two hours feasting our eyes on tempting food recipes, especially since we knew that all we would have for supper would be the usual menu, bacon and beans; yes, and dried prunes.

Our dogs were hungry too, as it was near their feeding time. So, after Clemy and I bade Aunty Fanny goodbye, our malemutes fairly flew through the snow.

We were about half way home, when all at once a little white jack rabbit crossed our path and darted down the hill.

Immediately, the dogs took after it, in wild pursuit—lickity split! Clemy, on the back runners, screamed at the dogs to stop, but they paid no heed.

Like a flash, we raced through showers of icicles and mushy snow—bumpity, bump! Past bushes, fallen logs, ruts and trees.

Suddenly, and with a terrific jolt, we hit a rock! Ella flew from my arms and in the same instant I was thrown just barely clear of the sleigh, landing under an avalanche of wadded diapers, wet snow, and yapping, quivering dogs.

"Clemy, Clemy," I shouted, "find Ella quick and help me!"

He came running from somewhere and frantically searched for Ella who had gone into a nearby snow bank, head first!

Quickly, he found the spot, pulled her out and propped her up in the snow. Then, he turned his frantic attention to me. The impact had only knocked the wind out of us.

Desperately, and with Clemy's help, I tried to free myself from that awful, tangled mess of harnesses, dogs and everything else, but the more

I struggled, the harder the feet of the dogs beat upon me, as they were still madly trying to pursue that poor frightened little jack rabbit!

"Help, help me, Clemy," I implored hysterically. Clemy was only seven years old; much too young to handle a situation like this, and the dogs sensed it. What a chaotic dilemma I was in!

By this time, Ella had found her voice and was wailing her lungs out. Still, I couldn't go to her, but at least I knew she was alive!

Finally in desperation, Clemy himself began to weep. Great helpless tears streamed down his anguished face. But he kept struggling to set me free. Intermittently, he pulled and tugged at the harness, and cried, and even kicked at the dogs in his frustrated agony. But still they were wildly unmanageable. I was becoming afraid, too, as sometimes dogs do go completely savage!

Then, all at once Clemy straightened. He rushed to the head of that frenzied heap of dogs and suddenly let loose torrents of terrible oaths that were indeed shocking to hear! His words were so bad they would have done credit to a profane old Sourdough. Why! Even I, in my state of helpless tangle, was speechless!

But the effect of those impassioned, unprintable words was electric. To my utter amazement the dogs immediately calmed. Obediently forgetting the rabbit, they quietly let Clemy untangle them—and me—and right the sled. Actually, the animals appeared ashamed and as meek as lambs!

Soon, Ella and I were back in the sled under the robes, ready to continue homeward!

As we approached our cabin we saw Ed coming hurriedly down the trail looking for us. Because of the lateness of the hour he had become very much alarmed.

"Edward," I exclaimed, as I jumped from the sleigh, "I hate profanity, but I tell you, it was the only thing that controlled the dogs. You should have heard your son swear!"

Later, when it was quiet in the cabin and Clemy was fast asleep, Ed laughed softly when I reviewed the sled accident in detail, and with some embarrassment softly repeated words that Clemy had used from his "Sourdough vocabulary."

"Vel," chuckled Ed, "those dogs understand swearing perhaps more than any other words. I honestly believe you would still be back there wallowing in the snow if Clemy hadn't resorted to that kind of language. But, Vel," he added, more seriously, "you may be sure Clemy realized the desperate plight you were in when he swore like that. Yes, you bet," added Ed, with a half-amused expression, "in times of great emergency very strong language is the most effective to use on these Alaska malemutes."

"Perhaps," I admitted reluctantly, "but I'm wondering what Clemy's grandmother and friends in Tacoma would say if they could hear him using such rough language."

"Oh," said Ed, looking quite serious, "when we return to civilization, don't worry, Clemy will know better than to talk like that."

"Oh I hope so," I said dubiously, "But Ed, as a matter of curiosity, do you ever swear at the malemutes?"

"Me?" laughed Ed, "Sure, of course I do, occasionally! Yes, Vel, at times a fella's got to let the dogs know who's boss. Naturally, tho', I try not to use that kind of authority in front of ladies!"

Chapter 22

PATSY AND PEDRO AND ANOTHER SUMMER

Pat, nicknamed "Patsy," was another one of Ed's good sled-dogs. This animal was of Alaska origin, but he seemed much milder than our other dogs and we soon discovered that he wouldn't fight unless actually driven to it.

One afternoon Ed returned home from a jaunt earlier than I had expected, and he had Patsy with him. The dog showed obvious signs of recent battle. His flank was torn and his ears were bleeding. Also several claws hung loose and bloody.

"Sure, Patsy was in a dog-fight!" said Ed, looking a little proud, "but he certainly came away the champion!"

"Oh, but poor Patsy's badly hurt," I said anxiously.

---

*By 1901 Arizona Charlie, world-famous actor, wild West showman, was putting on a much-talked-of show at the Savoy Theater in Dawson called, "The Cheechako Girls."

"No, they're only minor injuries," declared Ed, "a little warm water and salt will soon fix that up, and in a few days Pat'll be as good as new."

"But what happened?" I asked, as I hurried to get the water and salt solution.

"Well," said Ed, "it was like this: I had to go down Dominion Creek to see a fellow about something and of course Patsy followed me as usual. On the way I met a miner who also had a dog—a great big, fierce-looking fellow called, 'Big Boy'.

"The stranger and I exchanged pleasant enough greetings, but it was evident that our dogs immediately disliked each other. Almost right away they started snarling and snapping.

" 'Great Scott,' I remarked to the stranger, 'I ought to take my dog home before there's a terrible fight.'

"But the miner just laughed lightly, and said, 'Oh whatcha worrying about, Partner? Let 'em fight. It's good for 'em to have a little exercise.'

"Well, I could see that the man was actually egging his dog on by his encouraging attitude and the tone of his voice.

"Suddenly, before I could get Patsy away, the big fellow rushed him! In a twinkling he knocked Pat over into the snow. Such kicking, clawing and snarling with fur flying as I've hardly witnessed before! The dogs were just like two mad jungle beasts! First, Big Boy grabbed Pat by the throat, but Patsy somehow slipped out of his clutch, evading the awful death-grip. Big Boy then got a toe-hold on one of Pat's sore ears. But Pat tore himself loose. Then Big Boy got Pat by the other ear, and again Pat tore away. The next thing I knew Big Boy had clamped his sharp fangs into Pat's flank and was dragging him all around in the snow! Pat's blood spurted in all directions!

" 'Jumping Lucifer!' I shouted to the stranger, 'Your Big Boy is killing my dog! You've got to stop him!' But the man just stood there grinning with a satisfied smile. Suddenly, before I could find a rock or a club to drive Big Boy off, Patsy wriggled free. Like lightning he was up on his feet. He grabbed Big Boy by the throat, then by the nose, sinking his sharp fangs deep down into the dog's nose gristle. Then, our Pat began shaking that dog like a rat in the wind.

"Great Scott, I was glad to see that the battle had turned. But I could also see that the stranger's dog was going to be minus a nose pretty soon if something drastic wasn't done, and quick! I almost felt sorry for the brute. And, mind you, his master just stood there like a big dummy, staring with mouth wide open, not believing what he saw. Well, I couldn't stand it any longer, so I yelled, 'Pat, drop that dog. Drop him, I say; do you hear!'

"Of course, Patsy was infuriated and I thought, beyond the point of recall. I couldn't blame him much either. He certainly had good reason to be mad. The big brute had started the whole scrap in the first place. But at this point Pat musta' decided he'd taught Big Boy a severe enough lesson. Whatever it was, he was willing to obey my second stern command. Anyway, what followed proves that Pat isn't really a killer. He just gave one more last twist to the big bully's nose, then shaking himself free, he walked disdainfully away from the writhing beast!

"But, oh, it was a grisly sight! Big Boy's nose hung in ribbons."

"What happened then?" I asked, shuddering a little.

"Ha! The last glimpse I had of the stranger and his 'Big Boy' was of them runnin' down the creek together. Big Boy was howling bloody murder and was leaving a gory trail behind.

"Sure," added Ed, proudly, as he gently washed Pat's wounds, "you were the real champion! But I'm truly glad that you didn't kill that other dog—you just taught him a good lesson, and I hope he and his master will remember it for a very long time. It doesn't pay to be a big bully!"

* * *

Feeding our dogs was always a real chore. We had laid in a supply of special dog-bacon and Ed nearly always prepared the dog food just before our supper time. The mixture was made of dog-bacon, mush and flour, and, if we had any scraps, he would throw them into the stew also.

Naturally, the dogs were always ravenously hungry by nightfall. They would group around the cabin door in a semi-circle, sitting on their haunches like wolves, licking their lips while Ed was in the process of cooking their supper.

Each dog had a tin plate and when the "slum-gullion" was cool enough Ed would take the stuff outside and pour it into each individual dish. Then he would call,

"All right, boys, it's all yours. Come and get it."

Before he would finish the words, each dog would make a rush for his plate, snapping and snarling a ferocious warning to the others not to trespass. Then, whole mouthfuls of food would disappear in big gulps. Before the meal would be finished, quite often there would be quarrels over tiny stray morsels. Boris would usually be victorious if a real dog fight developed, for he was a powerful animal. With dog-supper over, usually they would curl up in the snow and sleep peacefully 'til morning. If it happened to snow heavily during the night the animals would be completely covered except for little air holes above their noses, marking the spot.*

PEDRO

Early in the spring of 1901, Edward finally realized that our dogs couldn't possibly haul enough wood to supply our cabin and the boiler house at the mine (2B Below Lower Discovery). So he bought a horse named Pedro.

Pedro was a lovable brown animal with wide soulful eyes that matched his color. All of us grew very fond of him and he quickly became the family's pet. Of course, he especially loved Ed.

But something very mysterious began happening almost right away after we acquired Pedro. Our mattress, which had bulged with a comfortable stuffing of fragrant wild hay, gradually grew thinner and thinner! Then, one day I knew why. Ed had been feeding some of our mattress to Pedro!

"Aw," laughed Ed, when I caught him red-handed, "soon we'll be getting fresh new hay from the hills! Vel, you should see how that horse comes running when I offer him straw from the mattress! Why, I think it's worth sleeping on a little harder bed, don't you?"

Well, that was that! I wouldn't complain of a thinner mattress if Ed and Pedro were happy! And certainly the horse was thriving and proving his worth. He hauled great quantites of wood for the mine and us, and we grew fonder of him with each passing day, for he truly was a very gentle, loving animal. Often, Clemy would come riding home on

---

*Many cheechakos think, after a snowstorm, that their dogs have wandered away, only to find them later, buried under a thick blanket of snow. Cold weather is no real hardship to Alaska dogs, for they are built by Nature to withstand very severe temperatures.

Pedro's back with Ed walking beside him.

When the snow began melting away, Ed turned Pedro loose at short intervals so that the horse could roam the nearby hill, and, too, he could forage a little food for himself. But always when Ed would whistle or call, the horse would come galloping to him.

One day, however, when Ed whistled and called, the horse didn't appear. At first Ed thought he must have strayed beyond earshot and would soon return. But the day grew late and there was still no Pedro in sight. Alarmed, Ed hurried down the trail.

Now and then he would stop and whistle and call for Pedro, but there was no sign of him anywhere. Finally, Ed met a stranger coming up the trail.

"Say, have you seen a brown horse?" asked Ed, anxiously.

"Why, yes," replied the man, "I saw one just about a half-mile back down the trail."

Ed thanked the stranger and hurried on. Soon he caught sight of Pedro through the willows. Ed whistled, expecting the horse to come galloping to him. But Pedro whinnied pathetically and stood still, waiting for Ed to reach him. When Ed approached closer he saw that the horse was badly injured and could barely stand. Then, Ed saw blood all over the ground.

He rushed to Pedro's side and discovered that he had a gaping gunshot wound in his back and it was bleeding profusely.

"Poor boy," cried Ed, as he tried desperately to staunch the blood, first with his handkerchief, then with parts of his shirt. Pedro, even in his terrible agony, tried to show Ed how very glad he was to see him. He whinnied softly and even tho' gasping for breath, tried to nuzzle Ed's hand.

But in a few minutes the horse staggered and fell to the ground. It was then Ed realized there was no hope of saving Pedro. The poor animal was mortally wounded and was dying. So, knowing that the end was very near, Ed sat down on the trail beside Pedro and gently cradling the horse's head in his lap, he talked softly and soothingly petted him.

Pedro, himself, seemed to realize that he was dying. Even in his last few moments he made a pitiful effort to show his great affection for Edward—tried to show his gratitude that his master had come to be with him until the end. And as Pedro's head sank lower and lower and his soulful eyes closed, he faintly whinnied a last farewell to his beloved master.

That night in our cabin Ed sadly described the death of Pedro. Clemy was tearful and completely unconsoled until Edward said tenderly,

"Little son, if ever a horse deserved going to animal heaven, it was our faithful Pedro. I'm sure he's there now in green pastures."

The following day the miners and Edward buried Pedro under the birch and willow trees not far from the river and under the protecting shadow of King Solomon's Dome.

No, we never could find out who killed poor Pedro, but one of the miners thought that it might have been a trigger-happy "cheechako" who was out hunting and mistaking our lovable brown horse for a deer, had shot him. The miners seemed to recall having heard gunshots earlier that same afternoon.

Later, Ed questioned the stranger whom he had met on the trail, but the man claimed no knowledge of the horse being wounded. He said he had only seen Pedro from a distance and that he had supposed the animal belonged to some miner in the close vicinity.

Not only had we lost a lovable pet, we lost a willing worker. And, besides that, horses in the North were scarce and very, very expensive!

* * *

By the middle of March the first hint of spring is signalled in the North by the appearance of a few birds from the South and the fall of large moist snowflakes which flutter to earth like petals from dewy white star-flowers. Soon the patter of soft rain can be heard, and the snow which has covered the frozen ground all winter long turns damp and perforated and is ready to melt.

Suddenly, vivid rainbows unfurl high overhead. When these appeared I could nearly always expect little Clemy to come shouting and running to the cabin in excitement, wanting to make sure that I, too, would see the lovely rainbows.

Spellbound and almost in awe, we would watch the delicate beauty and the subtly-changing colors, and delight in the anticipation of the wonderful coming of spring and another summer.

One day in April, after watching an especially beautiful rainbow

*Horses cost from $1,500 to $3,000 apiece in the early days.

spanning our valley, I said, "Clemy, God is the Creator of all that makes this beautiful display and He never forgets a promise. The rainbow in Noah's time many centuries ago meant a radiant colorful promise, a sign in the sky that never, never again would there be another terrible flood that would cover the earth."

Clemy was so impressed with the Ark story that he rushed indoors and drew and painted dramatic scenes of Noah's Ark, showing all the animals that he knew about in Alaska, including bear, rabbits, horses, deer, mountain sheep and malemutes. These, he showed hurrying into the Ark barely escaping the angry flood waters. He painted other versions too, and made bright rainbows over different landscapes. These he pinned to our cabin walls and invited his good friends, the miners, to see his Noah's Ark exhibit. He explained the Bible story—of the terrible storm and how the flood waters covered the earth and how old Noah had gathered the animals into the big Ark and saved them.

"Oh, Clemy," one of his friends commented, "you sure make me feel mighty glad that I didn't live in them turrible days, 'cause I can't swim and Noah wouldn't of took me aboard 'cause I'm a mean old swearing cuss!"

Quite a number of Clemy's pictures ended up on the cabin walls of the miners, and his pictures did brighten their quarters—even kept some of the cold air from coming through the knot holes.

After the spring rains ceased, like magic many wild flowers sprang up all over the hills, and then sometimes Clemy and I would roam the slopes gathering fragrant bouquets of blue bells, lupine, primrose, forget-me-nots, anenome and shooting stars. At the height of the flower season Clemy always had my precious cups filled with colorful blooms.*

In mid-summer, we took tin pails and tramped the hills hunting wild strawberries, blackberries, ruhbarb, thimble berries, salmonberries, wild raspberries and red and black currants.

Wild cranberries ripened very late in the fall and grew down in the low, boggy places. The cranberries were of a deep red color and made

---

*Other wild flowers in the North were: yellow violets, roses, foxgloves, iceland-poppies, columbine, monkey flower, spotted orchids, and all kinds of ferns. Then there were: adder's tongue, spiderwort, bracken, pasque-flower, Hudson Bay tea, and many varieties of moss. Many cultivated flowers grew in Dawson, too. Mrs. George Black, wife of Yukon's seventh commissioner, recorded that there were 464 different varieties of wild flowers in the North.

delicious sauce, an excellent accompaniment to wild meats.

Often, I made pies. One day when I wanted to make blackberry pie for supper, I discovered I was completely out of lard. I tried bacon grease as a substitute. With many misgivings, I baked the pie to a golden brown, and to my surprise and delight the bacon grease made a flaky delicious crust. Ed and Clemy smacked their lips and said they couldn't guess why it tasted so unusually good.

Yes, it certainly took all of my creative ingenuity to cook in the North, and I was learning to be a fairly good cook at last. They say necessity is the mother of invention and so it was with me and my cooking. I also supplemented our diet with fresh greens which grew wild on the hills. It seemed that we just couldn't get enough of these, and I often sent little Clemy out to gather them in late afternoon. They were a very tender, light green, leafy plant which we called "lamb's quarters."

These were quite plentiful and were a real joy to prepare and eat, especially if seasoned with salt and pepper, a dash of vinegar and hot bacon grease. Some folks called it "wilted Yukon lettuce."

Naturally, we were always ravenously hungry for all kinds of fresh foods. In the spring of 1901, a barge arrived at Dawson loaded with produce, having come down the Yukon after stopping at White Horse. This first barge of the season had, among other things, potatoes, onions and eggs. Of course, everyone in Dawson was eager to get a fair share of the fresh food, really drooling in anticipation! Only a few pounds of it was freighted out by packhorse to the little roadhouse on Dominion Creek.

Luckily, I happened to be on hand when the food arrived and I persuaded Selma, the cook, to let me buy some, if only a little taste! Reluctantly and rather grudgingly she sold me one precious dried onion and a scant pound of potatoes (three of them). In the States I could have bought a sack of potatoes and ten pounds of onions for what I paid for those few vegetables!

Trembling with anticipation, I rushed home and boiled the potatoes

---

*By 1902 the Fax Brothers were successfully farming on the outskirts of Dawson. They made a good profit on their potatoes, cabbages, parsnips and turnips. In West Dawson, across the Yukon River, there were several successful farms. The produce was large and delicious. During summer the sunlight was almost unbroken for about six weeks, causing the vegetables to mature rapidly. All produce was spoken for in advance. People hungrily watched the garden grow and sometimes thieves would rob the gardens before the produce could be harvested.

with their jackets on and lovingly cooked that one lone onion. I hovered over the kettle while the food was boiling and when Ed returned home I had the unusual treat all ready to serve. Needless to say he was very surprised and pleased. Never had potatoes and one onion become such a sumptuous banquet.

Chapter 23

SOURDOUGH TALES AND YUKON ROMANCES

One night, when bright stars were flickering and Northern Lights flashed in the sky, Edward and I hurried to get our cabin ready for a gathering of miners, as they were coming for an evening of talk and song. I was whisking through the supper dishes when suddenly there came an early knock at our cabin.

Edward rushed to the door and was surprised to see, not a miner, but Max Lange, our mail carrier.

"Why, Max, it's good to see you," exclaimed Ed. "We're having the fellows over, and I am awfully glad you dropped by."

"Thanks, Ed," said Max, stepping inside, "I'll be glad to see the boys and stay awhile. Was on my way to the Dome Roadhouse, but my malamutes suddenly played out. Thought I'd better stop and give them a rest. Your cabin did look cheery and inviting!"

"We could put you up for the night," I said. "We do have an extra cot."

"Thanks, I may accept your kind offer if my dogs are unable to travel," he said, as he pulled off his parka and loosened his mucklucks.

Soon the miners began arriving. They were delighted to see Max, as he was always very good company, and he knew all the latest Dawson news. He was literally the walking, talking newspaper of the Klondike.

The children were now fast asleep in their own little corner (behind

---

*Almost all miners lived on credit during the long winters and at "clean-up time" in the spring and summer months, debts would be paid at the bank or trading companies from gold sluiced out of the pay-dirt.

the pink cretonne curtains). The men sat smoking near the stove in a semi-circle, blowing smoke rings and looking quite contented. I settled down by the lamp near the window, with a pile of mending—socks, moccasins and mittens—listening to the men discuss late news of the world, gold, Dawson, adventure, romance! The men seemed to completely forget my presence, and that was the way I wished it.

One of the miners drew sly, hilarious mirth, and then masculine speculations as to what kind of a woman she would be who so brazenly had sent him a letter, a complete stranger, passionately begging him to marry her, and settle down on Dominion Creek to mine lots of gold and raise a large family. The Chicago woman had mentioned her various feminine charms with shocking frankness!

"Ha, that's no joke," laughed the miner. "Back in '98 there was actually a female expedition organized in New York for the sole purpose of grabbing husbands in the Klondike. The miners were pelted with love letters, saying the women were coming! The river boat, 'Mae West,' and several others, actually steamed up to Dawson that year bringing eager, hopeful Amazons. It was really interesting to watch those marriages. They seldom panned out. One gal even jumped into the Yukon soon after she and a miner got hitched!"

"Yes, you're right," agreed Max Lange, "those marriages seldom worked out. Now you take the famous 'Birch Tree Wedding'—well, it worked out just fine, and became one of the most unique and colorful romances of the North."

I put down my sewing to ask with bursting curiosity, "What on earth do you mean by a Birch Tree Wedding?"

"Ha!" laughed Max, "I thought you'd be interested in this one. All of the ladies are! It's truly the most talked-of marriage of the gold-rush.

"Well, I'll have to tell you about it: It happened like this. Back in '98 there was an excited group of stampeders who took off from Dawson for the Koyukuk River country where gold had been reported, way up beyond the Arctic Circle. Among the group was an intrepid school teacher traveling alone with her sleigh and dogs.

"It's hard to say just how the romance started, but anyway Aggie Dalton fell in love with a fellow-traveler, a stampeder named Angus McGinnis. Of course he returned her love and begged her to marry him. But that was a real problem! There was no preacher within hundreds of miles and the couple had no idea when they would meet one.

"It so happened that there was a religious fellow in the group who had a small Bible. His name was 'Frenchie Joe.' He very obligingly offered to perform the wedding ceremony which was, under wilderness circumstances, considered quite legal. There was one catch. It was only legal if the ceremony could be immediately recorded.

"So Aggie, being a school teacher, and mighty smart, thought of a novel way to record the marriage. She found a large white birch tree and with a penknife engraved on its trunk her part of the marriage record. It read:

> Ten miles from the Yukon, on the shores of this lake,
> For a partner to the Koyukuk, McGinnis I'll take.
> There is no preacher and we have no ring,
> But it makes no difference, it's all the same thing.

Under Aggie's record McGinnis carved his pledge:

> I swear by my gee-pole, under this tree,
> A faithful husband to Aggie I'll be,
> I'll love and protect her, this maiden so frail,
> From Sourdough-stiffs, on the Koyukuk Trail.

And Frenchie Joe finished the record by writing:

> For two dollars in cheechako money,
> I'll unite this couple in holy matrimony;
> He be a miner and she be a teacher,
> I can do this job as well as a preacher!

"Yes, you're right! That certainly was a unique marriage," I agreed. "But I'm sure the school teacher and McGinnis would want the benefit of a real preacher once they get back to civilization."

"All of the ladies react like you to the Birch Tree Wedding," laughed Max. "Well, it's one of my favorite stories, and I enjoy telling it."

"Say," broke in Turner, slightly changing the subject, but still on matrimony, "I heerd one of them gay-gals got married. Yes, sir! She grabbed herself a pretty nice feller, too! Then, she complained to the Mounties that the gals of the bright red curtains and red lamps next door just wasn't decent! She made such a fracas and all hell-fuss of it that the Red Coats finally ordered them gay-gals to go across the

Klondike River, to Louse Town, or else get clean out of the country. Can you imagine it? N'right in the dead of winter, too!"

"Yeah," drawled the miner, "things is sure changing in Dawson. 'Taint like it used ter be, back in '97 and '98 when fellers was a whoopin' it up! Them was the good ole days, all right! Yep, even the hotels is a-tryin' ter put on the dog—a-servin' them six course dinners, from soup ter nuts, just like they do in San Franciscy. If you don't believe it, just go take a look in the new Fairview Hotel and the Royal Alexander.

"But say, by gosh!" said Johnson, lowering his voice. "A feller tells me there's a lot of them painted dolls of the red lights still a-livin' in Dawson! Those rich, licentious wimmin' pays as high as $500 fer jes one of them flimsy, peek-a-boo gowns at Madame Trembley's fancy French Dress Shop. A lot of the wimmin' has got dozens of them purty, butterfly dresses, too! A number of the fellers have seen 'em! Lordy, jes ter think of all of them nuggets, and how them wimmin' is a-collectin' 'em. It ain't right!"

"Yea, and do you know somethin'?" said one of the miners, in a lower whisper. "Some of them gals who buys the peek-a-boo dresses, and some of them pretty clerks too, who sells 'em, sleeps in beautiful beds with pretty red covers and soft, satiny pillows? Sure thing—it's all upstairs, right there near the dress shop in that hotel. Them shiny brass beds, they tell me, looks like real gold, but it's all supposed to be kept a secret!"

"Humph! 'Taint no secret," broke in one of the miners. "Everybody knows! But they jest ain't supposed to talk. Why, they say them brass beds is jest like gold in the bank and . . . "

There was a long, awkward pause. I looked up from my sewing. The miner suddenly remembered where he was, flushed and didn't continue the tale.

"Say, Vel," called Ed, obviously anxious to change the scandalous subject, "I think it's time to have refreshments."

While the canned milk, with snow water for hot chocolate, was

---

*To a bigamist, who had a wife in Skagway, Whitehorse, and Nome, a judge asked, "How could you do such a thing?" To which the man replied, "Me have fast dog-team!"

*Madame Trembley went over Chilkoot Pass in the early stampedes, carrying a few dresses to sell. Her store in Dawson was the most fashionable and she was very much respected. She and her husband died in the 1950's.

heating, I cut the coarse-textured cake and listened nostalgically to the men harmonize. Someone had brought an old fiddle and Max gladly played the tunes, improvising as he went along.

They ended up by singing, "Tenting Tonight," "Nearer My God to Thee," and "Throw out the Life Line." What a relief the songs were from the dubious subject of the peek-a-boo gowns and brass beds.

The men ate ravenously, enthusiastically applauding my cake, and while they were smacking their lips over the last drops of chocolate, I slipped behind the pink cretonne curtain to check on the children. When I returned to the circle one of the miners was saying,

"Humph! That's Swiftwater Bill, all right, his same old confidence game. How're folks to know? 'Klondike!' It's the magic word. In England Bill got over a million for worthless stocks."

"Humph!" said Smythe, "I'll say he's glib; dresses like a dandy—in them expensive suits and flashy ties! Not bad lookin' neither. Some think he even uses perfume. Ugh!"

"Yep, that's Bill," laughed Ed, "and he always wears nugget jewelry and lots of diamonds, too!"

"And such big talk!" added Larsen, "He promises the moon and people scramble to buy his stocks. But Jack Smith, his partner, is mighty worried. He and Swiftwater own that Monte Carlo gamblin' casino. Says Swiftwater has gone through several fortunes already. Says gold is real bad for Bill.

"And, did you know that when Swiftwater was in Seattle he threw a big party at the Rainier Grand Hotel? It really made the headlines. Clad only in a skimpy bathing suit, he jumped into a champagne bath and splashes around. Then, he climbs out of the tub of bubbly stuff and showers everybody at the party with nuggets! They tell me his champagne bill alone that night was $1,500. Think of it, and all that champagne going down the drain! Would you believe it? He lights cigars with five dollar bills to impress folks, and throws gold coins helter-skelter to the crowds. Loves to be tagged, 'The Big, Generous Klondike King'. His partner says, 'Just watch Swiftwater, he'll surely be a pauper some day!' "

"Well, I'm watchin'," said Joe, "but he's still very rich!"*

"Yeah, but just keep watchin'," laughed Max, "Swiftwater Bill's in

---

*Swiftwater Bill did become a pauper. About 1910 he returned to the States and worked as a day-laborer laying ties for a railroad.

the Dawson limelight again, more than ever. I mean matrimonially. Yes, sir! Ever since he returned from Seattle the gals have sure been after him! Do you remember how he got rid of Wife Number Three not so long ago? His real reason was, he said, that she'd married him just for his gold. Now isn't that surprisin'? Remember how, last year, Swiftwater Bill put on a special act in his Monte Carlo show ridiculing his wife so unmercifully? Well, it was burlesqued by his wife's own sister, an actress!

"The poor wife! Every time she set foot in Dawson, she was nearly laughed off the streets.

"Well, after a while the fellows began to feel pretty sorry for Number Three Wife. Especially since it was the girl's own sister a-makin' all the trouble. But then the fellows began betting the sister would be Wife Number Four. Imagine betting on two women like they were race horses! Yep, that's the way they are—this gamblin' bunch of the green cloth!

"Ha!" laughed Max, "Swiftwater is one of them and don't you ever forget it! But there is a very recent Klondike episode all Dawson is still smiling about, which, I'll bet Swiftwater would darn well like to forget! It concerns a certain high-spirited, saucy young lady, named Nelly Daly.

"Well, it seems that Nelly had just barely arrived back in Dawson when Swiftwater Bill spotted her. He followed her all over town, and out on the Eldorado to a social event where he hadn't been invited! But that didn't stop him. He crashed the party and inveigled the hostess to introduce him to Nelly.

"A few minutes later, when the music struck up, without going through the formality of asking Nelly to dance, he grabbed her and pulled her out onto the floor. She danced with him all right, but when the music picked up speed and he was wildly whirling her, suddenly she jerked herself free and Swiftwater, losing his balance, went careening across the floor to the opposite side of the room, where he crashed with an awful thud! There he lay on the floor, sprawled like a clown, in an awkward daze, while everyone at the party roared with laughter!

"As soon as Swiftwater could pick himself up he left the party as mad as a hornet! But the following day, much to Nelly's surprise, he

---

*By about 1900 there were a few telephones in Dawson and there was one at the gold fields. By 1903, a direct telephone line was run across the Divide to the mouth of Gold Run Creek. Captain Olson was the manager of the Telephone Expansion Line. All copper wire was used. Fifty instruments were on the line.

St. Andrew's Ball, Dawson, 1902, a yearly event. Notice formal evening clothes.

A group enjoying a summer's picnic on Mid-Night Dome, high above Dawson City. Moosehide slide is to left, not in picture.

George W. Carmack, discoverer of gold in the Klondike, with his Tagish Indian wife and little daughter, Graphie Grace.

Ben Atwater, famous mailman, and his dog team. His runs often amounted to 1,000 miles.

came around by the telephone company where she was working as a substitute operator. It was just closing time. To Nelly's amazement, Swiftwater acted as though nothing had happened. Of course, she expected him to be very resentful. But what do you suppose he said? Well, you could never guess! It was, 'Nelly, my girl, I want to marry you!'

"Nelly was flabbergasted! She couldn't believe her ears! She tried to argue him out of the idea, but he, with his fast glib talk, was like a ferocious avalanche—not to be turned aside. He swore she'd be his true love forever and ever, and he would buy her anything—just anything—she desired!

"On and on he raved, adding all sorts of extravagant promises until poor Nelly was at her wit's end to know how to get rid of him. Everyone had left the telephone office. She was completely alone with this eager, egotistical nugget-covered suitor, who was used to having his way with women.

"But all at once she got an idea! 'Swiftwater Bill,' she said, sweetly, 'call my Mother. Her number is 29, Eldorado. When she answers, ask for my hand in marriage. If she consents, I'll surely marry you!'

"Now Nelly knew very well her Mother's opinion of the notorious gambler, so she had no fear of the outcome.

"With brassy confidence Swiftwater stepped into the telephone booth and called his prospective mother-in-law, while Nelly watched through the glass window with suppressed laughter. She couldn't hear the conversation, but she saw Swiftwater Bill's expectant face turn from flushed pink to vivid purple, and then she saw him shake with rage. Hurriedly, he banged up the receiver and came at her like a wounded bull.

" 'Nelly,' he roared, 'you tricked me! Half of the women of Dawson would jump at the chance to marry me! And here, I begged you! I have already engaged a special luxury yacht to take us down the Yukon, to Ruby. It was to be our wedding trip! Now you make me the laughing stock of Dawson!'

"With that last remark he bolted from the telephone company. They say Swiftwater took the trip downriver to Ruby—alone, without Wife Number Four. After that, for a time, Dawson was minus its notorious lover," laughed Max, mischievously.

"Well, to go on with the story: It seems that soon after Swiftwater

Bill's departure, Nelly met John Vogel, the handsome Klondike Nugget reporter. Vogel owns Nero, the Great Dane that delivers papers up to the Bonanza and Eldorado twice a week. I guess there isn't a dog as famous in the Klondike as this one.

"Well, to make a long story short, Nelly first saw Nero out on the Eldorado one day after Swiftwater left Dawson. Of course, she stopped to pet the big affectionate animal and when John Vogel met Nelly he promptly fell in love with her. The couple will soon be wed and they plan to take Nero to Seattle.

"Say," said Max, fumbling for something in his pockets, "here's a poem that Nelly wrote. John Vogel published it in the Klondike Nugget the other day. (Virgil Moore was editor-in-chief of the paper.) The miners figure that Nero has mushed about six thousand miles altogether, delivering papers. Listen while I read the poem," said Max, as he moved closer to the lamp:

> Everybody knows old Nero,
>   Our dear old faithful friend.
> Twice a week he brings the Nugget,
>   And on him we depend.
> So we call him, "Nugget Nero,"
>   How appropriate the name!
> And perchance if we miss our paper,
>   We're sure old Nero's not to blame.
>
> For four long years, nugget Nero's
>   Packed the Nugget up the creeks;
> And no matter what the weather,
>   Faithful fellow never kicks.
> On Eldorado and Bonanza
>   Nero's friends are not a few,
> And they always greet him kindly
>   On the day the Nugget's due.
>
> Remember, dear old Nero,
>   Every doggie has his day;
> And for faithful service
>   You surely must have pay.
> Soon the days of mushing will be over,
>   Into your kennel you can creep,
> And to those who come to call you,
>   Sing, 'Go away and let me sleep!'

> Could we find an artist, Nero
>   Who might sketch you as you are,
> And do justice to our hero;
>   We would sound his praises far
> For we love our Nugget Nero,
>   And a picture we would like
> Of the dog who brought our papers
>   In the far away Klondike.

"Oh," I told Max, "I think this love story with Nero as matchmaker is the happiest romance of the North! I think it's even more romantic than the 'Birch Tree Wedding.' "

"Yes, now, perhaps sweet Nelly will forget that awful day back in 1900 when the ice gave up the battered body of Fred Clayson*," said Max Lange, quite unexpectedly.

At the mention of Fred Clayson there seemed a sudden chill in the air. Hurriedly, I bade the miners a friendly goodnight, and as I was drowsing off, behind the curtain, I could hear quiet subdued voices droning on, and in varied conversation about people in the Klondike ——about Fred Clayson——Nelly, and then——George Carmack.

"Say, everyone feels mighty sorry for poor Kate Carmack, the little Indian wife of George Carmack!"

"What's it all about?" Ed asked.

"Well, it seems there's a new girl in Dawson who's come between the Carmacks and broken up their marriage," said Joe. "It's Marguerite Laimee, that rather pretty, dark-haired hussie who, they say, has followed all the new gold camps for the last few years. She even crossed the ocean to Australia. From there, sailed to South Africa—then, up here to the Klondike. Well, it seems she's struck it rich by grabbing the most famous Klondike King in the North! The Discoverer of Bonanza Gold!

"But it's funny! That girl surely knows her mining, too. Already, she's cleaned up a small fortune of her own. Every night, they say, she scrapes up the floor sawdust in her cigar store (on Front Street) and burns it, and then she pans real gold from the ashes—quite a lot of it, too! Gold dust is often spilled by careless miners, maybe forty dollars' worth a day!"

*See Chapter, "Three Men in a Casket of Ice"

"Well, I'm awfully sorry about the Carmacks," said Ed. "Most of us have seen them together in Dawson with chubby little four-year-old daughter, Graphie Grace. They all seemed happy! Kate was dressed nicely; obviously was trying to look like a white woman, and I'll say she was succeeding quite well, too."

"Yes, you're right," agreed Max, "but Carmack is sending Kate back to the Tagish Indian Village. Little Graphie Grace will remain with her father to be raised as a white woman."

"Poor little Indian woman!" said Ed, sympathetically. "For without Kate and her relatives, Tagish Charlie and Skookum Jim, Carmack might never have been the discoverer of Klondike gold."

"Yep, there's another example of how the yellow stuff has changed the life of a Klondike King," observed Larson. "Back in '98 and '99, the owner of rich Whisky Hill Number Ten, Hunker, fell hard for that frumpy little dance-hall girl. And it's common knowledge, too, that he offered her her weight in gold if she would come spend the winter with him in his cabin up on Hunker Creek.

"Well, by Jiminy! The girl consented. I think she actually fattened up just so she could get a bigger payment. Then, when she had received her gold, quite suddenly she came down with a very mysterious illness, and so Hanson took her to the Dawson hospital.

"Of course, everyone but Joe Hanson knew the way she was playing cat and mouse. On weeknights she would sneak out to dances. But on Sundays when Hanson would visit town, there she'd be on her hospital cot, limp and pale—too weak to travel up to Hunker.

"Well, by cracky! She fooled Hanson like that all winter! And as everyone predicted, she ran off with the other fellow, and this same man eventually ran off with the girl's ill-gotten gold! Of course the fellows kept telling Hanson how lucky he was to be rid of her. But Hanson took it mighty hard—would have taken her back, even married her! Well, the girl drifted down the Yukon to parts unknown and for a while Hanson was much wiser, and a whole lot poorer!"

"By George! Do you realize how much gold that girl got from Joe Hanson?" exclaimed Ed. "According to my figures it was a real fortune! If she weighed, say one hundred and twenty-five pounds, it was a mighty big sum! Figure $17 to the ounce of gold. Remember there are sixteen ounces to a pound. Each pound then would cost $272. Now multiply that by one hundred and twenty-five and you have it!"

*These tender lines written in 1888 by George Carmack show that "The Wanderer" had an affection for family and a love of home. Evidently Carmack was in his mountain habitat when he wrote the following verse:

CHRISTMAS THOUGHTS

I'm camped on a mountainside tonight
    One hundred miles from the sea,
And the smell of the caribou steak
    Is a grateful odor to me;
For the deer were fleet-footed and shy,
    Today, I've roamed the mountain's breast
Till the bearskin robes on my cozy bed
    Seems beckoning me to rest.
But a tall old spruce by the camp fire's
    Glow, bows his glittering top to me,
And seems to whisper, 'Tis Christmas
    Eve, and I'm your Christmas Tree.'
Then a flood of memories o'er me sweep,
    And my spirit afar must roam—
'Tis where there's another glittering tree
    In a California home.
There, all is light and life and love,
    And the children laugh with glee,
And I cannot but wonder with wistful pain,
    Are they thinking tonight of me?
But a whisper comes from the tall old spruce,
    And my soul from pain is free,
For I know when they kneel together tonight,
    They'll be praying for me.

—By George Washington Carmack
(This poem was published in the Dawson Nugget Newspaper in 1898)

*George Washington Carmack was born Sept. 24, 1860, at Port Costa, Calif., on a cattle ranch. He was from an old pioneer family that came West in 1849 at the time of California's gold discovery. When Carmack became a young man he got the wanderlust and his "itchy feet" took him to the Northwest. He explored the upper Yukon in 1885 and set up a trading post at Five Fingers. But he wandered again, back to the Alaska coast and became friends with the Indians at Lake Tagish where he met Tagish Charlie and Skookum Jim and the little Indian girl whom he married. Carmack has the distinction of having helped Maj. William Ogilvie in surveying part of the Canadian-American boundary line. In Carmack's little log cabin on the Discovery Claim on the Bonanza, he had a fine organ, as he loved music. Carmack also had a fine library that was the envy of the Klondike. George Carmack was a tall, handsome man of dark complexion. He had well-set, intelligent eyes and loved to talk about the latest scientific discoveries.

Chapter 24

THE NORTH STAR

Fool's Gold?

Ah yes, there was fool's gold mixed in with Klondike's black and gray sands. It glittered in the sluice-boxes, while the high hills seemed to lean back on their rocky heels and laugh mockingly at our fevered efforts and heartbreaking hardships.

As every school boy in the States dreams of becoming President, so every Cheechako and Sourdough dreamed of striking it enormously rich, like Alexander McDonald*, the great Klondike King. He had hundreds of crews of miners and laymen working for him, and now, he even owned Claim 2-B, Below Discovery, on Dominion Creek! Yes, all of us found ourselves working for this fabulously rich Klondike King. How could he lose? If any gold came from the mine, he got the biggest slice of it!

Ed and Joe worked in the mine, made the decisions, paid the operation bills and the miners out of the gold produced from the grudging earth, which was now yielding only small, spasmodic pockets of gold. What was left of the fifty percent yield was ours. At times it was only a very small pittance!

Of course, everybody knew that McDonald had once been a poor miner working in the Juneau mines, back in 1895. Certainly, Lady Luck had smiled her very brightest on him here in the Klondike. (How could any of us know that in less than ten short years he would be as poor, or poorer, than the rest of us?)

The names of the Klondike mine owners of great wealth were constantly before us. They were like a glittering, beckoning light, telling us that we, too, could strike it rich! Some of these men were: Frank and Clarence Berry, Antone Standar, Dick Lowe, James Morrison, Billy Leak, Ronald Morrison, Thomas Lippy, James Monroe, Andrew Hunker, Charles Hamilton, Charles Lamb, Charles Turgeon, Charles Johnson, Duncan Stewart, W. A. Miller, the Chittick Brothers and

---

*By 1911 Alexander McDonald was a poor man. He died alone and forgotten on Slough Creek, about sixty miles from Dawson.

others.

Well, of course, more than ever, Ed was alert for rumors of new gold strikes, in or out of the Klondike. Anywhere, to improve our struggle for existence! And now it seemed the great magnetic wheel of golden opportunity was pointing Northwest again, toward Alaska, in American territory.

It had pointed that way before, back in the late 1880's and '90's, when gold had been discovered up near Circle City and at Forty Mile, and then in 1898, at American Creek, Seventy Mile and in the Koyukuk regions. But these were soon climaxed by "The Wheel" swinging very far north to the tremendous discoveries along the coast of Nome in 1899 and in early 1900.

One day Ed was discussing with Joe the possibilities of large deposits of gold somewhere in the great Tanana region, or over in that general direction. To illustrate his theory, Ed began telling Joe about his 1897 and '98 Arctic Circle adventures:

"My party of men and I, on September 28th of 1897, left Dawson first by rowboat and then by a river steamer, to escape the terrible food famine in the Klondike. The steamer was packed to the guards with hungry fellows, like ourselves, who hoped to get out of the country before winter would set in. But at Circle City, suddenly, the ice closed in, and we were stalled for the winter. Joaquin Miller, the famous poet and gold-rush reporter, who had been sent North in 1897, by William Randolph Hearst, for the Hearst Newspaper Syndicate, was on the same steamer as was Captain Patrick Henry Ray, who had been sent in by the United States Government to make reports on the Dawson famine. My party of men consisted of: C. E. Tibbets*, Shelly Graves*, N. H. Bertram, W. L. Moore, R. H. Hill*, T. W. Calhoun, and of course Edward B. Lung.

"No, there wasn't much food there at Circle, but by continually tightening our belts we managed to keep body and soul together during those long cold months! And we never really lost interest in the possibility of new gold discoveries in the Arctic Circle. In fact, all we could talk about during those long, dreary months were Food, Home, and Gold!

*Tibbetts was a former sea captain of a small steamer from Juneau. He was the oldest in the group. R. H. Hill was a newspaperman. Shelly Graves was only 20. Steamer Weare was nicknamed, "Weaver."

"We hadn't been in Circle many days when we heard vague rumors of gold in a remote region called, 'The Tanana.' It was reported to be somewhere beyond many ranges of mountains, far to the west, in a wild, unexplored region.

"Old timers at Circle told us that the Tanana savages had been known to come there around Christmas for supplies, but that these Indians were quite unapproachable, and could be downright hostile! All the same, we were determined to go to the Tanana with the Indians, if we possibly could arrange it, even if the risks were great.

"Well, it seemed that luck was with us the day before Christmas, when an Indian Chief with three young braves entered the Circle City Trading Post to barter for supplies. Bertram, one of the fellows in our party, happened to be there at the post trying to buy something.

"Secretly, Bertram and another member of our party coaxed the Indians to our cabin, feeling sure they were the Tananas. And there, after we had given them valuable supplies and treated them to friendly cups of hot coffee, the chief promised to take us on their return trip to the Tanana, where, he told us proudly by sign language, White Man had never set foot, and where there was much gold—gold as bright as the sun! Of course, we were jubilant. As far as we knew we were the first white men ever to obtain a promise like that from the Tanana Indians. In return for this favor the Indians made us swear not to tell anybody of our plans. But from the beginning, our expedition was ill-fated!

"Strangely enough, it was ill-fated because of Thomas Edison's wonderful new invention, the talking machine. Well, to go back a little with the story:

"While the Indians were bartering at the trading company, having great difficulty being understood, a practical joker, a crazy-fool clerk, slipped behind the counter where a Gramophone was concealed. By snapping on a recorder, he was able to get a pretty good record of fierce shoutings, weird, high pitched Indian lingo, savage threatening, guttural mutterings, and even a few loud war whoops!

"As fate would have it, the next night was to be a Christmas benefit for Ryan, a poor fellow who had lost his feet through frostbite. And, as fate would have it again, my party of men and I had consented to be in that show.

"We never knew just why the Tanana Indians wandered into the 'Opera House' that night while the program was on. Perhaps it was the bright Christmas lights that attracted them, or the music. But, anyway, in they came, as big as you please, dressed in gorgeous fur parkas.

"However, the Indians didn't remain very long. During a pause in the program that stupid fool clerk brought in the Gramophone with the big black horn.

"Immediately, he set the thing up on the stage and turned it on. This was his idea of a huge joke, the big highlight of the evening—that record he had made of the Tananas at the trading post!

"Naturally, the Indians were terrified when they heard their own voices coming out of the box and horn! To the extreme amusement of all in the audience, except of course to my party of men and me, the Indians wildly bolted for the door and out of the building. Their fright created much hilarity among the audience.

"Twenty hours later, however, we discovered to our chagrin, that the Tananas had fled from Circle City, and had taken great pains to cover up their trail.

"But my party and I managed to follow their footprints through the snow—that is, until a blinding blizzard overtook us. Then, as we tried to make shelter, thirty hysterical fellows staggered into camp. They were half-frozen, and told us they'd been trailing us and the Indians too, since early morning.

"Well, we knew our chances of ever catching up with the Tananas were gone forever. Under our breath we cursed our stinkin' luck and also those blasted stampeders who had followed us. No doubt the Indians sensed a 'stampede in the making' and thought we had betrayed them. Anyway, our dreams of bright Tanana gold vanished with the last Indian footprints in the snow.

"Oh, it was a bitter pill to swallow! Strange, how an Edison talking machine, a fool clerk, thirty gold-hungry stampeders and a blizzard could change the course of a fellow's destiny! But that talking machine was really responsible for the whole adverse outcome. Because of it, the Tanana Chief and his Indians were recognized by those other fellows, who had followed us from Circle City. Unbeknownst to us, they, too, had been secretly watching for the Tanana Indians.

"So, it was on January 2, 1898, that my party and I, feeling pretty much disgruntled, packed our sleds and harnessed our dogs. We had decided to get out of Circle and go back to Dawson. A cold, hazardous trip lay ahead of us. For safety measures, we split up the party in two different groups, but would check on each other at designated points.

"With me were Billy Moore, Shelly Graves, and a fellow named Kain. We had four sleds and three dogs between us. I owned Chattel; Moore, Caution, and Kain, Jack. (Jack was bought from 'Italian Jack,' the famous Sourdough dog racer.)

"About a dozen parties left Circle the same day we pulled out. Among them were fellows we all knew—Casper Ellinger, George Eaton, Fred Gesche, O'Hara and LaDuke. Also, Pat Finnigan, purser of the 'Weaver,' who with his horses was heading back to Dawson. We knew he would have trouble with those horses and he did. The poor critters fell through the ice a few hours out, and he lost five of them.

"At first, Captain Tibbetts, with his party, and Captain Morgan with his, stayed close to us. Morgan's prize passenger was little Casey Moran, the popular showman from Dawson and Circle City. We knew Morgan would make better time than any of us, since he had a string of eleven fine dogs. Before leaving Circle we had all made bets about who would reach Dawson first. Well, the betting game seemed risky when we began encountering serious trail hazards.

"We caught up with many 'loners,' some with dogs, and we always stopped to check on them. Some were getting along nicely, others suffering from severe frostbite and other illnesses. Some were handicapped by very lame sled-dogs. We came upon a man who, in a fit of rage, was unmercifully beating his helpless dog with an iron chain. That, we had to stop! It was apparent the man had gone temporarily insane due to the hardships of the icy trail.

"Sam Wall, the well-known newspaperman, was foolishly traveling alone. One night he came staggering into our camp more dead than alive. But the next morning he was off on his own special mission, a quest for gold-rush news, and we couldn't dissuade him. His gold-fever frenzy was for news, just as Joaquin Miller's had been when he was frozen-in at Circle City with us. The famous Hearst reporter and poet had foolhardily set out on the ice from Circle City with Canovan two months before we started. We learned they had been caught in terrible blizzards while encountering mountains of ice; suffering from snow blindness. Once Canovan fell through the ice. Had it not been for friendly Indians, Joaquin and Canovan would have vanished from the

---

*Yukon Indians shoe sled runners with walrus ivory. Steel runners frost up and drag.

face of the Arctic!

"Always, at night, we tried to reach shacks along the Yukon, but most of the time we camped in tents. Mine did not furnish adequate shelter as it had numerous holes because of flying sparks from previous fires.

"One night my party of men reached Indian Sam's cabin. He was a friendly pilot for the Alaska Commercial Company's steamers, an intelligent fellow. He let us stay there for several days as the mercury had hit 60 below.

"While waiting for the cold spell to break, I mended socks and patched my tent. For diversion, I sang songs to the Indians. Also, I told stories of Buffalo Bill, Robinson Crusoe and Rip Van Winkle. Sam's relatives were highly intrigued with these tales and the Indians made a wonderful audience. When we left Sam's village I gave his squaw my silver thimble in exchange for a pair of much-needed Indian moccasins. To me they were worth their weight in gold. I had a good many miles to walk to reach Dawson. To her, the thimble was like the finest jewelry, and she was wearing it when I left Sam's cabin.

"Before leaving Sam's place we heard indefinite rumors of new gold discoveries up the Yukon, but they were vague as to exact location. However, when we went southward about 100 miles we caught up with scores of excited fellows who were mushing as fast as possible to Eagle City, Star City and a few small outlying creeks on American Territory, which had suddenly come into the limelight around the first of January. (Mission Creek, 70-Mile River and American)

"So, as a result of encountering this excitement, naturally my party and I debated whether we, too, should hit the stampede trail. But the stampedes had already been in progress for nearly three weeks which meant hordes of men had been in the area ahead of us.

"At first we couldn't work up any enthusiasm or real interest in this part of the Territory. Maybe it was because we were extremely trail-weary. We argued among ourselves that compared with the great Tanana these streams were probably very insignificant and obscure. However, when we reached the mouth of American Creek at Eagle City, suddenly, I caught gold-fever.

"I kept thinking, 'What if there are rich gold deposits in these American creeks? Here am I, an American citizen, passing them all by.' So, fired with new incentive, I tried to whip up enthusiasm amongst my group, but the fellows only gave me the horse-laugh. Besides, hadn't they walked over 270 miles since leaving Circle City?

" 'Why pile up the agony?' they bitterly asked, 'Haven't we already had enough blasted hardship—enough damned disappointments?'

"But I persisted. Finally, I persuaded Billy Moore* to start out with me, while the gang waited at Eagle City.

"We packed a few supplies and pushed up to the Discovery claim of Mission Creek. It was a disagreeable, uncomfortable hike. We wallowed through wet snow, for strange to say there were warm springs in there which melted the ice and kept the snow mushy.

"Well, it turned out to be a difficult twelve-mile trek in any man's language! I kept freezing my little finger and Billy suffered from frozen toes and nose. When we reached our destination, we found the richest ground all staked by the members of the new Alaska Placer & Coal Company (gold and coal). Near the Discovery Claim we ran into Tom O'Shea whose partner had gone back to get some precious beans left by mistake (a serious loss) at a spot on upper Mission Creek. Well, we couldn't be of help, so hurriedly Billy and I cut across back-country, safely reaching the 70-Mile River. Here again it was the same old story. Stampeders had been there ahead of us—by the scores! We learned that the Alaska Placer and Coal Company had managed to grab eighty acres of the choicest ground, an entire island below the falls, and twenty acres above the falls. Also, they had acquired rich ground on every tributary of the 70-Mile River, amounting to hundreds of acres! Then we met a fellow who said that the Company intended to bond all claims in the area. Well, there was nothing for us at the 70-Mile, that was very obvious!

"On our return trip from the 70-Mile we almost met our Waterloo. Billy and I got seriously lost during a sudden snow flurry. However, we plunged on in the semi twilight, hoping for the best. But in the fresh snowfall the stampede trail and our own footprints were wiped out, and the country, what we could see of it, looked totally unfamiliar and strange.

"For a while, Billy and I floundered through the wilderness, our spirits matching the winter's gloom! We knew not where we were head-

---
*Billy Moore was a man from San Francisco. He dabbled in politics in small towns near the Bay area. Was a carpenter by trade. He was not the Billy Moore, founder of Skagway.

Forty Mile, gold camp, at an early date, about 1894. (On the Yukon River below Dawson.) Miners in foreground.

Eagle City, Alaska, near Old Fort Egbert.

At Eagle, Alaska (Old Fort Egbert). Notice the old cannons.

Prehistoric mastodon tusks found in frozen ground in mines in the Klondike. (Courtesy of Dick Racine)

ing, nor where we would end up, but decided in any event we should keep moving. We dared not sit down to rest for fear of freezing. For the first time in many weeks I became panicky, and so did Billy.

"Well, I guess we would be wandering yet had not a wind whipped up, blowing the snow-filled clouds aside. And there, to our supreme joy, was the Dipper and the North Star, Polaris, hanging almost above us, like a great beacon, a guiding sign, seemingly put there just for us by a guardian angel.

" 'Moore,' I cried, 'Look! According to the North Star we're heading northwest—toward the Tanana. We should be traveling southeast, in the opposite direction, to get back to Eagle City!'

"Through chattering lips Moore agreed.

"Well, so, for a second time within a short period, there we were on a stampede for gold, and a second time too, we were thwarted by circumstances and foul weather! But, again, our lives were spared. Never was I so glad to see the Great North Star! By taking true directions from the North Star we were able to get back to our camp at Eagle on the Yukon River.

"After that harrowing experience Billy Moore promptly lost all interest in hunting gold, but somehow I was stubbornly unwilling to give up the search. My dander was up and I was determined to accept the stampede-challenge. Besides, I could use a good claim! So the next day I set out from Eagle City, again going into rough country, a little to the south this time. I traveled on snow shoes. At a small frozen stream I ran into fellows who had managed to dig through the permafrost and had several nuggets and a little gold-dust. And so, fired with new hope, I pressed on. But the farther I went the more I could see that I was probably too late. Apparently a lot of the stampeders had been grub-staked by the Syndicate and they had grabbed everything, just like a pack of hungry malemutes! It was unbelievable!

"However, after pushing through ten rugged mountain miles, I managed to find a piece of ground that had been overlooked. It was number 34 Upper American Creek. Hurriedly, I dug around and found just a hint of gold, just enough to swear to the Gold Commissioner at Eagle that I had found traces of it in No. 34. And—yes, I really had a good patriotic feeling when I drove my stakes in that ground on which was printed my name and number!

"While I was still up there, I met some fellows who spoke of more remote streams where probably the Syndicate hadn't reached: Liberty, Independence, and Fourth of July, but a fellow would be a crazy chump to risk it alone, and in the dead of winter.

"So I limped back to record* my new claim at Eagle City. There, I found Billy Moore and the rest of my gang comfortably bunked in with United States Gold Commissioner and Recorder, Barton. His cabin was extra comfortable and cozy warm, because he had plenty of coal, freighted from the rich veins of coal on the 70-Mile River, not far away.

"During my absence three in my party, I found, had caught the gold-fever too, and had actually gone on several small private stampedes of their own. However, no one had made any startling discoveries except to say that they had seen extensive veins of coal streaked with gold in the region, but it had all been staked by the A.P. & C. Company.

"While we were preparing to leave Barton's cabin for Dawson, a furious storm raged on the Yukon, and I was thankful that I was not out hunting gold! Two dozen homeless fellows crowded in with us at Barton's, and he tried his best to make us all comfortable although some of us had to sleep on the floor.

"Well, after several days the storm abated and we took off for Dawson. We were determined that no more stampedes, or anything else would sidetrack us. Many of the fellows who had left Circle City about the same time that we had, had also run up to the stampede creeks. Perhaps I was more fortunate than most of them since I had title to a strip of ground that might prove negotiable.

"On the trail again, we kept track of Weymouth and Fisher, Captain Tibbetts and party, and the Williams party. Also, we kept running into George Eaton and Tom O'Shea, traveling together. We caught up with O'Hara and LeDuke and then Ben Atwater, the mailman, with his fast sleigh full of mail, passed us. And for a time we traveled close to Henry Pinkus and his sleigh. It was full of candles for which he expected a dollar apiece in Dawson. Closer to Dawson our old friend R. H. Hill caught up and 'dog-trotted' all the rest of the way to the Klondike with us.

"Well, all the fellows we knew were finally within safe reaching distance of Dawson after traveling through temperatures ranging from

---

*In order to record a claim a person had to swear that he had found gold in the ground that he wished.

30 to 60 degrees below zero. We had had an exciting trip—full of adventure and real suffering, too. And, yes—turmoil! Billy Moore and Shelly Graves were no longer on speaking terms by the time we reached Dawson, but at least they were 'alive and kicking!' Of course, their feud didn't last once they were back in the Klondike.

"None of us could find out what became of the courageous stampeder who passed us a hundred miles from Dawson, double-tripping it (running on the ice)! Both feet were badly frozen and so were all of his fingers on both hands!

"My party and I pulled into Dawson Feb. 2, 1898, having been gone six whole months from the Klondike with nothing accomplished except that we had escaped the Dawson food famine at its very worst. —And yes, I had acquired a little gold-bearing ground on American Territory. However, it was well-known by this time that the A.P. & C Syndicate had gobbled up the richest ground, streaked with gold and coal in that territory, for hundreds of miles.

"Captain Morgan and Casey Moran were the dog-team winners to Dawson having reached the 'home-base' a full week ahead of any of us from Circle City.

"About ten days after reaching Dawson, I signed over the No. 34 American Creek claim to a Mr. Goodwin in payment for a debt. How glad I was for that claim! But, it is another story which I shall relate at some other time. That American Creek claim was only valued at $300. Thus ended my 1898 Alaska and Circle City gold-rush adventures."

With gold-glitter in his eyes, Ed pointed to a map in our cabin. "Joe, cast your eyes northwest to American Territory*, about seventy miles beyond Eagle. There, almost lost among the mountains are more small streams from which now come vague reports of gold. Then, look beyond those mountains about 200 miles. Somewhere in there are the headwaters of the great Tanana River—unexplored—intriguing and mysterious! Man, oh man! It's immense country! The Indians said, 'There's plenty gold,' and I really believed them! If only my party and I could have reached the Tanana from Circle City in 1897 we might have struck it very rich. No doubt there's a great *wheel of gold* in the Tanana as fabulous as the Klondike region. Who knows! Maybe richer!"

"You bet," agreed Joe enthusiastically, "Ed, I'm rarin' to go into that territory any time you say!"

Chapter 25

CALL OF THE TANANA AND FOREST FIRE

It was about noon of July 1, 1901, when Ed and Joe received the exciting word that there had been an important new gold discovery in American Territory at Chicken Creek, ninety miles away.

Ed and Joe quickly assembled outfits, bade me goodbye, and with packs strapped to their backs, stepped silently out of our cabin on Dominion Creek. Paul Hebb had sent the word that he would wait for them if they would hurry to Dawson. Of course it was to their advantage to keep the stampede absolutely quiet!

The following morning Joe and Ed, with their newly formed party, slipped inconspicuously out of Dawson. Crossing the Yukon in a small boat, they reached the opposite shore, near West Dawson, where they

---

*The Alaska Placer & Coal Company became immensely rich by late spring of '98 due to the huge holdings they were able to acquire around the first of January, 1898. Not only did they get the richest gold-bearing ground, they were able to get title to 20 acres of coal on the 70-Mile River; also on Mission Creek they held most of the coal veins. There were five partners who formed the original company. At the first news of the region's richness they rushed from Dawson with fast dog teams. They were: Lyman S. Burrell, Andrew Nelson, Richard Aggazig, M. L. Hamilton, N. N. Brown.

The coal strata in this particular area (for several hundred miles) were unique in that they were streaked with free-gold and gold-quartz. Star City, a short distance from Eagle, became the headquarters of the Alaska Placer & Coal Company after moving from Dawson City. Many of the officials of the syndicate were previously wealthy from their rich holdings in the Klondike gold fields, Yukon-Canadian territory. The company had several of their own steamers that plied the Yukon River. "Arizona" Charlie Meadows bought one-sixth interest and was the great publicity man for the syndicate. He built the famous Palace Grand Theatre in Dawson in 1899 and performed in it as well as put on Wild West shows in other parts of the world.

*In 1897 Mr. T. J. Hamilton and R. C. Johnston made a great petroleum (oil) discovery on the Mainland, just east of the mouth of the Copper River on Prince Williams Sound.

*The name, Northwest Mounted Police, was officially changed in 1904 to The Royal Canadian Mounted Police, by King Edward VII, in recognition for their splendid service to Canada.

*In 1897 gold was reported at Katzebue Sound.

*In 1897, on Cook Inlet, on Turnagain Arm, a gold camp called "Sunrise" was starting, as gold was being found in good quantities in the area of the Six-Mile Creek and in Resurrection Creek.

tied up the boat, then they struck out for the high ridge, going almost northwest.

Reaching the big ridge about noon, they followed a rather indefinite trail which ran along the divide. It was quite rough and showed little signs of use. They knew they had several days of hard hiking so set their pace accordingly.

Occasionally, they stopped to sip cool water from canteens, also, to drink in the primeval beauty of this gigantic country of deep, green canyons, rugged mountains, and glacier-fed creeks. This day, it was unusually warm—almost too warm for strenuous exercise. The temperature had hit about 90 degrees!*

Suddenly, a strange sight greeted their eyes. Straight ahead, about 500 feet, they saw a wagon loaded with hay! The wagon was leisurely jogging along, drawn by a team of white horses. An old man in a wide-brimmed hat sat in the driver's seat, slouched over as tho' fast asleep.

Ed and his party rubbed their eyes in astonishment, for how in tarnation could a wagon loaded with hay and drawn by horses ever have reached this ridge? And yet, there it was, jogging along in front of them as big as you please!

The men called to the driver, but there was no response. The drowsing driver just kept jogging along, never turning to look back.

The men walked faster—even tried running to catch up. But, the faster they went, the swifter the rider and horses traveled. Somehow, the hay-wagon managed to keep the same measured distance between them. And, too, there was a strange, eerie silence which was mighty unnerving.

"By Jove!" said one of the men, "I'd say we were seein' things—having some kind of strange hallucinations—if we'd been nipping at the bottle. But—I'll swear none of us has had one drop of hootch!"

Finally the men decided that the fellow, with the mysterious wagon, must be a mirage. They had played hide and seek with him part of the afternoon, as now and then, when the trail would lead around a bend the wagon would disappear, but when the trail would straighten out, lo, and behold, there would be that wagon.

Hours later, when the men decided to stop and make camp, the rider

---

*In summer, temperatures have been known to reach as high as 102 and 103 degrees in Alaska and Yukon Territory.

suddenly disappeared over the ridge!

"Sure, he's a mirage," said Ed. "The real fellow had to be miles away, maybe at Fortymile. Must have been just the right mixture of heat and dust-particles in the air to've created an unusual phenomenon like this, a reflection of objects in the atmosphere. Fellows dying of thirst on the desert are apt to see rivers and lakes, or maybe even big gold nuggets if they've been searching for gold!"

"I'm not dying for water," laughed one of the party, "but you can bet your boots I'm dying for a fat poke of yellow gold!"

The next day, of course, the hay-wagon with driver and horses were nowhere to be seen.

On the afternoon of the third day, Ed and his party looked down onto the headwaters of Sixty Mile River, a junction where Miller Creek flows into the main stream, not far from Franklin Gulch. Farther on, the men passed a tiny Mounted Police Outpost, a checking station, where all incoming travelers were required to stop and pay duty on certain kinds of equipment. From there, along the high ridge, the men continued.

Now, they were closer to many jagged peaks jutting up, like sharp needles, not more than twenty or thirty miles away. Almost due south, was Crag Mountain; to the east, was Mt. Nolan; to the northeast, Mt. Baldy; and nearly due north was the Fortymile Dome rising about 5,000 feet.

"Man, oh man, it's immense country! Feast your eyes on this!" Joe exclaimed. "And to think it only cost 02c an acre—$7,200,000 for all Alaska. What a bargain, and what a grand country it is! But Great Scott, I believe a fellow could wander for the rest of his life in here, if he should ever become lost."

"You said it!" the others chorused in awe.

With mixed emotions the men scanned the vast, untamed territory which had only belonged to Uncle Sam for thirty-four years to date (1867 to 1901)—Purchase of Alaska from Russia. Suddenly, patriotic ferver swelled in their breasts. Momentarily forgetting the stampede, they shouted to the mountains:

"Hurrah, hurrah for good American Territory! Hurray for Alaska!" Then the men listened to the echoes of their voices coming back across the ridges, and as the echoes died, Ed pointed to the northeast.

"About fifty miles, over that way, are the headwaters of American

Creek, Excelsior and the 70 Mile River. On my way back from Circle City, I visited them in '98, and of course, in them I hunted gold. It's an unusual area, rich in large coal veins streaked with gold-quartz. There's enough coal in there to heat a good many stoves and run large factories. But the best of the rich, accessible ground was all staked by the Alaska Placer and Coal Company, a rich syndicate, before I could reach the scene. Even though the syndicate owns the most accessible ground, there must be good territory that is yet available, but it's hard to reach, back in among the mountains. Chicken Creek is part of that vast complex of streams.

"See," said Ed, "there's the outline of that amazing elephant-like river, the Forty Mile. Notice how its rich tributeries radiate out like spokes of a big, uneven, lopsided wheel? The Forty Mile Dome acts as a center-hub, or starting point."

"Yes, but the big North feeder, or North Fork, comes in from a far different location," said Joe. "It rises in the Ketchumstock Mountains, way over there towards the Tanana. Man, oh man! What wouldn't I give to take a crack at that region, Indians or no Indians!"

"Men," said Paul Hebb, "we'd better start moving! An old miner in Dawson said we must cross over Glacier Creek, Poker, Davis, Woods, and a whole slough of small ones including Baby, Kat-Squaw, George, and Jack Wade* before we finally hit down onto Mosquito Creek. The old fellow gave me a map and said we must be sure to follow Mosquito Creek up-river 'til we reach the place where it branches to the right (north). This little branch is called Chicken Creek. It's right there, that all of the gold excitement is taking place. Unless my name is 'Mud,' we've certainly got to make tracks. Every second counts!"

At last, on the fifth day, Ed and his party reached the mouth of Mosquito Creek. They were surprised at the bigness of the stream, and were startled to see dozens of small rafts floating downriver, loaded with men. Obviously, they wore disgruntled expressions. Calling to them, Ed's party asked if they had been on the Chicken Creek Stampede.

"Sure," was the reply, "but there ain't nothin' available. Fellows galore up there—thick as mosquitoes! Didn't have a chance. 'Twas just

*An early stampeder died at Jack Wade Creek and was buried there. Later, a cheechako happened to pan some of the gravel taken from the grave and discovered gold. He staked the grave, removed the body, and named his new claim "THE GRAVE YARD CLAIM."

like the early Klondike days and big Nome stampedes—all gobbled up by the very early birds. Some of those birds on 'Chicken' got twenty acres apiece in quartz claims!"

"Well, anyway," called one of the men, sarcastically, "from what I could see of it, there was nothin' much but chicken feed, and—oh, yes—an awful lot of coal scattered around!"

With disappointment gripping them, Ed and his party hurried along the dusty trail. In spite of the discouraging reports, they were not willing to turn back. They had come a long way and would just have to see for themselves. However, when they reached the right Fork and rapidly walked along its banks, they could see that the men had been telling the truth. There were stampeders galore!

Already, they were mining and sluicing; some even building shacks!

After scouting Chicken Creek thoroughly, it was evident that all fifteen miles were completely staked. About $1.50 to the pan was the average yield. Certainly it was not to be scoffed at! It was true what the men on the raft had said about coal being everywhere. The richest pans taken were streaked with gold, black sand, and coal-particles. The miners were drying the coal-particles and burning it with wood for heating and cooking purposes. Chicken Creek had the same combination of gold and coal and black sand outcroppings that were in the territory around American Creek, Mission and the 70 Mile River where the Alaska Placer and Coal Company (syndicate) had managed to acquire such immense holdings in early January, 1898, Stampedes.

"Golly, ninety miles is sure a long way to come for nothin'," complained Joe in disgust. "Yep, probably a lot of those fellows are from the Syndicate, too. They came from Star City, Eagle, and even Dawson. Some of the 'Early-Birds' even poled up the Fortymile to Mosquito Creek!"

After serious consultation, Ed and his party decided to split up. Hebb and his friends would go one way, and Ed and Joe another. Ed and Joe pressed on towards the North Fork of the Forty Mile River,

---

*By 1906 and '09 almost all of Chicken Creek was bonded by a Syndicate. Dredges were beginning to go into the area, one especially at Walker's Fork. They were even getting up as far as Franklin Gulch.

*Miners in the area dreaded forest fires because of the coal-underground-strata. Sometimes coal veins would burn for years making the surface-earth too hot to walk on. Often miners would have their moccasins-soles charred by stepping on hot earth which would not show at first glance.

and as they went slowly along, they eagerly watched for signs of "float" and outcroppings of quartz. Steadily they advanced, always pressing towards the Tanana.

The mountains grew higher, the gorges deeper, the shadows colder, and there was the definite chilling breath of early fall on the wind.

"Joe, this is terribly risky!" Ed warned, with growing apprehension. "We'd be fools to try to get into the Tanana this late in the season, and with our meager supplies. Why, any time now, a snowstorm could whip up! In this part of the country it's been known to snow in mid-summer and then develop into early winter."

At first Ed couldn't reason with Joe, for it seemed that Joe was possessed with a feverish desire to reach the Tanana at all costs. Strangely, his flaming obsession was mostly inspired by Ed's own accounts of his Circle-City Tanana Indian adventures of 1897 and '98 and his party's quest for gold.

So, onward the two partners trekked, ever pressing towards the big, Ketchumstock Mountains, Joe eagerly leading the way, Ed reluctantly following. At last, they came upon a ragged, half-starved old miner, camped by a small stream.*

The old fellow hailed Joe and Ed as long lost friends, for he had not seen anyone for many weeks. The man had become lost in among the mountains and he told of harrowing experiences. Yes, he too, had been headed for the Tanana!

"Take it from me, boys, it ain't worth the terrible risk," he told them, candidly. "Ya' know when a fellow's got food and a good outfit he thinks gold is the most important thing. But just let him see his last piece of bacon sizzling away, then he's face-to-face with real values. Why, just the sight of you boys was worth more than all the gold in Alaska!"

Then, as the three talked further, the old man told of other goldseekers who had ventured guideless into the Tanana region, only they had come from the other direction. He recounted how, in '98, a Dr. Smith with his party, had come hundreds of miles across country from Valdez, on the west coast. They had left Portland, Oregon, in March of that year, by steamer, and after landing at Valdez, they had struggled over perilous glaciers; had forded dangerous streams; had built at least a

---
*There is a river named "Ketchumstock." A tribe of Indians by the same name inhabit this remote area. White man seldom visited the area.

half-dozen boats; had crossed the hazardous Copper River; climbed many nameless, rugged ranges until they had, at last, reached the big Ketchumstock Mountains. There, they stopped and broke down and wept. In order to scale this last high barrier, they had to abandon the very things that they needed most—food, clothing, supplies, and even blankets! Finally, more dead than alive, they staggered into a remote cabin on upper Franklin Gulch,* and there they told their story. They had been ten whole months on the way.

"Yep," continued the old man, "I remember that party very well, for they not only told of their struggles, they also told of seeing evidence of gold in that huge Tanana region over yonder. Well, the golden glitter finally lured me this summer. I thought I'd strike out for myself. I didn't mind being alone, for I'm a seasoned old Sourdough, or at least I thought so until I got lost in these blasted mountains!"

"By George! we must heed this man's warnings," Ed told Joe. "No! I'm not eager to sacrifice everything, maybe life itself. Yes, some day I hope to get into that territory, for surely there must be great quantities of gold . . . "

"You're not dreaming!" said the old miner. Maybe it'll be as rich as the Klondike."

On their homeward trek Ed and Joe camped at Walker's Fork. (A tributary of the Forty Mile.) Here, to their surprise, they discovered a man with wife, and two children—a boy of seven and a girl of five. Ed and Joe learned that the woman, before her marriage, had been a school teacher at Forty Mile. Now, she was using all of her spare time to teach her two children. But she told Ed and Joe she was not satisfied with results and was planning to send the children Outside the following year—"a great sacrifice," she said with tears in her eyes.

While Joe and Ed were having coffee, they looked over the school teacher's books. Among them was a copy of Caesar's Commentaries, written in Latin. Much to her delight, Ed read parts of the Commentaries aloud. This volume had been a favorite of his father's and had been kept in a conspicuous place in the Lung parsonage. (Ed's father, Rev. Lung, was a scholarly Baptist minister. He knew Latin, German and

*Franklin Gulch Creek is a tributary of the Forty Mile River. Some of the earliest miners settled on Franklin Gulch.

*Joe Latshaw returned to Dominion Creek, agreeing with Ed that his fortune definitely lay in the Klondike.

Hebrew, and some of his learning had rubbed off on his children.)

After a few days of prospecting in the area, Ed bade the family at Walker's Forks farewell. He told them that he had an uneasy feeling that he should return to his family as quickly as possible. But Joe, however, was not quite ready to leave American territory as he wished to further explore the area. It was therefore agreed that if Joe should find promising gold deposits, he and Ed would share as partners.

Now, Ed was hurrying homeward, along the high ridge. He had reached about the same spot where his party had last seen the mirage—"the phantom rider." All at once a black bear suddenly blocked the trail. Not wanting to tangle with old bruin, Ed shouted and threw rocks from a safe distance, but the bear was not willing to move on, for he had been royally dining on blueberries. After a great deal of rock-throwing and loud shouting, by Ed, the bear finally lumbered on down the mountainside and let him pass. Ed hurried along much faster, for he had been delayed by that stubborn old bear far too long!

Soon, he met a packer coming from Dawson. The two stopped and hailed each other as long-lost buddies, and, it being around lunch time, they decided to share their grub. As they ate, they talked, "chewing the fat," which meant exchanging news and views.

While the two were having lunch, Ed began noticing little white puffs of smoke off on the far horizon, to the east. And as he watched, minute by minute, the puffs became plume-like, growing bigger and bigger!

"Holy cats!" he cried, "That's the start of a forest fire!"

"It shore is, partner," the packer agreed, and it's over thar beyond King Solomon's Dome—most likely on the Indian River or Dominion Creek!"

"My God!" cried Ed in dismay.

Now he knew why he'd had that urgent premonition to hurry home! Quickly, he took his leave of the man and in seconds was racing like a deer along the ridge. Before an hour had passed, the sky over Dominion Creek had turned an ominous red. Soon, the smell of burning bush reached Ed. Cinders fell, and the red, bloodshot orb of the sun looked down on the Yukon with a baleful, malignant eye.

As Ed hurtled along the ridge, he reproached himself many times over for having been gone from home for so many days! Fear put wings to his feet. What would he find, when at last he would reach Dominion Creek? No! He dared not think.

* * *

That same day—back at Dominion Creek— my vacation came to an abrupt end when Clemy came running into the cabin to let me know there was a forest fire burning way down the valley. I rushed outside and discovered the fire was quite a distance away. But soon, a stiff breeze began blowing up the valley, in our direction, and the flames, like long red hungry tongues, licked at the hills. It being mid-summer, the valley was as dry as tinder!

No one could tell just how the fire had started, but we surmised it was caused by a careless prospector or hunter. Soon, dozens of miners from Lower Dominion Creek flooded the trail, bringing as much of their worldly possessions as they could carry. Hourly, the fire raged closer, even tho' there were crews of Mounties and miners fighting it with every means possible, including back-firing.

Quickly, Clemy and I packed all of our valuables into a valise, and placed it by the door. Then pulled furniture and everything to the middle of the cabin. Outside, we watched, waited and prayed! Ella was only a tiny baby, and so slept most of the time. But for Clemy and me, there was absolutely no rest or sleep. We were much too frightened for that, and besides, we had to keep a close watch in order to be ready to run to safety in case the fire swept dangerously near.

All of that first night we kept a nerve-wracking vigil. The sky turned blood-red; the air was stifling hot! We could hear poor, terror-stricken animals wailing and running past our cabin—headed for the creek. All through the night we could hear the echoing crash of burning trees, as they burned like torches and fell along the hillsides.

At last, two of our miners who had cabins nearby came to be with us to help in case we had to flee. Now the fire was burning perilously near. It was approaching just above us on the slope of the hill.

"Don't be panicky," the men counseled, with dry, anxious eyes, for they had been fighting fire. "We'll get you and the children to safety if the fire drops below the government trail. But we'll be in a tough spot if the fire jumps down this way and burns to the river and leaps to the opposite side of the valley," they added seriously. "But now, if that should happen, Lady, still don't worry, for we can all make a dash for a mineshaft and remain underground until the fire passes."

Well, of course the Mounties and miners kept back-firing and doing everything possible to stop the awful conflagration. But it seemed a hopeless maneuver and I felt for a certainty that in the end we would have to run for our lives and that we would be quite homeless! It seemed that all cabins on upper Dominion Creek were doomed to go up in smoke.

With anxious eyes I scanned the high King Dome Trail, wondering what, oh what, had become of Edward! He had only planned to be gone about two weeks. Oh, how desperately I needed him!

* * *

When at last Ed reached King Solomon's Dome and looked down into the Dominion Creek Valley and saw the vast blackened area and smoking hills, with fire still spurting here and there (looking like a real Dante's Inferno, he told us later), he was frightened beyond words.

From that distance, although the fire was now under control (only burning at isolated spots), he had no assurance that we were really safe. He literally ran down the mountain to reach us. When he finally bounded through the door and clasped us in his arms he nearly fainted from gladness and extreme exhaustion.

"Oh Vel, thank God!" he cried. "If I had lost you and the children, all the gold in Alaska could never compensate! It was a miracle, only a miracle that you and cabin were saved," he exclaimed over and over.

Needless to say, there were tears of great happiness, and thankfulness in our hearts that night, and while I prepared supper I gave Ed a quick account of the fire:

"Yes, indeed, it was a very close call! Just a few hours ago, when it seemed that all hope was gone and that we would have to flee, suddenly a miracle happened—the wind shifted and the blaze swept back down the valley, towards Lower Dominion Creek, literally choking itself out, for most of that territory had already burnt over."

Ed was so glad to be home again and so grateful that we were safe that now he tackled his "Lay" with renewed vim, and determination. At last, he was sure that our future was not off in the far, distant horizon; not even on American Territory. It was right here on Dominion Creek!

He set his jaw. Yes, he would search out a fortune. Dominion Creek would pay us for all our hardships and he resolved never, never to give up until it had done just that!

Soon we added a new crew of six miners to our claim. They were willing and eager to work underground with Ed and Joe for $10 a day. These were not high wages but for us to meet a payroll of $60 more a day meant a great deal of anxiety and skimping on our personal needs. Of course the men would get their pay first, before we could touch a penny of it. But we still could exist on bacon and beans, and greens and berries, and we still had our warm, cozy log-cabin intact; and, most wonderful of all, we still had each other to love and cherish and work for.

Many of the unfortunate Sourdoughs, who had been burnt out that summer on Lower Dominion Creek, had to live that winter in tents.

The following year, in mid-summer, when the men were at last forcing the grudging earth to give up about .60c to the pan in gold-dust, our valley smouldered under a misty, smoky, blue-grey haze. But the smoky look was only an illusion created by the soft buds of new fireweeds which always cover the hills after a fire.

Then, it was the next year, in August, that the hills went wildly aglow with waves of vivid scarlet! The fireweed-buds had burst wide open. And when the breezes blew briskly over the slopes, it seemed that real sparks flew from the throats of millions and millions of bright red flowers, and it seemed, too, that flames swirled and leaped and danced on the high winds, blowing towards our cabin!

Ah yes, the fireweeds, which so brilliantly covered the hills, were certainly a beautiful sight, but they were also a poignant reminder of that terrifying forest fire of the year before.

*On July 1, 1902, Felix Pedro, an Italian immigrant made the Tanana-first-gold-discovery in Chena Slough. A stampede followed and gold was found in three other creeks, later named Pedro, Cleary and Fairbanks. The tiny gold camp of Fairbanks sprouted into an exciting boom-town, and by 1904 it was a well established American city, getting some of Dawson's population.

*In 1896 W. A. Dickey and Mr. Monks made a perilous trip up the uncharted Sushitna River from Cooks Inlet and discovered Bulshaia which they named Mt. McKinley in honor of the American president. The Indians had always called it Bulshaia—meaning "Great Mountain." In 1898 a U. S. Government party of surveyors, headed by G. H. Eldridge, saw Bulshaia, or Mt. McKinley, and claimed it the highest mountain of the continent (20,300 feet). Another tribe of Indians called the mountain "Denalee."

Chapter 26

THE BANSHEE IN THE HAUNTED MINE

There was an ever changing population among the miners in the Klondike, so by late fall of 1901 we had quite a few new men working in our claim. Some of the old ones had left for parts unknown expecting to strike it rich. In a few cases we would hear from them, but more often, not.

The new miners were always curious about their predecessors and previous happenings around the claims. It was just a natural human curiosity, I suppose. Ed, in his experience with miners, had come to the conclusion that a good many of the professional ones were prone to be quite superstitious. Among his true stories Ed had a mine mystery which all newcomers liked to hear and one which delighted him to tell.

One evening near Halloween, Ed decided it would be an appropriate time to recount his favorite "hair-raiser" to a group of our miners and several visitors gathered in our little cabin for the evening.

While the candles burned low, he began:

"The winter of 1900 closed in with a rapid succession of sharp frosts and an exceptional snowfall. We had leased Claim 2-B Below Lower Discovery on Dominion Creek and were working like beavers night and day to have a large dump of pay-dirt ready for our spring cleanup.

"On the night that this story begins the thermometer registered thirty degrees below zero and promised to go lower before morning. I made the usual evening inspection of the boiler house, then paid a friendly visit to the men's bunkhouse where McMullen, Shaw, Johnson, Kelly, Anderson and several others were having a late supper-snack. The air was thick with the pungent odor of coffee, sourdough and steaming socks, drying around the stove.

" 'Hello, fellows,' I greeted, 'It's cold as blazes outside, but how you can stand the air in here is more than I can fathom!'

"The men all laughed. Kelly was fastening his heavy coat preparing for the night shift at the boiler house.

" 'Kelly,' I said, 'watch the steam points in number three tunnel. Last night the pressure must have fallen extremely low, for the points weren't working this morning, and today no pay-dirt was removed from that tunnel. Do you know what happened?'

"Kelly didn't answer right away, but reached over and took one last resonant swallow from his cooling coffee. I thought he looked a little pale. He was usually the picture of robust health.

" 'Can't understand it either,' he muttered, 'Ed, I'll be damned if I know what's the matter, but I'm a little nervous on the night shift lately. I dunno, but I actually hate to go down into those tunnels alone at night. Shucks, it's almost spooky! I'm almost beginning to believe in Banshees and supernatural stuff!'

"Kelly shook himself and looked embarrassed, then grinned, 'Oh, forget it. I'll see you in the mornin'.

" 'What ails Kelly?' I asked, after he had closed the door and left.

" 'Oh nothing,' answered Johnson, 'Guess he's a little too young for this kind of work, but he'll grow up. He should have stayed in the States and finished college.'

" 'Fellows,' I said, 'I'm giving you a pep-talk. We've got to keep those steam points thawing the muck in the different tunnels, otherwise there'll be nothing accomplished during the day. I'm worried. That mining syndicate down the creek has its eye on this claim for hydraulic-sluicing purposes and it's up to us to hold the claim and make it pay. I'm counting on you, boys.'

"The next day was extremely cold and several days following. We struggled through the wintry twilight with the usual routine of working in the tunnels and dumping the pay gravel on the surface. Tunnel number three yielded little.

"To my engineer, Smythe, a week later, I said, 'I'm greatly concerned. Our work's at a standstill and the men are awfully jumpy. I've questioned them, but they're very evasive. I feel there's something wrong.'

" 'Yes, I know,' Smythe answered, 'The men are acting mighty queer. I've noticed Kelly and Shaw especially. They seem quite upset lately. The fellows do a lot of talking among themselves, but when I come around they shut up. I think some of 'em are thinking of quitting. Shaw's one of 'em, and he's sleeping in the bunkhouse now. Says he's sick, but I have a suspicion it's something else. As he came off duty this

---

*Steam points are often six feet in length with a bore of 1½ to 3 inches in diameter. Steam points have solid heads which stand the blows of 6 or 8 pound hammers. The points are attached to hoses through which steam is forced. For efficient work, each point requires steam equal to 1½ h.p. boiler capacity.

morning he asked Kelly to take his turn tonight. You know this last week every man has had a turn at the boiler house, and it's supposed to be three nights in a stretch.'

" 'Well, I can't complain about that,' I said. 'They've been a dependable crew. And besides men are hard to replace these days. But I wish I could find out what the trouble is. I simply must get to the bottom of this!'

"That same afternoon I decided on the spur of the moment to visit the bunkhouse again. I found Shaw sleeping sonorously in his bunk. Night duty was evidently very hard on him, for he looked tired and pale. I stood surveying the room. Then my eyes lit on an old yellowed magazine lying on the table. Absent-mindedly I picked it up and began fingering through its well-worn pages. One page caught and held my eye, and one sentence stood out, for it was underscored in pencil:

" 'And with a loud, piercing shriek the Banshee disappeared in mid-air, leaving behind only a weird blue light in its place.'

"I laughed softly. Now, what had Kelly said? 'Banshee, Supernatural stuff?' So that was it!

" 'Someone's been having fun,' I thought.

"That night was crisp and cold, with a weak moon sending its pale shafts through the cabin window. I had not slept well, and guessed it was about midnight. Suddenly, I heard quick footsteps on the crunchy snow outside. I listened. They hesitated. Then came a rapid succession of bangs on the cabin door.

" 'Great guns, what's happened now?' I thought. Grabbing my clothes and draping them on, I rushed to the door. There stood Smythe.

" 'Ed,' he said, 'come quick! Kelly's passed out! Don't know what ails him, but he came stumbling into the bunkhouse a few minutes ago, woke us all up, mumbled something about a Banshee, and then fainted dead away!'

"In no time flat Smythe and I were at the bunkhouse. We could hear the men talking excitedly inside. We pushed open the door and sure enough there was Kelly lying across his bunk looking as white as a ghost. In a few minutes he came to, and weakly accepted some whiskey offered by Johnson.

" 'What's the big trouble, Kelly?' I asked when the color had come back to his face a little. 'Are you sick?'

"Kelly evidently had lost his speech or was too frightened to talk, for he didn't answer and his breathing was labored. The men glanced meaningfully at each other. Finally Shaw spoke up.

" 'Well, Ed, guess I'd better tell you. That mine is haunted. It's the Banshee. Kelly heard it again tonight, and we've all heard it, too, at different times. Beginning about midnight that signal bell rings almost every hour and there's a peculiar thumping, pounding sound deep down in the tunnels. Sounds like heavy footsteps and someone driving steam points. I tell you it's frightening. At first, we thought someone was playing a joke but now we're sure it's nothing like that!'

" 'How long has this been going on?' I asked.

" 'Oh, for nearly ten days.'

" 'So that's it,' I said. 'See here, fellows, there isn't any such thing as a Banshee. You've all been reading too much trash in that old magazine lately.' And as I spoke I saw the corner of the magazine sticking out from under Kelly's mattress.

" 'Well, Ed,' Johnson spoke up, 'that may be, but I was on duty the other night and I'll be jiggered if that damned bell didn't ring three times. Each time I was underground in a different tunnel and the last time I was in tunnel three. It gave me the chills to be way down there and hear that thing clanging. And you know the bell can't be rung except from the bottom of the mine shaft, or in the boiler house. Now, I'm a man of strong nerves, but I don't mind saying I was glad when I passed the bell rope in the shaft and got up the ladder into the boiler house safely. I searched all around the entrance to the mine and around the boiler house, too, but there wasn't a sign of anyone.'

" 'Well, fellows,' I said, 'looking at my watch, 'it's 12:45, I'll take the rest of the night shift. All of you had better get some sleep.'

"I stopped at the cabin to get a heavy coat and the last Dawson newspaper, the Klondike Nugget*. As I walked to the boiler house it began to snow. The pale moon had slipped behind some heavy clouds.

" 'There'll be a good coating of snow by morning,' I predicted to myself. 'Winter has set in with a vengeance!'

"The first thing I noticed on entering the boiler house was that the steam gauge showed extremely low pressure, so I stoked up the fire,

---

*The Klondike News went bankrupt in 1903. Dawson had three newspapers, the Klondike News, the Klondike Nugget, and the Yukon Sun. Later, there was the Dawson Daily News, 1908.

made myself comfortable in a chair and tried to read.

"It was now getting warm in the boiler house and I must have dozed, for suddenly I was recalled to consciousness by the sharp sound of 'Clang, Clang!' I jerked to my feet. Had I been dreaming? No, it had been the bell overhead which was controlled by a rope from the mine below.

"For a moment I stood transfixed, watching the rope which came through a small hole in the floor. All at once the rope gave a quick jerk. 'Clang,' went the bell again. I stood rigid, watching the rope as it crawled from the floor up the side wall to the ceiling where it was fastened to that bell.

" 'Great Scott!' I said to myself, 'those fellows were right! There is something queer going on here!' Lighting a lantern, I hurried outside. It had stopped snowing. I looked in all directions but saw no one. The entrance to the main shaft was just a few steps away. I paused a moment and listened. All was quiet and dark below. I stepped onto the ladder and went straight down into the mine, 30 feet. When I reached the bottom, I sent the beams of my lantern in all directions, calling, 'Who's there? Who's there? Speak up, who's there?'

"There was no answer—only the hollow echoes of my own voice. From the main shaft I glanced into the five separate tunnels which branched out, spoke-like, in all directions.

" 'Sufferin' cats, this is preposterous!' I muttered, a little nervously. I stepped directly under the bell rope in the main shaft, holding the lantern high, tracing the bell rope with my eyes as it ran parallel with the ascending steam pipe up the shaft, where it disappeared under the floor of the boiler house. I was standing where a man would have to be to pull that rope! It was pulled only in the daytime by the miners working underground, to let the engineer in the boiler house know when a bucket of pay-dirt was ready to be hoisted to the surface.

"Puzzled, I began cautiously investigating the tunnels. Each passageway was about forty feet long, but somehow each one seemed longer than the last.

" 'It would be simple to hide down here and hit a fellow over the head,' I said to myself uneasily. 'Surely nobody wants this claim that much! The shadows looked large and threatening. Once I stumbled and thought someone had tripped me, but I quickly discovered that it was because of a small tool left by one of the miners.'

"I reached the end of number three, and stopped to adjust the steam points which were hooked into the muck and were slowly melting it for excavation. In our mining operations we were now at the very lowest strata of the valley. The floor of this tunnel was very near bedrock. Only a short while before, my men had pulled out the huge jawbone and teeth of a Mastodon, buried, God only knows how many thousands of years ago! This tunnel had also yielded the best showing of gold. What next would it produce?

"Since finding the remains of that Mastodon, many times in my imagination I had tried to picture what this huge extinct beast must have looked like. I was thinking about Dinosaurs and the Mastodon when all at once my ears caught a low, deep thud, like a heavy football! It was followed by another, and another! I stood at rigid attention listening as cold chills ran down my spine. There was still another sound which echoed through the tunnels—ping, ping, ping! It sounded as if someone were driving steam points. Then, as if in answer, and as if in warning too, the strident signal bell went Clang! Clang! Clang! I broke into a nervous cold sweat!

"In a few seconds I had dashed the full length of the tunnel, and stood under the bell rope in the main shaft. I examined it carefully, but it looked exactly the same as it had before. Then, I quickly cast the beams of my lantern to the floor for any possible clues, but there were none. Only a few footprints were visible and I was sure they were my own.

"In my hasty inspection of the main shaft I noticed the sump-hole which was located part way under the archway of tunnel one. It was half filled with seeping water.

" 'Must have the pumps working on that sump,' I noted hurriedly.

"I scrambled as fast as I could up the ladder. Yes, I had to admit that the situation was perplexing and nerve-wracking! Were those tunnel sounds made by beast or man, or were they supernatural? No, they certainly couldn't be supernatural. But if man made, who in hell was responsible, and why was he ringing that bell? And how in blazes did he disappear so fast from the scene?

"It occurred to me that if anyone had gone down into the mine,

---

*Remains of Mastodon were found about 1905 in a small melting glacier on Hunker Creek. Flesh and hide of the animal was still well preseved. Even the brown curly fur was still on the animal.

after I had come on duty, I would know it because of the freshly-fallen snow which would show plainly any new footprints. So—I held the lantern close to the ground and thoroughly searched the area, especially the entrance to the mine and around the boiler house. But there were no footprints, only my own. I was sure of it!

"As morning approached I was more than exhausted. I had made one more nerve-wracking trip into the mine. However, the bell had remained silent and there were no more unusual sounds in the tunnels.

"It was seven o'clock when Smythe came to relieve me, and I was extremely glad to turn over the boiler house to him with all its puzzling problems. When I told Smythe that I, too, had heard the hair-raising tunnel sounds and also that the bell had rung, he looked quite grave.

" 'Can't understand it, Ed, either someone's playing a dirty trick, or the place is really haunted.'

" 'Well, I intend to soon find out,' I said. 'Tell the boys I'm taking night shift again tonight. Right now I'm going to my cabin for much-needed sleep.'

* * *

"Toward evening I awakened refreshed and ready for the night's vigil. After supper I walked to the bunkhouse and found the men sipping coffee as usual. They greeted me in a friendly manner and waited expectantly for some comment, which I purposely held back. Finally, McMullen couldn't stand it any longer.

" 'What did you hear last night?' he blurted.

" 'Oh, some faint pounding noises, and of course, the bell,' I said undramatically, trying to keep my voice matter-of-fact.

" 'Just what we've all heard,' broke in Shaw excitedly. 'I tell you, Ed, that mine is haunted! Better take my gun along tonight. You may need it!'

" 'No, No! You can't shoot a Banshee!' gasped Kelly. 'In Ireland my uncle tried to shoot one, once, but the thing vanished in midair with a terrible shriek!'

"The men glanced at one another and all laughed a little nervously. If any of them were 'in the know' I couldn't detect it.

" 'Well, boys,' I said unceremoniously, 'I must be going. I'll see you in the morning!'

"That night I was expecting a strenuous nerve-wracking vigil, and was fortified with coffee, sandwiches and the Dawson paper. But I couldn't concentrate on reading. The evening and early morning hours dragged by without event, and although I spent a great deal of time listening, there were no unusual sounds. The bell was absolutely silent. All was dark and quiet in the mine. Only the distant howl of a wolf, answered by the barking of a dog, sounded on the cold, brittle air. I was slightly disappointed as I had sat at wide-awake attention, tensely keyed up all through the night.

" 'What luck, Ed?' Smythe asked as he greeted me in the early morning.

" 'Nothing at all. The Banshee took off last night,' I replied.

" 'Maybe it decided to leave for good,' volunteered McMullen, who had come along with Smythe.

" 'Say, I've got a message for you, Ed,' said Smythe. 'McCaffery, down the creek, sent word this morning that he wants to see you. Says it's terribly important.'

" 'Tell him to come to my cabin about four this afternoon,' I said.

* * *

"Late that day McCaffrey rapped at my cabin door and for a full hour we talked seriously. When he left I was deeply puzzled and very thoughtful.

"It had been snowing all that day and toward evening a cold wind came up, swirling the snow. As I walked to the mine it was difficult to see anything but close objects. When I reached the boiler house I was grateful to see Smythe who was waiting for me.

" 'Hello, Smythe,' I said. 'Something mysterious has happened. McCaffrey tells me his signal bell rang last night. Said it happened at intervals. Said his night watchman was pretty much frightened.'

" 'Sufferin' cats,' exclaimed Smythe, 'So that's where the Banshee was! This is really spooky, Ed! Sure you don't want me to keep you company tonight?'

" 'No,' I said emphatically, 'I'll manage all right!'

"Smythe slowly shook his head as he carefully closed the door, leaving me alone for the night.

"I began the usual routine of stoking the furnace and checking the steam gauge for the different tunnels, but the time seemed to drag slowly by. There were no unusual sounds from the mine. Gradually, my thoughts began to turn to stories I had heard about supernatural happenings.

"Some people really believed in ghosts and spirits and midnight was the fearful hour when such creatures were permitted to visit their favorite haunts.

"I began to wonder if the dead really could return to this earth. Some thought so. Otherwise, spiritualists would be completely discredited. I had heard of their methods of recalling departed spirits. It was always accomplished in a darkened room with the medium calling the spirit by name. I had heard that the returning spirits manifested themselves in various ways, such as strange knockings on tables and chairs and for the privileged few, an occasional apparition.

"When I was quite young my father, being a Baptist minister, had warned me to shun such stories and beliefs as coming from the Devil himself. Still, it was a fascinating, sometimes entertaining, sometimes frightening subject! I wondered . . .

"Now it was almost time to check the mine. I glanced at my watch. It was nearly twelve, the witching hour. I lit my lantern and put on a heavy coat. It was odd, but I was beginning to have a strange, eerie feeling.

" 'Guess it would have done no harm to let Smythe stay tonight,' I thought.

"I stepped outside and cautiously looked around. It had stopped snowing but the wind was beginning to blow. For a moment I hesitated at the top of the shaft. Then, clutching the lantern in one hand and with the other tightly holding onto the rungs of the ladder, I began the steep descent into the mine. I felt a queer premonition of something about to happen. Felt it in my very bones! Right now I wasn't at all eager to go into any of those tunnels! Almost at each step I paused and listened, peering downward into that black opening beneath. At last I reached the bottom of the ladder and stepped onto solid earth. I began slowly walking towards tunnel number three. That feeling of apprehension was mounting! I could actually feel the little hairs along my body bristle and quiver.

"Suddenly, without any warning, something hit me a terrific blow on the back of the head. There was a flash of light, and stars! Then, I dropped into complete darkness—and oblivion.

"When I regained consciousness I was lying on my back at the bottom of the main shaft. At first, I couldn't remember what had happened. Then, I recalled that awful blow on the head. I was numb! My head throbbed and I was stiff and cold all over. Oh, it was dark down there! And, confound it, where was my lantern? No doubt broken to bits!

"Gropingly, I felt around for the ladder. At last my fingers touched it and I stepped up. Then, something *soft and clammy* brushed my face!

" 'Oh, Great Scott!' I yelled, 'this place is haunted!' I literally sprang up the ladder! At the surface, I broke into a run toward the bunkhouse. Near the door I glanced back over my shoulder. No, no one was pursuing me, and what would the men think if they could see their boss fleeing in panic? As I walked back to the boiler house, the blue faced moon pushed its way into the wintry sky. Seemed that it was focusing right on me!

"Slowly I re-entered the boiler house. It was exactly as I had left it except that the place had grown quite chilly. Yes, the fire had almost gone out. Quickly, I threw small chunks of dry wood into the furnace as the steam pressure was down to zero!

"Another hour passed all too quickly, and it was time again for the mine inspection. By this time my nerves had calmed somewhat as I had told myself over and over again that 'there was no such thing as a Banshee.' But I thought of Smythe and fervently wished I had allowed him to stay. 'He certainly could have been of real help this night!' I told myself uneasily.

"Resolutely, I pulled on my coat and lit the extra lantern. I left it burning on the table while I stepped outside to survey the landscape. That pale, mysterious, uncertain moon had dodged behind a cloud, leaving a peculiar bluish glow which reflected deep into the snow. The very atmosphere was weird and unearthly. I shivered and hurried back to the boiler house to get the lantern.

"Carefully, I climbed down into the mine, one hand clutching the frosty ladder, the other casting the beams of my lantern in all directions trying to see into the farthest underground corners. Again, I felt that strange, eerie feeling—the flesh was beginning to creep along my spine.

"At last I reached the bottom of the ladder and stepped out a few feet onto solid ground, holding the lantern high. I was now under the

Miners thawing the gold-bearing muck and gravel in deep, underground tunnel with steam-points, 1899.

Ed Lung, right, starting out with the Goodwin party from Dawson to Skagway in 1898, completing his 1,000 mile trek over the ice.

Sun-dogs in the sky—a phenomenal sight in the North.

Stampeders on the Trail of '98, between Lake Linderman and Bennett.

bell rope and I looked up to inspect it. Suddenly, I saw the rope sag and jerk and heard a sharp Clang! Clang! in the boiler house. I was frozen stiff in my tracks! Couldn't move a muscle, and as I watched, a strange bluish light descended into the shaft and glowed along the bell rope. Simultaneously, there was a peculiar pounding sound, faint at first, then increasing in volume, echoing through all five tunnels. Then, a heavy thud, thud, thud!

" 'Oh, Great Caesar's ghost!' I yelled, 'the Banshee! The Banshee! It's the Banshee!' "

* * *

"Next morning Smythe greeted me anxiously. 'Any luck, Ed?'

" 'Yes,' I replied, wearily, 'I came face to face with the Banshee last night and he nearly finished me off. But Smythe, be a good fellow. Please let me get some sleep. I had a strenuous time last night and I don't feel like talking about it just yet. Tell all the boys to meet me at the bunkhouse tonight.'

"Smythe looked a little puzzled and hurt. 'All right, Ed. You're the boss,' he replied, 'but I can hardly wait to hear about it.'

"In the bunkhouse that evening the boys were waiting anxiously. The familiar smell of coffee, sourdough and steaming socks greeted my nostrils as I opened the door. The men all gathered around me and waited expectantly.

" 'Well, boys,' I said slowly, 'I saw the Banshee last night!'

" 'You—saw—the Banshee?' whispered Kelly incredulously.

" 'Yes, I saw the Banshee,' I said, 'He hit me over the head with a terrible wallop and left me lying at the bottom of the shaft. It's just a wonder that I'm here to tell about it!'

" 'My God!' breathed Shaw, 'What did he look like?' Shaw had turned a dead white.

" 'Well, fellows,' I said, 'I can't say exactly, but he seemed almost formless. He was awfully dark and blurry, soft and clammy, and he had a horrible odor, like something dead! The light in the shaft was very dim, but the Banshee seemed to float through the air without any difficulty and then he vanished right through the floor of the shaft, in front of my very eyes!'

" 'Saints protect us!' groaned Kelly, crossing himself. 'What are we gonna do about that ghost?'

" 'I don't know, Kelly,' I said, 'unless we close up the shaft. But I don't imagine that it would keep the Banshee away from his favorite haunt. Yes, believe me, men, I'm worried, but I won't give up this mine. Will you fellows stick by me, even though it means taking an awful chance?'

"I watched the semi-circle of men. Their faces were a study of mixed fear.

" 'Well,' began Shaw, 'I had sorta thought of quitting this week. You see I have a sweetheart in Skagway, and I know she wants to see me in the worst kind of way.'

" 'Oh, is that a fact?' I asked. Then I turned and gave Smythe, at my left, a sly wink. Anderson, next to him, caught it too.

" 'Oh, come on, Ed,' he drawled, 'Why scare the pants off us like this? Now what is that Banshee, really?'

" 'All right, boys,' I chuckled, 'I'll let you have it straight. Brace yourselves for a real shock. The Banshee which I saw under the light of a stray beam of blue moonlight is nothing but melting muck, falling from the location of the steam pipe and hitting the bell rope with enough force to jerk the rope and ring the bell in the boiler house. It happens this way only at night because that's when there's heat in the big steam pipe. You know the steam is always turned off during the day. Sometimes, the muck falls and hits the steam pipe in the main tunnel and causes that pounding sound which echoes through the connecting pipes to all the tunnels. As you know, pipes are a very good conductor of sound and especially so if the muck happens to contain heavy gravel. The horrible odor you smelled was tunnel gas from the ancient swamp under the mine. As the muck thaws it releases gas little by little. No doubt there were a lot of animals trapped there millions of years ago. You all know about the Mastodon.'

" 'Well, I'll be damned,' exclaimed McMullen. 'As simple as that! You mean it was only muck that made the bell ring and knocked you out at the bottom of the shaft?'

" 'Yes,' I laughed, 'but it packed a real wallop. No doubt there was a good-sized rock mixed with the muck that hit me, and falling maybe 20 feet, it's no wonder it knocked me cold!'

" 'Yeah?' put in Kelly, 'Then why didn't we see the muck on the floor of the shaft?'

" 'Simply because it always fell into the sump-hole where the water concealed it,' I said. 'So you see, the Banshee did actually vanish through the floor of the shaft! And that reminds me, fellows, we've got to get the pumps working on that particular sump hole.'

" 'Yes, but why did the steam always register so low?' asked Shaw, still not absolutely convinced.

" 'Simply because each man was either too scared, or too preoccupied with the Banshee to keep the boiler fire properly stoked,' I repled, 'Now does that clear up the mystery of the Banshee?'

"The men all nodded, and I noticed a sheepish expression creep over their rugged faces.

" 'Well, Ed,' said Shaw, 'I guess after all I'll wait until spring to go out to Skagway. My girl surely can wait that long.'

" 'Good,' I said, 'And now, fellows, I have to pay a visit to McCaffrey, down the creek. I promised to let him know if I caught the Banshee.'

"Before closing the door I paused a moment and looked at Kelly, 'I believe it's your turn in the boiler house tonight,' I said, 'And be careful, boy, when you go down that shaft. Don't let the Banshee conk you on the head. He's a dirty customer!'

Chapter 27

RUGGED WAYS TO RICHES AND ROMEO

Late in the afternoon, one day in fall of 1901 when I was making biscuits for supper, suddenly I had a frightening premonition that my husband was in very grave danger. Anxiously, I glanced at the clock. It was just twenty minutes to five, almost time for his return home.

Without stopping to brush the flour from my hands, I knelt down right where I was by the table, and asked Almighty God's protection.

That evening at supper Ed didn't seem hungry. He just sat staring out of the window.

"What's wrong, Ed?" I asked anxiously. "You've scarcely eaten and the biscuits are cold."

"Vel, I have no appetite," he said reluctantly. "I hate to tell you this but I must. Less than an hour ago I had a very close brush with death—I'm still shaken up over it. It happened like this:

"I was way down underground in the mine on my knees near a sumphole with Killim. We were digging to get some pan-testings to see how the gold was running. Well, I knew it was getting late so I said to Killim, 'Please look at your watch and tell me what time it is.'

"Killim stood up, pulled out his watch, held it under the lantern and said, 'Twenty minutes to five.'

"I replied, 'Then we'll work until five o'clock and call it a day!'

"A couple of minutes later, Killim screamed, 'Ed, look out!'

"Like a flash, I threw myself backwards. Lucky I did! A ton of rock and muck fell right where I'd been kneeling! If I had hesitated one split second, or jumped the wrong way, I would have been killed instantly! There's absolutely no doubt of it!"

"Oh, how awful!" I cried. "It was exactly twenty minutes to five when I had a very real warning of you in imminent danger. Oh, I was so relieved when you walked through the door!

"But Killim!" I exclaimed. "Where did he come from? Why, he isn't one of our miners!"

"He wasn't, but he is now," said Ed, seriously. "He just came from Dawson this afternoon looking for a job and I hired him! He stayed down in the mine with me and it was fortunate that he did, for if I had been there alone in that spot, I would never have known what struck me!"

BOB

There was an old miner on Dominion Creek whom everyone called "Bob." No one seemed to know his full name and we just let it go at that.

He was a very unkempt, sloppy individual, and could easily have passed as a tramp. Occasionally he came to our cabin and while there, would hungrily feast his eyes on everything: the white cottonwood floors, my little handmade rag-rug, the pink flowered curtains at the window and the ruffled ones around the base of the bed. He seemed absolutely fascinated with everything in our cabin!

One of the things that worried me most about old Bob was that he never wore suspenders. His trousers were held up by a rope which was knotted and wound around his middle. Over this contraption hung a roll of heavy fat. Somehow I always felt real concern about the strength of that rope!

Another thing that bothered me terribly was that Bob wouldn't be in our cabin many minutes when he would begin to warm up and perspire profusely. After that, a real scratch-fest would follow. He would loosen his heavy woolen shirt at the collar and furtively dig around under the folds and scratch his anatomy. Occasionally he would appear to capture some minute, crawling little beast and kill it!

Out of the corner of my eye I would watch with real apprehension for we had already had several severe seiges of gray-backs and body-lice (fleas, too,) and I felt sure old Bob was responsible.

I had had to sterilize all of our clothes, using boiling water, and I had worn my hands raw in the process. Therefore, Bob's visits were a constant threat and something to be dreaded! Finally, I guess, Bob suspected that he wasn't really welcome any longer and so he stopped coming to our cabin.

(Years later, Old Bob surprised us with a visit in Tacoma. He was actually so neat and clean and dressed up that I didn't recognize him!)

THE WOMAN FROM DAWSON

There were very few women living on Dominion Creek in the early days but in the upper valley there were three that I knew of—one was Aunty Fanny, the good-natured middle-aged miner's wife who lived about a mile away. Then, there were the two young women who had come to work at the new Dominion Creek Roadhouse which had recently been built. They were employed as cooks and housekeepers. However, If I wished to see them I had to go to the roadhouse as they were much too busy with their daily work to have any time for social calls.

So it was with real pleasure that one day I heard we were to have new neighbors—a man and his young wife—and they would be just two claims away. Of course I was elated as I was hungry for feminine companionship.

I waited a reasonable time, the shortest possible, then dressed up in my very best Klondike clothes and eagerly called on Mrs. Smith. Although it was the middle of the afternoon, the cabin, I noticed, was in bad disorder and seemed generally ill-kept. "Well, whose cabin wasn't untidy at times?" I thought charitably.

However, I found Mrs. Smith very pleasant. (She was about my age.) She was rather plump, had a round face and a very sweet smile, pretty teeth and dimples—really a fascinating person—I thought.

Her chatter was quite entertaining, too, and she seemed to know a great deal about all of the prominent people of Dawson, even spoke of some intimately. Naturally, I, being so cut off from town, was interested in her patter. Well, I was sure we were going to be very good friends.

For a week after my visit I waited anxiously for her to return my call. Then in about two weeks she did come to visit, but I noticed that she was quite ill at ease. I thought nothing of it. She talked a lot about her husband and in such an affectionate way that I got the impression they were newlyweds and were a most devoted couple! Right away, too, I could see that she had taken a real fancy to Clemy, and he, in turn, seemed to adore her.

During her visit she said to him, "Little man, why don't you haul freight on your new sled? I'll pay you for hauling different things to the roadhouse, as I have friends up there."

Clemy was intrigued with the idea and told her that he would haul her freight for only a quarter a load. (The smallest coin in the North.)

"Fair enough, Clemy," she laughed, showing her beautiful white teeth and pretty dimples.

While Clemy waited at her door, Mrs. Smith went into her cabin and wrote a note to a man at the roadhouse. Then she took a large paper bag, put a rock in it, and blew the bag up, then tied the top with a string. Carefully, she carried the bag outside, pretending it was very heavy. This she placed on Clemy's sled in the "freight box" and ceremoniously handed him a note to be delivered to a certain male-boarder at the roadhouse (a person whom Clemy knew). She told Clemy that now she considered him a real mailman like Ben Atwater, the well-known mailman-freighter who made such spectacular runs to the Coast with his famous dog-team.

"Go slow, little Clem," she cautioned, "don't lose my precious load.

And be sure to deliver the bag and letter right away!"

Clemy, of course, was puffed up with real pride over his new job. It was a mighty important errand he was running for our pretty new neighbor. But several times on the way, when he paused to check on his load, he noticed "the freight" appeared a little smaller!

By the time he reached the roadhouse the bag had shrunk to about half its original size. This surely was puzzling! Then when he examined the bag more closely he discovered the trick she'd played. Naturally, he was quite indignant, yes—and hurt, too!

All the same, he marched up to the roadhouse, located the man, gave him the letter, then announced briskly:

"Your friend, Mrs. Smith, shipped you a bag of air and a rock. I'm the freighter and the mailman. You owe me a quarter, and you must unload your own package."

The man read the letter sheepishly, then hurriedly paid Clemy the quarter. He took the bag from the sled and told Clemy to wait a few minutes while he wrote a return message.

A half hour later Clemy stood at Mrs. Smith's door with the letter. Tartly, he demanded a quarter for his services and told her in a halting little boy's way that he wasn't freighting bags of air "no more," and that he had decided to give up the mailman business forever. Mrs. Smith fumbled around for insincere words of apology and Clemy, unsmilingly, accepted them and the money, but he was a disillusioned, tearful little boy when he returned home and told me all about it. It was only a few days later when my husband came home and said reluctantly:

"Vel, it's a shame about Mrs. Smith! Today, I learned she isn't Smith's wife at all. She's one of those women from Louse Town—an Alley Woman—belongs to the White Chapel Group—you and Clemy musn't go near her cabin and Clemy musn't carry any messages for her!"

"Mrs. Smith" only remained on Dominion Creek a little while after that, then moved on. We never saw her again. No doubt, she left for more profitable fields.

CAN CANS

Tin cans, we rarely threw away. We used them in so many ways: to melt snow, to cook dog food, to carry water, to make lanterns, and the largest cans were often used to make stoves for trail-traveling. Some miners even used cans as receptacles, for storing nuggets and gold-dust. Many cabins had secret places hollowed out beneath log-floors or in walls where "canned-golden treasures" were hidden and where they were generally safe from theft.

Of course, oil cans were the most highly prized because of their square or oblong shapes. On long trips the miners carried stoves made of two, five-gallon oil cans riveted together; one was used for burning fuel, the other served as an oven. A third, smaller can formed the chimney. This homemade equipment was light-weight to pack and easy to cook on or bake simple meals in.

Lanterns were often fashioned from smaller cans, preferably square ones. The top and one side would be cut away, then, a hole would be punched in the bottom of the can to hold a candle. This style of lantern could be made in only a few minutes and would throw a steady and bright light, the three sides of the tin-can acting as reflectors. This kind of lantern would burn more slowly than would just a plain candle stuck in an open holder or candlestick. It was very, very important to be frugal with candles as they were quite expensive, a dollar apiece! A tin-lantern could easily be carried, suspended from a long wire handle. To make a handle, the ends of a strip of wire were bent and inserted into the two top sides of the tin can (in perforated holes).

Miners often used this sort of lantern on stampedes. It was dependable in all kinds of weather, as the flames would rarely blow out. Even in our cabin we often used tin can lanterns, as they were safe and economical to operate.

* * *

Getting drinking water was a real problem for in wintertime the streams were usually frozen over. However, there was a small spring flowing from the hillside on the opposite side of the valley which remained open almost all through the winter. It, no doubt, contained quite a variety of minerals as the sides of the spring were heavily coated with light green and reddish-brown deposits. Whatever the minerals were, they seemed entirely harmless and so we drank the water with no ill effects.

To get water for household use, Ed would tie three ten-gallon cans onto the sled, then he would harness the dogs and away he would go down the valley to another spring about a mile away. We could count on this stream remaining open nearly all winter long. The water was not palatable to drink but we were glad to have it for washing dishes and clothes, and also for frugal sponge-baths.

Of course when the mercury hit 50 degrees below zero absolutely all water froze solid. Then it was necessary to resort to melting snow but this was a tedious process as a ten-gallon pail of snow only made about a fourth of a pail of water and it took a surprisingly long time to melt it even over the hottest fire!

Washing very soiled clothes was something to be dreaded! So, as a matter of necessity, we wore our clothes as long as we possibly could. When I had begun cabin living and after I had struggled through several Klondike washings I felt a great deal more charitable towards those who appeared to live in the same old clothes all winter long without the benefit of laundry!

Wash-day certainly took a great deal of endurance and the patience of Job. I postponed the wash-day-anguish for as long as possible, especially in the wintertime.

When I would finally decide that I could no longer delay the ordeal; with a homemade washboard and two galvanized washtubs, dark brown soap and heavy sad-irons, and with lots of wood, a very hot stove and oh, such a limited amount of water, I did the family laundry. Truly, it was the rugged pioneer method! How my back and hands ached on those blue wash-days! After that, we lived in a cloud of vapor from drying clothes around the stove. It was impossible to hang washing out in winter for the clothes would freeze as stiff as boards in only a few minutes.

Whenever we needed a fresh supply of wood, Ed would bring the dogs inside the cabin in order to get them in harness. If they could, they would sneak away before the ordeal. Somehow, with their uncanny instinct, they always seemed to sense the wood-getting-expeditions. It was obvious they dreaded these trips like fury! Once in the cabin, if possible, they would crawl under the beds and hide. It was all Ed could do to drag them out amid the commotion of yapping, cuffing, and snarling. When he would finally corner them, they would sit on their haunches and roll their eyes and shiver while he adjusted the harnesses. It was almost funny to watch their doleful expressions when they realized that they were trapped and couldn't escape the wood-gathering ordeal.

Well, I couldn't blame them much. It was quite a long climb up the mountainside to where the trees grew. It was difficult to know which part of the trip the dogs dreaded most: going up, or coming down.

"Oh Edward," I said on one occasion after I had watched the dog-team come downhill at breakneck speed, "why don't you turn the dogs loose after they've pulled the heavy go-devil up hill?" (sledge)

"Can't, Vel. They would run away and not come back for days! I need them to haul the wood home when I reach the bottom of the hill! And by Jove!" he remarked proudly, "I do believe I've got the best racing-dogs in the whole Klondike, especially when I'm hauling wood down hill!" he added with a laugh. (Ed never had a mishap on his down-hill excursions as he dragged a log as a break.)

ISAIAH

One day several Dominion Creek miners talked Ed into going on a fifty-mile stampede. They were just about ready to take off when Ed accidentally stepped on a rusty nail.

Frantically, after trying to convince Ed that he should stay at home, but to no avail, I looked around the cabin for some kind of medicine. All at once I recalled that there was mention in the Bible (somewhere) of how Isaiah, the prophet, had told King Hezekiah to bind figs on his wounds. Now, I happened to have a Christmas package of dried figs which mother had sent from Tacoma. So I grabbed a fig, scraped the seeds out, dampened it with warm water, and then bound it onto Ed's sore foot. Over the bandage he pulled his woolen sock and heavy boot. Then, hastily, he departed on the stampede.

For some time after he left I had grave misgivings about that fig-plaster. I knew what a badly infected foot could mean out in the wilds. But when Ed returned a week later, to my surprise, he was in good shape. His foot had healed rapidly while in constant use and it had given him absolutely no trouble! With grateful thanks to old Isaiah, I

---

*Italian Jack was famous during gold-rush days for his powerful string of sled-dogs. He won many contests for the speed of his dogs and their remarkable strength. (Dawson)

tried to locate that special Bible passage, but I never could find it a second time.

Well, anyway, I had learned something—the fig remedy was a success, even tho' the gold-stampede proved a dismal failure!

LUNG'S PREHISTORIC TEETH AND TUSKS

There was a great deal of excitement one day on 2-B Below Lower Discovery when Joe and a miner, who were working far underground in one of the tunnels, unearthed some very large teeth and tusks of a huge prehistoric animal. The men worked carefully and brought the bones to the surface. After much discussion, the men decided the bones were the remains of a mastodon like others they had found before. Bones of the extinct mastodon (which millions of years ago roamed the North) were a great curiosity, and while not an entirely uncommon discovery, they always created a stir of excitement and a lot of imaginative speculation.

After all of our miners and others on Dominion Creek, too, had viewed and examined the mastodon relics, the bones were brought into our cabin and placed in a corner. However, in only a short time, and almost before our eyes, the huge tusks rapidly began disintegrating. No doubt their resting place in the frozen muck for untold centuries had been the means of preserving these bones for our wondering eyes. The pity of it was, the tusks were returning to dust!

Ed carefully watched the mastodon jaws and teeth for signs of deterioration and decided that they were in fair enough condition to ship Outside. Carefully he wrapped the relics in cloth and moss and shipped them to Tacoma, Washington, to the University of Puget Sound where they were kept on display in a glass case for many years.

Of course, at the college there was a card telling where the mastodon teeth had been found and by whom. Many of our friends in Tacoma made special pilgrimages to see the prehistoric relics and some of them humorously called them, "Lung's Teeth."

* * *

One day in November Ed announced enthusiastically, "There's to be a Dominion Creek-entertainment at Caribou this evening. Slavin's

'Hardly Able Orchestra' will supply the music with Max Lange as violin soloist. Art Buell, the Dawson Nugget cartoonist, will make sketches of folks and some may get into the newspaper. It should be a lively, very interesting evening. Maybe Dr. Slayton*, the famous palmist, will be there, too, and we could have our fortunes told! Yes, Vel, they want us to bring Rover to do his Talking-Dancing act, too. It'll all be great fun, and so, let's hitch up the dogs tonight and take the children," said Ed, persuasively, with one of his most charming, boyish smiles.

"I don't think we should take the children out at night in such cold weather, but anyway, you go with Joe," I told Ed, half-reluctantly.

"But I dislike leaving you," my husband informed me, then added, "However, if you insist, I will, but please press my best woolen trousers. Joe says there's to be a dance after the program."

"A dance!" I exclaimed, slightly taken back.

"Great Scott, Vel, I don't particularly care about dancing," replied my husband, half embarrassed, "but you know how much Joe loves to waltz and do the polka. You know it would take a team of horses to drag him away once the dancing starts."

"Oh yes," I agreed, "you're right about Joe being fond of dancing!" But I thought to myself, "Well, a dance certainly does put a little different light on the evening." However, before I could think of a logical reason for my husband not to go, he had rushed out-doors like an excited schoolboy.

In a jiffy he returned with a pailful of fluffy snow. This he put onto the back of the stove to have bath water. Then, as if he feared I might reverse my decision about him going to Caribou, he raced off to the mine, saying he wished to leave everything in good order for the man on night duty.

The fame of young Art Buell of The Dawson Nugget spread to the Outside. Slavin's orchestra, which Art Buell humorously named "Slavin's Hardly Able Orchestra," was well-known in the Klondike. This orchestra was directed by A. R. Slavin, cousin of Frank Slavin, the well-known British heavyweight pugilist champion who, among others, was also in the Klondike during the gold-rush. Frank Slavin went over Chilkoot Pass in 1897. Mr. and Mrs. Amos R. Slavin owned No. 28 Below Upper Discovery, Dominion Creek.

*By 1904 Arthur Victor Buell, called "heavyweight cartoonist of the Golden North," and Joseph Andrew Clark of Brockville, Ontario, had their own show. They traveled to the creeks, Buell making quick sketches and Clark lecturing and doing the "art spieling." They became well-known and drew large audiences.

*Dr. Slayton was a lady palmist from Portland, Oregon. She was world-famous. She spent a season in Dawson and vicinity.

Naturally, I wasn't too happy over Ed's obvious enthusiasm about the evening's program, especially the dance for Joe's benefit! But I knew how impossible it would be for me to attend. Also, I knew how hungry Ed was for entertainment. He did love gaiety, lively music and groups of people. It was a drab, hard life he was living, working long hours, day after day, down, deep underground. Yes, I decided, it would probably do him good to go and certainly Rover's Dancing-Talking act would add to the evening's entertainment. So I would remain with the children; I would keep the home-fires burning. Little Clemy was always very good company.

That afternoon I gathered more snow to add to Ed's bath water. Then late in the afternoon I rummaged through the clothes-box and found his best trousers. They were badly wrinkled, having been stored away for many months. Carefully I turned them *wrong side out*, laid them on the table and, with hot sadirons and a damp cloth, I succeeded in pressing in two very deep creases from top to bottom on each pant-leg, front and back.

After I had finished, naturally I felt very proud of myself, as I had never pressed my husband's trousers before. Then I laid them carefully over the back of a chair, awaiting his return.

Mentally, I patted myself on the back for my new achievement; here I was actually getting my husband spruced up for a dance!

By evening I had everything in readiness; a brimming pail of warm bath-water, hot supper, and oh yes! Ed's freshly pressed trousers!

He came rushing home and was tremendously pleased with the amount of bath-water I had managed to get as he knew what an effort it was to gather snow and melt it.

Soon Edward was bathing behind the flowered curtain. I could hear him splash and happily whistle some of the popular dance-tunes and some that he would need for Rover's act. Pretty soon he interrupted his whistling to call out, "Now, Vel, please hand me those trousers!"

Eagerly he reached for them, but in a few seconds something like an earthquake was going on behind the curtains and a muffled exclamation of anguished surprise.

"Sufferin' cats! Vel, what in blazes have you done to these trousers? Good Lord," he cried, as the curtains parted, "Look at these monstrous things!"

"What's wrong?" I asked, quivering a little in my moccasins, for it didn't take half an eye to see that my husband was enormously displeased about the trousers. But why?

For answer he stepped out under the lamplight so that I could get a good look at him, and them. Then, suddenly I saw what was wrong. Deep ripples extended from the waist to the bottom of each pant-leg, both front and back!

"Oh!" I gasped, a little defiantly, in order to hold back the tears. Then all at once I saw the funny side of the situation. I couldn't help it—I just leaned back and laughed and laughed!

Edward looked at me reproachfully, even accusingly.

"Yes, in those pants," I said, "you will be a fit subject for a good cartoonist!"

"Vel, how could you press the creases on the *wrong side!"* he exclaimed in half-injured voice. "Just look at me! The fellows will all give me the horse-laugh! And Great Scott, Vel," he added, grinning a little, "I almost believe you did it on purpose. If you did—well—I really can't blame you much, since you knew I was getting ready for a dance!

Hurriedly, Ed took off the trousers and laid them on the table and then I saw how to press men's pants. And so, with a damp cloth and sadirons (that weren't nearly hot enough by this time), Ed tried to remedy the ridiculous mistake I had made. But try as he would, the obstinate creases continued to turn in, or remained wrong-side-out.

Finally, in desperation, he put on the offending things. It was either that or stay at home! Hurriedly he swallowed his supper and then he and Joe and Rover were off for Caribou.

Grudgingly, I had admitted to myself as I watched my blonde, Teutonic husband in the last throes of getting ready, that he was really quite a handsome fellow. Yes, in spite of the odd looking trousers! Naturally, I wondered if some of the young, pretty women of Dawson would attend the dance. Would voluptuous Kate Rockwell (Klondike Kate) be there, or some of the other equally attractive young women like Cad Wilson, or the Oatly sisters? Art Buell, himself, a popular young blade, would no doubt bring a bevy of vivacious, beautiful girls for the performance and dance.

After Joe and Ed, and our dog-actor had departed, I locked the cabin door. Then I threw myself down to rest for a bit. It had been a strenuous day! I hadn't really wanted to go to Caribou at all on this particular night and I smiled again at the thought of those ridiculous trousers! If I knew Edward, he would be extremely uncomfortable and miserable all evening—and I really couldn't be too awfully sorry!

Now Ella was asleep in the "children's corner." Clemy sat by the fire whittling a sailboat from a soft piece of wood. Chilly November winds whistled around the cabin sending loose snowflakes flying against the window pane.

I knew that in Tacoma brilliantly colored leaves would be swirling merrily down C Street and Pacific Avenue on this cold autumn night. Yes, I had to admit I was just a wee bit homesick.

For a while Clemy sat by the fire, or until his hands grew tired and his eyes, heavy; then he said his prayers and I tucked him into bed. After that I stirred up the fire and put on more logs. Certainly I was not at all sleepy. Besides, I had a batch of sourdough bread to bake. This would keep me busy for several hours, maybe until Ed would return home.

Now, all was quiet in the cabin, only the smell of baking bread filled the air. I sat staring into the fire which glowed in a cozy way through the half-opened grate. Then I began day-dreaming, blissfully living over my gay, young womanhood-days in Tacoma ten years earlier when I had dressed in beautiful evening clothes and had gone to formal dances, the opera and Shakespearian plays. During my reverie I forgot all about my shapeless Indian moccasins; my work-worn hands; my coarse clothing, as absentmindedly, I opened the oven and turned the bread—yes, I knew all of the operas—could sing some of the leading roles myself, and I knew all of the Shakespearian plays, too.

I could see Modjeska, the gorgeous Polish actress as Lady Macbeth— washing, washing her hands, trying to remove the bloodstains! Then, I could see wonderful Sarah Bernhardt as Cleopatra and as poor Camille. How I had wept over the death scene as Bernhardt had made Camille so very real!

Suddenly I burst out laughing, for I remembered how, after the theater plays, I would re-enact some of the most dramatic scenes for the benefit of a young relative from Oregon who had come to live with us. (Cousin Eltha)

But my favorite play was Romeo and Juliet. How I liked to play-act that balcony love scene and extra-dramatize it! My cousin would laugh until she would hold her sides, then she'd beg me to stop acting like a comedian . . . "spoiling a perfectly beautiful love-scene," she would say.

Then off we'd go to the kitchen to see what the maid had left in the icebox for a midnight snack: usually ham or chicken sandwiches. We'd laugh and giggle in the kitchen, then tiptoe up the long winding staircase so as not to waken the sleeping household.

Again I could see my father (long since dead these many years) standing in the parlor under the gaslight reading Shakespeare to the family. He would suddenly stop and look straight at me to see if I was listening. Sometimes I was, but more often I wasn't. My father had an uncanny way of telling how much by my glassy stare. "Vel," he would say, "you must learn your Shakespeare. You must be cultured!"

My dear father was tall, dark, slender, and handsome. His father was French and his mother, English. His family had lived in Montreal. I had named our little son "Clement" after the family name.

Such a glorious bass voice my father had! I could hear his rich tones yet. He had never used his voice professionally, but he had generously given of his talent in the large churches of Portland, Seattle, and Tacoma. Gaily he had laughed and said he was too busy to be an opera singer when the critics had suggested it. No, he enjoyed singing and that was all! He was a very successful business man[*] and had loved his work. He had served as a Councilman of Tacoma and many had thought he would some day be Mayor and maybe Governor, but his sudden death had cut short his useful career,[*] also, it had cut off the Clement fortune.

Now I smiled as I thought of Edward. He had met me after much planning on his part: One day soon after his arrival in Tacoma from the east, he had seen me riding down Main Street in my father's carriage.

"Who is that young lady?" he had asked.

"Don't you know?" a friend had replied. "Why, that's Velma Clement, one of Tacoma's belles."

"There goes my future wife," Ed had announced with determination.

I smiled as I recalled the beginning of the romance—how a fine looking young man had hurried to pick up the fuzzy, little grey kitten that had happened to cross my path just as I was about to go up in the

---

[*]During the latter part of 1880 and early 90's Horatio C. Clement owned the Hotel Abbott which he later changed to "The Grand Pacific." His cousin, Edward H. Clement, was editor of the Boston Transcript. Another cousin was Judge Clement, who lived in Brooklyn, New York, where he served on the bench.

elevator of my father's hotel (The Grand Pacific).

"Oh," I exclaimed, "what an adorable kitten!" Somehow, Edward was there and he gallantly handed the kitten to me with appropriate words, introducing himself as Edward Burchall Lung, a Baptist minister's son from New York.

A year later Ed and I were married! Two years after that, the awful depression, then . . . rumors of gold in the Klondike—1897! I remembered the heart-pangs when Edward told me goodbye. He wouldn't be long in the Klondike. I remembered our sentimental, heart-rendering promise—"to look at the North Star each night and think of each other." Even yet, the North Star meant Edward, and it always would!

Suddenly my reverie was broken by a frantic knock at the cabin door and the night watchman called in an anxious voice:

"Mrs. Lung, never mind to open the door, but what shall I do? The pump has stopped working in the mine."

"Is it very serious?" I asked.

"It sure is! By morning the shaft will be flooded!"

"Then hurry to Caribou. Find Ed and Joe at the dance and tell them what's happened," I advised earnestly.

Realizing the extreme seriousness of the situation, the miner took off on the run for Caribou. When at last Ed and Joe arrived home, they didn't take time to change their best party-clothes. They spent the rest of the night ankle-deep in mud and ice-water, trying to repair the pump damage.

And so my lovable Edward, my "North Star," my "Romeo," dressed in his ridiculous trousers with the creases pressed wrong-side-out never really got to step the "Dance Fantastic" with Klondike Kate nor with any other queen of the North on that eventful, almost comedy-like evening which both of us would long remember, and which would have made a hilarious theme for a light opera, or would it have been Shakespeare? The night watchman (I found out afterwards) reached Caribou just as the orchestra struck up its first lively dance tune!

The next day Ed was far too weary to give me much of an account of that eventful evening at Caribou but in his own mind, I'm sure, he thought the outcome was some sort of retribution! Nor could I find out whether Art Buell had made a cartoon of Edward in his ridiculously funny trousers. Anyway, I did learn afterwards that our remarkable dog, Rover, stole the show with his "Talking-Dancing Act," as he always did when he had an appreciative audience.

Chapter 28

A SLEIGH RIDE TO DAWSON AND BLIZZARD

One day Ed announced that in a few days we were going to Dawson, as Rover had been invited to do his "Talking, Laughing, Dance Act" at a talent show at the Dawson Amateur Athletic Club. Of course, all of us were elated for the chance to go to town, as it would give us a fine holiday and an opportunity to do some shopping. Clemy was excited about the trip, too, as he had a small poke of gold to spend.

For two nights, in the cabin, Ed put Rover through his act and the children and I had the fun of watching these rehearsals. Rover hadn't forgotten any of his act; in fact, he'd greatly improved the illusion of a talking dog, and his laughing had taken on a more human sound. (He was still trying to imitate Ed's voice.) And, yes, he'd even added a few steps, dance-prance, of his own and could remain on his hind legs minutes longer than before.

The morning we were to leave for the trip, the temperature hovered at one degree below zero which was not considered very cold for winter. Anyway, we dressed in our warmest clothes, including fur parkas, fur ear muffs, and fur caps.

Soon, we were ready to take off, or "mush the trail." Edward had packed the sleigh with a few necessary things for the ten-day trip. He then wrapped the three of us, Ella, Clemy and me, in the wildcat robe, and calling to the dogs, he cracked the whip and yelled, "Boris, Queen,

---

*The Dawson Amateur Athletic Club was conceived by Clement Burns. In 1902 the new building was finished. It was 200 feet by 100 feet and would seat a large crowd for all kinds of sports and shows and other entertainment. National Curling contests and hockey games were held there and the D.A.A.A. became nationally known. Before the big club house was built, meetings and entertainments were held in a large warehouse.

Nelly, Pat, Rover, mush on!" And away we went, loose snow flying, with Edward running behind, only jumping on the back runners where there was a downhill grade to the trail. He yelled to Boris the leader, "Gee," if he wanted him to turn right, and "Haw" if to the left.

It was splendid traveling weather—invigorating and crisp and the snow was hard packed. Occasionally, Pat would turn in the harness to see if we were coming. But he always got a little nip on his flank from the long whip as drivers of dog teams never allow their dogs to look back while in harness as it can be extremely dangerous to passengers and dog teams alike.

At Dawson, we stayed at the Klondike Hotel, on First Street, near the river, and the following night the talent show was to take place in a large warehouse that had been converted into an auditorium. On the improvised stage that night, much Dawson talent was displayed: singers, dancers, musicians, skaters, elocutionists, and it was a wonderful show. But our Rover became the star of the evening when he waltzed out onto the stage dressed in Clemy's little red jacket and Ed's miner's hat. Of course Ed was with Rover, providing music with his merry whistle. The crowd went wild with enthusiasm when suddenly Rover stopped his dance to say in a loud hoarse voice that he "wanted to go home with mamma and papa and Clemy!"

Then, when the applause had died down, Rover danced to the edge of the stage and laughed at the top of his Husky voice, at the audience, in that peculiar unearthly tone, long and loud! Everybody was astonished, and delighted at this wonder dog from Dominion Creek!

After the show, people crowded around Ed, Clemy, and me, to pet Rover and compliment Ed on his marvelous dog. Rover received their adoration and compliments like an old trouper. As a reward that night, Rover was served a nice big chunk of juicy bear steak and slept in our room. Yes, he had been the Star of the Evening and we were all happy and pleased. A man had wanted to buy Rover right there at the auditorium, but of course Ed would not part with his remarkable sled-dog-pet.

The rest of the time in Dawson was spent as a holiday, sightseeing, shopping, calling on friends, the Jene Allens, owners of the Klondike Nugget newspaper, the Jim Slaydens from Tacoma, and, too, we visited Mrs. Cash Chittick, formerly Mrs. Daly. She was now a new bride, having recently married one of the finest men in the Klondike and a well-to-do Eldorado mine owner. Well, it was a wonderful week. We had even gone to the Sunday Service at the Methodist Church. But now, we were eager to get back to our little log cabin on Dominion Creek. So with our sleigh loaded with extra things we started back on our homeward trek. The first night out we stopped at the Grand Forks, and the second day, about noon, we reached the junction of upper Bonanza and McCormack's Creek. Then began the long strenuous climb to the ridge. The grade was so steep that it was very difficult for our dogs, and in places Ed had to push the sleigh, or pull with the animals. Boris developed a lame paw, and so Ed put Rover at the head of the team and let Boris run beside the sled. Part of the time, Clemy and I walked in the snow to lighten the burden.

At last we gained the top of the ridge and followed a narrow trail which went right along the very top of the sharp divide. This marvelous view of the Klondike always made me catch my breath!

But suddenly the weather had turned too cold to further appreciate the beautiful scenery! Ominous clouds were gathering and the wind began whipping into a furious gale. It was one of those strong penetrating winds which cuts straight to the bone.

Clemy and I and baby Ella were snug in the sleigh, but poor Edward! He had to run behind in the gale while trying to urge the poor half-frozen dogs to a faster clip. Yes, a frightening storm was almost upon us! Not only was I worried about Ed and the dogs, I was concerned about Ella. She had been poking her face out from under the sheltering folds of the sleigh robe all afternoon in order to see what was going on, for she was by nature an inquisitive child, and now there was an odd, peculiar expression to her face. Finally, I called to her father to halt the dogs so that he could have a look at her.

When he saw Ella's face he gave a terrified cry, and pointed to her nose which was white and hard.

"Vel, it's frozen," he cried, in panic. "Oh my God, her whole face is frozen!"

I was frightened beyond words! Many people had lost hands and feet through frostbite. But a baby's face! Ed grabbed a handful of snow and rubbed it briskly over her marble-like features. It was the only thing to do under the circumstances.

Naturally, she screamed and yelled and the icy wind caught her

---

*In severe cases of frostbite, amputation is the only way to save the patient.

breath, but in spite of the hazards of frozen lungs, Ed kept right on rubbing with snow until her flesh had turned from stark white to pale pink. This was an indication that the blood was beginning to circulate normally again.

To make sure that Ella was safe Edward took off his fur parka and wrapped it securely around her face, but exposing himself like that to such weather was a very dangerous thing to do.

Fortunately, at this point, we knew we couldn't be far from the King Solomon Dome roadhouse, high on the summit. We made a wild dash and reached it just as snow began falling in blinding sheets.

Safely indoors, we thanked our lucky stars for the shelter of that little roadhouse, while we listened to the howl of the blizzard striking along the ridge!

Of course, the first thing we did after checking Ella's face again was to look Ed over to make sure that he hadn't suffered frostbite too. When we were satisfied that he was all right, all of us warmed ourselves by the big round stove while the Negro cook, who was so accommodating, prepared a hot meal. As he served it, he exclaimed:

"Lawsy me, if it ain't de same lady dat I seen once a year ago, wid dis little boy! And now deres a real, live baby-girl! Folks, I know you'se all is mighty glad to get in out of dat bad storm, and I knows, too, you are mighty tired and hungry. Praise de Lord dat you'se did make it safe to dis mountaintop and dat de little baby's face is unfrozen!"

Fortunately by the following morning the storm had passed. After breakfast we said goodbye to the innkeeper and his Negro cook and began the long steep descent down the mountainside.

It took all of Ed's strength to hold the dogs in check, for the straining animals were more than anxious to get off the mountain and reach home as another storm was brewing, and they sensed it.

Soon we passed the Mounted Police barracks at Caribou and in short order reached our cozy little log cabin. Like all good Sourdoughs, Ed had left a big pile of kindling and dry wood by the stove ready for action, and in no time we were warming ourselves by the fire and drinking hot chocolate and saying how very good it was to be home again, especially after such a nerve-wracking adventure! Truly, our cabin seemed like a palace and even the scorched outing flannel on the walls and around the stove looked good to us!

For many days after the storm on the ridge, I shuddered when I thought of Ella's frozen face and poor Edward running behind our sleigh with only a sweater for protection.

Yes, over and over, I thanked God for helping us reach the roadhouse in time, and I blessed the dogs, too, for their fine teamwork and faithfulness. In our hour of great peril, Rover, our wonderful show dog, worked like a friend and earned forever our love and gratitude.

Chapter 29

A THOUSAND MILES OVER THE ICE AND TRAIL OF '98

On long winter nights the miners would often drop by our cabin for a friendly chat. They would crowd close to the Klondike stove and talk about home and gold-rush adventures. Often the subject would turn to winter Yukon travel and to Soapy Smith, Skagway's underworld chief, a heartless criminal who cared little for the suffering he had caused the stampeders on the trail of '98.

"Well, sir," said Ed, knocking the ashes from his pipe, when the subject of Soapy Smith came up. "I guess there's hardly a sourdough among us who came over the passes from Skagway who didn't have a close brush with Soapy Smith before he finally met his fate. It's well known how Frank Reid sacrificed his life to rid Alaska of its worst vulture.

"You might say that the prelude to my encounter with Soapy's men really began way up at Circle City, in early 1898, where my party of men and I had been frozen in for the winter of 1897. After some very nerve-wracking adventures in the Arctic Circle, we pulled out of Circle City Jan. 2, 1898, and headed back to Dawson over the frozen Yukon. It was a hazardous trip, taking nearly six long weeks and was 350 miles. But after a week's rest in Dawson I was determined to hit the trail for Skagway and home. I was not able to persuade my Circle City group to go with me this time, so I was forced to hunt up a new group.

"That week in Dawson I learned that Ben Atwater, the old-time

Yukon mail carrier, was forming a party to go out over the ice. I contacted him, but he wanted the exorbitant fee of $400 for the privilege of traveling with him. That was too rich for my blood! I knew it would be very foolhardy to attempt that 650 mile trip alone, so after much inquiring around I heard that a Mr. Goodwin was forming a party to take to the coast. I contacted him. He, too, wanted a fee, so having very little cash, I signed over my American Creek claim which I had so recently staked out on my way out of Circle City. I valued it at $300.

"The next day Goodwin introduced me to Jim S. Denharn of Sacramento and David LaSalle of Denver. These pleasant fellows I soon discovered were to be Goodwin's other passengers. 'Passengers' of course meant we were to camp together, eat together, walk and run together (dog-trot) and help with the sled and other chores.

"Well, we passengers grew quite concerned over the haphazard way in which our guide was making preparations for that long strenuous journey. We were three days late getting started (Feb. 15, 1898), and we had only been out on the ice a few hours when our worst misgivings were confirmed. Goodwin's incompetence began showing up in big capital letters! He seemed absolutely ignorant of the country and how to cope with it. From that time on we had to supervise him! Indeed, he was so afraid of the ice that he was glad to shift all responsibility onto the three of us. Hourly, we made decisions which meant our very survival as the trail in spots was a holy terror. In places, huge blocks of ice barred our way, some as high as houses. In other spots there was hidden open water. The weather was bitterly cold and often we staggered through blinding snowstorms in order to reach government cabins which had been built at twenty mile intervals along the Yukon for government officials, or anyone else who desperately needed them.

"Part of the time we camped on the ice, either because the cabins were already full, or because we couldn't quite reach the shelters before exhaustion overtook us. Naturally, it's impossible to be constantly exposed to very severe weather without suffering unmentionable body discomforts. Just staying alive and keeping the human system functioning was a major problem. Icicles hung from our noses and chins and our whiskers were frosty most of the time.

"For several days the mercury hovered at 63 and 64 degrees below zero! Even so, with caution and good sense we managed to keep moving on the ice. We had only been on the trail eight days when we glimpsed a remarkable phenomenon, which few Cheechakos have the thrill of seeing. The day was Feb. 23rd, at 9 a.m. The mercury was at 55 below zero, when all at once Old Sol, which had been sulking below the horizon all winter, began putting on a spectacular show.

"Six sundogs suddenly appeared slightly above the horizon and were grouped above the real sun's hiding place, in kind of a half-circle, looking almost as bright as the sun itself. A sight like this, I'd been told, is a reflection, a sure sign of ice crystals in the air. They're a warning not to stop and rest especially if a strange inertia and drowsy feeling overtakes a traveler.

"Soon after the appearance of the sundogs, LaSalle and I had a serious time with Goodwin. He began complaining of terrible fatigue and sleepiness and was lagging behind. Then he disappeared behind a snow bank. We rushed back and found him curled up in a frightening stupor. It would have been his last sleep had we not jerked him to his feet and spanked him into life again!

"That night I wrote in my diary of the happenings of the day:

> Feb. 23rd (55 below zero)
> Beautiful appearance in heavens from 9 to 11 a.m. Sundogs!! Made the cabin 2 miles from meat raft. Met Mr. Terry, cousin of Father Nash of Tacoma. Very cold! Froze my little finger on right hand. Goodwin was terribly played out! Found Miller party had been here. Trail very winding. Traveled a good many miles to make a direct distance.

"The Miller party had shoved off from Dawson just the day ahead of us. Dr. William Misner (from Tacoma) was in that party and we had promised to try to overtake the group, or at least watch for their trail marks—a mighty good idea, we thought. A real safety measure. Other parties behind us were doing the same thing for us. It was the only way anyone would know of the disaster of a party should anything happen.

"On the day of the sundogs, we had been fortunate to reach shelter and a meat raft. The raft had been wedged in the ice since late fall of '97. It had been on its way to starving Dawson, and it was a pity that it never reached the hungry city. For some reason it had been abandoned to the elements!

"Well, it seemed that the 'elements' had mostly been the crows and wolves! They had dined royally, like kings, all winter long. We did a great deal of feasting too. None of us could remember when we had had fresh beef, and when we were ready to leave we stacked the sled with as much meat as it would carry. Two days later, even though we now had more nourishing food, we were becoming extremely trail-weary. Bickering and quarrelsomeness broke out, and increased with each weary mile, especially between Goodwin and LaSalle on one particular day. I wrote in my diary, with shaking hands, after a very savage 'tea pot' tempest:

Feb. 25, 1898–25 degrees B.– Friday
Goodwin and LaSalle had a row this morning! Made about 22 miles. Am now camped about 8 miles from Pelly R. We are badly crippled up. Goodwin has blisters on his feet. LaSalle has sore leg. Jim has game leg & I have rheumatism in left leg. Trail is drifted in; had to use snowshoes again. Found good camp at last!

Feb. 26, 1898–30 degrees B.–Saturday–Pelley Post
Made Ft. Selkirk at 11 a.m. We were only 5 miles below. Could have made Pelley last night if we had known how near we were. The old Indian whom I saw last summer at a pt. about 15 miles below here, came in the cabin; had the same dirty suit of moose skin & was still eating lice; gave him some tobacco & bread & fired him out of the cabin. Bought 10 lb. sugar ($10.00) of two men who were camped up Pelley R. Miller party left here this A.M. Did not see them.

"That night we stayed at Selkirk, but the following day we had a horrible scare. Jim Denharn broke through the ice twice. For some reason, unknown, the ice was very thin in this area. Many air holes and even open water showed up. These dangers were so concealed by snow and thin ice that a man could suddenly step through without any warning:

Feb. 27, 1898–28 degrees B.–Sunday
Left Pelley Post at 7:45 a.m. Made 25 miles & struck Miller's old camp. Trail is in very bad condition. Lots of open water. Jim broke through twice. Saw place where Dr. Misner fell in. The dogs are in fairly good condition & are working hard. The country now is not so mountainous & is more of a table land. I am in good condition, except a cold. My nose is sore yet, and peels. I wonder if it will ever stop peeling. (One day nearer Dear Velma.)

"On Feb. 28, the next day, Jim Denharn had another close call. He broke through the ice again and Goodwin became hysterical. It seemed that the devil himself was pursuing us. That particular day had been our very worst since leaving Dawson:

> Feb. 28, 1898—20 degrees B.—Monday—Lewis River
> Broke camp at 7:30. Made 25 miles. Found lots of open water, fortunately did not get our feet wet although we had to cross some very tough places. Jim had another close call, a large piece of ice caved in under the sled, just pulled him out in time. The trail is very bad along this point. We tried to make Rink Rapids, but could not. In Miller's old camp. The weather is fine & scenery grand. Now out of the mts., among the small hills & tablelands.

"On March 1st, eighteen days after leaving Dawson, just three miles above Five Fingers, we spied a small cabin back among the trees. We hastened to it as we wished to inquire about the Miller crowd and found that a Mr. and Mrs. Craft were spending the winter there. Cordially they invited us in, and while having hot coffee we heard all of the latest news as Mrs. Craft was a very talkative woman. In some uncanny way she knew what was going on, both up and down the Yukon.

"No, she hadn't seen the Miller party. 'But, friends,' she said, 'there were two men who left our cabin less than a hour ago. They (Dickson and Roberts) have with them a seventeen year old boy whose name is William Byrnie. Poor lad! Don't see how those men will ever get the boy to the coast the way they're traveling. Think of it! They have only one sled and scanty equipment—and the boy walks on crutches. Just about a month ago the awful thing happened, and it cost the lad the loss of his feet and legs.'

" 'How did it happen?' we asked in horror.

" 'Well, as you might guess it was due to frostbite,' Mrs. Craft answered, with tears in her eyes. Then she went on to tell us what had occurred: 'It seems that the boy and his uncle, Mr. Maguire, had come North with the T. B. Cory party. Cory was a newspaperman and he had made up the party in Seattle. They had come over the Chilkoot Pass in the fall of 1897, and with them were Nunan C. Fisher, Syd Barrington and Colonel Green. Like many others they traveled light—didn't bring enough food—were complete greenhorns, didn't know frostbite from fleabites! But they reached Dawson safely. When the Dawson famine was at its very worst in midwinter, Maguire and the boy started back up the Yukon. When they reached the Pelly River, Mr. Maguire suddenly caught a second dose of gold-fever, as he had heard of a spot up the Pelly River where there were reports of gold. Of course, the two were traveling light; had no stove, no tent, nor did they have enough warm clothing. One night they were caught in a heavy freeze and William Byrnie hovered over the open fire. He didn't notice that sparks had burned holes in his socks and trousers. He didn't even feel the first beginning of frostbite. When he did a few days later, it was too late. His ankles and feet had turned black. Gangrene had set in and there was nothing to do but amputate.

"A doctor 'of sorts' did the job at Fort Selkirk in January, and as soon as the boy was able to be on crutches the pitiful party started up the Yukon, leaving the gold-crazed uncle behind—the uncle who by now had really deserted the boy!"

"Naturally, hearing of this tragedy had a very sobering effect upon my party and me. Goodwin, I noticed, became more high-strung and harder to deal with. We had only gone about a half mile from the Craft cabin when we caught up with the pathetic group described by Mrs. Craft. The Byrnie boy was crutching along between Dickson and Roberts, who were trying to steady him while one of them was also trying to keep the sled in tow.

"We pulled up and offered assistance, but they thanked us and waved us aside, saying they had been told to watch for Captain Morgan who would be coming along soon, and who they hoped would pick them up, or at least sell them a dog or two. William Byrnie was extremely brave—tried pitifully to make light of his affliction—said that now he wouldn't have to worry about getting his feet wet; said that he might return to Dawson another year and hunt for gold on artificial legs.

"After making sure that there was nothing we could do to help the Plucky group, we bade them goodbye with a feeling of apprehension for their safety. They bravely waved us on and said not to worry about them, but we knew their optimism was forced. Their fate was all in the hands of Providence. However, we felt sure that lively Mrs. Craft would widely broadcast their predicament and seek aid.

" 'Good Lord,' I remarked to Goodwin and the others, after we left the Byrnie boy, 'such courage as that young man displays is Heroic!

And those men are heroes to undertake a terrible trip like this so that the boy may get to a good doctor in Seattle.'

"That night, after we had made camp, I scribbled the events of the day in my little red diary, writing in sequence of the things as they happened:

> March 1, 1898—15 Below Zero—Tuesday
> Passed Rink Rapids and Five Fingers. The latter was frozen solid. Trail went up right hand side. Had good chance to examine the rocks which are a conglomerate mass of granite quartz, all having the appearance of being through a fire. No doubt this was a waterfall at one time. Made cabins 3 miles north of Five Fingers. Stopped in at Mr. and Mrs. Craft's cabin. Very talkative woman. Boy there from Chicago who had his feet frozen Jan. 3rd at Pelly—had his two feet amputated. Was helped along trail by Dickson and Roberts of Seattle. (Mr. Roberts was a well-known detective from Seattle. Somewhere along the line the two men joined the Cory party. It was reported later that the gold-crazed uncle, Mr. Maguire, had even suggested that William Byrnie commit suicide.)

"Traveling on the ice was so difficult that by March 3d we had only progressed fifty-five miles from Mrs. Craft's cabin. In places the trail was so bad that it was necessary to zig-zag back and forth across the river to avoid the danger spots. Exhaustion and numbness were constantly with us. It was too cold to sit down to rest, and it was too cold to even quarrel. Always, we watched for signs of the Miller party, and always we thought of that plucky little group coming somewhere behind us. When unhappy complaints occurred among us, I would mention the Byrnie boy. It was all that was needed to jerk my companions into tolerance of the other fellow's failures.

"As we traveled farther south we began meeting scores of stampeders headed for Dawson. Many were suffering from frostbite, lameness and snow blindness, but nothing would stop them from reaching Dawson, even tho' we told them that everything was already staked in the Klondike. Our advice fell on deaf ears. They would be millionaires! They would be the lucky ones! Hadn't the papers been printing glowing gold rush tales? Yes, the historic trail of '98 had surely begun; thou-

---

*William Byrnie, whose legs had been amputated, did reach Skagway safely and was taken to Seattle, and then home to Chicago.

sands were on their frenzied way. These eager gold-fevered men were just one leap ahead of the multitudes that were not far behind them on the great, exciting trail of suffering and hardships.

"Often we stopped to chat with the different groups and always inquired about the whereabouts of the Miller party. They were making fair mileage on ahead, we learned.

"When a fast-moving group would catch up from Dawson, we would (with terrible dread) inquire about the Byrnie party. It seemed they were 'inching along' and would accept no aid. Finally, a man overtook us who reported that Dan Eagen, a young prizefighter called 'The Montana Kid,' was coming behind us with his dog team. He had sold two of his best dogs to Mr. Dickson and Detective Roberts. Now the injured boy was riding the sleigh. This was very good heart-warming news, and all of us rejoiced!

"On March 4 it was our good fortune to reach a government shelter at the mouth of the Little Salmon River where a Mr. McGregor and two other men from Seattle were encamped. They had been there for some months sinking a thirty foot shaft, but no gold as yet had shown up. I was especially grateful to Mr. McGregor for putting us up for the night as I was suffering from a very severe sore throat. McGregor dug down into his medicine kit and generously gave me quick-acting pills. Yes, I had been more ill with fever than I was willing to admit. Yet I knew I had to keep going. Nothing was going to stop me from reaching the coast!

"The next evening we stumbled towards another government shelter, frozen to the bone. But now I'll let my diary tell the story:"

>March 5, 1898—20 degrees A.—Saturday—Little Salmon
>Left L. Salmon cabin at 8:30 a.m. Ran into a snowstorm. Badly disappointed upon reaching 24 mile cabin, as the government party was in possession, so we had to make camp below cabin. Passed Lake Creek six miles back; hear there is a stampede on there. Met three of the Mounted Police who had staked. Went with toboggans. Last six miles we made after dark, wind in our faces & snow.
>
>March 6, 1898—20 degrees A.—Sunday—Big Salmon
>Wind blew hard all night & trail was drifted in so that we only

---

*The Miller party also reached Skagway safely, as did the "Yellow Kid," Wilson Mizner. Also Dan Eagan, "The Montana Kid," made good time to Skagway.

made 10 miles today. Found Dr. Misner's cabin at Big Salmon. All of the men here have staked Walsh Creek and Lake Cr. They claim good prospects. Sorry we did not stop & stake on Lake. Would go back but trail is horrible & it is 18 miles. Misner gave me some quinine for my cold—which I need.

March 7, 1898—Monday
Left Big Salmon Cabin at 8 a.m. Found trail badly drifted. Hardly made 15 miles. Met two parties of stampeders, all tired out. Camped at 4:30 p.m. Sundogs in the heavens, very peculiar in appearance!

March 8, 1898—18 degrees A.—Hootalinqua—Tuesday
Trail was worse today. Needed snowshoes today as well as yesterday. Passed Cassiar Bar at 11 a.m. Made Canadian Gov. cabin 5:30 p.m. Gov. party with mail we met at 4 p.m. Mr. Herdman was with them. Had copy of the new mining laws. Made 22 miles today. Snowed 3 inches last night. Moccasins wet, my cold is not broken yet.

March 9, 1898—25 degrees A.—Wed.—30 Mile River
Had experience with 'a Hog' last night. (Evans, policeman, who fired us out of Gov. cabin No. 24). If we had known he was only a 'duffer' would not have gone. They were on stampede to Lake Cr. We left Hootalinqua 9 a.m. Made 22 miles today. Camped same place with Mont. Kid who left Dawson last Dec. He fell in the river 5 miles up from here*. We will have to be careful tomorrow. Put my mucklucks on as snow was wet.

March 10, 1898—25 degrees A.—Thurs.—30 Mile R.
Broke camp 7 p.m. Sold pr. moccasins $5.00. River open at upper end for last 8 miles. A little dangerous, could see the big rocks sticking up. Reached Canadian Gov. post at foot of Lake LeBarge at 1 p.m. Delivered letter to Capt. Stearns, sent by Fyffe from Post at Hootalinqua. Hear a good deal about Walsh Cr. & Lake Cr. Made a run of 10 miles (on Lake LeBarge) in afternoon. Camped almost same place as we did last July. Had row with Jim

---

*Dr. Misner left the Miller party at Big Salmon to remain until the weather turned milder, in the spring. Indeed, he was very much needed as a medical doctor by the Stampeders, who constantly suffered various maladies.

*Old Yukoners nearly always carried long ice-poles which could be quickly turned and held onto should they crash through the ice. Ice-poles were the means of saving lives, especially if there was someone to give a helping hand from a firm position on the ice.

this A.M. at breakfast. Snow squall in afternoon; head wind. Sun shone behind storm clouds. Beautiful sight.

March 11, 1898–10 degrees A.–Friday–Lake LeBarge
Heavy head wind. Broke camp 8 a.m. Made run to middle of island, took lunch with policeman who is on his way to Dawson with mail. Two policemen passed us were from Big Salmon. Caught them at Indian Village where we bought 3 lb. caribou meat. Our provisions are nearly gone; got some bacon from police, made camp with us, were freighting with 7 horses. This has been our banner day; made 28 miles. Had a heavy head wind to buck all day. Good trail though.

March 12, 1898–3 degrees A.–Sat.–50 Mile River
Broke camp 9 a.m. Heavy snow squall. Passed two parties freighting their stuff in. My throat is almost closed. Can hardly speak, so hoarse! Passed Tahkeenah R. at noon & had lunch. Got into White Horse at 5:30 p.m. Hardly knew the place, so silent and still compared to the roaring torrent & turbulent waters that go rushing through in the summer. Got some horse meat for dogs. The weather is getting very warm.

March 13, 1898–5 degrees B.–White Horse–Sunday
The great and mighty White Horse rapids, frozen solid; ice piled up in ridges & only a faint sound of water coming from a crevice. Followed trail on old tramway. Crossed river at Squaw Rapids below canyon & followed new tramway which they are building & comes out 1 mile above canyon. Passed party of two. Shultz told us to go to his tent & cook our dinner, which we did. Had fish, potatoes & onions. Good Sunday dinner, all feeling well. Made McIntosh cabin 7:30 p.m. Had good supper. Feel better now. Hear that Charley is on the way to Skagway. (McIntosh had oxen.) (Charley Lung my brother in Tacoma.)

March 14, 1898–5 degrees B.–Monday–Lake Marsh
Mr. McIntosh treated us royally, gave each three cigars apiece. Had racket with Charley Goodwin about paying for my meal according to contract. Left cabin 9 a.m. Had wind in our favor. At lunch, rigged up a sail & we piled on & rode to Six Mile River. Stopped at Can. Gov. cabin. Am out of grub. They gave us supper & will give us breakfast. Hear that a man named Lung is in Skagway. (Miller passed McIntosh cabin last Thursday. Atwater passed Wed. camped on Island in Mud Lake.) (Wonder if it is Charley.)

March 15, 1898—Zero—Tuesday—Six Mile River
Lake Tagish. Has been a beautiful day. Crossed Lake Tagish & am now at empty cabin 2 miles up Lake Bennett. We met, today, oxen for the first time. They pull 3 tons. Lots of horses & a few mules on the trail. We are fast knocking the miles out & each day puts me nearer dear Velma. Can find out nothing about Charley—so many people & they do not keep track of each other. We will go over the Dyea Trail, no doubt.

March 16, 1898—3 degrees B.—Wed.—Lake Bennett
Made the run to head of Bennett. Met Wilson Mizner, "The Yellow Kid," two miles from head of lake. Am stopping at a tent hotel, have had a good supper & a fair cigar. Godson, the customhouse man, is here. Will have to clear. Quite a town here, about fifty tents and five log houses. Wish I had my outfit ready to start out.

"Well, at last we had reached the head of Lake Bennett! It had been a long hard pull towards the coast and I had noticed that, as we approached closer to our goal, the nerve-wracking tension among us had somewhat eased. There was less bickering and hard feelings. I for one was grateful for having had the opportunity to travel with these men; I knew from my Circle city experiences that an extended camping trip—especially when surrounded by terrible dangers and accompanied by severe hardships—can often bring out the very worst in human nature. I knew, too, that I would always hail these men as good old Sourdough friends.

"At Lake Bennett I was truly amazed to see what had happened since I was there in '97. The place was buzzing with activity—a temporary city! Tons and tons of freight were piled along the shore, even though only a few days earlier an avalanche had roared down the mountainside, depositing huge amounts of snow on the east, or left-hand, side of the lake, burying many tons of supplies. Lucky it was that all campers had been in the forest whipsawing trees for boat-building, or there would have been considerable loss of life.

"The morning after reaching Lake Bennett, I tried to persuade Goodwin*, LaSalle and Denharn to change their plans from going over the old Chilcoot route to the new White Pass. But the men were deter-

---

*It was Mr. Charles Goodwin who was our "trailmaster." He was a fine fellow when off the Yukon Trail.

mined to go via Lake Linderman, to Chilkoot and Dyea. Somehow, I couldn't face Chilkoot this trip. I had nearly died on the summit the year before, and the pain of the Ptomaine poisoning still hung like sharp swords in my memory.

"There had been much drama up there on old Chilkoot, since I had last seen it; yes, even a little comedy, too, I was to find out from my friend, Archie McLean Hawks, the Chilkoot Tram engineer. Around our campfire at the lake that night, he recounted a ludicrous tale:

" 'Nelson Burnett, the arrogant Tramway manager, had run into a lot of trouble with a red-headed lady-packer. Bennett had ordered her off the right-of-way a number of times, of course, in his overbearing way. But the lady had disdainfully ignored his orders, which infuriated Bennett beyond words!

" 'One morning, however, his Irish wrath hit the breaking point. The tent hadn't been moved! He had threatened to tear it down next time around.

" 'It was at an early morning hour when he stood at the flap of the lady's tent and ordered her to get up and get dressed, because he was surely going to tear her tent down. Of course, Bennett accompanied his command with a lot of profanity.

" 'Suddenly, Nelson got the hothead's answer. The tent-flap flew open, and too late Nelson saw the terrible thing coming—the liquid contents of the thundermug! He tried to dodge, but he wasn't quick enough. Right then and there he was christened 'Old Thundermug.' And Ed,' Archie Hawks laughed, 'the nickname has stuck. And, it's a story that's being told with much relish along the trails in this section.'

"All along the way, since leaving Dawson, I had been on the lookout for my brother, Charles Lung, who might be heading North. I had had word that he might join the '98 Stampedes. I had sincerely hoped he would change his mind about coming North, but I knew that if he did make the trip he would come by way of the White Pass. That was another reason why I wished to go over the White Pass route to Skagway.

*It was Nelson Bennett who ordered the men to continue work on the tramway the day of the awful Chilkoot avalanche on April 3, 1898, when so many of these men lost their lives. The Indians had warned Bennett of an impending avalanche disaster, but he wouldn't listen. When the men objected to working that day Nelson Bennett threatened to fire them. Seventy-two people were buried alive under the avalanche.

"On the morning of March 17, 1898, at Lake Bennett, at exactly 8:30 a.m., I waved goodbye to Goodwin and party and stepped out briskly onto the snowy trail, pointing south. My muscles were as hard as steel—a thousand miles over the ice from Circle City! Yes, I had come a long way and I had developed a great deal of stamina. I feared no man. But, oh it was good to feel my feet firm on good solid earth again, with no danger of slipping under that rotting ice! Soon, I would be over the pass and at Skagway where I would board a vessel home.

"The trail was crowded with people all pressing Northward! Chilkoot Pass could now be seen at a point through an opening in the mountain range, perhaps a dozen or more miles away to the west. I was traveling on a high broad plateau surrounded on three sides by glacier-clad mountains. The scenery was glorious to behold!

"I reached Middle Lake around noon, after passing a series of lakes. I sat on a rock munching hardtack and dried salmon, watching the crowds of gold-seekers trudge by. There was a place nearby called Log Cabin or Balsome City, where there were hundreds of tents. A temporary settlement. From there a trail branched to the east, to Lake Teslin and Lake Atlin, where there were supposed to have been some rather good gold discoveries. Many scores of stampeders were headed that way too.

" 'Why, Ed Lung!' two voices called from out of the crowd, 'We're mighty glad to see you!' Looking closely I recognized Mr. Mattison of Tacoma and Mr. Shelgren of Lake Bay, Washington.

"Great Scott, but we were glad to see each other! And there by the lake we had a jolly good visit, they telling me news of home and I news of Klondike.

" 'But say,' said Mattison, 'aren't you headed the wrong way, Ed?'

" 'No, sir,' I told them, emphatically, 'I've chased Dame Fortune all over the North. She's shown me some mighty fine scenery and given me high adventure, but never rewarded me with much gold. Sure, I'm carrying some gold, but it's mostly for selling the best dog a man ever owned—good old Chattel, the malemute I sold in Dawson after he had helped me over the trail from Circle city.

"Before my friends from Washington bade me goodbye they began warning me about Soapy Smith's gang on the White Pass and in Skagway. I listened to their warnings, but somehow felt no real alarm, even tho' I was unarmed and traveling alone.

"As I came closer to the entrance of the pass I noticed that the plateau was rapidly narrowing and was compressed between strange pyramid shaped mountains that were encrusted with thousands of huge jagged boulders. The boulders looked as if they had been gouged from a deep quarry by a giant hand and thrown helter-skelter all over the mountains.

"In just a few miles, I was on the White Pass summit. The approach had been very gradual and deceiving, and I knew that on the other side I would encounter very precipitous heights. There, at the summit stood the Northwest Mounted Police Barracks and Canadian Customs, and also the American Customs; both country's flags flying high, almost side by side.

"I had very few valuables to declare and so passed through both Customs. But it was there that I got my first real detailed warning about the Soapy Smith gang.

" 'Fellow American,' said one of the U. S. officers, 'I must seriously warn you—Soapy Smith's men are very active on the Pass. They are particularly interested in men like you, who are returning from Dawson. These crooks are more numerous around Porcupine Hill. They work in twos and threes and are often disguised as travelers, miners, packers, business men and even preachers! Sometimes, they keep bonfires burning near the trail and offer rest and warmth to weary travelers. Be careful who you take up with. On Feb. 15th eight brutal murders were committed, and on March 7th there was another one on the trail. If you encounter traffic snarls, please don't fall for strangers who suggest friendly little card games while waiting for the trail to clear. Soapy Smith has many traps, and in Skagway be doubly alert. It's Soapy Smith's stronghold!'

"Gratefully I thanked the officer for his warning. Also, I inquired if Charles Lung, my brother, had registered at the summit, but the officer could not find his name among the signatures. 'Keep inquiring,' he advised, 'Your brother may be somewhere below, on the trail, or at Skagway.'

"I hurried on down the pass, meeting scores of exhausted people trudging up through the snow. It seemed that they were swarming the pass. On any available level spot they camped. What a bedraggled, miserable looking army they were! But their dreams were lined with gold, and none of them seemed to complain. And, Holy Moses! Even a few women with small children were scattered in among the crags. It was a well-known fact that only one in five could ever hope to reach the Klondike—only one in thirty would ever find gold. How would these women and children fare on the Yukon Trail? I hardly dared think of it.

"Well, it was quite apparent they all expected to be glittering millionaires! Some had even brought rakes with them to scrape the gold out of the creeks!

"Along in early evening, footsore and dog-tired, just above Porcupine Hill, I came to the 'White Pass Hotel,' which was actually a crude shack.

"Stepping inside, I asked the bartender for a night's lodging and supper. I guess I showed obvious signs of long arduous travel. I was wearing my weathered reindeer parka, fur cap, fur gloves, black miner's shirt, stained corduory pants and yellow moccasins and I had grown a very heavy beard. Yes, I confess, I did look shaggy!

"The bartender shook his head, answering gruffly that he was just fresh out of beds. But quickly added that I could have my supper there.

"While we were talking, a rough-looking character from one of the sidetables came sauntering over and asked,

" 'Partner, how are things in Dawson? Lots of gold, eh?'

" 'What makes you think I'm from Dawson?' I asked curiously.

" 'Say, you can't hide it, fellow!' laughed the man. 'Dawson is stamped all over you. Why, you even smell like Dawson,' he remarked, sarcastically, showing a row of uneven, vicious-looking white teeth which resembles those of shark. Then, he slapped me on the back and offered to share his bunk with me.

"Well, of course I didn't like the idea of sleeping with this evil-looking fellow! And, too, I had noticed his group of tough-looking companions when I first entered the inn. They were playing cards but when they spied me they put down their hands and began sizing me up.

"Remembering the grim warnings of my friends at the lake and from the Customs officer, I thought, 'Maybe these men belong to the Soapy Smith gang!' And so, not wanting them to know that I suspected anything out of the way, I politely thanked the stranger and said I might have to accept his kind offer. Then I ate a leisurely supper of coarse bread and stew.

"The stew was stringy and had a peculiar sweetish taste. I very much feared that it was the flesh of some poor packhorse that had given up the ghost out on the trail. But, being famished, I put these awful thoughts aside and finished supper, downing it all with several gulps of hot coffee. Then I paid the innkeeper one dollar. Afterwards, I stood up, stretched myself lazily and said casually, 'It's a fine moonlight night. Guess I'll just get myself a little breath of fresh air before turning in.'

"The air was frosty and crisp and I walked briskly around the inn, clapping my hands together, forward and backward, in order to keep warm.

"I was very much agitated and undecided as to what to do! However, I felt certain that if I were to sleep in the roadhouse with that loud-mouthed fellow I would be minus my gold in the morning—yes, and maybe my life! I knew full well that I couldn't tramp all the way to Skagway either, without rest, and it was utterly impossible for me to camp out as I didn't have enough equipment. Goodwin had kept most of the supplies for the trek over Chilkoot.

"Well, I began walking slowly down the main trail, feeling perplexed about my predicament. As I moved along, suddenly I caught the faint jingle of sleigh bells and I surmised that a freighter was coming up the grade from Skagway.

"I hurried forward. When the stranger saw me he was quite startled, for a lone hiker out so late on the trail without equipment was an unusual sight. The man proved to be a packer as I had thought!

"When I greeted him, at first he seemed very uneasy. I knew he suspected me of being one of Soapy's men! Hurriedly, I introduced myself as Ed Lung from Dawson. Then it was he became quite friendly. We walked back up the trail together and I offered to help him unpack the horses at this destination. He said he was storing everything in a barn which was at a little distance from the roadhouse. Here, he told me, he managed to keep hay for his animals and also used the place for sleeping quarters.

"After I had helped with the horses the grateful packer asked, curiously, 'Friend, now where might you be sleeping this cold, wintry night?'

"When I told him the roadhouse was full, and that I had no bed, he replied wholeheartedly, 'My friend, you're surely welcome to sleep here in the hay. It will be much warmer than sleeping out in the snow on

'Yukon feathers' (evergreen boughs). Yes, sir, I have plenty of extra blankets and I always keep the barn doors locked.'
"It was exactly what I hoped he'd say. Gratefully, I accepted his welcome invitation.
"Next morning I was up bright and early. As I entered the roadhouse for a quick breakfast whom should I meet first thing but my sharp-toothed friend of the night before!
" 'Partner,' he said, with a disagreeable hissing voice, 'Where *were* you last night? Damn it, I waited up for ya'. I didn't get a wink of sleep just worryin' about you.'
"Well, naturally, I made some very lame excuses—said I was sorry, and was preparing to barge out of the roadhouse when the fellow stopped me.
" 'Partner,' he said, 'will you do me a big favor? Will you deliver a letter in Skagway?'
"Well, naturally, I was taken back at this unexpected request, but being very anxious to get away from the fellow, I quickly consented. Besides, it would have been a bad breach of northern etiquette to have refused.
"So I took the missive, stuffed it into my vest pocket and started on my way.
"Altho' it was yet very early (morning), I certainly was not alone on the trail. The date was March 18, 1898, and the hour 6 a.m. (According to my diary.)
"Already, there were scores of early-risen stampeders struggling up the grade, driving dogs, horses, mules, cows, oxen, bleating sheep and goats. On the animals' poor backs were strapped ungainly packs of miscellaneous supplies. Some were even pulling very heavy sleds. It was a queer, unbelievable sight——people blue with the cold, animals frightened and groaning under terrible burdens! Howls of malemutes echoed from canyons, answered by screams of tortured horses, who were beaten by sticks, or long snake whips to make them put forth greater effort in getting extra-heavy loads* up the steep grade for their cruel, gold fevered masters!
"I passed scores of bearded, frantic-eyed men, they themselves loaded down like animals. And the crowds pressed harder and harder against

---

*In 1898 it was Canadian law that no stampeder could enter Yukon Territory without 1,000 pounds of food supplies.

each other, and up the snow-draped crags! Below, yawned deep chasms filled with glaciers and melting snows.

"The trail at the very widest was not more than four feet; in other spots, only two or three feet wide.

"In stretches, where the trail permitted, I jumped on my sled and rode downgrade. However, I had several hair-raising, close calls; especially when I took a shortcut and nearly crashed into a ravine.

"Often, I paused to ask strangers if they had met a Charles Lung anywhere along the trail, but most of the stampeders gave me that 'iceberg' stare, thinking perhaps I was one of Soapy's men!

" 'Is he a Chinaman?' one fellow ventured to ask.

" 'No, he's a German and he looks like me. Blue eyes, blond hair—and about my height,' I told him.

" 'Nope, haven't seen him,' replied the stranger, curtly, eying me suspiciously.

"As I made my way farther down the grade, I began noticing that the trail had a coating of horse manure. I gleaned from conversation that hundreds of horses had been on the grade, and still more hundreds were coming. But the poor animals! There were no meadows for them to feed in. Only moss and stunted, gnarled trees. Men suffered, but surely the horses endured the heart-breaking tortures of the damned. Added to their terrible agonies was snow blindness, split-hooves and frost-bitten lungs. (No wonder there was an almost unbroken chain of decaying horse-flesh all along the trail of the White Pass by the summer of '98!) Some of the dead ones I saw lying in their harnesses right where they had fallen. Man and beast were stepping over them, or on them, stamping them into the earth, a sickening, pathetic sight!

"Well, at last I was approaching Skagway. Only one more hill and I would be there. What a thrill it would be to see the Pacific Ocean once more.

"When I reached the outskirts of town, it was then that I thought of that confounded letter and my promise to deliver it to Jeff's Parlor, No. 317 Holly Street. The place wasn't hard to find, as obviously it was well patronized. (It was a saloon.)

"Quickly, I pushed open the door and strode inside. The letter was addressed to a Mr. Y. M. Hopkins. I walked up to the bar and crisply asked for the gentleman.

" 'You're looking at him, partner,' said the burly bartender, with a crooked smile, as he took the letter unceremoniously from my hand. He tore it open and read its contents, then he loudly thanked me for delivering it, and at the same time he offered me a drink, saying as he poured the whiskey:

" 'Partner, I thank you for bringing this important letter. Now, I'm going ta treat ya' to a fine glass of Scotch. It'll be on the house, and it's a jolly good welcome to Skagway!'

" 'Thanks,' I told Mr. Hopkins, 'but I don't drink whiskey. Delivering that letter was just a Sourdough favor. Now I must be on my way.'

" 'Oh, but you must stay for your drink and meet the boys,' Hopkins persisted, and as he spoke he motioned to some rough-looking characters who were leaning on one end of the bar. Immediately, they crowded in close.

" 'Hey boys, this is Ed Lung,' said Hopkins, "He's just come in from Dawson. Let's show him some real Skagway hospitality.'

"The men crowded closer, all loudly acknowledging the introduction at once, slapping me boisterously on the back while inquiring about Dawson, the Bonanza, the Eldorado and even Circle City and American Creek. And, while they asked questions, they were pressing me closer and closer against the bar. The smell of whiskey was nauseating!

"Suddenly, I had a terrible feeling that I was in a trap. Why in blazes had I so foolishly promised to come to this place? Surely, it was Soapy Smith's hangout and these his men. It was then I thought of what the Customs officer had said about Soapy, in Skagway. I had heard, too, of miners losing their gold in places like this. First, a fist fight would start over a trivial dispute. A scuffle would follow and the victim would be hit over the head. Later, he would awaken in some dark alley, beaten and robbed, if indeed he would awaken at all!

"Well, I was determined that that wasn't going to happen to me! So I said again that I must be going; that I had to catch a steamer home.

" 'Aw, fellow, there ain't no steamers leavin' this time of morning,' drawled one of the men. 'Now just relax. Leave it to us. Be a good sport. Tell us all the news from Dawson and we'll sure get you on the next steamer headed south—yes, the one that leaves tonight. Here's your drink. After you've had it, we'll take you out in the back yard and show you a trained eagle. Man, if you're really patriotic you'll surely want to see this one! Then, after that, we'll all have breakfast together and celebrate the Gold Rush.'

" 'No thanks,' I said with determination. 'I had my breakfast up on the pass.' I was beginning to feel quite desperate, but I knew I dared not show it to these cut-throats.

"So, I took a deep breath and suddenly, with great energy, I pushed through the men, and leaped for the door. In an instant I had bolted through the doorway. Immediately, I could hear angry shouts behind me.

"Well, I didn't waste any time looking back. I just kept running, pell-mell, as fast as I could, in the direction of the waterfront. And as I ran, I felt for my money belt containing my gold-dust. Thank heaven it was all there! And thank heavens, too, it was broad daylight!

"When I reached the dock I took another deep breath, and halted. There, riding at anchor, was the steamer Victoria. Quickly, I saw the captain and asked for passage.

" 'Sure, mister, we can squeeze you in,' he said. 'At 3 P.M., sharp, we pull anchor. Be here a few minutes early, before we sail.'

"But there was one drawback to my leaving on the Victoria. Somehow, I felt a responsibility towards Goodwin, LaSalle and Denharn. We had sort of an agreement among us that whoever reached Skagway first would wait for the others. I had expected to find my gang waiting for me at the dock, as the Chilkoot route is shorter by 15 miles than the White Pass trail.

"Well, I waited in vain for Goodwin and party, and to my utter disgust and profound disappointment I had to watch the Victoria cast off for Tacoma. Losing that boat meant at least three days' delay in getting home.

"After the Victoria left, I scouted the town looking for my brother. But there was no sign of him. Anyway, it was like looking for a needle in a haystack! Skagway was bulging at the seams—at least a thousand people a day were arriving.

"The following day I watched for the Goodwin party and also again scouted the town for Charles. But I had no success in finding him, nor in finding any of my friends. Then I looked up Shelly Graves' brother. Shelly was one of my Circle City friends who had stayed on in Dawson. While the brother and I were visiting, Mr. E. O. Sylvester, the well-known merchant of Skagway, bumped into us.

"When I recounted the episode of the roadhouse and the letter, both Graves and Sylvester sucked in their breath, and Sylvester exclaimed,

'Good Lord, man! They nearly got you! Those were Soapy's men, both on the pass and in the saloon. Citizens of Skagway are practically helpless about the protection of you Stampeders. We ourselves can hardly tell the difference between friend or foe, as Soapy has a secret political gang. However, we do know some of his most notorious henchmen. One of the worst is Yeah-Mow Hopkins, who came from Chinatown, San Francisco. Why, that big brute would just as soon strangle you as look at you!

" 'The roadhouse letter* is a favorite trick of Soapy's. If you had slept in that roadhouse, or stayed in the saloon five minutes longer, Yeah-Mow would have had you!'

"Well, the more I thought of it the more the chills ran up and down my spine. Indeed, I fully realized how very lucky I was to've escaped. For, by now, I could have been a dead man, another victim of the Soapy Smith gang!

"While talking to Graves and Sylvester, I learned that definite preparations were being made for a White Pass railroad, which would follow in many places the gold rush trail. In fact, crews of men were now working on the right-of-way. But men in Skagway were hotly arguing that the project just couldn't be done——and, of course, some of them were Soapy's men!

" 'What will Soapy Smith's men do when people ride trains over White Pass?' I asked, 'Won't that cut down on Soapy's criminal activities?'

" 'You bet it will,' said Sylvester, 'But he can't stop 2,000 workers who are in the mountains ready to begin the job. Many of them are armed. There's no doubt of it, Soapy and his gang must be run out of town, and we've formed an organization to do just that!'

"After talking to Sylvester and Graves, I was more than anxious to

---

*In some of the Soapy Smith roadhouses a portrait of a man would hang on the wall. The eyes would be removable so that a victim could be watched through the picture.

*In early spring of 1898 a party of staff officers for the Canadian Bank of Commerce landed at Skagway with many thousands of dollars in banknotes. The notes were divided up among the officers, in kitbags, and stuffed in among the personal belongings in order to fool Soapy Smith's men. The party of staff officers decided that the Chilkoot Pass route was less risky as there were fewer men of the Soapy Smith gang on that pass. The officers got over the pass safely and reached Dawson with the money intact. There the bank officials set up a tent and did business while a building was being erected.

A goat team headed for Dawson, 1898, at Dyea, Alaska.
(Photo by Hegg)

Dredge on claim No. 90, Bonanza Creek, near Dawson.

Joe Latshaw and Ed Lung, left, with a group of miners on claim No. 10 Above Lower Discovery, Dominion Creek. Rover, the trick dog, sitting by Ed Lung.

Claim No. 9 Above Lower Discovery, Dominion Creek. Ed Lung and Joe Latshaw with miners. Ed in sluice box at top; Joe in open cut with big Louie. It proved to be a rich claim.

get out of Skagway. There was an evil atmosphere about the place! I checked again to see if Charles had landed in Skagway, but there was no evidence that he had, and while I waited at the dock, Goodwin and his party arrived. It was with great relief that I welcomed them, as I had feared Soapy's men might have waylaid them. While we had a jolly-good meeting right there on the dock, they had much to tell of their trip over Chilkoot. It had been an eventful one, but they had not encountered any of Soapy's men. That same day, I wrote in my diary:

> March 20, 1898–Sunday–Skagway
> The boys came over from Dyea. The Pakshan landed this a.m. We took passage. Am now sitting in my cabin. We left Skagway at 3 p.m. Mr. Garvin of Garvin & Chandler is on board. Fare is $50.00 to Tacoma. We do not stop this side of Vancouver. This steamer is an old China Str., iron hull, a staunch vessel. I had a close call from Soapy Smith's gang, Skagway.

"Well, I arrived in Tacoma, Washington on March 26, 1898. No one could possibly imagine the great excitement of getting home. The family had not received any mail from me for six months! All of my concern for my brother joining the gold-rush had been needless, as he had decided to give up that rugged trip North.

"Yes, it was good to get home! I had come a thousand miles over the ice (from Circle City) and another thousand miles by salt water to reach my home. Little did I dream, then, that I would be headed back to the Klondike on the 'Trail of '98' in only a few short weeks, and that I would be fired with gold-fever to search for the Ancient Channel of the Bonanza* River, where there could be a Mother Lode of dazzling treasure in nuggets and yellow dust!"

---

*Most of Soapy Smith's descendants live in Southern California.
*Read "Black Sand and Gold" for story of the Ancient Channel.

Chapter 30

THIEVES IN THE CACHE

In early summer of 1902 I took Clemy and Ella and went Outside in the company of Mrs. Chittick and Mrs. Jene Allen. (The Allens owned the Klondike Nugget Newspaper.) Needless to say the trip was a strenuous one as little Ella was only eighteen months of age. But my two friends helped with the children when things became too difficult. When we reached Tacoma it was a joyous homecoming for me as well as Clemy. Of course Mother and Ena welcomed us with open arms and loved the new baby.

Altho' I was overjoyed to be back in Tacoma, before many days had elapsed I was longing for my little log cabin in the North. Most of all I was homesick and yearning to see Edward.

In anticipation of my trip back North, I made a special trip to Vancouver, B.C. to the Hudson's Bay Company and gave them a sizable order for canned goods and foodstuffs amounting to hundreds of dollars. Also, from the same Company I bought quite an assortment of clothing and a few household furnishings, such as a tan and green rug, a fur robe, a table cover, some new window curtains and many pretty pink rolls of wallpaper.

By purchasing all of my supplies at the big Hudson's Bay store, and by making arrangements to travel on a Canadian vessel, too, naturally I would not have to pay duty in Yukon territory on these things. The clerk assured me that when I was ready to sail, my purchases would be on the steamer.

When finally the last of August* came I was glad to be on my way back to the Klondike.

Edward met us in Dawson and was almost pathetically happy and relieved to see us, as we had come in on one of the last steamers of that

---

*King George VII of England was crowned Aug. 12, 1902. He was to have been crowned June 26th, but he fell from a horse and was injured. Dawson celebrated the coronation in grand style, with a parade, speeches and band music.

*The Semi-Weekly Nugget reported in Aug. 13, 1902 that mountains Redoubt, Diana, and Augustine, on Cook's Inlet continued to smoke. Also, that the Cocos Island Treasure-hunt was fruitless.

season. The trip down the Yukon had been a rugged one—just as it had been in '99 when I had first gone North with little Clemy. But the Captain of the Casca was a veteran of the river boat line—very skilled!

"Oh, it's great to see you and the children again," exclaimed Ed, hugging us fondly after we got off the steamer. "And oh, it's good to see all of the big crates of canned goods and other things. Yes, you bet, Vel, we'll eat like Kings," he said, smacking his lips in pleased anticipation. "No indeed, we won't go hungry this winter!" (I had brought in a wide assortment of canned vegetables, meats, fruits and also a number of slabs of bacon, hams and dried beef. I almost believe I had enough to start a small grocery store! It was worth a small fortune in the Klondike.)

After Ed had thoroughly checked over everything, he had the crates hauled to a windowless cache in Dawson which he had rented for our temporary use. Before leaving the vault-like structure (built of sturdy logs), he saw to it that the heavy door was securely locked.

Well, I was in seventh heaven to be home again in our cozy little log cabin. Dominion Creek Valley seemed like real Paradise!

While waiting for the snow to fly and pack so that we could get our winter supplies from town, Ed and I decided to fix up the cabin with some of the household things which we had managed to haul ourselves. It took both of us to do the job of putting the wallpaper on over that scorched outing flannel. Using the kitchen table, we laid the paper out and cut it in proper lengths and then applied the paste; I held the strips up against the walls while Ed smoothed them down with a big brush. Of course it was a messy job and we had many good laughs during the process.

Ella, being an inquisitive toddler, was constantly into everything! During the wallpapering job she was a pasty, smelly, sticky mess!

Once she fell onto a nicely cut strip of wallpaper, tearing it badly, and another time upset the paste-pot, spilling it on herself and all over the floor. But at last when we were finished, and had scrubbed Ella and the cabin floor shining clean, we stood back and surveyed our papering job.

It certainly did look nice, we agreed; made the cabin look like an oversized doll-house with that rosy-glow restored which I had loved so much before the cabin fire. In Vancouver I had carefully selected wallpaper with a profuse design of pretty pink roses over a paler pink background. Yes, so once more the log cabin was our lovely "pink-heaven," papered with hundreds of roses! Even tho' there were a few paper wrinkles showing here and there, the place did look wonderful!

One day in October Ed announced that the snow was hard-packed enough to take the dog-team to Dawson to get our supplies. He only expected to be gone four or five days.

Three days later I heard our dogs yapping on the trail, sleighbells jingling. Joyously, I rushed to open the door to welcome Ed home. For a moment he stood in the doorway, looking very ill.

"Oh, Ed, what is it?" I cried as I caught a glimpse of an empty sleigh behind him.

"Vel, oh, Vel," he groaned, "it's the cache! Everything was gone. Thieves had forced the door and taken absolutely everything! It was completely empty! Nothing left! Oh, what will we do this winter? Vel, Vel!"

I was terribly shocked and panicky, too, but I smiled as bravely as I could and soothed my husband, saying that we would surely manage somehow, yes, somehow! But I knew it was a serious misfortune. We would have to live again, like the previous winter, on bacon and beans and whatever we could scrape up. Poor Ed, tho'! How hungry he had been for the various new kinds of food, and I had anticipated preparing mouth-watering dishes from that large assortment of groceries. I had even brought in a small barrel of pickles and another one of pickled pig's feet, the latter of which was one of my husband's favorite delicacies!

Who on earth could have done such a mean, despicable thing? Of course Ed immediately reported the theft in Dawson. No doubt the thieves had been watching my shipment and had robbed the cache right after we left it, and by now, were probably way down the Yukon on the American side. Soon after that the price of extra heavy padlocks in Dawson jumped to $25 apiece! (The police never located the thieves.)

Ah, yes, there was no doubt of it! Dawson* was fast changing. It had been an unwritten law that personal belongings, including food and gold, were sacred property. When I first went North people could leave cabins and caches unlocked, feeling absolutely secure that nothing would be taken. Even glass jars and tomato cans filled with virgin gold could be left standing on shelves or tables, in plain sight, with no fear of theft. But, sad to say, this had all changed with the coming of more civilization!

*Dawson was a much bigger city in 1902. It had a few government buildings (the Governor's Mansion), an electrical power plant, four newspapers, several churches, a library, a court of law, a water-works department, schools and several gold mining syndicates.

By 1902, Dawson had most of the recreations of larger cities on the Outside: She had carnivals, banquets, concerts, lectures, grand-balls, plays, steamheated club rooms, billiard rooms, a swimming pool, a bowling alley, base-ball games, hockey games, a curling club, and ice skating. A number of Churchmen were in Dawson, including the Salvation Army. Evangeline Booth, of the Salvation Army, was in Dawson for a season in 1902.

Dawson's first ice-rink was in a slough back of the Mounted Police Barracks. It had a wooden foundation and was tent-covered. There were about 45 members the first year. Base-ball was a great summer sport as there was so much daylight. Often, the games lasted past midnight.

When the last boat would leave for the Outside, the winter social whirl of Dawson would begin. By 1902 the people were dressing well. Many of them were refined and intelligent and of good education. They read good books and had a library in town to draw on— "The Carnegie." Most of the people who lived in Dawson grew to love it, and boasted that they knew the "spell of the Yukon."

The Governor's mansion was a large Victorian, three-story building, facing the Yukon River. Major William Ogilvie was Yukon Territory's first Governor.

In summer, many wild flowers dotted the hills, and in Dawson, people were finding that they could grow all kinds of flowers, some, head-high; Roses, candytuft, geraniums, pansies, poppies, delphinium, dahlias, nasturtiums etc. grew easily.

In 1902 the valleys of the Bonanza, Eldorado and Hunker were beginning to look different. The private claims were being snapped up by the big syndicates which were putting "gold-digging" machines to work in the valleys. These large dredges, made of wood and steel, moved slowly, like great prehistoric monsters, from pond to pond, chewing up the gravel and spewing out the gold—of fine, or flour-gold quality. These seemingly insignificant gold particles the early miners had let slip through their fingers in their delirious quest for quick riches. Already in 1902 the dredge-monsters were beginning their slow advance up the valleys on trips that would last over half a century!

Joe Boyle, the sparring partner of Australian heavyweight boxing champion, Frank Slavin (both of them in partnership in Dawson), was already acquiring mining properties from the old sourdoughs for his dredge company called, "The Canadian Klondike Mining Company." Later, Boyle was to be known as the famous "Mining Dredge-King." After the first World War he sold out to the Yukon Consolidated Gold Corporation. Another huge dredge company called "The Yukon Gold Company," belonged to the Guggenheims. They owned hundreds of Klondike claims and their headquarters were at "Guggyville," in the Klondike Valley. Their dredges were nick-named "Guggies."

The first Klondike claims were called, "Poor Men's," because they could be worked without the aid of machinery. The look of Dawson in 1902 was less frontier-like. The city had settled down to a stable metropolis and capital of Yukon Territory.

Chapter 31

MYSTERIOUS TEN ABOVE LOWER DISCOVERY

Early in mid-winter of 1903 I was becoming quite frail and so it was increasingly difficult for me to do the cabin work and adequately care for our three small children. Perhaps my waning vitality was the result of a number of things. Under primitive conditions, in late January, I had given birth to my little son, Paul. He was now only two months old. Previously (through the winter), I had been in a weakened condition because of a very limited diet owing to loss of our food supplies which had been stolen from our cache in Dawson. And then too, I had never quite recovered from that long, strenuous trip to the Outside in the summer of 1902 at which time I knew for a certainty that a little one was coming. (son Paul)

Added to all of these trials, claim No. 2-B Below Lower Discovery was rapidly falling short of gold-production. In spite of this depressing fact our four miners had to be paid. Naturally, it was a constant anxiety.

At last the 1903 spring clean-up was over, and it was then apparent to Ed and Joe that it was useless to try to squeeze any more gold from that claim. The feeble pay-streak seemed to have vanished completely! In 1902 Ed and Joe had taken a lease on No. 4 Below Lower Discovery. It, too, was yielding little returns.

Ed and Joe held a serious conference and decided to give up the two claims. They had their eyes on No. 10 Above Lower Discovery. Ed and Joe had traced ownership through the bank and discovered that No. 10 belonged to Fernand de Journel, a Frenchman.

Graciously, and with much enthusiasm, de Journel granted my husband and Joe a lay. The papers were signed August 4, 1903. And then on August 14, 1903, at 11:30 a.m., the document was registered at the Dawson office of the Gold Commissioner. (W. R. Humelt was the Commissioner who signed the papers.) The terms of the Lay-Lease were to be 50% of the claim's gold. Ed and Joe were to have full control of the mine until it was worked out. All of this, of course, was stated in the lease.

Well, it seemed like a marvelous opportunity. Who could tell? Maybe that elusive pay-streak would turn up in great richness in this particular claim, for after all, wasn't it right in the very shadow of King Solomon's Dome, the heart and hub of the Klondike gold-fields?

But there was something rather strange about this piece of ground, too. The claim had stood idle for some months. Why? No one seemed to know, exactly. We had only a short distance to move to claim No. 10 and had very little to take in the way of equipment as all machinery belonged to the bank. We only owned some steam points and various lengths of hose and of course our household furnishings.

When the first of September came, we regretted leaving our snug little cabin (on No. 2-B) which had been our "pink flannel heaven" and was now papered with rose-pattern-wallpaper. Edward and I made many trips back and forth to the other cabin and when all was moved out of cabin 2-B, we took one last look at it, then closed the door. It was to be the very last time that I was ever to see the interior of that pink-rose doll-house except in my house of memory.

The log cabin on Claim No. 10 Above Lower Discovery was very inferior to the one on 2-B! Apparently it had been built by a prospector in a desperate hurry for winter quarters. The rough logs, with bark still clinging, were uneven and mud-caked. Much of the stringy moss which had been used for chinking up the cracks, hung loosely. Yes, it was a poorly built cabin, all right! (Never was I so cold as I was that winter of 1903.)

Instead of the usual one big room, the builder had made two small ones; one for the combination kitchen-living-room, the other for the bedroom. In the kitchen stood a large partly worn out stove which probably had been in some cookhouse. The bedroom was dark and small. Into this we crowded our beds and several chairs. An airtight stove stood in one corner of the bedroom. It proved to be almost usless as it smoked and gave off very little heat. The whole cabin was dismal, both inside and out! And besides that, it was very low-roofed, so low in fact that it was almost lost among the high mounds of rocks and heaps of old tailings from previous clean-ups.

When at last we were settled, my work became greatly increased. Now I began cooking for several of the miners and of course Joe Latshaw was a steady boarder.

At this point Ed and Joe began mining in real earnest and on a much larger scale. We now had a crew of ten men working for us among whom were represented a half dozen different nationalities.

Gradually, as winter came on, the days grew shorter and colder and soon our unattractive cabin, with all of its ugly surroundings, was covered with a soft mantle of snow.

Our busy day began at five a.m., by the alarm clock. First, Ed would hurry into his clothes and build a fire in the cook stove, then I would follow. By five thirty a.m., I would begin frying sourdough pancakes, but before that, I would make a large pail of fresh coffee, as the men liked a quick warm-up when they first entered the cabin, and another one, just before leaving for the mine. Our work-whistle blew promptly a 7 o'clock.

After the men were out of the way Clemy would quickly climb out of bed, then dress and wash his hands and face in warm snow-water. Always, I looked him over to make sure that he was clean and properly dressed. While he was eating his breakfast I would pack his lunch in a small tin pail.

When he had finished breakfast he would pull on his heavy sweater; over that, his parka, then put on his woolen mittens and red stocking cap. Always he would give me a hasty kiss and away he would run to catch the sleigh-bus on the government road, a short distance above our cabin.

The sleigh-bus was usually right on time and took him to the Caribou school, three miles away. On the return trip it would usually be dark before the sleigh would bring him home again. (In mid-winter.)

After Clemy would leave for school, I would dress the two small children (Ella and Paul) and give them breakfast. They spent the rest of the day in a large dry-goods box. I kept the box in the middle of the floor as a playpen. Here they were safe, for they couldn't climb out. This gave me a chance to do my housework without interruption. Seldom the children cried. Somehow they seemed to amuse themselves and it was a good thing they did, for I don't know what I would have done with fretful, crying babies as my life was so full of necessary things that just had to be done! My life was so regimented by now that it seemed I had no time at all for myself, none to rest or relax.

My afternoons were usually spent in baking loaves and loaves of sourdough bread. The men were very fond of sweets and needed the sugar for energy, so I tried to concoct some kind of pastry for at least one meal a day, usually the noon one which had to be ready promptly at 12 o'clock. Ed and the men worked hard from 7 a.m. until 6 p.m. and required plenty of hearty food.

That winter on Number 10 we were so busy and fatigued from our strenuous routine that Edward and I never went moonlight-sleigh riding, nor even bothered to rush outside to watch the brightly flashing Northern Lights whenever they put in their spectacular appearance.

As the months wore on, I was so very weary and so extremely cold, too, that I did everything, just automatically! Nothing was really neglected. But oh, I was so very cold that it seemed I was numb from head to toe and to the very bone! My husband tried desperately to seal up the cracks of the cabin, but in spite of his efforts, when the wind blew down from the Rockies and swept across the valley, that freezing air would penetrate through our cabin, making it drafty and cold, almost like the inside of a frigid icebox.

Poor Edward grew thin and worried! It just seemed I was more dead than alive! Some nights when my work was done and the children asleep, I would slip off my felt moccasins and crawl into bed, too exhausted to further undress.

Ed always went to the boiler-house after supper to check with the miner who happened to be on night duty. It was this man's job to keep the steam pressure up and also to reset the steam-points underground in the different tunnels in order to keep the muck continuously thawing so that the following morning quantities of melted earth could be hoisted to the surface and deposited on the dump above ground to await the spring clean-up.

Often finding me fast asleep, with my clothes still on, Ed would begin talking softly, or until I would be sufficiently awake to finally prepare for bed. But many times he would have to assist me.

Three of our miners discontinued coming for meals when they learned that the work was too much for me. However, Joe still took meals with us as he was like one of the family and would eat just about anything! Besides, the children looked forward to having their "Uncle Joe" with them and he did try to be helpful.

But at last, the climax came! One day I fainted dead away on the floor and Ed found me. When I opened my eyes panic was written all over his face. He knew, and I knew that I couldn't continue much longer like this.

For several weeks after that Ed stayed home and took care of me and the children while Joe ran the mine alone.

It was at this particular time that a very kind, sympathetic lady, hearing of my plight, sent me a quart of fresh milk* every day, for six weeks. Early, each morning, a young man delivered it and it was carefully wrapped in straw to keep from freezing. Gradually, I began to improve in health.

Never, never, can I be too grateful to Mrs. Thompson for her wonderful gift! I really believe she saved my life and perhaps that of little Paul, too, for I was still nursing him. She and her husband owned what had proved to be a rich claim on Dominion Creek. They had sent Outside for horses and most valuable of all, a cow,* which was, to my knowledge, the only one on Dominion Creek. During this time my older children continued to live on Eagle Brand or condensed milk and they were holding their own, healthwise.

Near the middle of March, the slanting rays of the sun which had been submerged below the horizon all winter were now shining on the hilltops once more. How I looked forward to seeing the sun reach down into the valley and longed for the feeling of its warmth on my heat-starved body! Of course, in due time, the snow did go away and we were living again among grey rocks and piles and piles of ugle sand-dumps, but of this I couldn't complain. It was just good to feel alive again and adequate to the challenge of our strenuous existence in the North.

As the days rolled by, soon, I almost forgot the sufferings and hardships of that winter. I was now twenty-nine years of age. Surely I would have many good, useful years ahead of me yet!

I reminded myself many times that there was much to be thankful for. The hill of pay-dirt was thick and high and I was sure it contained good quantities of gold, because I had seen some of it. Pretty soon we were to be rewarded for our hard winter's work.

As the very last patches of stubborn snow thawed away and dripped rivulets from the hillsides, and as Dominion Creek roared with melted ice-water, the miners busied themselves in the sunshine on the banks of the river, making and repairing and then laying many feet of sluice boxes in grand preparation for the final steps of retrieving the gold—the

---

*Fresh milk in Dawson was $20 and $30 a quart. H. L. Miller brought the first cow to Dawson on a barge in 1898.

gold which had come so very hard from the dark, frozen depths of the earth.

The small pond, fed by the river, and now dammed up, was high enough to feed water into the sluice boxes. Soon the dam would be opened and just the proper amount of water allowed to pour through the sluice boxes. Then, the men would begin "shoveling in" the precious dirt from the dump.

In very early spring Fernand de Journel had paid us several visits and had seemed most anxious that we make all possible haste with the clean-up. He had spoken words of encouragement and praise for our work and he had been very pleased when he had taken samples of the gold. He reminded us that half of it all would be ours, according to our lay-contract.

Well, at last, by the middle of May everything was in readiness for that important event, "The Big Clean-Up."

Ed and I stood by the sluice box, eagerly watching, while the men began putting through the first shovelfuls. The gravel began traveling towards us, pushed by the force of the water. The suspense was great—almost more than we could stand!

Suddenly, there was a stranger at our elbow: a tall, suave, well-dressed man who introduced himself as Mr. ————, a lawyer from San Francisco. He ordered us to halt the clean-up and startled us by saying he was the real owner of this mine and not Fernand de Journel of Dawson. He told us that there had been a nasty mix-up concerning title to No. 10 claim and that de Journel, the bank, nor anyone else, had the legal right to grant a lay, but he, himself. He declared he had come to take what was rightfully his—the claim and the gold.

Well, my husband and I, at first, thought the stranger was a liar, or maybe he was just a practical joker. Then we were shocked when he swore he wasn't fooling—that it was all absolutely true.

Incredible! How could this nightmarish situation exist? We had worked ourselves to the bone, feeling absolutely secure under what was supposed to be a legal lease.

Of course Ed and Joe were outraged and furious when the lawyer told them, vehemently, over and over, that they had no legal claim whatsoever to the gold on top of the ground (in the dump) or under the ground.

"Stand back!" Ed shouted to the lawyer. "You can't touch this gold. I don't know your crooked angle, sir, but I'm going to see that justice is done. We've labored all winter long to bring up every speck of this gold. Stand back, I say!"

Never before had I seen Edward so furiously wrathful! The lawyer used much profanity, then departed for Dawson in a violent rage, saying before he left that he would prove he was the real owner. Ed and Joe also rushed off to town to prove that he was not the legal owner, that he was a crook, an imposter.

But while in Dawson, Ed and Joe learned that there had certainly been some bad legal tangles over the claim and this had been going on for the last three years. There had been a series of double mortgages, renewals, and agreements of sales with a number of Klondike people involved. All had fought fiercely over this rich piece of ground.

Then Fernand de Journel had stepped into half-ownership, but his claim to No. 10 had been precarious due to personal debts and mortgages and miner's liens against the property. In our Lay-Lease, de Journel had given us the right to work the entire claim until the gold would be worked out.

Now it seems that during the last year this lawyer from San Francisco had been in cahoots with a gambler and confidence man and through them had managed to pick up the two mortgages to the mine. One was Fernand de Journel's and the other his partner's. One mortgage had come into the possession of the lawyer through a crooked business deal.

Once the lawyer had the deed of ownership to number 10 he adroitly got around our lay-lease contract and clean-up-time clause on a technicality, even though our lease said that we could stay on the claim and work it until the gold ran out!

Little did we dream of the turn of events or of how very important it was to get that gold out of the dump and rush the clean-up! But spring in the North is something human beings can't rush. The clean-up depended on melted ice-water and warm sunshine!

"Ah, if it were anyone but this fellow we might be able to help you so that you would not stand to lose so much," said the assistant bank president sympathetically, in talking to Ed privately.

"You see, Ed," he continued, "to complicate things further, Fernand de Journel borrowed money here at the bank, giving us a note to be paid from the gold to be taken out of claim 10. Of course you know the bank must be paid for its loan, so now, settlement must be made between the bank, de Journel, and this lawyer-fellow. Sorry Ed, it seems you may stand to lose on the deal unless the lawyer will honor the Lay of his own free will. But of course, he probably will not."

Well, Ed was not to be so easily turned aside, nor would he be soothed or reconciled. At the Gold Commissioner's office he raised such a furor of protest that it rocked the gold-interests of Dawson, and as a result the bank hurriedly sent out a representative to be on hand at every clean-up. Of course the belligerent lawyer had immediately returned from Dawson to harass and stand guard over us in a hostile, menacing way. Ed could tolerate the bank's representative, but could scarcely endure the presence of this overbearing, threatening lawyer, who fiercely claimed that after the bank got theirs he was going to take over the claim immediately and run it to suit himself.

Ed and Joe just as fiercely declared that they were going to take the matter to a good attorney in Dawson and legally force the lawyer from San Francisco to honor their lay-agreement.

Naturally, Ed and Joe and the sharp-tongued fellow exchanged some very bitter, vitriolic words and once nearly came to blows as Ed's patience was at the near-breaking point.

Now the man actually accused Ed and Joe of being claim-jumpers. Think of it! Claim-jumpers, when we had held a lay to the mine for over ten months! This man was placing us in this position because we were remaining on the claim and were fighting for our rights! We had brought the gold out of the earth, now he wanted us to leave the premises. Only an unscrupulous attorney would dare resort to such abuse!

Ed indignantly retaliated, accusing the lawyer of being a scoundrel. Joe said that the fellow had planned to let us put in a season's work and then had timed his arrival at just the crucial moment—the big clean-up.

In a horrible huff the lawyer departed for Caribou, saying before he left that he meant to have us arrested and thrown off the claim. I was, oh so embarrassed! And all of this in front of our miners!

Soon Sergeant Hilliard of the Mounted Police came over to see us. He had put on civilian clothes so that his coming would not be so conspicuous or humiliating.

Courteously, he told Ed he had come to talk over this unusual and distressing situation. Reluctantly, he also said he had a warrant for Ed's and Joe's arrest.

When Ed gave Hilliard the true facts of the case and then showed him his Layman's paper and free miner's license and the Lay-lease, Mr Hilliard made no arrest. However, he, being our friend, advised Ed and Joe to tread carefully as it was a very nasty situation.

"Oh Edward," I implored, "let's abandon the claim. Obviously, we are caught in a bad legal situation and are terribly wronged. We'll never get much, if any part of this gold . . . I'm afraid, oh so afraid!"

But I could not sway my husband and make him deviate from his course. Joe stood firmly with Edward. They had set their hands to the plough. They would see it through to the bitter end with a righteous stubbornness that is so common to the Teutonic race. In other words, the two men were positive the lay would be honored by Canadian law.

That spring, during the rest of the clean-up, the situation was an unbearable nightmare, for every day, when the miners started running the pay-dirt through the sluice boxes, there stood four, grim-faced men—Edward, Joe, the bank's representative, and the obnoxious lawyer who never missed an opportunity to arrogantly proclaim the gold in the sluice boxes as his—all his!

But Ed and Joe, with set jaws and knotted fists, stood firm on their Laymen's rights. They would not allow the lawyer, nor even the bank's representative to handle the gold.

After each sluicing, the black sand and gold was scooped up and hurriedly brought to our cabin and immediately turned over to me for safekeeping.

"We will trust Mrs. Lung," said Sergeant Hilliard, "for after all she is our little minister on Dominion Creek and we will trust Ed Lung and Joe too, for we know them to be honorable men!"

And so, as usual, in the evenings, after the work of the day, I dried the black sand, or pay dirt on top of our stove. All the while I worked, as I stirred and stirred the sandy mixture, I hoped and prayed that we would receive our just share of the gold. After supper Ed and I would sit together at the table, side by side, with magnets in hands, drawing off the black sand, ending the process by blowing away the finer black-dust particles. Joe often helped, too.

After each session we would weigh and sack the gold. Of course we kept an accurate account of the number of pans of sand and of each resulting ounce of gold-dust. We found it was running quite rich, as was expected.

But, as the days dragged on, we worked with worn, tired fingers and heavy hearts. What would we receive for all of our efforts?

On June 1, 1904, Ed sent the very first shipment of gold from the mine, almost twenty-two ounces of it to the bank at Dawson. A few days later we received a memorandum dated June 3, 1904 and headed Dawson, Y. T.

> For E. B. Lung.
> Dear Sir: We beg to acknowledge receipt of 21.65 ounces of gold-dust from you on account of F. de Journel, No. 10 Above Lower Discovery, Dominion Creek.
> Yours truly,
> T. K. May, Ass't. Manager

Finally, after a number of shipments of gold, we were ordered to halt the clean-up. Then every single speck of gold was turned over to a business arbitrator in Dawson (appointed by the bank). The gold we had sent had been a sizable sum.

A few days later, Ed was informed by the arbitrator, by mail, that after the wages of all the miners had been paid, and after the bank's note had been redeemed from the gold in F. de Journel's account, they were sorry but there would be nothing left for us.

Then, there were polite apologies from the arbitrator with an added message saying that the lawyer from San Francisco would no doubt take over the claim as it was now legally his. Also, that we should vacate the cabin within a few weeks to save further trouble. Ed received the news with ashen face and Joe with livid, pent-up anger.

Words can never fully describe our terrible shock and distress when the real impact of the message beat into our minds. A whole year's work gone for naught. Wasted! Where would Ed and I go with our children? In a few short weeks winter would be upon us. It was much easier for a lone man like Joe to bunk up with others, but what would we do?

Poor Edward! The outcome of it all was almost more than he could bear. For a few days I feared for his sanity. In Dawson he had been led

*Gold was worth about $17 per ounce from most of the Dominion Creek mines.

to believe, for a time, at least, that justice would prevail. Now, deep despair seized him, especially after he had gone to Dawson again (a third time) to consult Harry H. Bleaker, a well-known attorney, who told him candidly there was absolutely nothing to be gained in a lawsuit. Of course Ed appealed to the United States Consul, Henry D. Taylor, but there was nothing he could do, nor could T. Sidney Marshall, Commissioner of Affidavits at Dawson, do anything to help us.

"Now," I thought, "maybe we would leave the North. Yes, this certainly would be the time." But at last, after a few days, Ed's devastating disappointment acted as a springboard.

He persuaded Joe to go on a prospecting trip. "Yes, of course," I agreed, "a prospecting trip is just exactly what you both need! It will be a change of scenery and you might find gold." (This would give me a good chance to rest and recuperate. Goodness knows—I needed it badly!)

For weeks all of us had been like tightly wound springs, ready to snap in a moment of extra strain.

Yes, I'm sorry to say, I had been a distraught eye-witness as to how yellow gold could bring out the snarling beast in man. This particular fellow was crazed beyond all reason by the lust to possess number 10 which he had come by so dishonestly. And he had had no pity on us—no, none at all!

Well, at last that heartbreaking episode was over!

Ed and Joe hurried to Dawson and rented a small boat for their prospecting trip. Then they paddled down the Yukon to a little river called the Twenty-Mile. Here, Ed and Joe poled up what turned out to be one of the most turbulent of streams, especially so, since the river was swollen and deep from a recent, heavy summer rainstorm.

As the men swung around a sharp bend of rocks in the river, the rapids boiled so fiercely that their boat began to ship water and capsize.

Knowing that Joe couldn't swim a stroke, and knowing too, that the boat would probably only remain afloat with just one of them in it, or clinging to it, Ed jumped into the icy water, frantically calling to Joe to stay with the boat.

Of course Ed was a fine swimmer, but it was all he could do to keep his head above water. Finally he managed to reach a log in the river and from there, half-drowned, he pulled himself up onto it and then to the slippery bank beyond.

Joe, in the meantime had swept downriver out of sight, for at least a mile. At a sandy spot he was able to land. There, he tied the boat to a stump and grabbing the water-tight clothes-bag he ran along shore looking for Ed, knowing that if he could only find him, Ed would be in desperate need of dry, warm clothing.

When Joe at last found Ed, he was chattering on the bank, half frozen from his icy swim.

Hurriedly, Joe got a fire kindled and soon he and Ed were warming themselves by the flames. The two partners thanked their lucky stars that they had escaped the river and had found each other. In this desolate spot they could have become hopelessly lost, and who would have known what had become of them? (Back in the cabin at this particular hour I had an urgent premonition of terrible danger for Ed and Joe, just as I had had when the ton of muck fell in a tunnel (at Claim No. 2-B), just barely missing my husband's head by inches! Again, as then, I fervently asked Him for His special protection.)

It wasn't until the following day that Ed and Joe felt sufficiently recovered from their bout with the river to have the courage to search for gold.

After taking numerous samples in nearby tributaries they found infinitesimal traces of the yellow metal. It winked at them in a few of the samples of sand which they tested.

"Oh, it's the same old story," Ed told Joe, in exasperation. "Almost any place we dip our pans here in this blasted country we usually come with a glint of gold. And yet the lode could be several hundred miles away, yes, maybe even in the Tanana!"*

Of course, at this point Joe was all for heading North, towards the great, beckoning Tanana region, just as he had been in favor of doing during that fruitless Chicken Creek stampede, back in 1901.

"Listen, Joe," said Ed, "first let's go back to Dawson. Let's see if we can procure No. 9 Above Lower Discovery on Dominion Creek. I hear it belongs to a French syndicate called 'Le Syndicat de Lyonnais du Klondike.' The syndicate is controlled by a French Count. While in

---

*Vague rumors had come that gold had been found in a place called "The Chena Slough" in the Tanana Valley. Felix Pedro had been there in July of 1902 and had made the discovery. (The city of Fairbanks was to spring up a few years later.)

Dawson I happened to hear that number 9 was for sale.

"Yes, Joe," continued Ed, "that elusive pay-streak could very well be centered deep under No. 9. I'll tell you something, Joe:

"When we were working No. 10 I found faint indications of a new stratum showing up at the end of one of the new tunnels. I took my chisel and picked at it, in the wall. I felt sure we were reaching something promising near the boundary line of de Journel's claim and the one beyond. Of course, this fact I never divulged to that cheating lawyer.

"Yes, Joe, I would bet my boots that there's an exciting strata of gold hidden in No. 9. An Ancient Channel! It could be chuck full, maybe a Mother Lode! Let's hurry back to Dawson and try to get that ground before it's grabbed by someone else."

"Sure, Ed," said Joe. "I'm with you a hundred percent, as always,"

When Ed and Joe called on the affable Frenchman... "Yes, he would sell, but it would have to be for fifty thousand dollars."

"Fifty thousand dollars!" gasped Ed and Joe. "Why man! That's a staggering figure!"

"Well, how much can you raise?" asked Alfred Tarut sympathetically.

"Not more than one thousand dollars between us," answered the two men, with disheartened tones. Alfred Tarut shook his head.

"No, boys, the claim is worth all of fifty thousand," he told them, firmly. "I represent Le Syndicat de Lyonnais du Klondike, and they must be paid more than what you offer."

"Come on, Ed, let's go to the Tanana, then," said Joe, abruptly. "This is the time to strike out for a new land."

Bidding the Frenchman a quick adieu, Ed and Joe hurried down to their little boat, but they didn't get in and head North for the Tanana. Instead, they sat on the bank on the Yukon, talking in low tones.

Ed again said he wished like "Sixty" that they could own No. 9, and again said he felt certain that a treasure lay buried there. "Yes sir! I would almost stake my life on it," he told Joe. "And besides," he laughed, in a lighter vein, "if you'll take another fellow's opinion of it, Big Louie, our French Canadian miner, told me he actually saw the tip of the rainbow, on several occasions, dip low and touch that particular spot and move along a little. He says there's got to be a pot of gold buried right there at No. 9! So Joe, let's go back and see the Frenchman. I have a feeling he'll come way down on his price."

Alfred Tarut seemed quite pleased to see Ed and Joe the second time and surprised them by saying, "Well boys, you may have No. 9 Above Lower Discovery for twenty thousand dollars."

"Impossible," said Ed, "we can't pay anything like that! We told you honestly how much money we could raise."

Then the Frenchman smiled his charming smile and answered, "Boys, I like you tremendously. You may have the No. 9 claim for five thousand dollars. You may pay the Syndicate one thousand dollars now, and then from future clean-ups you may finish the payments with 10% interest until the four thousand dollars are paid off. My friends, what better deal could I possibly make you?"

With warm thanks and hearty handshakes, Ed and Joe accepted the unusual offer. It took all of the assets they could scrape up between them to make up the down-payment, but they came home the proud possessors of a claim—a claim that was to prove a rich one; and if Tarut could have known what they would find at bedrock in one particular section of that mine, he would never have sold for less than twenty thousand dollars!

---

*By 1909 the Canadian Government had what was called an "ASSURANCE FUND." Complaint of irregularities in claim titles, land fraud, omissions, mistakes, or misfeasances were looked into by the Minister of Finance. He rectified and paid settlement-sums to plaintiffs on exemplication or certified copy of judgement rendered. Registrar of Titles for Yukon Territory in 1909 was Napoleon Laleberte. He kept records in what was called "The Day Book."

*Dominion Creek had the distinction of having two Discovery claims: Upper Discovery and Lower Discovery. Albert Fortier, Camille Corbell, Frank Pijon and Max Landreville were the men who staked Lower Discovery almost at the same time that another group of men were staking a discovery claim several miles away, above them. That group was composed of Tim Conolly, Mr. Dnieper, Louis Corky and a few others. To save controversy, the Gold Commissioner allowed the recording of the Two Discovery claims.

Chapter 32

RIFFLES OF RICHES AND KLONDIKE KINGS

It was now early winter of 1904. All hands had willingly helped make the big move from the ill-fated No. 10 to the promising No. 9 Above Lower Discovery. The change had meant many long hours of hard work, but at last we were settled and things were now beginning to hum around the mine, for soon midwinter would be upon us. There was a certain eager expectancy in the air that was both invigorating and electric. And I noticed that Ed walked with a brisk new step of assurance, for each time that he had made a sample-test of the pay dirt it had loomed up more promising, especially in that certain location near the No. 10 boundary line.

We were now living in the roomy cabin which the French Count had once occupied. Everything about the cabin was fine and good. In fact, it was a very luxurious cabin for being so far out from Dawson.

The logs were nicely peeled and polished to a rich honey color and the cracks were well sealed. The cabin had an air of real refinement, and I loved it from the first moment that I saw it. Yes, the cabin would keep us snug and warm and protected from the icy blasts that were sure to sweep down from the Canadian Rockies.

Even the miners' cabins were cozy and well built, and were furnished with comfortable bunks and warm stoves. Then too, there was a splendid mess-hall and well-equipped kitchen. The mess-hall and kitchen were housed together in a separate building which stood close to the miners' quarters. It was a long, oblong-shaped structure, also made of peeled logs. Inside, was a table running almost the full length of the dining area. Brightly colored, cherry-red oilcloth covered the table, giving the place a cheery, gay appearance. Also, there were long benches stretching along the table on either side of the room.

About the same time that we made our move to No. 9, a very nice Scotch lady, Mrs. McPherson, came North to be with her husband and so Ed pursuaded her to take over the mess-hall cooking job. I was extremely relieved for I was finding the heavy work almost too difficult. The miner's wife was a big strong, healthy, jolly person, with a merry laugh and the men liked her and appreciated her cooking efforts.

When she blew the whistle they would come running to the mess-hall, and stand in line for a quick turn at the washpan and a chance to smooth down their hair with the "community comb." The bench, washstand and mirror were placed just outside the mess-hall door. But, of course, in wintertime the miners skipped the outside washup ritual.

When the mess-hall door was thrown open the miners would make a wild dash to their places at the table, then noisily begin devouring their food, very much like hungry wolves! If soup or porridge was served they would loudly suck it in, or inhale the hot liquid mixture partly through their beards, and they would keep up a continuous unpleasant snorting sound until that part of the meal was finished!

Most of the men were so eager for their coffee, they wouldn't wait for it to cool, and so would pour the steaming liquid right into their saucers and proceed to drink it that way! They rarely talked at the beginning of meals; they were too intent on getting their fair share of the food.

We took our meals at the mess-hall most of that winter, and I found it a great relief from the drudgery of everyday living. How long had it been since I had had such luxury? Four long years! But the eating habits of the men were no end of distress to me. Especially so, because Clemy watched them with such admiration, aping their every mannerism! These Sourdoughs were absolutely perfect in his young eyes. They were his adored heroes and before I knew it he, too, was inhaling his soup and grabbing and snatching his food and loudly wolfing it down; also drinking out of his saucer, just the way they did. And then one day I even caught him trying to chew a plug of tobacco! Of course, the wad made him awfully sick, and it was then he agreed that he was a little too young to "chew." It was for the older Sourdoughs and he'd wait until he was much older!

Desperately, I tried to talk him out of his Sourdough table manners, too, but it was useless, for there was that constant daily example in the mess-hall. And I could hardly rebuke him in front of his idols, his very good friends the "dear old Sourdoughs."

Secretly, I wondered if the handsome French Count had carelessly fallen into Klondike mess-hall habits; because, in the North, it seemed so very easy to slip away from the nice refinements of civilization and just go primitive! It was gratifying to note that my husband's good manners had never lapsed. He was careful, thoughtful and courteous.

This, I believe was due to his fine early training.

But now, what to do about Clemy? In every respect he was growing into a real little Sourdough—was taking on all of their habits, both good and bad, and of course, it was the latter that I was so concerned about.

After a few months Clemy's table manners grew so atrocious that I finally decided that it was time to resume family living. Of course, this was a hard decision, and was a terrible blow to Clemy to be separated from his beloved miners at meal time. But I knew he was forming eating habits that would stay with him for the rest of his life. Of course, we had almost all nationalities respresented in our group of miners and with each nationality there was, no doubt, a wide difference in concept of table etiquette.

* * *

One day, late in February, Ed was sitting on a box in the boiler house reading a Dawson paper, The Yukon Sun, published Feb. 20, 1904. This particular weekly edition had just arrived from town. The six Russians who worked for us gathered eagerly around Ed and in broken English began asking questions. Japan had just attacked Port Arthur!

Even before the news of the Russian-Japanese war, Ed and I had begun to suspect that our Russians were escaped prisoners from Siberia. For, at times, they were quite evasive and furtive about their country. But they were intensely interested to know the latest news and it was necessary for someone to read it to them since they couldn't read English themselves.

To please them Ed read aloud everything in the paper concerning the Russian trouble. At the moment, the big news was about the Japanese making a sneak attack on Port Arthur while Commander Alexieff was happily celebrating his birthday with a party of high-ranking Russian officers. Of course, the party had been a sumptuous affair!

Ed continued reading everything in sight, but when these items were exhausted, just for fun he began making up little imaginary stories of his own, saying that the Czar was going to demand that all escaped prisoners from Siberia, now in Yukon Territory, be rounded up and sent home immediately to fight in the war with Japan.

Of course this figment of Ed's imagination was all a little joke. But he never changed his grim expression. Often he glanced up from the newspaper and was amused at the apprehensive looks he received. After he had finished his Czar story, he folded up the paper and looked very solemn, for he had ended by saying that an extensive search for all escaped Russians was to be carried out by the Mounted Police within a few days.

One by one the Russians made quick excuses to go back to their cabins. That night they kept us awake with loud, excited talk, punctuated by fierce shoutings. Evidently they were drinking vodka and were violently discussing a serious matter.

"Say, I wonder what ails those Russians," I remarked to Ed. "Whatever it is, they seem to be pretty much upset."

"Oh, they've probably heard some kind of bad rumors," said Ed, with a nonchalent, mischievous grin, "but no doubt they'll calm down and forget it. You know how excitable and temperamental these Russians can be!"

The next morning the six Russians casually told us they were going to Dawson on business. My husband thought they merely wanted a little vacation and would soon be back. There was no mention of not returning.

However, two weeks passed and they had not shown up. Now Ed was puzzled, for they had sent no word in explanation and he had completely forgotten his "weird" little newspaper stories.

Then one day a Russian whom they called "The Student," came to see Ed and in an anxious voice inquired, "What in heaven's name, Mr. Lung, did you tell my fellow- countrymen? They came to Dawson very much agitated; and they got outfits and hurried off to the American side. They said they had to flee the country before they were picked up by the police and sent back to Siberia!"

Sheepishly, Ed remembered his Czar story. Needless to say, he was quite embarrassed and then, too, he had lost six very good miners.

"Well, at least," sighed Ed to me later, "it does go to prove that our Russians were escaped convicts; but somehow I can't think they had committed very serious crimes. Sorry to have caused them so much distress. I'll bet by now they have gotten themselves pretty much lost in

---

*In 1901 William Yanert, a retired U.S. soldier, founded Purgatory. He lived there alone until his brother joined him in 1910. They called it "a hell of a place" and erected their patron saint on the banks of the Yukon.

the wilds of Alaska—maybe even in Purgatory*— 150 miles down the Yukon, below Ft. Yukon. It's a lonely place and they could feel safe there!"

* * *

Some of our men preferred night work, and would go on duty at seven in the evening. By this time, 1904, my husband had four pair of horses and enough men to handle the heavy plough-shovels which we had recently acquired.

With horses and shovels they could work to bedrock much faster, using the "Open-cut" method, as it was called. Of course, the ground had to be thawed first before it could be ploughed up, farmer style.

When at last the miners came close to bedrock (thirty or forty feet), the horses were discarded. Now, the gravel which had been exposed had to be carefully dug up and sorted and saved in piles and the larger rocks put into special piles for scraping. It was in this particular rock-stratum that the richest gold-dust was often found.

One day while the miners were working in the open cut, suddenly there appeared a labor agitator. He got right down into the pit where the men were digging and began talking loudly about working conditions. Obviously, he was intent on stirring up a lot of ill feeling.

At first Ed ignored the intruder's presence—that is, until he saw that the men were becoming confused. Then, quietly, Ed went to the stranger and requested that he please not talk to the men during working hours. But the fellow just laughed insolently in Ed's face and continued his venomous attacks on all mine owners, shouting to the men:

"You're not getting a square deal. None of you miners are! Now what are ya' gonna do about it? Say, if you're smart you'll walk off this place and strike for higher wages." (Ed was paying the men $10 a day plus giving them room and board.)

Big Louie Moreau, our new young French Canadian (head miner) was working in the open cut with Ed. In angry disgust he listened and with scowling disapproval to the troublemaker's inflammable rantings.

"Ed," Big Louie whispered, "what are ya' going to do wiz thees here fellow?"

"I don't know yet, Frenchie," whispered Ed, "but on second thought, when I give the signal you get Olie and go after him and run him off the claim. I'll give that fellow just five minutes more to leave, and if he hasn't gone by then, you go after him, Boy. If you can't scare him away, pick him up and move him bodily!"

Once more Ed asked the man to leave, but the disagreeable fellow swore at Ed and continued to ignore his request. Ed looked at his watch; the five minutes were up. He signaled Big Louis. That was all the young Frenchman was waiting for.

Throwing down his pickax, but at the same time grabbing up his shovel, he called to the husky Swede to help him clean up on the fellow.

With war whoops that sounded like Comanche Indians and charging bulls, the two miners rushed at the troublemaker, waving menacing shovels, both Frenchie and Olie screaming something pretty terrible in their own native tongues.

When the fellow saw them bearing down on him he went white. He knew the jig was up and, like a scared rabbit, scrambled up the ladder, climbing the deepest part of the open cut in no time flat!

Big Louie and the Swede (Ed said afterwards) looked like two ferocious barbarians about to commit murder. Much to the amusement of all who saw him, the man kept running long after he had gained the top of the mine. And he continued running down Dominion Creek, apparently much too frightened to stop to look back!

That same evening Ed called a miners' meeting in the mess-hall and when the noise of chatter had died down he raised his hands for silence.

"Men," he said, "you all heard the stranger today. Now, we want peace and harmony here on this claim. I simply cannot pay more than ten dollars a day, and some of you know it for you've been with me a long time. If I hit the big gold-streak there'll be a bonus for all. If any of you are dissatisfied and don't want to wait, please speak up right now and I'll weigh out your pay in gold-dust and you may leave."

No one spoke up. Slowly, they all filed out and returned to their cabins. When the whistle blew next day every man was in his place in the open cut ready to work. Everyone worked with renewed vigor and enthusiasm.

Again, there was that intangible feeing of vibrant expectancy—as tho' on the eve of a big discovery! It seemed that Dominion Creek waited breathlessly and hushed for something to happen. Even Little Clemy said he knew something exciting was about to happen!

That night, tired and damp, Ed brought to our cabin a sample of paydirt, taken from a deep stratum exposed by the open cut.

"Look, Vel," he said, with glittering eyes and obvious relish, "See the big particles of rich yellow gold in this pan, smilin' up from that black sand? Man, oh man! It's like bright yellow polka dots resting on black satin! Look at those yellow babies! Oh, are they beauties!

"Yes, I tell you, it's rich ground. It may exceed our dearest dreams—our biggest expectations. Joe is sure we're hitting the old river bed, an ancient channel. If it's true, and if the richness continues, we should be tapping the main channel tomorrow. Yes," concluded Ed, "tomorrow will tell the story."

* * *

"Tomorrow" was really the beginning of the big spring clean-up and the men were working like Trojans to bring up as much good earth as possible.

This day I was in our cabin only a short distance from where the momentous event, the reckoning with Nature and her payoff, was about to take place. Again, I sensed that electrifying vibrancy in the air!

From my cabin window I could see the men "shoveling in" the pay dirt. I could see the water being turned on to carry away the unwanted particles of gravel and rocks so that the black sand and gold only, would be caught in the riffles at the bottom of the sluice-boxes. And I could see Clemy bobbing up and down among the miners, mostly getting in their way.

I was hurrying to make blueberry pie for our supper and when it was finished I would go down to the sluice-boxes to see what was in them. A well-practiced eye could almost evaluate the gold showing in the boxes even at that early stage of the process.

As I worked with my pie, I recalled a similar "Big Clean-up Day" just the year before, when the lawyer from San Francisco had suddenly swooped down upon us like an ugly vulture! I recalled how he had gloatingly claimed all of the gold in the sluice-boxes as his—all his!

What an evil, horrible day that had been! What a catastrophe the following events had seemed! Yet, had not these seemingly tragic events occurred we would certainly not have come into possession of this wonderful No. 9 piece of ground! So, after all, it had been for our good, altho' at the time it appeared the Devil himself had taken over. And what had become of the "Devil" himself? Well, a few months after he had taken our gold and run us off the claim he had disappeared.

As I formed the lower piecrust, patted it down, then opened a can of blueberries, I hummed one of my favorite hymns, "The Doxology," "Praise God from Whom All Blessings Flow." Yes, how grateful I truly was for everything! It was now very apparent that through all of our adversities we really had been under the care of His watchful eyes and in the hollow of His loving hands.

Now I had finished my pie; had chucked some wood into the stove; had put the pie into the oven and was just brushing the dough from my hands when I heard a wild cry.

Rushing to the window I saw Big Louie. He was jumping and hopping up and down in what appeared to be some kind of insane animated dance. He waved his long arms frantically in the air and feverishly shouted something to Edward, who also was shouting and dancing up and down in the same kind of elated senseless way.

"Mon Dieu! Mon Dieu! Look at eet," shouted Louie, pointing with quivering hands towards the sluice-boxes. "Ed, mon ami—just look een the bottom of that sluice-box. Eet ees filled with gold! You've struck eet! You've struck eet rich!"

For a moment I stood transfixed. I couldn't move a muscle and I could feel my voice "gone" in my throat. The pent-up, long, anguished years of struggle suddenly rushed upon me. Could it be that now they were ended?

Big stinging tears blurred my vision and dripped down to the floor.

Then Clemy came running into the cabin. Rudely he grasped me by the apron, pulling me outside toward the sluice-boxes, hysterically jibbering and laughing as he hurried me along.

"Oh, Mother, Bamba, Mother'" he cried, "We've hit the pay! We're rich—rich at last!!" Then he began sobbing for sheer joy.

Ed's arms were around me as I leaned over with quivering mixed emotions and looked down into the riffles of the sluice-boxes.

Joe was standing nearby, happily examining a good-sized handful of damp shiny nuggets.

"Ah yes," I cried, "it's gold—almost pure gold in sections—praise be to God!"

All at once I felt something grip me! I was all but overcome with a queer, terrifying emotional sensation. Yes, I felt as tho' I would faint or swoon dead away.

No, not at this moment, I thought wildly; no! no! I must not give way. I must not let my husband guess my secret! I must not reveal it! It was no time for Ed, or anyone to know. This was Ed's big day, his triumph—this day for which he had striven and suffered and waited for seven long years!

Later I would tell him my secret. Later I would tell him that there was for a certainty another "Little One" on the way. With both hands I gripped the sluice-box; and for a few brief seconds it seemed there was a shimmering vision of a child's face floating above the wet particles of gold. The child smiled and beckoned, then quickly vanished through the riffles.

The miners had gathered around the sluice-boxes. All operations had ceased. All were laughing and slapping Ed and Joe and each other on the backs, rambunctiously congratulating each other on hitting the jack-pot, saying that old Sourdoughs like themselves could certainly tell when they were coming to the big pay. Why, they could literally smell the gold in the ground!

Big Louie was still in motion (French style) saying excitedly, with eloquent gesticulations,

"Ed and Joe, do you remember how those rainbows moved across the valley, and how they bent low and deeped down at one end and touched thees very spot? Remember, how I say to you, 'Just look eet thet rainbow! She ees trying to tell us one beeg secrete.' Watch her, she ees trying to say, 'There ees gold right there under that Number 9 Claim. Oui, a great beeg pot of eet!' Oooh, la, la——la!"

* * *

That night I served my family and Joe a light supper in our cabin and I knew that no one would mind a little thing like a partially burnt blueberry pie! There was so much to talk about, and so many things to plan that food was far from our thoughts.

Ed and Joe were partners and of course they would share and share alike. As I looked at their happy, but careworn, faces and at their calloused, gnarled, workworn hands and then at their rough miner's clothing, I felt that there were no two men anywhere in the North who more richly deserved success than they. Yet, the North at first had seemed cruel; had made them wait a long, long time—had made the gold come unusually hard.

And yet I knew for all of this, Ed and Joe would always have more appreciation of what the earth had finally given them. Yes, they knew what it was to strive and sacrifice and suffer and even go hungry—and so did I!

How much would there be? Well, it would take many months before Ed and Joe could actually tell. But praise the Lord! The gold was there, and it was running eleven and twelve dollars to the pan—maybe more! Now I knew that one of these days we would pack our things and return to Tacoma.

Ed and Joe talked late that night and from my bed behind a faded pink French brocaded curtain I listened happily. As I drifted off to sleep I whispered prophetically,

"Yes, one of these days there will be another 'Little One' in our midst and Ed and Joe will be Klondike Kings!" (I figured we would be in the Klondike perhaps another year or two and then we would return to civilization. Little did I know!)

Chapter 33

FAREWELL TO THE NORTH

One day, late in summer of 1905, out of a clear sky, my husband said firmly, but gently:

"Vel, I just can't let you remain in the North any longer. The birth of our fourth child fills me with terrible anxiety so you must go back to

---

*By 1904 Dominion Creek was coming into its own. The Yukon Sun was headlining the achievements of the miners and their rich returns. Also Bear Creek was spotlighted. The Berry and Field Company was making news and Joe Boyle's concessions were acclaimed at Bear Creek. In Dawson there was excitement about the discovery of a quartz vein traceable from a point near the Moosehide Indian village, extending under the Yukon River to a point where the quartz out-cropped at West Dawson.

the States while there's yet time. In Tacoma you'll have the best of medical care. Yes, you must be ready to leave Dawson before the ice closes in!"

Of course I remonstrated with my husband; said I didn't want to leave him, that I wasn't fearful, but his mind was thoroughly made up and I couldn't sway him. So my big trunk was brought out and I began packing my meager belongings and those of the children.

While in the flurry of last-minute preparation, there came a knock at our cabin. It was a lady whom I had never seen before. Her arms were piled high with all kinds of children's clothes—little dresses, petticoats and tiny infant's garments. She hastened to explain that she had been sent to deliver the little clothes for the children and and the new baby-to-be and that it was not charity but a special token of appreciation from all of the women* on Dominion Creek for the good work I had done among the miners. She said the valley-folks would always remember me as "The Little Preacher."

At first I was overcome with surprise and pleased emotion and could scarcely speak. Deeply touched, I managed to find my voice enough to thank the stranger and invite her in for a cup of tea.

While the tea was brewing she spread the little garments out on the bed so that I could see them more fully. Truly, they were dainty and beautiful—all hand-made! I told the kind lady that I could never adequately express my grateful thanks to the ladies of Dominion Creek for their generosity and thoughtfulness. The stranger was pleased and said she would deliver my message.

Later, when Ella came in from play and saw the lovely dresses—some with ruffles, ribbons, and bows, she danced and skipped around the cabin in her great excitement and happiness; then she grabbed the fanciest one and tried it on. Poor little girl! She had hardly seen feminine clothes as she had spent most of her four years in boys' overalls!

In several days the children and I were ready to leave our cabin-home. The big trunk which now contained the beautiful gifts, except those which were to be worn on the trip, had been sent on ahead to Dawson by freight-coach, and so, after regretfully saying good-bye to our miners and neighbors, Edward and I and the children climbed to the government road and caught the stagecoach* for Dawson.

*By 1905 more women had come into the Territory.

FAREWELL TO THE NORTH

Soon the horses began the steep ascent to King Solomon's Dome. It was one of those fine, crisp days with the first tinge of frost in the air. When we gained the top of the ridge we could see for hundreds of miles—ridge after ridge—to the South, West and North, and to the East, the magnificent Rocky Mountains towering in all of their white, glistening glory. It was a panorama so marvelous I could scarcely imagine anything to equal it anywhere else in the world!

For just a few minutes the stage paused at the summit and I looked wistfully down onto Dominion Creek which had been my home for the last six years. It was then I realized just how much I had come to love this beautiful valley and Oh, how much I regretted leaving it!

There was a choking lump in my throat and hot tears swimming in my eyes as, silently, I bid each familiar mountain, rock, and tree farewell, and the dear little log cabin nestled there in the valley. Then the stage started down the steep road to Dawson, reaching town and the Regina Hotel in the early evening after a very hard day's ride.

Next day I shivered when I watched the mighty Yukon struggling with its load of gathering ice. It was late September now and before many days the Yukon would be a solid mass of formidable ice.

Ed had been able to get reservations on one of the last steamers leaving Dawson for the city of Whitehorse. From there we would travel by White Pass railroad to Skagway—then it would be home, to Tacoma, by steamer and train.

That last day while waiting for the boat which was scheduled to leave Dawson before noon, Ed gave Clemy an American quarter to buy something to take on the boat as a special treat.

Clemy hurried off to a nearby store and came back with five candy-cigars, the very most he could possibly get for his money! Then we strolled over to the fire station to view the exciting new fire engine. Near the station on Front Street, chained to a post, was a little black bear. He was a very tame, friendly cub—a real pet of everyone in town.

When the little fellow smelled the candy cigars he stood up on his hind legs and put his paws on Clemy's shoulders, sniffing him, trying to locate the enticing sweets. Then he dropped his paws to the ground and searched through Clemy's pockets but Ed, anticipating what might hap-

---
*The Orr and Turkey Stage Coach Company ran the stages from Dawson to the creeks. They began the route about 1901, making daily trips to The Grand Forks. By 1904 the government had made a road to Dominion Creek.

pen, had deftly slipped the candy away. Of course the children who were gathered nearby were delighted with the cub's antics and there were some adults taking pictures.

We had been told that our steamer would be late in leaving the Aurora Dock, but pretty soon the captain of the steamer, Victorian, tooted the whistle which meant "All aboard." The children and I scrambled on ship and told Ed a hurried, tearful goodbye; when the boat pulled away, the children and I, leaning at the rail, waved and waved, for as long as we could see our dear Edward.

After Dawson had faded from view I went into my stateroom and, throwing myself down on the bed, I wept bitterly. Somehow I couldn't be reconciled to leave my husband at this particular time. Bravely, with tears concealed in his eyes, he had said in parting that a year would pass quickly; that he would come Outside with plenty of gold; that we would be reunited; and that I had better start making plans for our dream-house—that beautiful white cottage with a picket fence and bright flowers around the door.

Well, I was crying, crying—a year was a very long time!

There was a large knothole between my stateroom and the one next to it. Presently I heard a gentle knock on the stateroom door. Drying my eyes quickly, I called, "Yes, who is it?"

A sweet woman's voice replied, "I'm your neighbor, please do let me come in." I opened the door and there stood a very refined, attractive-looking, well-dressed young lady.

"Oh, my dear!" she exclaimed, "parting from your husband has been very, very hard on you, and I understand you're going to have another child. Please, I want to help; let me look after your small children while you relax and rest. I promise to take good care of them."

The young lady was so sympathetic and concerned about my welfare that I gratefully accepted her kind offer, and gradually, thanks to her, my panicky feelings subsided and I grew more calm. For two whole days she took full charge of the children, coming after them right after breakfast. From my stateroom window I could see them walking the decks, hand in hand. It seemed she was trying her best to amuse them in every possible way. I was surprised that they had taken a shine to her, immediately, and were so utterly content as they were unaccustomed to strangers. The young lady certainly had an unusual, winsome charm. Clemy liked her too, but he, of course, spent a great deal of the time with me since his father had asked him to look after me. However, I noticed that each time he came to the stateroom he seemed to be carefully searching through the luggage. At last he asked:

"Whére is my little sack of candy-cigars?"

"Oh, Clemy," I told him, "I have a terrible confession. I threw the cigars to the bear just before we boarded the steamer. I was afraid they were made of such cheap material they would make you ill."

Big tears of disappointment filled Clemy's eyes but in a moment he smiled bravely and said seriously, "But I had never seen long candy-cigars before and I wanted to pretend they were real and smoke with the Sourdoughs aboard-ship."

"Oh, Clemy," I said, "I'm dreadfully sorry, so when we reach Skagway I'll buy you some real peppermint stick candy and I'll even try to get you more candy-cigars."

The ride up the Yukon to Whitehorse was, as was to be expected, exciting! We were bucking the current and often small chunks of ice hit the prow of the boat, but our captain was very cautious and skilled and we never traveled after dark.

The third day out the young lady didn't come for the children so, thinking she might be ill, I began inquiring about her. No one seemed to know her whereabouts. Finally I questioned the purser. He hesitated a moment, looked embarrassed, and said:

"Oh, Madame, that woman is a dope fiend! I really do hate to tell you this, but we've had to lock her up in an upper stateroom. She's been there for over twelve hours, raving mad for morphine. If it were possible we would send on ahead to Whitehorse to have the drug ready. Right now we're quietly asking all passengers if they have any of the stuff to tide the poor girl over."

Naturally I was dreadfully shocked at this terrible news for I had blissfully entrusted my little children to her care. Of course I broke into a nervous chill.

When we reached Whitehorse, the first passenger off the steamer was the young addict. She was carried on a stretcher by the deck hands. Her face was set and white; her eyes wild and glazed. She looked as if she had passed through a hideous nightmare. (Often since that day I've wondered who she really was, and then too, I've wished that I might have thanked her for her kindness and sympathy although there were those among the passengers who thought she could have been feeding my children dope—an awful thought!)

The next morning, early, we left the town of Whitehorse by train, by-passing Miles Canyon, the Lewes River, Lake Marsh and Lake Taggish. Soon we came within view of Lake Bennett. It did not seem possible, in looking over the lake on this fine day, that such a beautiful body of water could really be as treacherous as I had experienced it on my way going North in '99!

After traveling along the cliff of the lake (left side) for its full length, we finally reached the upper end where we began the long, gradual climb to the White Pass summit.

At the summit the Canadian Customs officers came aboard to search everyone. They were looking for undeclared gold which some people might be guilty of trying to smuggle out of Yukon Territory. This would be the last whack at departing travelers before they would leave Canada.

All ladies were told to go into one special coach for inspection, the men into another. There, believe me, we had absolutely no secrets from the matron!

We even had to remove our shoes, loosen our corsets, and let down our hair so that the stern-faced policewoman could thoroughly search every inch of us. Everyone taking gold out of the county was supposed to have declared it and paid the tax before leaving their port of departure. If smugglers were caught, their gold was immediately confiscated.

Well, no one, apparently, in our crowd was found guilty of evading the Canadian Customs for soon we were turned over to the American Customs who also went over us with a fine tooth comb. But at last we had passed through that unpleasant double ordeal and were on our way again, now in American Territory.

The distance from the Summit to Skagway is only a little over twenty miles, but it is a very steep, spectacular descent. Winding hairpin turns gave us two hours of breath-taking views. But the most spectacular view of all was when we passed over the high, new cantilever* bridge which spanned the famous Dead Horse Gulch.* Looking down, we could see the whitening skeletons of hundreds of dead horses that had been sacrificed by the stampeders. Also, from this point, to the right,

---

*The Dead Horse Gulch cantilever bridge wasn't fully completed until about 1900. First train passengers rode part way around rim and into the canyon with the aid of switch-backs. Bridge is 300 feet above canyon.

A late steamer going against the ice floes on the Yukon, near Dawson.

Horse-drawn sleigh which began travel between Dawson City, Y.T., and Whitehorse about 1904. (Courtesy, Dick Racine)

Robert W. Service, famous Poet Laureate of the Yukon, 1906.
Made the gold-rush come alive in poetry.

Robert W. Service and his cabin in Dawson, about 1908, when he was
a clerk at the Canadian Bank of Commerce. Previously, he
lived at Whitehorse where he wrote his first poems.

FAREWELL TO THE NORTH

across the gulch, were portions of the torturous, old, gold-rush trail of '98 etched against the canyon's sides. But gone were the miseries of the trail, for it was completely deserted now.

Our small narrow gauge train had tremendous power, both for climbing and holding back on the grades. There was a terrific drop of altitude in spots and the little Duchess Engine puffed and held back her cars on the 36-inch width track with giant compression. At last, in the late afternoon, we chugged into Skagway—the city which a few years earlier had been called "the most lawless spot on the face of the earth." Now it seemed like almost any other fast-growing frontier-seaport.

Our trip from Skagway by steamer to Vancouver, B.C. was uneventful. In Vancouver we transferred to a passenger train for Tacoma. But it was on this train that we became quite a curiosity, for Ella and Paul had never seen cows, pigs, chickens, ducks, or geese.

From the train window they now saw many of these animals, especially when we passed numerous farms. Of course the children went wild with ecstasy over each wonderful new sight and would screech and yell out their delight, much to the amazement and amusement of all the passengers in our coach.

When we passed an orchard full of red apples Ella became greatly excited and yelled, "See the baked apples! Oh, see the baked apples!" She had never seen fresh apples before and to see them growing on trees was something to scream about. Clemy drew attention from the passengers when he showed his poke of gold and talked of Dawson and the Klondike like a seasoned old miner.

The children and I arrived in Tacoma in early evening and went straight to the home of my mother and Ena who welcomed us with open arms and tears of joy. At last we were safely home from the Klondike! At last! At last!

The following spring a golden-haired, blue-eyed daughter who looked like an angel was born to me. Then it was that I appreciated the wisdom of being Outside, for in order to successfully have this child I needed special medical care which I could not have had in the North.

I named the new baby "Rowena," after my own sister, Rowena. (Ena was her nickname.) Altho' I couldn't know it then, this precious child was destined to become a well-known artist—a painter of Indians of the Pacific Northwest—and her name was to be in "Who's Who of American Women Artists." (Rowena Lung Alcorn)

Chapter 34

BRICKS OF GOLD AND ALASKA FORGET-ME-NOTS

Encouraging letters came from the Klondike all through the winter and following summer. Ed wrote that Joe and he and the miners were working like beavers and that the pay-streak was beyond their expectations. He wrote, too, that they were having a "flock" of visitors. One, a budding young Yukon poet, down for a few days from Whitehorse named Robert W. Service, who had recently written, "The Spell of the Yukon," a poem everyone was talking about. "And he's quite a walker," said Ed. "Made it out from Dawson in record time. Got here just as I was taking burnt biscuits from the oven. I offered him lunch and he ate with relish, burnt biscuits and all. After lunch I drew his shadow on a sheet hanging on the cabin wall. The sun cast a fine silhouette. It is my first attempt at portrait drawing. Will try to bring it home, also will try to get a copy of 'Spell of the Yukon.' "

Time has a way of passing. It was late summer of 1906. Then Ed wrote with joyous exhilaration that he and Joe had hit the jack-pot—a big bang-up affair, and that they were now at the assayer's office in Dawson having their gold melted up into gold bricks to be sent to Seattle where the U.S. Government would buy them. He also said that he was selling the sled-dogs to the man taking over the claim and that Rover would have a good home in Dawson where he would be happy and continue to entertain the miners with his "talk, laugh, dance act." Ed said he hated to part with Rover but felt that the dog would be much happier in the North.

At last, late in the fall, Ed arrived in Tacoma. It was a noisy, hilarious greeting he received from our children. With mixed emotions of great joy and thankfulness I welcomed him back to the family and put Baby Rowena into his arms.

"Why! This pink cherub has eyes like wild forget-me-nots* of Alaska," exclaimed Ed, hugging her fondly. "And do you know," he laughed mischievously, "she's half American and half Canadian. Yes, you bet! She got her first spark of life in Yukon Territory." Ed had

*The official Alaska flower is the wild forget-me-not.

brought nine bricks of gold—his share of the claim. Each brick was worth about $9,000, enough to start a good real estate business with a nest egg left over. Soon, we had a comfortable home for our growing children, and in a few years another daughter joined our family. We named her Helen, after her Aunt Helen of New York.

Ed and I soon forgot our rigorous struggles in the North and only remembered the country with affection. When Joe would come to visit and spend an evening, as did some of our other Klondike friends, we would usually gather 'round the piano for an old-fashioned sing. Our children had good voices and we formed kind of a family chorus. Ed and Joe always loved to sing together in the Klondike and now, somehow, their voices blended better than ever. When we would exhaust our repertoire, many times we would talk of "the good old days in the Klondike."

The children loved stories of the North and Clemy often joined in, for he had a gifted, vivid way of telling things. At school he was much in demand during the story hour as he was the only child in school who had been in the gold-rush.

After school, many times, I would look through a window and see children in our yard cutting grass, piling wood, or weeding the garden so that Clemy would have more time to tell them stories of the Klondike. Sometimes they would refuse to go home when called and then Clemy would diplomatically say, "Sorry, kids, story is to be continued 'til another time."

Now Clemy was fast becoming known as one of Tacoma's most promising young artists. He attracted quite a lot of attention through his public art exhibits, especially when he showed a large sketch of his conception of how the huge steamer Titanic* must have looked as it sank beneath the waves, taking 1,517 souls to their deaths after the steamer had hit an iceberg going full speed ahead in the North Atlantic Ocean, 1600 mile northeast of New York. Clemy's large picture of this

---

*The Titanic sank April 15, 1912, after hitting an iceberg. The steamer was on her maiden voyage from England. Only a little over 700 people were saved, mostly women and children who were picked up in lifeboats. The Titanic was the largest and most luxurious to date, and had been considered unsinkable. Her passengers included socialites from both continents and scores of financial tycoons, among whom was a male member of the Guggenheims, of Alaska fame. John Jacob Astor lost his life on the Titanic as well as many other very wealthy men. The Titanic was the greatest maritime loss ever recorded. It was a British steamer of the White Star Line.

appalling tragedy was on display in the big Broadway Street window of Rhodes Brothers Department Store in Tacoma.

Yes, I should have known he would become an artist, because as a child, he had tried so hard to reproduce the things that interested him (with his limited art materials) in the Klondike.

But one day tragedy struck a heartbreaking blow. Clemy was suddenly stricken with polio at the age of sixteen, making him a pathetic cripple. He continued to paint and his talent blossomed and matured. Then one day, a year and a half later, his lovable soul slipped away beyond the sunset.

After the loss of our beloved Clemy, our lives limped along. There was his empty chair; his paint brushes; his unfinished canvasses. I busied myself with the family, trying to forget that I had lost my beloved first-born child.

People were still interested in the North. Often I was introduced as "The Little Preacher of the Klondike." I finally consented to teach a young ladies' Bible class at the First Baptist Church in Tacoma. Often fifty young business women would attend. Many times they asked to hear about my church work among the miners. Sometimes I would weave in stories about Clemy. Somehow, it helped ease the pain of losing him, to tell about his life in the Klondike, and how as a little boy he always added his voice to the hymns in the Sunday services at the Dominion Creek roadhouse.

Ed was now successfully launched in a strenuous business career. The years quickly sped by. He had won a fine reputation in Tacoma for his integrity and ability in the business world. Often, he was asked to be master of ceremonies at civic and church affairs, and on many of these occasions he had requests to tell his Alaska-Yukon adventures. People loved to hear them, and surely Ed had had his share of adventure!

Because of his hard work in the Klondike and because he was an expert accountant, he had learned the valuable lesson of handling money carefully and wisely. His heart-breaking experience with the dishonest lawyer on Claim No. 10 Above Lower Discovery had left its mark. He demanded absolute honesty in all business and personal dealings.

In the 1920's, Ed gave up his real estate business and became the secretary-manager of the Tacoma Association of Credit Men and of the Tacoma Wholesaler's Association, a real honor. He proved to a "lion" in

Will Rogers stopped at Dawson City on his flight to the Orient with Wiley Post in summer of 1935. Afterwards, while trying to make a landing at Point Barrow, they were killed. Photo shows "Apple Jimmy," well known Sourdough of Dawson with Will Rogers. (Probably the last picture taken of Rogers.) (Courtesy of Margaret McRea)

Gold melted up into bricks and stored in a Dawson bank waiting for shipment. (Courtesy, Dawson Artscraft)

Edward Burchall Lung as he looked when he went to Fairbanks, Alaska. (Note the nugget stick-pin—Klondike gold.)

Fairbanks, the golden heart of Alaska. A Fourth of July celebration in 1913 on Cushman Street.
(Courtesy, Frank Clark)

his work and was greatly respected and trusted by friends and business associates.

Always, since his return from the Klondike, he had yearned to see the great Alaska-Tanana region where Fairbanks now stands. The good Lord let him have that wonderful opportunity in the summer of 1936 (June 17 - July 9). Ed was a happy delegate with thirty-two Chamber of Commerce members who went on a tour called, "The Tacoma Chamber of Commerce Alaska Goodwill Tour."

Among the prominent representatives were the Mayor of Tacoma, Mr. George A. Smitley, and Dr. Edward H. Todd, president of the College of Puget Sound. Also Joseph W. Quick, attorney for the Western Council, N.P.R.Y., went along, as did Lawrence Johnson, vice-president of the First United Mutual Savings. Mr. T. A. Stevens, secretary-manager of the Chamber, arranged the trip. Some of the other important members who went to Fairbanks were: Robert H. Hyde, Edward Griffin, C. C. Garland, E. C. Richards, S. M. Collins and Harry R. Lawton. The last three mentioned were on the board of the Alaska Development Committee.

A well-known newspaperman, Otto Perlit, of the Tacoma Daily Times, was an important delegate, as was Col. Gordon L. Finley and Dr. Horace Whiteacre, prominent physician and former Chamber of Commerce president. Also traveling with Ed was his old friend, S. S. Waterman, sales manager of the St. Paul and Tacoma Lumber Company.

In Fairbanks the men from Tacoma were royally received and entertained. The booklet, printed on gold-gilt paper and distributed to Alaskans, said: (excerpts)

"Fairbanks, we salute you—We have come to make acknowledgments. The trail of 1898 marks the beginning of your growth. We wish to contribute to your prosperity... Your commerce clears our ports, enriching our people... We are here to find in what manner Puget Sound and the State of Washington can better serve you. You have inherited a new, a raw country, and have achieved the '49th State.' (In 1936 people were already calling Alaska "The 49th State," although it did not officially become that until 1958 under President Eisenhower.)

So, at last, Ed had a great dream fulfilled. And those on the trip to "The Golden Heart of Alaska" were proud and pleased that he was with them—a real Sourdough in every sense of the word—to add color and history to the trek. No, Ed never got to dig for gold in the Tanana. But he saw where Felix Pedro, an Italian immigrant, made the momentous discovery in the Chena River on July 22, 1902, which made Fairbanks the center of the Gold Mining Empire. And Ed had another wonderful dream come true—he saw the great mountain called by one tribe of Indians, "Bulshaia," and by another tribe, "Denalee" (Denali). It was the great mountain that Dicky and Monks had discovered in 1896, and named Mt. McKinley. It was the mountain that Ed and his party had heard about while they were at Circle City in 1897 before they tried to go with the Indians to the Tanana in quest of gold.

Time raced along. Six years later, in early September of 1942, the year after Pearl Harbor, Edward was stricken suddenly with a severe stroke, a heart-breaking blow! (Pearl Harbor Japanese attack Dec. 7, 1941).

Good old Joe Latshaw, like a Guardian Angel that he always seemed, now in his eighties, came faithfully to encourage and help "Eddy" over this last, rough trail. He sat for hours by Ed's couch, cheering him and calling him back to health. It was touching to see the two old Sourdough partners together. For many weeks Ed was in low spirits and had many dark days, but at last he was beginning to conquer his crippling illness. Of course, it was necessary for him to retire from active business, and so, six months later, when he could walk with a cane, we bade goodbye to good old Joe and all of our friends and relatives and moved to Santa Barbara to be near our three children, Ella, Paul and Helen. (Ella, a singer; Paul, a chemistry teacher; Helen, a singer.)

Among the letters that followed us was one from a business associate written in September soon after our arrival in beautiful Santa Barbara:

Tacoma, Washington
Sept. 25, 1943

My dear friend Ed:
I was pleased to hear of your safe arrival in the sunny South, and I suppose by this time you have taken root to a degree. Just so you don't allow the roots to become so firmly lodged as to

---

*Mr. Josiah H. Latshaw married in Tacoma. His grandson, Harvey Warren, became a noted stage artist. His stage settings for "Hello, America," have received national acclaim both in New York and Las Vegas.

keep you from returning here once in a while... that is the thing.

We're having "Zebra" initiation and a membership* dinner Tuesday evening. Surely wish you were here to assist in the initiation. Kay Ewart, Vern Day, and Warren Watts are the candidates. A bunch of us met Thursday night to make plans and go over the ritual.

You know, Ed, I've missed you a whole lot since you have been out of the office. You have been the source of a great deal of what I have learned in credit work. Throughout 18 years, I had come to depend on your availability whenever I needed advice. It was a great help to a beginner to have counsel every day.

You've made a still greater contribution to my life in a spiritual way. I do not know a finer example of integrity in the business world than you have provided. I have been amazed many times at your ability to see clearly what was right and honorable in a perplexing situation. And the thing that impressed me, was that you always chose the right path without the least hesitation. You didn't seem even to be tempted to do the wrong thing. The character you have expressed has been a real inspiration to me in my effort to be Christian in my business relations. If I succeed in approaching the excellence of your example, I shall feel that I have paid you back for providing it. I am satisfied that the good life is the only successful one, and I believe you are a success. I hope these words will give you some pleasure, for they are sincere appreciation of my enjoyment in our friendship.

I look forward to seeing you again, Ed, whenever either of us shall travel far enough in the direction of the other. In the meantime be sure you have my best wishes for your happiness and renewed health.

Sincerely,

CARL O. PANKS

Because, during the years, we had had a large family to care for in Tacoma, the little white cottage with the picket fence and bright flowers around the door, which had filled our dreams and hopes in the Klondike, didn't come to actual fulfillment until we were aged and living in Santa Barbara.

---

*Edward Burchall Lung was voted honorary secretary-manager for life of The Tacoma Association of Credit Men and The Tacoma Wholesalers' Association.

And now, as my dear Edward and I walk arm in arm together here in the warmth of California, we often reminisce about our exciting gold-rush days. And then, sometimes when Ed dozes in his chair, my mind is filled with deep and pleasant reverie.

Like a flash, my memory whisks me back to the Klondike and once more we are young and are walking through the Valley of Gold. Oh! what a sheaf of fragrant memories! And then I see our little log cabin—our pink flannel heaven, where we were so happy. And, again, I see the figure of a small boy with his dog—searching, searching the hills. It's Clemy, dressed in a parka and a red stocking cap, searching, searching for the "Ancient Channel and rainbow's pot of gold."

And now, when I think of the great Alaska-Yukon Territory, with all of its rich treasures stretching far to the North, gradually beginning to have a network of highways and airlines, my mind turns back to the torturous trails of 1897, '98 and '99, and again I see thousands of intrepid stampeders, my husband with them, bent low under heavy packs, struggling, struggling, up over Chilkoot and the White Pass. Now, I think of all the new inventions and modern advantages that have come to the territory, and I am glad that I have lived to see these things come to pass.

Recently, Edward and I celebrated our fifty-fourth wedding anniversary. We realize that we have lived long and useful lives, and too, we know that life has been unusually good to us. True, it has given us "Black Sands of Sorrow," like the loss of our beloved Clemy, but life has also given us many happy years of Gold. And, as we go bravely and serenely towards the sunset of our lives, we keep our eyes fixed on wonderful Polaris—the North Star.

Yes, we are happy to be among the honored members of *The International Alaska-Yukon Sourdoughs, the Pioneers of The Last Frontier of America!*

THE END

At the summit of White Pass is the Canadian-American boundary line. Northwest Mounted Police and U. S. Army officers stand guard—flags side by side, flying high.

AT EIGHTY-TWO

By Robert W. Service

The last of living is the best;
The olden years are golden years,
When there will come a rhythmic rest
Beyond the tempest and the tears;
When memories of wine and song
Are bravely buried in the past,
And we to home and love belong,
The best of living is the last.

The shawl and slipper days are good,
This I can stalwartly affirm,
As I defy in mellow mood
The petulance of waiting worm,
For now I am my utter own,
Playing the pantaloon with zest,
A monarch on an armchair throne,
The last of living is the best.

And so, sweet people, have no fear,
I tell you from a brimming heart,
Old age is rich with hope and cheer,
You may rejoice ere you depart.
A childwise calm will come to you,
The pain and passion overpast,
Ah, you will see my say is true,
The best of living is the last.

GOOD-BYE, LITTLE CABIN

By Robert W. Service

O dear little cabin, I've loved you so long,
And now I must bid you good-bye!
I've filled you with laughter, I've thrilled you with song
And sometimes I've wished I could cry.
Your walls have witnessed a weariful fight,
And rung to a won Waterloo:
But oh, in my triumph I'm dreary to-night—
Good-bye, little cabin, to you!

Your roof is bewhiskered, your floor is a-slant,
Your walls seem to sag and to swing;
I'm trying to find just your faults, but I can't—
You poor, tired, heart-broken old thing!
I've seen when you've been the best friend that I had
Your light like a gem on the snow;
You're sort of a part of me—Gee, but I'm sad;
I hate, little cabin, to go.

Below your cracked window red raspberries climb;
A hornet's nest hangs from a beam;
Your rafters are scribbled with adage and rhyme,
And dimmed with tobacco and dream.
"Each day has its laugh," and "Don't worry, just work."
Such mottoes reproachfully shine.
Old calendars dangle—what memories lurk
About you, dear cabin of mine!

I hear the world-call and the clang of the fight;
I hear the hoarse cry of my kind;
Yet well do I know, as I quit you to-night,
It's Youth that I'm leaving behind.
And often I'll think of you, empty and black,
Moose antlers nailed over your door:
Oh, if I should perish my ghost will come back
To dwell in you, cabin, once more!

How cold, still and lonely, how weary you seem!
A last wistful look and I'll go.
Oh, will you remember the lad with his dream!
The lad that you comforted so.
The shadows enfold you, it's drawing to-night;
The evening star needles the sky:
And huh! but it's stinging and stabbing my sight—
God bless you, old cabin, good-bye!

INDEX

A

A.P. & C. Co. 236, 237
A. J. Goddard, Steamer 48
"A Lady's Secret" 192
A Wedding 141
Adams, Alec (Dawson Actor, Preface) 137
Adams Hill (Gold) 96
Addict (Young) 33
Aerial Tramway 28
Agitator, Dominion Creek 324
Ajax (Barge) 17
Alaska Coast 57
Alaska Commercial Co. 71, 73, 75, 87, 111, 170, 233
Alaska Dogs 81, 212
Alaska Indian Legend 23, 70
Alaska Map 14
Alaska Placer & Coal Co. 234, 238
Alaska Scenes 1, 3, 4
Alaska Territory 14
Alexander McDonald Hotel (Burned) 76
Alexieff, Commander of Russians 322
Alger, Russel (U.S. General) 203
Alice Steamer 19
Alki Steamer 17, 163
Allen, Jene (Mr. & Mrs.) Owned Klondike Nugget 277, 302
Alley Girls (White Chapel) 82
Amazons (Hunting Husbands) 218
American Creek (Alaska) 229, 233
Americans (Dawson Population) 88
American Territory 60
Anaconda (Gold Claim) 102
Ancient Channel 86, 90, 96, 97, 100, 342
Anderson, Charlie 102
Angel Light 127
Anglican Log Church 56
Annie Wright's Seminary 5
Anvil Creek (Nome) 175
Apollo (Greek Sun God) 50
Apple, C. J. (Tinsmith) 157
Arctic Circle 218, 229
Arctic Express Co. 157
Argonauts Preface, 55
Arizona Charlie (Meadows) 77
Armour Packing Co. 205
Artna (Gold Claim) 102
Asbestos 69
Ash, Harry C. 66, 97
Ashly, Thomas 104
Assayer's Office (Dawson) 336
Aster, John Jacob (Titanic Wreck) 337

Atlin Lake 37
Atwater, Ben (Famous Mailman) 58, 236, 264. 280
Augustine, Mt. Cook's Inlet 302
Aunty Fanny 202
Aurora Borealis 127
Aurora Dock 332
Aurora Saloon 72, 140
Australians (Fifteen) 87
Avalanche 26
Ayers, W. E. 104

B

Bacon, Constable, Mountie 155
Baggs, Doc. 20
Balsome City (Log Cabin) 292
Bank of British North America (burned) 76
Banner Line (River Boats) Pat Galvin 105
Banshee 252, 256, 261, 269
Baptist Church, First, (Tacoma) 338
Barbary Coast 20
Barbier, Mr. 115
Barna, Marie (Opera Star) 204
Barrett, Joe (Gold Discovery on Hill) 112, 113, 120
Barrington, Captain 49, 75
Barrington, Syd 284
Bartlett, Michael (Freighter) 122
Barton, U.S. Gold Recorder (Eagle) 236
Battle of Manila 67
Bean, Mr. 15
Bear Creek (Nuggets) 169, 329
Beck, George H. (purser) 8
Beck, Joe (Upper Discovery) 106, 113
Bedrock 324
Beeman's Chewing Gum 205
Below Discovery 119
Bench Claim 120
Bennett City 39
Bennett, Lake 33, 37, 38
Benton, Mr. 99
Bering Sea 174
Bernhardt, Sarah (Great Actress) 205, 273
Berry Brothers (Frank & Clarence) 97, 101, 228
Berry Claims 97
Bertha, the Adder 139
Bertram, N. H. 113, 229
Big Boy (The Horrible Fighter) 210
Big Clean-Up Process 84
Big Louie (Frenchman) 318, 324, 325, 327

347

348 TRAIL TO NORTH STAR GOLD

Big Salmon River 53
Big Thing Mine 44
Bigamist (With Fast Dog Team) 220
Binford, Thomas; Publisher, Portland, Oregon (Acknowledgments)
Binford, Thomas; Binfords & Mort Publishers (Acknowledgments)
Birch Creek 57
Birch Tree Wedding 218
Bishop Bompas (Of The Yukon) 42, 43, 56, 57
Bijax (Barge) 17
Black, Mrs. George (Wife of 7th Commissioner 215
Black Sand 84
Black Sand, Coal & Gold 242
Black Sand and Gold 314
Blair, John (Actor) 204
Bleeker, Harry H. (Attorney at Dawson) 164, 316
Blickensderfer (A First Typewriter) 126
Blizzard 231
Blue Clay 180
Bob (The Dominion Tramp) 262, 263
Bob (The Snarler) 202
Bodega Saloon 72
Bonanza 1, 18, 83, 95, 96, 100, 104, 110
Bonanza Valley 83, 84
Booth, Evangeline (Salvation Army) 304
Boris (Malemute Dog-Team Leader) 129
Boulder Hill (Gold) 96
Bowers, Charles 20, 22
Boyle, Joseph 134, 329
Bracket, George 23
Brady, Governor of Alaska (1898) 31
Bratsberg, Bert & Thora Preface
Breeze, Captain 66, 101
British American Commercial Co. 105
Brothers, John 104
Brown Bear 107
Buel, Art (Klondike Nugget Cartoonist) 78, 270 & Preface
Buffalo Bill's Hut 117, 233
Bulshaia, Mt. (Indian Name for Mt. McKinley 340
Burnett, Charles 119
Burns, Clement 276
Byers, Captain Tom Preface
Byrnie, William (Frozen Feet) 284, 285
Byrnteson, John (Nome) 275

C

Cain, John 89, 94
Calhoun, T. W. 229
Cameron, Alex 113
Cameron, Rhoda (Famous Actress) 205
Canadian Air Lines Preface
Canadian Bank of Commerce 114, 172
Canadian Boundary Line 60
Canadian Customs Officer 36, 334
Canadian Rockies 110, 320
CanCan Girls 77
Candle 131, 196
Candy Cigar 331, 333
Candy Tom 20
Canovan, Mr. 232
Cans (tin) and their many uses 266
Cantly (Klondike Mining Inspector) 113, 115
Cantwell, George (Dawson Photographer) 73
Canyon City 30, 46
Cape Nome 131, 173, 177
Cape Rodney 176
Carboneaux (French Count) 101
Carcross 42
Caribou Crossing 41
Caribou Settlement, Dominion Creek 113, 114, 141, 209, 279, 313
Carmack, George 42, 55, 56, 57, 97, 98, 100
Carmack, Kate 42
Carnegie Library (Dawson) 304
Carrier Pigeons 73
Carter's Liver Pills 91
Casey's Rock 51
Cashman, Nelly (Angel of the Gold Camps) 179, 180
Cassiar Bar 51
Catholic Mission 68
Cedarstron, Baron Relf (Swedish Nobleman) 204
Center Creek (Nome) 175
Chamber of Commerce (Tacoma) 339
Chamberlain, Al 111, 115
Chamberlain, Elmer 66
Champs 133, 137
Chattel (Best Dog) 292
Cheechako Hill (Gold) 97, 100
Cheeseman, Mrs Roy W. (Acknowledgments)
Cheechakos 24, 100, 109, 212, 282
Chena River (Near Fairbanks) 340
Chicago 16
Chicken Creek, Alaska (Gold Discovery) 238, 241, 317
Chief Isaac 70
Chilkat Indians 57, 59
Chilkat Island 8
Chilkoot Pass 16, 37, 38, 78, 291
Chilkoot Pass Avalanche 291

INDEX

Chilkoot Pass Trail 19, 28, 37, 342
Chilkoot Tramway 30
Chinaman Yee 20
Chittick Brothers 238
Chittick, Cash Mr. & Mrs. 277, 302
Christmas Benefit 230
Christmas (Dominion Creek) 194, 195
Christmas Dinner 156
Christmas Tree 194
Churchill, Lady Randolph 203
Circle City 62, 229, 230, 231
City of Gold (Dawson) 63, 80, 163
City of Seattle, Steamer 17, 19
Clam Shells 97
Clancey's Saloon 24
Clapp, C. W. 102
Clara Nevada, Steamer 8
Clayson, Anne 14, 153
Clayson, Bill 161
Clayson Fred 14, 101, 152, 160, 163
Clem (Clemy) 2, 7, 11, 44, 63, 100, 165, 169, 196, 204, 207, 208, 337, 348
Clement, Horatio C. 67
Clement, Mrs. Horatio 2
Cleopatra 273
Closeleigh Settlement 45, 48
Cloud of Glory 143
Coal & Gold 242
Coal Mine on Yukon 55
Coal On the Yukon 236, 241
Cocos Island Treasure Hunt 302
Collins, S. M. (Fairbanks Tour) 339
Colossal Discovery (Gold) 96
Combination Theater 134
Confidence Game 221
Conolly, Tim (Dominion Gold) 319
Conrad, Frank 104
Conrad Gold Camp 44
Constantine (Mountie Captain) 88
Cook, Fred Preface
Cook, Joe (Roadhouse Owner) 111, 161
Cookbook 207
Cook's Inlet 302
Copper River 244
Corbell Camille (Dominion Gold) 319
Corona, Steamer 9
Corby, Frank 141
Corby (Mountie Sergeant) 60
Corky, Louis (Dominion Gold) 319
Cory Party 264
Cottage City, Steamer 17
Courtesan 16
Cow (First in the Klondike) 310
Craft, Mr. & Mrs. (At Five Fingers) 284
Crawford, Mr. 47
Credit Men 328

Crime on the Yukon 58
Cromer, Mr. B. 13
Crowly, W. M. 104
Crystal Theater (Pantages) 190
Cub Bear (Dawson) 331
Curling Game and Other Sports 276
Currie, Mr. 111
Cushman, Mr. 115
Customs 37
Czar of Russia 322

D

Daily Alaskan Newspaper 21
Dalton, Aggie (School Teacher) 218
Dalton, Jack 97
Dalton Trail 57, 58
Daly, Nelly 14, 51, 152, 157, 222
Daly, Mrs. 82
Daly Cafe 65
Dante's Inferno 247
David Harum (Book Title) 153
Davis, Grandma 6
Dawson Amateur Club 276
Dawson Artscraft Preface
Dawson City 236, 286
Dawson Dude 61
Dawson Fires 71, 72, 73
Dawson Food Famine 237
Dawson, George Mercer 68
Dawson Landlords 82
Dawson Stampede 170
Dawson (West) 238
Dawson, Y. T. 34, 43, 61, 62, 63, 77, 90, 99, 108, 164, 171, 173, 304, 325, 329
Dawson's Painted Girls 79
Day, Vern (Zebra Initiation) 341
Dead Horse Gulch 334
Dear Little Cabin 116
Debney, Charlie 66, 115
Denharn, Jim S. (of Sacramento) 281, 283, 284
de Journel, Fernand 306, 312
Denali (Mt. McKinley) 340
Dene Indians 57
Densmore, Mr. 208
Denver, Colorado 18
Desperate Plight 209
Devil 326, 327
Dewey's Victory in Manila 111
Dexter Creek (Nome) 175
Diamond Jim Brady 188
Diamond Ring (Stolen) 158
Diamond Tooth Gertie 68, 187
Diana Mt. (Cook's Inlet) 302
Diaries (Gold Rush) 73, 90, 282, 287, 288, 290, 301
Dickerson, Marie 205
Dicky and Monks (Discovered Mt. McKinley) 248

Dickson (Mountie Counstable) 157
Dickson, Mr. (Diary of 1898) 286
Dime Novels 11
Dines, John (Mining Recorder, Dawson) Preface
Dipper 6
Discovery Claim, American Creek 234
Discovery (Gold) 57, 100
Dixon's Pencils 205
Dnieper, Mr. (Dominion Gold) 319
Dolly Dimples, Burro at Smuggler's Cove 32
Dominion Creek 1, 83, 103, 113, 118, 119, 248, 331
Dominion Creek Roadhouse 216
Dominion Hotel 79
Dominion Valley 110, 303
Donaghy (Attorney in Dawson) 164
Donovan, Jack 97
Dope Fiend 333
Douglas Isle 10, 14
Dowie, Fran (Show Producer) Preface
Dredges (Klondike) 304
Duchess Engine 33, 34
Duffield, Blanche 205
Dugas, Dawson Judge 164
Dupont, Aime 203
Dwyer, Frankie 22
Dyea, City of 25, 26, 30
Dyea Indian Village 31
Dynamite 8

E

Eads, Murry (Owned the Flora Dora Hotel) 78
Eagle Brand Milk 201, 310
Eagle City, Alaska 233, 235
Eagon, Dan (Young Prize Fighter) 287
Eames, Emma (Opera Star) 204
Eastman's Kodaks 205
Eaton, George 232
Edison Talking Machines 205, 230
Edison, Thomas (Inventions) 67
Edison's Projectroscopes 67
Edward 65, 196, 208, 275, 314, 327
Eisenhower, President U.S.A. 339
Eldorado, Bonanza, Quartz & Placer Mining Co. 101
Eldorado Queen (Mine) 102
Eldorado River 1, 18, 83, 97, 100, 105, 110
Eleven-Mile Post 35
Elijah 143
Eliza Anderson Expedition 108
Ellinger, Casper 232
Emery, Mr. 119
Ena (Rowena Clement) 3, 335
England 164
Ensley Creek 60

Enterprise (Meat Grinder) 206
Eskimos 109
Eureka (Gold Claim) 102
Evil Aura 33
Ewart, Kay 341
Excelsior, Steamer 17, 19
Expert Accountant 338
Exploding Bullets 72

F

Fair View Hotel (Plush) 79, 101, 220
Fairbanks, Alaska 217, 248, 338, 339
Fairbanks, Lulu (Former Alaska Weekly Editor) Acknowledgments
False Bed-rock (Nome) 180
Family Caravan (Lung) 83
Fan-Tail Trail 37
Farming (near Dawson) 216
"Fat Little Poke" 122
Fathers of the Nome District 175
Fawcett (Gold Commissioner, Dawson) 88, 106
Fax Brothers (farmers) 216
Fay, Mr. (Skagway Bartender) 26
Fernand de Journel 311, 312
Field, Mary (Actress & Sister of Diamond Tooth Gertie) 68
Finley, Col. Gordon L. (Fairbanks Tour) 339
Finnigan, Pat (Purser) 232
Fisher, Bud (Boatmaster & colorful Old Sourdough) Preface
Fisher, Mr. 236
Fisher, Nunan C. 284
Flame Act (Klondike Kate) 77
Flash Fire (Cabin) 181
Flora Dora Hotel Casino 78
Flora, Steamer 48, 54
Follner, E. F. 58
Footprints 231, 255
Forest Fire (Dominion Creek) 245
Forget-me-nots (Alaska State Flower) 336
Forks of Gold 100
Fortier, Albert (Dominion Gold) 319
Forty-Mile 62, 97, 98, 157
Foster, "Slim Jim" (Soapy Smith's Man) 20
Fourth of July Creek, Alaska 236
Franklin (The new typewriter) 206
Franklin Gulch 244
Fraser (Gold-Rush settlement) 37
Fraser, A. H. 58
Free Drinks (Saloon) 66
French Hill (Gold) 96
Frenchie Joe (Stampeder) 219
Frenchmen on Dominion Creek 113, 141, 167

INDEX 351

Fricks, Mr. 119
Fritz (sled-dog) 129
Front Street (Dawson) 66, 321
Frostbite 232
Ft. Selkirk (Old Hudson's Bay Fort and Trading Center) 56
Fugitives of the Yukon 157
Fussel, Capt. & Mrs. 155, 162

G

Gage, Mr. 101
Gaisford, Euly 98
Galvin, Pat (from Montana) 104 (Klondike Steamer King)
Garland, E. C. (Fairbanks trek) 339
Garnets & Rubies 83
Gaslight Follies Preface
Gastineau Channel 15
Gauvin Brothers (Wilfred & Alfred) 104
Gay Hill 86, 87
"Gee" turn right (dogs) 277
George W. Elder, Steamer 17
Gertie, Diamond Tooth (Actress) 77
Gesche, Fred 232
Gibb, James A. (Sentinels of the North Pacific) 3 & Acknowledgments
Globe (claim) 102
"Glory Hole" (Juneau) 16
Goddard, Miss 203
Gold 52
Gold Bottom Creek 1, 83, 87, 174
Gold Bricks 336
Gold Camp 68
Gold Commissioner (Dawson) 313
Gold Discovery 68
Gold-fever-frenzy 232
Gold-fevered men 287
Gold Fields 82, 85
Gold Hill 96, 99, 101
Gold Mining 84
Gold Mining Empire 340
Gold Rush Diaries 109 (Ed Lung's)
Gold Run River 110
Gold Stampede 69
Gold Stampede (Dawson) 169
Gold Stampede, Nome 173, 174
Gold (Tanana) 229
Golden Heart of Alaska (Fairbanks) 339
Golden North Hotel 24
Golden Rule 136
Golovin Bay, Alaska 175, 177
"Good-bye Little Cabin" Robert Service 343-4
Goodwin, Charles 281, 290
Goodwin, Nat (Actor) 204
Gould, Howard (multi-millionaire) 203

Gould, Jay (multi-millionaire) 203
Governor's Mansion (Dawson) 304
Gramaphone 74, 231
Grand Forks 83, 97, 100
Grand Pacific Hotel 275
Grauman, Sid (newsboy; later, Theater King) 80
Grave-yard claim (Gold) 241
Graves, Shelly 229
Graves, Thomas (Cache robber) 157, 158, 161, 162, 164
Great Diva, Nordica 204
Great Panic 2
Green, Col. 284
Green (Pugilist from San Francisco) 134
Greentree Hotel (burned) Dawson 76
Griffin, Edward (Fairbanks trek) 339
Guggenheims (Klondike) 304, 337
"Guggies" (Klondike) 304
Gun Fight 25
Gypsy Organ Grinder 24

H

Haines Landing 57
Half-castes 82
Hamilton, Charles 228
Hamilton (Steamer) (Rammed by the Ice) 62
Hand, Fred (Acknowledgments, Sourdough Alaska Yukon President 1969)
Harper, Arthur 56, 69
Harper and Ladue Milling and Mining Co. 69
Harper's Landing 56
Harris, Richard 14
Harrison, James V. 72, 114
Hartwell, John 104
Harum, David (Title of Book) 153
"Haw" (Turn left, dog team command) 277
Hawkins, E. C. (Railroad Engineer) 35
Hawks, Archie McLean (Chilkoot Engineer) 28, 291
Hearst Newspaper Syndicate 229
Hearst, William Randolph 229
Heartbreaking experience 338
Hebb, Paul 66, 72, 74, 111, 172, 176
Hebert, Tom (Freighter and Former Mountie) 181 & Preface
Held, Anna (Opera Star) 204
Helen 337
Hell's Half Acre (Louse Town) 82
Henderson, Patsy 42

Henderson, Robert (Canadian Gold Discoverer) 110
Heney, Michael (Famous White Pass Railroad Engineer) 35
Hepburn Tramway 45
Hershaw, Mr. 114
Hill, George 113
Hill, R. H. 229
Hilliard (Mountie-Sergeant) 141, 313, 314
Hinkley, Bill 112
"Hiyu-Skookum Girl" (Indian Princess) 70
Holly Street 21, 24
Holmes, Burton (Lecturer) 205
Holy City 145
Homemade Broom 116
Homemade Chairs 116
Homemade Hairpins 182
Hootchikoo (Mounted Police Station) 155, 159
Hopkins, Mr. Y. M. 197, 300
Hudson Bay Flour 181
Hudson's Bay Co., Vancouver, B.C. 302
Hudson's Bay Trading Post 56
Hueston Orchestra (Dawson) 71
Humbolt, Steamer 17, 19
Hunker 1, 110
Hunker, Andrew 228
Hunker Creek 175, 185
Hunker Theater 187, 189
Hyde, Robert (Fairbanks Trek) 339

I

Independence Creek (Alaska) 236
Indian Chief 6
Indian Children 52
Indian Dogs 52
Indian Footprints 231
Indian Legend 70
Indian Moccasins 233, 273
Indian Papoose 38
Indian River 105, 110
Indian Sam (Steamer Pilot) 233
Indian Skeletons 69
Indians (Ketchumstock Tribe) 243
Indians (Tanana) 230
Indians, Yukon 1
Ingersol Dollar Watches 205
Inside Passage 1, 7, 8, 9, 10
Irish Prince 35
Iron Horse (Train) 24
Isaiah and the fig plaster 268
Iselin, Mrs. Oliver 203
Island Post 162
Islander, Steamer 9, 17
Italian Jack (Famous dog-team racer) 232, 268

J

Jack-Pot (Gold) 336
Jack Wade Creek (Gold) 241
Jackson, Turner 20
Japan 322
Jeff's Oyster Bar 21, 24
Jewel Song 204
Joe Latshaw 314, 317, 337, 340
Johnson, Charles 228
Johnson, Lawrence (Fairbanks Trek) 339
Johnson, Mike 119
Jones, Senator P. 15
Jourgensen, Mr. 47
Judge, Father William (Catholic Priest) 76
Juneau, Alaska 10, 13, 14, 16
Juneau, Joe 14, 15
Juneau, Mt. 14
Juneau, Solomon 17
Juneau Wharf 25, 26, 28

K

Kahlenborn, Randolph 74
Katzabue (Gold) 238
Kehoe, John (Found the Corpse) 161
Keller, Frank 101
Kerry's Saloon 71
Ketchikan 13
Ketchumstock Mts. 241, 243
Kid West 163, 164
King George VIII 302
King Solomon Hill (Gold) 96
King Solomon's Dome 105, 109, 123, 331
Kirkpatrick 69
Kiwanis Club, Dawson Preface
Kline, Jack 58, 148, 162
Klondike 1, 5, 39, 52, 163, 342
Klondike City 81
Klondike Famine 229
Klondike Gold Rush 176
Klondike Hotel 79, 277
Klondike Kate 77, 184, 185, 189, 190
Klondike Kings 7, 16, 19, 24, 61, 78, 79, 99, 101, 166, 188, 329
Klondike Meat Market 76
Klondike Mines Railway 103
Klondike Region 110
Klondike Stove 116
Klondike Wheel of Gold 110
Knife Indians 57
Knox Gelatin 206
Knutson, Michael 101
Knutson's Nugget 101
Kopanski (Mary Pullen) (Acknowledgments)

INDEX 353

Koyukuk River (Gold) 218
Kulsin (Indian Boy, later named Patsy Henderson) 42
Kyle, Mr. 115

L

La-Ha-Na (Casino and Hotel, Dawson) 72, 144
La Moore, Gussie (Actress, Dawson) 61
Ladue, Joseph 57, 68
La Duke, Mr. 232
Lady Lily 11, 12, 13, 16
Lady Luck 55
Lady Preacher 139, 330
Lake Bennett 37, 334
Lake Linderman 38
Lamb, Charles 104, 228
Lampkins, Web 104
Landerville, Max (Dominion Creek Gold Discoverer) 310
Lange, Max (Yukon Mailman) 151, 161, 218, 270
Lapiere, Alphonse 98
Largest Diamonds 58
LaSalle, David (of Denver) 281
Last Chance Creek 71
Last Dollar Claim (Gold) 102
Latshaw, Joe (Ed's partner) 64, 73, 77, 90, 119, 124, 126, 131, 139, 185, 189, 196
Last Frontier of America 342
Lawton, Harry R. (Fairbanks Trek) 339
Lawyer from San Francisco 113, 331
Leak, Billy 228
Lebarge, Lake 49
Le Syndicat Lyonnaise du Klondike 113, 317
Lewis Island 9
Lewis, Mr. 115
Lewis River 44
Liberty Creek, Alaska 236
Licker, Bud 119
Lillian Davenport 16
Lind, Jenny (Swedish Nightingale) 204
Lindberg, Jefet (Gold Discoverer) 175
Lindshom, Erick O. 175
Lippy, Thomas 101, 228
Little Blanche 87, 110
Little Brimestone Creek 72, 107, 110
Little Chief Gulch 126
Little Duchess Engine 18, 335
Little Moonlight Creek (Gold) 175
"Little One" 328
Little Salmon River 53
Little Skookum Gulch 100

Lloyd, William R. 72, 114
Locke, Captain 10
Log-Cabin 37, 194
London, Jack 42
London Times 57
Long-Nose Snoopy Nelly 168
Long, Joe 114, 115
Longwell, Mr. and Mrs. 114
Lord Selkirk 56
Louse Town 75, 81, 82, 170
Louse Town Trail 83
Lowe, Dick 102, 104, 228
Lowery's Chocolates 206
Lucifer 138, 139
Lung, Edward Burchall 185
Lung, Ella 201
Lung, Paul 306
Lung, Velma 3
Lung's Prehistoric Teeth and Tusks 269
Lynn Canal 10, 30, 34

M

Macauley Tramway 45
Madame Trembley's Dress Shop 62
"Maddest gold-rush" 96
Mae West, Steamer 218
Magnet Hill (gold) 96
Maguire, Mr. (Uncle of William Byrnie) 284, 285, 286
Malemutes 3, 207, 208, 209, 211
Manchester, Duchess of 203
Marlow, Julia (great actress) 204
Marriage Record (Birch Tree) 219
Marsh Lake 44
Marshall, T. Sidney (Commissioner of Affidavits) 316
Martin, Ike (murdered) 58
Martinsen, Ole Preface
Mary Ellen Galvin, Steamer 105
Mastodon (Prehistoric animal) 254, 269
Mathews, Mr. 15
Matson, John (Sourdough) 190
Mattison, Mr. 292
May, T. K. (Ass't Bank Manager) 315
McCall's Magazine 206
McCook, J. C. (U.S.A. Consul) 67, 88
McCormacks Creek and Forks 105, 110
McDonald, Alexander 90, 96, 98, 99, 101, 105, 106
McDonald Building 72
McDonald, Pete (Built Pavilion Theatre) 71
McDonald, Rev. R. 57
McFarland's Dump 112, 114
McFee's Saloon, "Bill" 66, 140
McGill University (Montreal) 161

McGillacuddy, Ella 169, 175, 181
McGinnis, Angus 218
McGrath, Mr. 26
McGregor, Mr. 287
McGuire, Judge 70
McKay, David 97
McKay, Jim 101
McKay, Mrs. Clarence 203
McKinley, William, President 248
McKinnis, Col. 97
McKinsie 15
McNamee, James 104
McNutty, Dick 101
McQuesten, Jack 62
McRae, Dan 101
McRae, Margaret (School teacher) Preface
McPhee, William 76, 139
Mead, John 66
Meadows (Settlement) 37
Meadows (Actor, Arizona Charlie) 77, 238
Medicine Man 69
Meeker, Ezra (Oregon Trail Fame) 74
Melba, Nellie (Australian Opera Star) 204
Mennen's Talcum Powder 205
Methodist Church, Dawson 94
Methow River 98
Mexico, Steamer 8
"Midas Touch" 99, 105
Mikado's Kingdom 205
Miles Canyon 44, 186, 334
Miller Creek 100, 240
Miller, H. L. (owner of first cow) 310
Miller, Joaquin (Poet) 70, 229, 232
Miller, Juanita Preface
Miller Party 282, 283
Miller, W. A. 228
"Million Dollar Claim" (Klondike) 100
Miner's meeting 325
Minto 56, 155, 159, 161, 163
Mirage on a mountain trail 239
Misner, William, Dr. 4, 33, 282
Mission Creek 233
Mitchell, Belle (Dawson Fire) 73
Mizner, Wilson 22, 80
Modjeska (Polish actress) 273
Monroe, James 104, 228
Montagne, Lady 203
Montana Mine 44
Monte Carlo Casino 72, 79, 155, 190, 221, 222
Monte Cristo Hill (gold) 96
Monte Cristo Island (fake gold-rush) 60
Montreal 161, 274
Moore, Billy (Building Contractor, San Francisco) 113

Moore, Billy (Old Sea Captain, Skagway) 32
Moore, Virgil (Editor of Klondike Nugget) 224
Moore, W. L. 229
Moosehide Indians 69, 70, 329
Moosehide Slide 68, 69
Moran, Casey (Showman, Dawson) 232
Morford, Kirkpatrick, Harper & Ladue Co. 97
Morford, S. O. 97
Morgan, Capt. 232, 285
Morrison, Frank 66
Morrison, James 97, 228
Mother Lode 15, 100, 106, 112, 118
"Mountain Hero" (Mine) 44
Mounted Police Barracks 45, 57, 75
Mounted Police Outpost 240
Mounties 3, 72, 155, 157, 159, 161, 162, 186
Mt. McKinley (Dicky & Monks discovered) 248
Mud Lake 44
Muir, John 15
Mulrooney, Belinda 101
Mulrooney Roadhouse 101
Munsey's Magazine 203, 204, 206
"Mush the Trail" 276

N

Nash, Thomas J. 72, 114
"Nearer My God To Thee" 221
Neil, M. J. 102
"Nellie, the Pig" 139, 140
Nelly, the malemute 66, 127, 128, 129, 165, 169, 178, 179
Nero, Great Dane Dog (newspapers) 224
New Century, The (typewriter) 206
New York, N. Y. 204, 205
New York World Newspaper 21
Newton Creek (Nome) 175
"Nigger Jim" 70, 71
Nome 229
Nome Stampede 76, 171, 174
Nora, Steamer 39
Nordica, Lillian (great Opera Star) 203
Nordling, Otto (Acknowledgments)
North Star 7, 235, 342
"North Wind" Skagway 17
Northern Lights 3, 127
Northern Saloon 66, 72
Northwest Mounted Police 49
"Nudes" 79
Nugget Shop 24
Nuggets (big) 101
Nuggets (on hill) 95

INDEX

O

Oatley Sisters (Actresses & Singers) 70
O'Brien, George 152, 157, 159, 160, 161, 164
O'Brien, Thomas (newspaperman) 70
Ogilvie, Ezekiel 100
Ogilvie, Major William (Governor) 60, 96, 101
Ogilvie, Settlement 60
O'Hara, Mr. 232
Oil Discovery (Copper River) (1897) 238
Oskvig, L. P. 140
"Old Brutus" 87, 96, 98, 111
Old Sand Bar (gold) 96
"Old Thunder Mug" (Chilkoot Pass) 291
Olson, A. M. Preface
Olson, Jack and Arlene Preface
Olson, Ole (telegraph man) 158, 161
Olson, Rev. 200, 201
Olympic Mountains 6
Opera House (Circle City) 230
Opera House (Dawson) 185
Ora, Steamer 73, 74
Oregon 6
"Oregon Mare, The" (Actress, Dawson) 187, 188
Oregon-Bannock-Piut Indian Wars 28
Orifero Hill (gold) 96
Orr and Turkey Stage Coach Co. 331
O'Shea, Tom 106, 111, 234
Ottawa, Canada 106
Otter (sea, fur) 4
O'Sullivan, Denis (Actor) 204
Outside 82, 123, 192, 335

P

Padlocks 305
Palace Grand Theater, Dawson 77, 137, 181, 185, Preface
Palmer, Joe 20
Panks, Carl O. (Tacoma) letter 341
Pantages, Alexander 79, 187, 180
Papering the cabin 303
"Pappy" 202, 206
"Paradise" 303
Paris, France 62, 98
Paris (Little) 113
Parka 196
Pat, sled-dog (Patsy) 129, 209
"Patent Leather Kid" 190
Patti, Adelina (great Opera Star) 204
Paul (son) 201
Pay-dirt 84
Pay-streak (gold) 96, 100, 336

Pedro Felix (Discoverer of Tanana Gold) 248, 340
Pedro (Lovable Horse) 212
Pelky, Thomas 104
Pelly River 57, 285
Pennycuick, Captain (Mountie) 156, 157, 159, 160
Percentage Women, Dawson 79
Permafrost 85
Perlit, Otto (Tacoma Times Reporter) 339
Petersburg 13
Phantom Rider 245
Phiscator, Frank 101
Pianos (Weber, Aeolian) 206
Pichon, Mr. 104
Pierce, Dr. 24
Pijon, Frank (Dominion Gold) 319
"Pink Flannel Heaven" 130, 182, 342
Pinkus, Henry (sold candles) 236
Pioneer Tales 6
Platinum 183
Plunger (Mine) 102
Pocket of Gold ($60,000) 114
Poke-of-Nuggets 186
Polaris, the North Star 7, 66, 103, 235
Pollard 6
Pooley, John 44
"Pork Trail" 159, 160
Port Arthur 322
Portland, Oregon 163
Portland, Steamer 17, 19, 101
Portlock, Al (Story teller) 114
Posey, W. T. 102
Powers, James (Actor) 204
Premonition 317
Presbyterian Church, Dawson 88
President Eisenhower 339
President McKinley 248
Prichard, Mrs. (Coffee Stand) 83
Princess Sophia, Steamer 9, 10, 78
Pringle, Rev. John 136
Profanity 208
Projectoscopes 67
Prospecting Trip 316
Prudential Insurance Co. 206
Puget Sound 6, 14, 109
Pullen House 32
Pullen, Mrs. Harriet 18, 23
Purchase of Alaska 240

Q

Quartz Creek 110
Quebec (Little) 106, 113
Queen Charlotte Sound 7
Queen Dome 87, 105
Queen Of Hearts 186
Queen of the Klondike 77

356   TRAIL TO NORTH STAR GOLD

Queen (Sled-dog) 129, 192
Queen Victoria 59
Queen Victoria's Birthday 59, 119
Quick, Joseph W. (Fairbanks Trek) 339

R

Rainier Hotel 221
Rainbow Gold 328, 338
Rainbows and Gold 165
Rajah of India 34
Rambler & Columbia Bicycles 206
Ray, Patrick Henry (Captain of U.S. Army) 229
Ready Bullion Gold Mine 14
Red Coats (Mounties) 219
Red (Frisco) 20
Redoubt Mt. (Cook's Inlet) 302
Regina Gold Mine 102
Regina Hotel (Dawson) 79, 331
Reid, Frank (Skagway Engineer) 27, 28, 29, 280
Reliance (Fort on Yukon) 62
Relief Ship to Dawson 203
Relf, Lynne (Casket of Ice) 155, 158, 161
Resurrection Creek (Alaska Gold)
Rhodes Brothers Dept. Store (Tacoma) 338
Richards, E. C. (Fairbanks Tour) 339
Rickard, Tex 79
Rideout Steamer (On Yukon) 174
Rieger, Jimo J. (Capitalist) 102
Riffles (Gold) 326, 328
Riggs, Tommy 115
Rink Rapids 55
Rip Van Winkle 233
Roanoke, Steamer 17
Roberts (Detective from Seattle) 287
Robin Hood of Alaska 28
Robinson Crusoe 233
Roche, Mrs. Burke 203
Rockers 84
Rockies (Mts.) 309, 331
Rockwell, Kathleen 77, 184, 185
Rockwell Settlement (Juneau) 15
Rocky Point 34
Rogers, Allen (Acknowledgments)
Rogers 1847 Silver 205
Rogers, William 74, 85, 94
Romeo and Juliet 273
Rosalie, Freighter 4, 16, 17, 152, 159, 163
Roseburg, Oregon 31
Ross, Malcolm Preface
Rough Riders 41
Rover (The Trick Dog) 129, 149, 151, 276, 277, 278

Rowan, Constable 26
Rowan's Widow 26
Rowena Lung 335, 336
Royal Canadian Mounted Police (Acknowledgments)
Ruby Sand 176
Ruby Settlement (On Yukon) 223
Rupert, Alaska 13
Russian-Japanese War 322
Ryan (Mountie Corporal) 155, 156

S

Safety, Port 177
Salmon River 98
Sampson (U.S. Commander of Fleet) 203
San Francisco 19, 22
Santa Barbara, Calif. 340
Savage, Dr. C. C. 102
Sawdust King of Dawson 57
Sawtooth Mountains 34
Scantily-Clad Girls 72
Scarlet Woman (Caribou) 201
Sea Otter 4
Sears, Roebuck 205
Seating Bill 95
Seattle, Wash. 4, 19, 101, 163, 190, 221, 222, 224, 336
Secret, Lady's 328, 334
Seitz, J. D. 102
Selbrede (U.S. Marshal) 25, 26, 31, 32
Selkirk, Fort 58, 161
Selma (Girl at the Roadhouse) 181, 194
Selwyn Creek (Mounted Police Barracks) 68
Sembrick, Madame (Opera Star) 203
Service, Robert W. Preface, 336
Seventy-Mile Creek, Alaska 233
Shah of Skagway 21
Shakespearian Plays 273
Shaw, Mr. 87
Sheep Camp 30
Shelgren, Mr. (of Washington) 292
Sherry Hill (Gold) 96
Shipment of Gold 57
Shipwreck 175
Siberia (Escaped Prisoners) 322, 323
Signal Bell 197
Silver Bow Basin 15
Silver Thimble 233
Simpson, Ed 66
Sitka 8, 15
Sixty-Mile 68
Skagway, Alaska 5, 9, 17, 18, 19, 33, 156, 157, 334, 335
"Skagway Charlie" 32
Skagway Harbor 23
Skagway newspaper 22

INDEX

Skagway River 30, 34
Skagway Trail 19
Skookum Barge 177
"Skookum Fellow" 85
Skookum Jim 42, 100
Skookum Gulch (Big) 101
Skookum Gulch (Little) 66, 101
Skookum House 42
Slavin, Frank 70, 134, 304
Slavin, John 115
"Slavin's Hardly Able Orchestra" 269
Sled-Dogs 276, 336
Sluice Boxes 98, 311, 314, 326
Smith, Jack 221
Smith, James (Governor of Yukon Territory) Preface
Smith, Jefferson Randolph 21, 23
Smith, Dr. & party 243
Smith's Premier Typewriters 65, 206
Smitly, George A. (Mayor of Tacoma) 339
Smuggler's Cove 31, 32
Smythe, Mr. & Mrs. Harold & Barbara Preface
Snake River, Alaska 175
Snow Creek (Nome) 175
Snow Man 170
Soapy Smith 17, 18, 26, 27, 29, 58, 156, 157, 280, 292, 293, 298, 300
Soapy Smith Show 24
Soapy Smith's Games 20
"Soapy's Lambs" 28
Sophia, Steamer 10
Sourdough Bread 122, 181, 308
Sourdough Hill (Gold) 96
Sourdough Starter 123
Sourdoughs 104, 109, 116, 321, 322, 328
Spanish-American War 41, 111
Sparks, Joseph (Actor) 204
Spirit Thermometer 197
Spokane, Wash. 187
Squaw Rapids 47
St. John 145
St. Michaels 108, 175
St. Nicholas Hotel 24
Stabbert, C. F., Capt. (Medical Marine Missionary) Acknowledgments
Stacey, William K. 39, 47, 76, 169
Stage-Coach 185
Stampeders 231, 234, 235, 238, 241, 286
Stampedes 20, 88, 241, 242, 268
Standar, Antone 97, 105, 228
Stanley, William 101
Star City, Alaska 233
"Star of Fortune" 94
Starke, Hans 114
Steam-Points 97, 250
Stearns, Capt. (Mountie) 288

Stevens, T. A. (Went to Fairbanks) 339
Stewart, Duncan 228
Stewart, J. D. 25
Stewart, Jack 114
Stewart, Josephus 44
Stewart River 98
Stickney, Mr. 99
Stocking, W. L. 102
Stoddard, John (Famous Lecturer) 205
Stratton, Steamer 68
Student, The 323
Sulphur Creek 72, 87, 107, 110
Sun-Dogs "Old Sol" 282, 288
Sunrise Gold Camp (Cook's Inlet, Alaska) 238
"Susie Blue-Nose" 139, 140
Swanson, Father (Catholic Priest) 112, 115
Swede Creek 60, 89, 90, 91
Swedes (Three) 95
"Sweet Chariot" 143
"Sweet Home" Bend, Oregon 190
Swiftwater Bill 60, 106, 188, 221, 223
Syble, Steamer 163
Sylvester, E. O. (Merchant of Skagway) 299
Sylvester's Warehouse 26
Syndicate, French 114

T

Tacoma Chamber of Commerce 339
Tacoma Fellow 85
Tacoma Hotel 85
Tacoma, Washington 1, 98, 273, 329
Tagish Charlie 42, 100
Tagish Indians 38, 41, 44
Tagish Post (Mounties) 157
Tanana Chief 231
Tanana Region 229, 230, 233, 237, 243, 244, 317
Tarut, Alfred 318, 319
Taylor, Henry D. (U.S. Consul, Dawson) 316
Taylor, Sheriff 22, 25, 26
Ten Commandments, The 32
"Tenting Tonight" 221
Teslin, Lake 292
The Big Clean-Up 311
The Little Cheechako Artist 59
"The Mexican Mine" 14
"The Nudes" 78
"The Old Rugged Cross" 139
The Rock of Gibralter (ad) 206
"The Snarler" (dog) 202
"The Tigress" 89
"Theater King," Alexander Pantages 189, 190

358 TRAIL TO NORTH STAR GOLD

Theodore "Teddy" Roosevelt 41
Thieves 305
Thirty-Mile River 49, 50
Thirty-Seven Mile Post 37
Thistle Creek 59
Thompson, Mr. 66
Thompson, Mrs. 310
Thompson, W. E. (Dawson Doctor) 164
Thorn Arm, Alaska (gold) 13
"Throwing Gold" 189
Tibbets, C. E. (Ship Captain) 229
"Tigers," Soapy's 22
Titanic (sinking) 337
Tivoli Theater (burned) 72
Tobin, Emery F. (former Editor of Alaska Sportsman Magazine) Acknowledgments
Todd, Dr. Edward (Pres. College of Puget Sound, Tacoma) 339
Tombstone 180
"Tooya" Indian Boy 54
Topeka, Steamer 17
Tracey, Fred (Singer & Theatre owner) 72
Trail of '98 286
Trail-joke 35
Trail, "Pork" 159
Trapper's Paradise (Furs) 54
Treadwell, John (gold) 15
Treadwell Mine (gold) 14
Treaty of Paris 111
Trembley, Madame 62, 220
Tremon's Store (burned) 72
Tripp, "Old Man" 20
Turgeon, Charles 228
Turnagain Arm (Cook Inlet, Alaska ... gold) 238
Typewriters 206
Typhoid Fever 76

U

Ugly Chief 69
Unalaska 109
Uncle Joe Latshaw 309
Union Pacific, Portland Extension 74
University of Puget Sound 269
Uranus Mine (gold) 44

V

Valdez, Alaska 243
"Valley of Gold" 103, 342
Van Duren, W. L. 190
Vancouver, B. C. 10, 302, 335
Vanderbilt Reef 10
Venus Massager 206
Venus Mines 44
"Vic," Queen 59
Victor Sewing Machines 205

Victor Talking Machines 205
Victoria, B. C. 36
Victoria (claim) 102
Victoria Rock 59
Victorian, Steamer 332
Vigilante Committee, Skagway 27
Vogel, John (newspaper reporter) 224

W

Wade, S. C. (Crown Attorney) 164
Walker's Fork (gold) 244
Wall, Sam (newspaperman) 70, 232
Walsh, Major W. L. (Northwest Mounted Police Commissioner) 88
Walsh (Private Detective) 161
Ward, Everett 104
Warden Hotel (burned) 76
Warren, Harvey (Noted stage artist) 240
Waterman, S. S. (St. Paul Lumber Co., Tacoma) 339
Watts, Warren 341
Waugh, Henry 97
Webster, Mrs. (Nurse) 114, 199, 201
West Dawson 216
West Devil's Rock 8
West, Mrs. (from Seattle) 74
Western Champagne (Aunt Fanny's cabin) 205
Westerner, The 65
Weymouth, Mr. 236
"Wheel of Gold" 85, 237
Whiskey-bottle windows 116
White Chapel (Red Light District, Dawson) 82
White, Garfield (Famous Canadian Actor) Preface
White Lemmings 54
White Pass 16, 24, 34, 342
White Pass (Yukon train) 32
White Pass Railroad 300
Whiteacre, Dr. Horace (Pres. Chamber of Commerce, Tacoma) 339
Whitehorse City (its founding) 48, 74, 333, 336
Whitehorse Rapids 44
Whiting, "Doc" 28
Wholesalers' Association, Tacoma, Wash. 338
Wick, John 104
Wiedemann, Thomas 108, 112, 114
Wien Air Lines Preface
Wilder, George 20
Willamette, Steamer 17
Willamette Valley 6
Williams, Fenwick 76
Williams party (on trail) 236
"Willie Irwin," Steamer 49, 68
Wills, H. T. (Dominion Creek) 115

INDEX

Wilson "Cad" (Actress) 74, 185, 187
Wincroft, Mr. 74, 75
Windless 84
Windsor Hotel 48
Windy Arm 43
"Wise Mike" (pet burro) 108
Witch Hazel, Steamer 49
"Wizard of Deceit" 18
"Wonder Claims" (Ancient Channel) 97
Wood Col. Stewart T. (Hdqts. Ottawa, Canada) Acknowledgments
Woodruff, Harry 204
Woods, Zachery T. (Mountie Supt.) 157, 158, 160
Worden, Mr. 101
Wrangell, Alaska 13, 180
Wright, El 74
Wynkoop, Mr. 74, 76

Y

Yanert, William (U.S. Soldier) 323, 324
"Yeller Stuff" (gold) 60
Yellow Babies 326
Yellow Kid 22
Yukon Crossing 56
Yukon, Fort 60
Yukon Gold Co., Guggenheim's 304
Yukon Ground Squirrel 54
Yukon History 56
Yukon Outfitting Co. 24
Yukon River 54, 159, 161, 162
Yukon Sun (Newspaper) 322, 329
Yukon Trail 294

Z

Zebra Initiation 431